POLICY MATTERS

Economic and Social Policies
to Sustain Equitable Development

POLICY MATTERS

*Economic and Social Policies
to Sustain Equitable Development*

edited by
JOSÉ ANTONIO OCAMPO
JOMO K.S.
SARBULAND KHAN

Orient Longman

Zed Books
London and New York

TWN
Third World Network

Published in association with the United Nations

Policy Matters was first published in 2007.

Published in Association with the United Nations

Published in the Indian Subcontinent, South East Asia (except Malaysia and Singapore), West Asia, China and Africa by
ORIENT LONGMAN PRIVATE LIMITED
Registered office: 3-6-752 Himayatnagar, Hyderabad 500 029 (A.P.), India
Email: info@orientlongman.com *Website:* www.orientlongman.com
Other offices: Bangalore / Bhopal / Bhubaneshwar / Chennai Ernakulam / Guwahati /
Hyderabad / Jaipur / Kolkata / Lucknow / Mumbai / New Delhi / Patna

Published in the UK, Europe, USA, Canada and Australia by
ZED BOOKS LTD
7 Cynthia Street, London N1 9JF, UK and
Room 400, 175 Fifth Avenue, New York, NY 10010, USA
www.zedbooks.co.uk
Distributed in the USA on behalf of Zed Books by
Palgrave Macmillan, a division of St Martin's Press, LLC
175 Fifth Avenue, New York, NY 10010, USA

Published in Malaysia and Singapore by
THIRD WORLD NETWORK
131 Jalan Macalister, 10400 Penang, Malaysia.
www.twnside.org.sg

Published worldwide by the United Nations and distributed worldwide
via the UN specialized network of agents.
United Nations Publications
2 United Nations Plaza, Room DC2-853, New York, NY 10017, USA.
http:/unp.un.org *Email:* publications@un.org

United Nations' sales number: E.06.IV.6
ISBN: 978-81-250-3064-5 Pb (Orient Longman)
ISBN: 978 1 84277 835 7 Hb (Zed Books)
ISBN: 978 1 84277 836 4 Pb (Zed Books)

A catalogue record for this book is available from the British Library
US CIP data is available from the Library of Congress

Cover designed by Andrew Corbett, Cambridge, UK
Typeset at Tulika Print Communication Services, New Delhi, India
Printed in India by Orion Printers Private Limited, Hyderabad 500 004

Contents

List of Tables

List of Figures

Preface

In mid-September 2005, the United Nations summit meeting—to review progress towards achieving the Millennium Development Goals (MDGs), set following the 2000 Millennium Summit—reiterated the international community's commitment to achieving the political, economic, social and environmental targets established at previous international summits and conferences, especially those held since the 1990s. Together with the General Assembly, the Economic and Social Council (ECOSOC) of the United Nations has been seeking to elaborate the coherence of this emerging United Nations Development Agenda and to accelerate progress towards achieving its goals and targets, as measured by various statistical and qualitative indicators.

Drawing from a selection of papers presented at the United Nations Department of Economic and Social Affairs (UN/DESA) Development Forum on 'Integrating Economic and Social Policies to Achieve the United Nations Development Agenda', held at the United Nations in New York on 14–15 March, prior to an inter-ministerial meeting convened by ECOSOC, the chapters in this volume seek to advance the debate towards this end. In particular, they seek to integrate economic and social policies for development by directly addressing the challenges and pitfalls posed by existing conditions, not least because of the policy reforms and institutional changes of recent decades have been associated with slower economic growth as well as greater inequalities in much of the world. Efforts to advance such policy and institutional coherence must necessarily tread in moot terrain, and the purpose of this book is to advance the debate.

In the first chapter, José Antonio Ocampo advances a holistic, but nuanced view of 'Markets, Social Cohesion and Democracy', in which he elaborates on some challenges in achieving policy coherence. His chapter analyses the means by which we may improve relations among the market, social cohesion and democracy, as they do not necessarily or automatically come together. He offers three guiding principles for improving democracy and its relationship to economic development by viewing democracy as an extension of citizenship, recognizing the diversity of democracy, and developing strong and clear macroeconomic rules complementary to the advancement of democracy. This perspective maintains that the economic system must be subordinated to broader social objectives and, hence, that economic and social institutions must be subject to democratic political choice. In particular, he analyses the role of both national and international institutions in creating robust democratic institutions.

Frances Stewart and Gustav Ranis then elaborate on the possible dynamic linkages between the economy and human development in the second chapter. Their contribution empirically confirms the significance of various links in each of two chains or cycles over time: first, from economic growth to human development, including economic growth itself, the distribution of income, the ratio of social expenditure ratio and female education; and conversely, from human development to economic growth, including both human development itself and the investment rate. Their most important conclusion, concerning the importance of proper sequencing over time, suggests that economic growth, an important input into progress on human development, is itself not sustainable without prior as well as concurrent human development. Thus, they take issue with the common policy advice that progress on human development must wait until economic expansion makes it affordable.

Giovanni Andrea Cornia then reviews the consequences of the policy reforms of recent decades for income distribution in the third chapter. He analyses the impacts of domestic liberalization and external globalization policies for within-country income inequality. Noting that the models invoked to justify such reforms usually predict declines in inequality, his review of the evidence shows that inequality often rose following the introduction of such reforms. He explains this discrepancy by noting actual conditions, including institutional weaknesses, structural rigidities, inefficient markets, e.g. characterized by asymmetric information, as well as persistent protectionism. Such conditions undermined the likelihood of the models' optimistic conclusions being realized as they are based on over-simplified abstractions of reality as well as restrictive assumptions.

In chapter four, Bernard Hoekman and L. Alan Winters consider the stylized facts and major research findings of the substantial literature on trade and employment. They note that research investigating the links between international trade and trade policy with labour market outcomes has generated a number of stylized facts, but many questions remain open. A common finding is that many of the short-run consequences of international trade and trade reforms have reallocated labour or wage impacts within sectors. Wage responses to trade and trade reforms are generally considered by the authors to be greater than their employment impacts, but [they/authors] insist that trade can only explain a small fraction of the general increase in wage inequality observed in recent decades.

In the fifth chapter, Eddy Lee also considers the implications of trade liberalization for growth and employment in developing countries by reviewing both multi-country and country studies. The studies considered suggest very contrasting effects of trade liberalization on employment, indicating that both country-specific and contingent factors may be important in determining its consequences. Differences in the implementation of trade liberalization seem to be particularly important, with a coherent set of supportive macroeconomic, structural and social policies especially helpful. The rather different findings, interpretations and conclusions of these three chapters clearly show that the debate over the welfare implications of international trade and trade liberalization is far from over.

Next, in chapter six, Graciela Kaminsky reviews the impact of greater international capital flows for both financial stability and growth following the heated debate over the explosion and dramatic reversals of capital flows to emerging markets in the 1990s. She reviews the characteristics of international capital flows since the 1970s and research since the 1990s on international investor behaviour as well as both short- and long-run effects of international liberalization on financial markets and economic growth. Kaminsky notes that the debate continues—while many argue that globalization has gone too far and international capital markets have become extremely erratic, others continue to insist that financial globalization has enabled capital to move to its most attractive destinations, thus fuelling greater growth.

In chapter seven, Jayati Ghosh offers a more critical review of the economic and social effects of financial liberalization in developing countries. She critically reviews the theoretical arguments in favour of such liberalization and considers the political economy context for the adoption and spread of such measures. She elaborates on some consequent problems for developing countries, especially financial fragility and greater propensity to crisis, as well as deflationary macroeconomic and other negative developmental effects. She concludes that developing countries must ensure that their financial systems are adequately regulated to more effectively serve their own specific needs and requirements, especially developmental priorities.

In the eighth chapter, Erik Reinert warns that aid, even if ostensibly for development, may inadvertently result in 'welfare colonialism', which will only serve to undermine the possibilities of the real economic transformation necessary to achieve economic development. Hence, he disputes the current development policy focus on poverty reduction as erroneous. Historically, successful economic development policy—since the late fifteenth century—has achieved the necessary structural transformation by reducing reliance on raw materials and agriculture, and by advancing specialized and sophisticated manufacturing as well as services subject to increasing returns. Reinert fears that the current MDGs' welfare emphasis is heavily biased in favour of palliative—rather than developmental—economics, by seeking to alleviate the symptoms of, rather than attacking the real causes of poverty. The resulting 'welfare colonialism' has consequently increased the dependence of poor countries, thereby hindering, rather than promoting, long-term developmental structural transformation.

Next, Francois Bourguignon and Mark Sundberg consider some problems in scaling up aid to developing countries to meet the MDGs by 2015 in chapter nine. Their list of macroeconomic and structural constraints to significantly raising aid flows includes inadequate infrastructure, consequent competitiveness problems, real exchange rate implications, labour market difficulties, fiscal limitations, governance challenges as well as the volatility and fragmentation of aid flows. The impact of such constraints on the cost-efficient sequencing and composition of scaled-up aid flows is considered using a dynamic computable general equilibrium (CGE) model applied to Ethiopia. The authors' main conclusions are that accelerating growth—through productivity enhancing infrastructure investment and improved governance—is key to achieving the MDGs. They argue that large increases in aid risk undermining competitiveness and future growth, while skilled labour constraints require careful aid sequencing, which in turn limit the scope for frontloading, as currently advocated in some quarters.

Alessandro Prati and Thierry Tressel then consider the most effective monetary policy for aid-receiving countries. Their chapter ten analyses how monetary policy can enhance the effectiveness of volatile aid flows and finds that monetary policy is effective in reducing trade balance volatility. They argue for a counter-cyclical monetary policy with regards to aid—it should slow down consumption growth and build up international reserves when aid is abundant, and deplete them to finance imports and support consumption when aid is scarce. If foreign aid also affects productivity growth, monetary policy should take this productivity effect into account in responding to aid flows.

Lance Taylor and Roberto Frenkel consider real exchange rate policy in the broader context of designing monetary policy for development, especially employment generation. As the exchange rate affects the economy through many channels, it has diverse macroeconomic and development impacts. Their chapter eleven focuses on the consequences for resource allocation, economic development, finance, external balances and inflation to highlight the potential use of exchange rate policy as a developmental tool in conjunction with its other uses, often in coordination with monetary policy.

In chapter twelve, Nanak Kakwani and Hyun H. Son suggest how the targeting efficiency of a government programme for a particular socio-economic group may be better assessed by using a 'total-group pro-poor policy (PPP) index', in order to capture its impact for the group. Using their own index, the study uses international comparisons—drawing household survey data for Thailand, the Russian Federation, Viet Nam and fifteen African countries—to investigate not only the pro-poorness of government programmes geared to the poorest segment of the population, but also of basic education, health and infrastructure service delivery.

Finally, Thandika Mkandawire makes a strong case against targeting in poverty reduction efforts, instead favouring universalism. As Amartya Sen has noted, targeted programs for the poor tend to be poorly funded and less likely to secure the necessary political support in order to be adequately financed and sustained. There is also considerable evidence, including World Bank research, that targeting measures have generally been costly and ineffective. Yet, Mkandawire notes, the Bank continues to favour targeting for the numerous poor while opposing the selective targeting of desirable new economic activities to be promoted.

November 2005 JOMO K. S.

1
Market, Social Cohesion, and Democracy

JOSÉ ANTONIO OCAMPO*

Developing countries are familiar with the dramatic gap between the expectations raised and the outcomes actually achieved by the reforms undertaken to broaden the role of the market in economic processes, and with a similar gap between expectations and outcomes associated with the extension of democratic regimes. This phenomenon reflects a more widespread problem: how to generate a good relationship between the market, social cohesion and democracy in a globalized world. The tensions among these elements are manifest in both industrialized and developing countries, but it is in the latter that they are particularly acute.

Latin America provides the best, if not the only, example. This was the developing region in which the adoption of market reforms coincided at a very early stage, and in a generalized fashion, with the consolidation of representative -. This coincidence was judged by some authors as a signal event in the history of Latin American democracy (see, for example, Domínguez and Purcell, 1999). It allows us to see more clearly how both the economic and political reform processes are linked to the frustrations expressed by the citizenry. In fact, as is evident from the regional surveys by *Latinobarómetro* (2004), while in 2004, 72 per cent of the population considered democracy to be the only system that would allow their countries to become industrial economies and 53 per cent considered it the best system of government, only 29 per cent felt satisfied with its functioning. Similarly, although the majority of the Latin American population thought that the market economy was the only system through which their country could become developed (60 per cent), the percentage showing satisfaction with its results was even lower than in the case for democracy (19 per cent).

This chapter analyses ways in which better relations between the market,

* This chapter has benefited from discussions over the years with some friends and colleagues, especially Carlos Vicente de Roux, Eugenio Lahera, Manuel Marfán, Ernesto Ottone and Juan Carlos Ramírez, and from discussions with Dante Caputo, Arturo O'Connel and Guillermo O'Donnell during seminars held within the framework of the UNDP project on Democracy in Latin America (UNDP, 2004), for which an earlier version was prepared.

social cohesion and democracy can be built. It begins by offering three guiding principles for a better relationship between the economy and democracy. The second section examines the role of national institutions in improving that relationship. The third section presents some succinct considerations regarding international institutions, and the fourth draws brief conclusions.

PRINCIPLES FOR THE RELATIONSHIP BETWEEN THE ECONOMY AND DEMOCRACY

Democracy is the Extension of Citizenship

The point of departure of this chapter is that *democracy means much more than a democratic regime.*[1] A democratic regime can be defined in terms of electoral institutions, mutual balance and control of powers, responsibilities of the majority and rights of minorities. Democracy has a wider meaning, rooted in the extension of the concept of equality before the law and, therefore, of the rights associated with citizenship, which can be understood in a broad sense as *civil, political and social citizenship.*

This powerful concept of democracy can thus be identified with the modern and richer view of citizenship that goes beyond civil and political rights. It ties democracy to the effective expansion not only of civil and political rights, which guarantee individual autonomy before the state and participation in public decisions, but of economic, social and cultural rights, which respond to the values of equality, solidarity and non-discrimination (ECLAC, 2001).

These interrelated views of democracy and citizenship also underline the universality, indivisibility and interdependence of human rights, an understanding that has emerged largely as a result of a long historical process. In terms of their character, enforceability and mechanisms of protection, civil and political rights are governed by legal statutes that differ from those that refer to economic, social and cultural rights. Nonetheless, they are all part and parcel of the fundamental rights of people, recognized by corresponding international declarations and covenants. Furthermore, where there is limited or no progress on economic, social and cultural rights, civil and political rights, laboriously attained in many cases, tend to lose significance for the poor segments of society.

The recognition of equality of all individuals before the law is perhaps the most important achievement of the modern era. It was associated with the development of modern capitalism, which demanded recognition of those who transact in the market as equals before the law. In economic thought, this -has had a contemporary renaissance in institutional economics, which has put emphasis on both equality before the law and respect for property rights as essential elements for reducing transaction costs and, consequently, for the proper functioning of markets (North, 1990).

However, a considerable historical literature, both political and economic, has highlighted the tension that also exists between social equality and property rights, inasmuch as property rights effectively consolidate the inequality in the distribution of wealth and income generated by the functioning of markets. The focus on this tension accounts for the ambivalent relationship between liberal thought and democracy, that still exists today (see, for example, Bobbio, 1990).

Resolving the tension—albeit never fully—between equality and property rights has been possible only through a gradual evolution of political citizenship, which has incorporated the principles of social citizenship throughout history. The development of these principles has led to redistributive policies that compensate inequality generated or reproduced by market forces. At the same time, it has led to economic regulations that directly target the relationship between the functioning of markets and the distribution of wealth and income. In this way, the expansion of social citizenship has implied the expansion of the regulatory and re-distributive roles of the state. Proponents of free markets consider these interventions to be a source of "distortions" in the functioning of markets, or even blatant restrictions of property rights. In fact, different schools of economic thought are deeply divided on this question.

As a corollary, these state interventions must be analysed in relation to their effects on the functioning of markets as well as in relation to the benefits they generate (Atkinson, 1999). This means that the efficacy of these interventions depends on their capacity to reduce inequalities generated by market forces and also on the benefits which society derives from a greater degree of equality and social cohesion. These benefits could include the positive effects of better income distribution on economic growth as well as the investment appeal of a society characterized by higher levels of social cohesion and political stability.

In highly unequal societies, overcoming the tension between the above principles becomes especially complex. First and foremost, ensuring equal opportunities is in itself difficult because disadvantage is not due to any one single factor, but to a combination thereof. That is why the provision of equal opportunities demands positive action for those in dissimilar situations.

Moreover, equality of opportunities is an insufficient objective. In fact, merit as a factor of mobility gives rise to social ascent or descent and, in the long run, generates inequality of opportunities. On the other hand, if a society provides inadequate opportunities to a broad segment of the population during the earlier stages of their lives, the result can, to a large extent, be irreparable losses. For example, malnutrition during childhood can make it difficult to attain the minimal levels of education necessary to secure a decent opportunity in the job market. This accounts for the need to have policies that may compensate for the inequality of life trajectories, and not only of opportunities.

In this view of democracy and citizenship, social equality is an objective in itself, as the true expression of the collective aims that move societies and, therefore, as a basic principle of social cohesion. Therefore, the defence of economic, social and cultural rights and their gradual redefinition in more complex forms (Borja, 2002) become the very purpose of development.

The indivisibility of these rights raises, nonetheless, complex issues. For example, the political declaration of "the right of everyone to an adequate standard of living for himself and his family, including adequate food, clothing and housing, and to the continuous improvement of living conditions" (Article 11 of the International Covenant on Economic, Social and Cultural Rights) does not allow for the creation of wealth or for distributing what is non-existent. Its instrumentation must be compatible, therefore, with the level of development achieved and, as we shall see, with the fiscal situation prevailing in each society in order to avoid resulting in unfulfilled expectations or macroeconomic imbalances, which may affect, through other channels, the very social sectors that are meant to be protected. Equity, in this sense, must be understood as involving the creation of targets which the society may be in a position to effectively achieve, given its level of development. That is to say, its point of reference is *that which can be realized*, but nothing less, and therefore aims at *maximizing the realizable*.

This having been said, it is necessary to bear in mind that the counterparts of rights are the responsibilities and obligations of the members of society who stake their claims on the corresponding social benefits (Palme, 2000). These responsibilities include the contribution (according to capacity) to production, compliance with tax obligations and participation in the public sphere.

Democracy Is Diversity

The second essential concept for analysing the relationship between the economy and democracy can be formulated simply as: *democracy is diversity*. Citizenship is meaningless when citizens lack options for making choices. Fortunately, history shows that even market economies are characterized by diversity due to the existence of different "varieties of capitalism", to use the term expressed by Albert (1993) and Rodrik (1999) expression.

In fact, despite the trend towards strengthened market relations, the modern world continues to exhibit variations in the mix between the state and the market. In the industrialized countries, models range from the limited welfare state of the United States to the elaborate welfare states of the European continent (Alesina and Glaeser, 2004). In Latin America, we find countries that allocate 4–6 per cent of gross domestic product (GDP) to social spending, and others, like Uruguay, which allocate more than 20 per cent (ECLAC, 2004: chap. 4). There are models of radical privatization of state enterprises, and others where such a process has been limited. Also, there are different models for restructuring social security, with varying components of solidarity and different mixtures of public and private participation.

Moreover, this view enjoys the backing of the notion that even though the basic functions of the institutions may be the same, the particular form they adopt varies (Rodrik, 2001). This reflects the fact that institutional development demands an active process of learning, which gives rise to different outcomes. It implies that institutional development ("institutional capital"), as well as the building of mechanisms of social cohesion ("social capital"), are essentially *endogenous* processes. Indeed, this is a characteristic that they share with human capital and technological capacity ("knowledge capital").

On the other hand, this view militates against market fundamentalism, which holds that there is only one desirable model of development applicable to all countries under all circumstances and sees the "market economy" as being antagonistic to state interventionism. The importance of this view has declined during the last few years, thanks to the recognition accorded to institutional development and, therefore, to the state being complementary to the market, and to the recognition of the crucial importance of "ownership" of national policies for the effective deployment of development assistance. It must, however, be underlined that these principles often clash with the conditionalities attached to international financial cooperation (see the section on international institutions below).

A revisionist view is that of "generations of reforms", which holds that, to overcome the problems experienced by developing economies with the liberalization processes, it is necessary to complement the first generation of reforms with a second one. The lines between the "generations" of reforms have become confusing. Even the first generation reforms, associated with economic liberalization and macroeconomic discipline, have been subjected to different interpretations and emphases in their implementation, inviting wide-ranging polemics. The "second generation" of reforms has as many meanings as there are possible interpretations of what appropriate institutional development (their major focus) should be. The need to improve the results of reforms in terms of equity and to place this objective at the centre of policy agendas, may be seen as a call for a third generation of reforms.

This is not the best way to deal with the need for change. The concept of "generations" of reforms implies linear and universal processes in which the achievements of previous stages prevail in unmodified forms as foundations for building new floors of a building. However, the fragility of some foundations can lead to problems that can only be resolved at later stages. This is, for example, what occurs in the cases of liberalization that result in higher levels of macroeconomic instability, destruction of productive and technological capacities that are not replaced by new ones, or increasing dualism in the productive structures. In such cases, it will be necessary to "reform the reforms" (Ffrench-Davis, 2000; ECLAC, 2001).

The same terminological confusion underlies the idea that it is necessary to "consolidate" the reforms. There is a minimum substrata around which a certain degree of consensus exists: a consolidation of macroeconomic achievements with respect to the reduction of inflation and the improvement in public sector accounts; an opening up to the opportunities offered by integration into the international economy; a broader participation of the private sector in the development process; and the need for more efficient states. All these terms, however, have different meanings for different analysts as, in fact, there is no single model of macroeconomic management that could guarantee stability (including, as we see later, differences of what is meant by "macroeconomic stability"). Moreover, there is no single way to integrate into the international economy or to combine the efforts of the public and the private sectors. These differences are reflected both in the industrialized and the developing world, where the diverse solutions to the problems posed by this minimum consensus are, at times, more important than the supposed homogeneity of the "market economy".

In reality, the idea that there must be some unique pattern, style or model of development applicable to all countries is not only ahistorical, but also damaging and contrary to democracy. Support for democracy is linked to the recognition that democracy generates a diversity of solutions to the problems of the people.

Democracy and Clear, Strong Macroeconomic Rules Are Complementary

A positive evaluation of diversity should not lead us to lose sight of the fact that, on more than one occasion, some policies have destroyed the foundations on which economic systems function, thereby falling into the category of "economic populism", to use a concept suggested a few years ago by Dornbusch and Edwards (1989).

Although this concept has not been used in a systematic manner in contemporary debates, it is used—as we do here—to refer to macroeconomic practices that result in temporary prosperity but that inexorably lead to crises due to the unsustainable nature of the public and private spending they entail. The concept has also been used to refer to policies aimed at redistributing income through forms of economic regulation that distort the functioning of markets, but it is difficult to differentiate such a meaning of "populism" from state intervention in a broader sense.

The concept of "economic populism" has thus been rightly criticized for its lack of precision and unclear relationship to the concept of populism developed in political science, where it refers to particular forms of mass mobilization based on the promises of social welfare. Actually, "economic populism", as defined above, has been practiced in more than one case by non-populist political regimes, including dictatorial regimes and even by seemingly very orthodox economic authorities. This is true, for example, of countries that have used periods of euphoria in international capital markets to accelerate financial liberalization. Accompanied by overvaluation of national currencies and other macroeconomic imbalances, this can unleash accelerated expansion of public and private spending and, later, deep macroeconomic crises. It might be better, therefore, to refer to these policies as "facile macroeconomics" rather than "populism".[2]

However, the most important corollary of this ambiguous process is that the progress of democracy and the establishment of clear and strong macroeconomic rules should not be seen as antagonistic, but rather as complementary. There are at least two strong reasons for this. The first is that, for any public policy to be efficient and sustainable, there has to be consistency between the different goals established by the authorities. In actual fact, the lack of consistency has been one of the main reasons for the painful adjustments in macroeconomic policies during the 1980s and the more recent crises in the developing world.

The second is that all forms of macroeconomic instability are costly, not only in economic but also in social terms. The regressive effects of inflation—and especially high inflation—have been amply registered in the developing world. The same holds true for the effects of exchange-rate crises, as capital flight guarantees adequate protection to the rich, while exchange rate adjustments, exacerbated by capital flight, redistribute the burden of external debt servicing to other social sectors.

The "lost decade" of the 1980s in large parts of the developing world and the strong macroeconomic ups and downs of the 1990s made it clear that *real* instability (i.e. acute business cycles) also carries high social costs. Recessions provoke a disorganization of social services provided by the state; a rapid rise in unemployment and poverty rates which decrease only slowly during later periods of economic recovery; permanent loss in human capital of those unemployed or underemployed, which could lead to their structural unemployment or underemployment and, in critical conditions, drop-outs from schools, which becomes a permanent loss of opportunity. Furthermore, real instability severely punishes smaller enterprises through their unstable access to credit, among other factors.

Consistency of policies with macroeconomic stability, understood in a broad sense (see below), is therefore necessary to achieve development objectives. Actually, when the economy is undergoing recession, unemployment, increasing inflation or a balance-of-payment crisis, long-term programmes and objectives tend to become subordinate to short-term macroeconomic policies aimed at overcoming different manifestations of macroeconomic instability. A context characterized by stability and consistency of policies broadens the temporal horizons of individuals, firms and authorities and, therefore, facilitates the proper functioning of democracy.

Stability and consistency of policies are necessary, but not sufficient, conditions for better social performance in a democratic context, however. In particular, many of the structural targets formulated during the period of economic reforms in the developing world lack clear social dimensions or even have negative implications—particularly when they are aimed at reducing the size of the state at the cost of sacrificing social policy. The conflict is, therefore, not between social policy, on the one hand, and macroeconomic stability and consistency, on the other, but between macroeconomic inconsistency and long run priorities (United Nations, 2001).

Moreover, as the foregoing discussion indicates, low inflation and sustainable fiscal accounts are components of macroeconomic stability and consistency, but they are not synonymous (Ocampo, 2002; 2005). This is an important consideration because the emphasis on macroeconomic stability in recent years has focused on these two aspects. Among other examples, in the run-up to their crises of the 1990s, Mexico and several South-East Asian economies registered equilibrium or even a fiscal surplus and low inflation rates while having an exchange-rate misalignment and an unsustainable current account deficit associated with large private sector deficits (Marfán, 2005). In other cases, where inflation and fiscal policy were also controlled, the most serious problem related to the high share of short-term external debt.

All this points to the importance of attaining higher levels of macroeconomic stability, in a broad sense, which includes not only fiscal sustainability and lower levels of inflation, but also stability in economic growth and in external accounts, as well as sound domestic financial and external balance sheets. It is clear that attaining price stability or rapid growth with overvalued exchange rates is costly in the long run, as are pro-cyclical policies which accentuate the effects of external financial cycles on the domestic economies, or a very narrow application of the objectives of price stabilization which ignores the costs of transition that anti-inflationary policies may entail. The formulae for achieving stability, in this broader sense of the term, are not unique and can result in multiple trade-offs, best resolved by democratic institutions.

NATIONAL INSTITUTIONS

Market, State and Society

The foregoing analysis shows that it is necessary to find a new balance between the market and the public interest. The definition of the realm of the "public interest" takes us, in turn, to classical discussions of the functions of the state or, in the terms of the contemporary debates, to institutional development.[3] There are several possible taxonomies but, for the purpose of this chapter, we can use a very simple one that classifies the public functions/institutions relevant for an analysis of the relationship between the economy and social cohesion, in two broad groups: those that ensure the proper functioning of markets and those that ensure consistency between their functioning and social cohesion.

The former can be classified, in turn, in four sets of functions/institutions, which are certainly interrelated: (i) institutions to *create markets*, i.e. those focused on reducing transaction costs (information, negotiation, oversight and control) among economic agents, including granting property rights (in a generic sense which includes not only private property but also its limits, and collective property rights in the diverse forms that we will analyse below), and on developing legal institutions to check violations of these rights or possible conflicts of interests; (ii) institutions for *the provision of public goods*, in a general sense of the term, which includes the adequate supply not only of pure public goods in terms of welfare economics (goods that are non-rival and non-excludable in consumption) but also of those that generate positive externalities and enhance the proper management of the public *commons;* and, on the negative side, the reduced supply of "public bads" and of goods generating negative externalities; (iii) institutions for *microeconomic regulation*, particularly in relation to non-competitive market practices, whether on account of the presence of scale economies or information problems; as regards the latter, since there is never factual information regarding the future (only mere expectations about the future course of events), markets involving an inter-temporal dimension (financial and technological markets, in particular) are essentially imperfect;

(iv) institutions for *macroeconomic regulation and design of structural strategies and policies,* aimed at avoiding short-run macroeconomic imbalances (recession and unemployment as well as inflation, and unsustainable fiscal or balance-of-payment accounts, and risky public or private sector balance sheets) and creating appropriate conditions for long-term growth (adequate incentives and financing of innovation, accumulation of human capital and investment, as well as development of complementarities and production linkages).

The functions mentioned include elements of social policy. Thus, human capital generates high externalities that play an important role in economic growth. Labour market regulation is another central element in macroeconomic regulation and can contribute towards proper macroeconomic regulation. However, market operation can give rise to very different distributive results. The concept of a "Pareto optimum" of welfare economics is the most concrete expression of the way in which an "efficient" outcome, from the point of view of markets, can be consistent with different distributions of the benefits. This concept is therefore insufficient for an analysis of the relationship between the economy, society and politics.

The functions/institutions which aim at making the workings of the market consistent with social cohesion can also be classified in four categories: (i) those which guarantee adequate provision of goods and services that a particular society considers should be provided for all of its members, either because of the influence they exercise on their capacities or on their welfare, and that we will call *"goods of social value"*[4]; (ii) *redistributive institutions,* which aim at raising the structure of wealth ownership and income distribution to levels considered desirable or at least tolerable by society and at establishing rules for the functioning of markets, especially markets of factors of production, which could guarantee such outcome; (iii) those related to *conflict management* generated by the functioning of markets and to the framing of agreements for their management and eventual elimination; (iv) those relating to *participation* in decision-making processes, not only relating to distributive outcomes but also to the very functioning of markets. The latter is essential because, as we have seen, it gives rise to different distributive outcomes, and, generally, it is not possible to achieve the desirable distributive results without influencing the functioning of markets. It is worth recalling Sen's observation (1999) that the exercise of political citizenship and the specific channels offered by democracy are not only rights which contribute to the well-being of people, but they are also the most effective means by which to guarantee that the social objectives of development are adequately represented in public decisions. As we will see below, institutions of participation also include those associated with the contribution of civil society to the fulfilment of all public functions, either as a partner of or substitute for the state.

In the framework of citizens' rights, "goods of social value" express economic and social *rights*. From there, it follows that these goods are simultaneously rights and commodities and express genuine *social preferences* which go beyond the individual preferences, the starting point of welfare economics. Actually, such a definition is arrived at through political processes and expressed as constitutional and legal norms. In recent times, the constitutions of Brazil, Colombia and South Africa, among others, concretely express this concept, indicating that such "goods of social value" are part of the social covenant underlying political institutions. Moreover, as the possibility of access by the whole population and the very definitions of such goods and rights broaden over time, achievements in different historical periods must be interpreted in relation to the potential that exists in a particular society at a specific point in time. It implies, furthermore, that making such access a reality, when possible, is an ethical imperative.

The basic functions of public policies are, therefore, related to how to guarantee the proper functioning of markets and the consistency between the latter and social cohesion. In this wider sense, "public policies" must be understood as all forms of collective action in pursuit of the common interest rather than as action exclusively by the state. Accordingly, the "public domain" must be conceived of as the meeting point of collective interests rather than as being synonymous with state activities. In other words, *the public domain" belongs to society*, and not to the state, which is the principal, but not the only instrument that society can employ to achieve the objectives of collective development.

In fact, although natural leadership falls on the state, the institutions that may be developed to carry out the public functions outlined above must take into account not only the "market failures" which lead to these functions but also the "government failures" (and those of other forms of collective action). The latter includes problems associated with imperfections of the mechanisms of representation ("agency" problems, as they have come to be called), the introduction of non-economic and non-social (bureaucratic or clientele) rationalities in the functioning of institutions and the reflection of dominant economic and social interest in their operation (i.e., problems related to political economy), opportunities generated by state intervention for capturing rents and information failures equally affecting government action.[5] During periods of state crises, when these shortcomings become marked, it is necessary, therefore, not only to look for improvement in the functioning of the state apparatus but to open up new opportunities for the participation of civil society in the exercise of public functions.

This approach underscores the importance of creating a strong institutional framework—a high *institutional density*—with active participation of multiple social actors and adequate accountability to the citizenry—i.e. a high *democratic density*. It creates room both for state institutions and civil society and, in each case, for local as well as national, international and supranational institutions, as a result of the profound restructuring of the domain of "the public" that has taken place in recent decades. It means, in other words, that all sectors of society must participate more actively in democratic public institutions, while at the same time developing multiple institutions of their own, which may strengthen the relation of solidarity and social responsibility, thus consolidating a culture of mutual understanding and collective development.

Development of Integrated Economic and Social Policy Framework

Market reforms offered only a limited role to social policy and, in particular, paid no attention to the distribution of wealth and income and, therefore, to the distributive effects of such reforms. On the other hand, equity was central to the alternative proposals formulated by, for example, the United Nations Economic Commission for Latin America and the Caribbean (ECLAC, 1990; 2001). Over the past few years, concern for income and wealth distribution, the productive assets of the poor, the need for a system of social protection and the effects of macroeconomic instability among the vulnerable sectors have enriched the policy agenda (see, for example, Birdsall, de la Torre and Menezes, 2001; Kuczynski and Williamson, 2003; De Ferranti and others, 2004).

This is a positive development. Even these recent contributions, however, have not entirely overcome a basic problem of social policies promoted during the reform period: the emphasis on the instruments (targeting, equivalence criteria between contributions and benefits, decentralization, private sector participation), instead of on the principles that ought to guide their design (universality, solidarity, efficiency and integrated character, in accordance with the ECLAC formulation (see ECLAC, 2001)). This has become problematic in some cases, e.g. when private participation in social security systems (health and pensions) has not been based on principles of solidarity, when targeting has been used as an instrument for reducing public sector spending rather than as an instrument to guarantee the access of the poor to certain fundamental services (and thus facilitate the application of the principle of universality) or when decentralization has not fully taken into account regional disparities.

Principles are important because they underline the fact that, as already mentioned, social policy is a basic instrument for social cohesion and, therefore, its design must be based on more than economic rationality. In any case, as we can see in the recent literature on the positive economic and political links between income distribution and economic growth, emphasis on income distribution and social cohesion does not preclude economic rationality (Ros, 2000: Chap. 10; World Bank, 2005). Actually, a principal corollary of this literature is that inequality may be an important obstacle to economic growth in Latin America and Africa, that is fast becoming a problem in some parts of Asia, and more generally, that social cohesion is a source of competitive advantage being supplied in increasingly scarce quantities.

The main problems of the recent formulations lie, however, in two areas: inadequate acknowledgement of the need to mainstream social objectives in the design of *economic policy* and disregard for the fact that economic and social institutions involve more than pure economic rationality. The choice of such policies, therefore, must be an explicit decision of citizens through adequately structured democratic institutions. Actually, in a more fundamental sense, political institutions that facilitate the exercise of democratic choice in selecting economic and social institutions are among the most important in any society. They give full meaning to the term "ownership" of development policies, a concept very much in fashion in recent international debates. In any case, as has been underscored in the first section of this chapter, it is obvious that political "voluntarism", political populism and "facile macroeconomics" have never served as adequate paths for economic and social progress and, therefore, the options chosen must, as we have seen, obey principles of rationality and macroeconomic consistency.

The idea that social objectives ought to be included in economic policy is contrary to the model of "leader/follower" that characterizes the design of macroeconomic policies today, according to which the latter is determined first, and social policy is left to address their ensuing social effects (Mkandawire, 2001). The importance attached to designing "safety nets" in place of broader systems of social protection, with an emphasis on the application of principles of universality and solidarity—and, ultimately, the creation of modern welfare states—is also a reflection of the vision of social policy's being subordinate to market reforms.

This is also characteristic of many other debates, especially those on labour market regulations. Undoubtedly, the need for institutional designs that can facilitate adaptation to changing economic circumstances ought to be taken into account in the design of labour institutions; however, traditional labour market flexibility (and, especially the flexibility to lay off workers) is only one of the possible alternatives, and one that can be applied in varying degrees and through different modalities. Its weak points relate to its negative effects on the accumulation of social capital by firms, on workers' commitment to the success of the enterprises they work for and on the harmonious relations between the workers, owners and managers of the enterprises. In recent debates, it has been increasingly felt that this flexibility ought to be accompanied by increasing investment in workers' training and strong social protection. Other alternatives include cooperation between workers and enterprises to enable adaptation to changing circumstances through social dialogue both in their own work places and at local and national levels. Moreover, labour market flexibility should never be considered a substitute for adequate macroeconomic policies that generate employment. In an unstable macroeconomic environment, additional flexibility may result in a marked deterioration in the quality of employment with unclear benefits for the quantity of formal employment, which is intended as its main objective.

In view of the link between economic and social development, it is necessary to design integrated policy frameworks that take into account the links among different social policies and between economic and social policies. Many analysts have pointed out the lack of appropriate institutions in this area, including those involved in the recent World Commission on the Social Dimensions of Globalization, which in its 2004 report called for "policy coherence", both at the national and the international levels. These integrated frameworks ought to start by designing rules to ensure the "visibility" of the social effects of economic policies and by asking macroeconomic authorities (including autonomous central banks) to regularly examine the effects of policies on the main social variables (particularly employment and income of workers). Similarly, finance ministers should be asked to include an analysis of the distributive effects in any budgetary or tax reform initiative they present to their legislative authorities. Likewise, public entities entrusted with technological, industrial or agricultural policy ought to evaluate regularly who the beneficiaries of their programmes should be. These exercises must be considered only as starting points for designing efficient coordination systems between economic and social authorities, in which *social objectives are effectively mainstreamed into economic policy decision making*, i.e. into monetary, fiscal, production and technological policies.

Besides these considerations, the recognition that economic and social institutions have multiple objectives, and some that go beyond their economic role, is essential. Thus labour market institutions have objectives that go beyond the creation of formal employment. As has been pointed out, the quality of employment, the promotion of cooperation between workers and enterprises and the distributive effects of those institutions are equally important objectives. On this question, it should be noted that labour market liberalization has been one of the principal forces behind the tendency towards the deterioration of income distribution in a broad range of countries and that centralized negotiations of salaries has acted as a defence mechanism against this tendency in a few countries (Cornia, 2004). Moreover, beyond their role in negotiations on labour conditions, trade unions are one of the most important mechanisms of social participation.

Fiscal Covenant and State Rationality

Public finances are central to all democratic processes. The strength or weakness of public finances reflect the strength or weakness of the "fiscal covenant", which contributes to a legitimization of the role of the state and to a definition of the area of governmental responsibilities in the economic and social spheres (ECLAC, 1998). In fact, the absence of a generally accepted pattern of state functions erodes the consensus on the quantity and composition of the resources that the state has to manage, as well as on the rules for their allocation and utilization. Therefore, political agreement between different social sectors on what the state should do helps to legitimize the level, composition and direction of public spending, and the tax burden necessary for its functioning.

Seen in this context, the "fiscal covenant" must include five distinct elements: (i) clear rules of fiscal discipline, accompanied by adequate tax revenues to finance the functions that society assigns to the state; (ii) transparency of public expenditure;[6] (iii) the design of efficiency criteria for the management of state resources; (iv) acknowledgement of the central role played by the public budget in the provision of "goods of social value" and, more generally, in the distribution of income; and (v) the design of balanced and democratic fiscal institutions, which include room for citizens' participation.

The first of these criteria must be reflected in targets for balanced budgets or deficits that are sustainable in time or, alternatively, in limits on public debt, within a multi-year budgeting framework that serves to make the action plans of the state more orderly. This operation should not, however, be inconsistent with the use of fiscal policy in the short run to smooth out the business cycle.

In any event, budgetary rules must be accompanied by an adequate allocation of resources for the fulfilment of the basic functions that society assigns to the state. In fact, many developing countries have a tendency to burden the state with objectives while providing it with too few resources to fulfil them, thus giving rise to unsustainable fiscal imbalances and non-compliance of governmental programmes, both of which are damaging for democracy. This reflects the absence of a culture of responsibility of the citizenry vis-à-vis the state and, especially, tax responsibility—in other words, of a culture of civic responsibility which, as we have seen, is the counterpart of citizens' rights.

That is why, in countries where tax rates and, consequently, levels of public spending are relatively low compared to international patterns, the "fiscal covenant" almost invariably requires a raising of the tax burden and, in particular, a strengthening of the less developed tax sources (direct taxes in general). The lack of a culture of tax responsibility also encourages the tendency to overburden tax legislation with exceptions. Hence the convenience of limiting specific benefits, of including in the budget an estimate of the costs of the tax benefits established by legislation and, of course, of severely punishing those who violate tax norms.

Fiscal institutions must pursue the above-mentioned objectives simultaneously. They must strive for fiscal discipline, but also guarantee income levels compatible with the functions of the state arising from the democratic process and offer incentives for the proper use of public sector resources. Placing these responsibilities on the shoulders of a few organs of central power—especially strong finance ministries—has not proven to be adequate in practice, because it does not ensure that a culture of discipline and proper use of resources permeates the entire structure of the state. It even encourages confrontations within the state and a search for quasi-fiscal practices to evade controls exercised by finance ministries. Even more debatable is the idea of assigning this function to an autonomous power—a fiscal board—which, among other things, could be considered an institution that would deprive democracy of one of its most essential elements. Indeed, in any democracy, nothing can replace the basic functions of the parliament in defining desirable levels of income and public expenditure, or its accountability in ensuring the proper use of resources by each organ of the state and by leading government officials. Accordingly, the promulgation of fiscal responsibility laws and adoption of explicit fiscal rules is the most appropriate approach for achieving fiscal discipline. This is equally the case as regards the proper use of resources and, indeed, all actions geared towards improving public sector management.

One of the most important corollaries of this analysis is that balanced and democratic fiscal arrangements require specific actions to strengthen the weakest entities within the budgetary process: the legislative power (in most countries), the sub-national governments and the citizenry. This implies that it is necessary to promote a broad democratic debate of public sector budgets. The creation of budgetary offices in parliaments as well as mechanisms for citizens' participation in budgetary debates (including participatory budgets), and the involvement of civil society in debates regarding annual or multi-year fiscal plans (as part and parcel of debates on development plans and strategies) are democratic virtues which must be promoted.

Policies on Property Rights

As has been extensively analysed in the recent institutional literature, while there is no market without property rights, neither is there a market which functions in an institutional vacuum. Institutional development leads, however, to the creation of regulations that, in some way or another, restrict property rights.

No other area of economic analysis gives rise to so many differences among various schools of economic thought as this one, especially on two specific issues: the limits that society must impose on large private property (or, according to the formulation used in some institutional contexts, to define the "social functions of property") and the scope of state ownership. This theme also covers at least two other dimensions: the promotion of small private property and alternative forms of property rights (cooperative and communal).

The limits to large private property are related mainly to the strong association between a mal-distribution of wealth and a mal-distribution of income. Therefore, one set of limits to private property rights relates to the levels of inequality in wealth distribution which a society is willing to tolerate and to the imposition of taxes on incomes from capital or from wealth as compensatory mechanisms against existing inequalities. A second set is related to the possible abuse of market power that large firms can exercise, as well as the abuse by large shareholders and executives of companies vis-à-vis small shareholders; the corresponding rules of "corporate governance" are thus part of the rules for the proper functioning of markets. The third set of limits refers to the capacity of economic power to expand its influence beyond markets, thanks to its preferential audience in the political system or to the control it exercises on other typical spheres of power in contemporary societies, the mass media in particular. Constitutional and legal rules which define the relationship between economic and political power as well as between economic power and the control of the mass media are, therefore, an essential component of policies on large private property (or factor in their absence).

In the production of public goods, in the wider sense in which we use this term, or when the control of a particular economic sector confers huge power in a particular economy, one of the options promoted by some political movements and schools of economic thought has been state ownership. The indirect regulation of private firms active in these sectors is one option, but regulatory authorities may encounter serious problems of asymmetric information and difficulties in avoiding the "capture of regulation" by the economic power that controls the respective sector. For this reason, direct ownership by the state can be an attractive option.

However, evidence indicates that this option also faces problems associated both with "government failures" and with the lack of definition of effective property rights (in this case, *public* property rights). Both problems lead to the control of public sector firms or of some of their operations by specific interests (control of their bureaucracies and/or company contracts by specific groups and, in the extreme, corruption), thereby resulting in the *private* appropriation of public enterprises. To this, we must add the absence of "hard" budget constraints facing these firms, which can translate into inefficient management (although this is not the only possible outcome). A similar problem to that which characterizes large private enterprises may also arise, although with a twist: political control can generate excessive economic control. All of this means that the rules guaranteeing the effective *public* character of the state enterprises and their proper economic functioning are an essential part of a policy on property rights in the broad sense of the term.

The defence of collective assets and commons has acquired increasing importance given the awareness of the importance of the environment, but it covers a broader group of subjects, amongst which the protection of the remaining urban and rural commons is noteworthy. The problem cannot be solved with a private allocation of the required assets or commons, mainly because the lack of some markets (for environmental services, in particular) would generate inefficiencies in the allocation of resources; the lack of information on the specific nature of externalities that they generate would, by itself, reduce the efficiency of any regulation; and also because private control of resources could generate the capture of the regulatory entities.[7] The problem is more complex because the allocation of private property rights over some assets can give rise to the general presumption of rights on such assets or services in cases where property rights are not clearly defined. One of the most relevant cases in point is ownership of land, since proprietors consider that environmental resources that are associated with it, such as water or shifting flora and fauna, are integral parts of their rights. This underscores the need for clear constitutional and legal norms regarding collective assets and commons and the creation of effective defence mechanisms for the collective rights over them.

Promotion of small private ownership is the least controversial element of a policy on property rights. Accordingly, it can be argued that the form of private property that is more akin to democracy is widely diffused ownership.[8] In line with this principle, related policies are the promotion of access to ownership of housing, support to small enterprises, both rural and urban, support to small shareholders and—something more debatable today than some years ago—the participation of workers in the ownership and management of enterprises (which in modern terminology can be conceived of as a means through which workers acquire some property rights to the firm they work for).

The promotion of small private property must be closely linked to support to associative forms of ownership (cooperatives) which small property holders use to exploit economies of scale in related activities (in acquiring inputs or marketing of their products, for example) and, therefore, to compete with large firms. The promotion of these alternative forms of property rights also arises from the coexistence of modern economies with communal organizations, such as the indigenous communities, as well as from the advantages that alternative forms of property rights entail as expressions of a larger domain of "the public" (Moulián, 2001).

Democracy, Public Debate and Technocracy

These reflections lead us finally to the one related directly to the concept of democracy as diversity: an effective democracy is *not* possible if the themes of economy and social organization are not part of its agenda. To eliminate such subjects from democracy is to leave it bereft of one of its fundamental dimensions.

This concept, however, conflicts with some of the most commonly shared ideas in contemporary economic thinking, which can be referred to as "technocratic ideology". Behind this ideology lies a deeply pessimistic vision of democracy as a system of competition for the concession of privileges granted by the state—for capturing rents, to use the most common expression. In the face of this reasoning, it is desirable to develop economic institutions that are isolated from democracy and even protected from it. There is also, in this regard, an undercurrent of intrinsic oligarchic tendency, in a very Platonic sense of the term—of the "government of the wise"—which is shared in one way another by all schools of economic thought that give a central role in economic decision-making to economic knowledge and to the elitist group that controls it—the technocracy (Ocampo, 1992).

Without ruling out the importance of solid technical institutions for the proper functioning of the state, and without failing to acknowledge the scientific underpinnings of all economic analysis, the truth is that the latter is always coloured by ideology, which divides economics into antagonistic schools of thought. For this reason, economics must be subjected to politics and, in particular, to democratic political processes, as it is through the latter that society settles its ideological controversies.

This type of reasoning has three basic implications. First, it is difficult to conceive of proper democracies without solid political parties that offer citizens alternative options for economic and social order. Without this ideological competition, politics will, in the worst of scenarios, become pure clientelism and, in the best, electoral competition among potential "public managers". Might it be the case that the increasing incapacity of politics to mobilize people is associated with the elimination of this basic substance of politics? Reversing this trend, and injecting more substance into democracy, is essential to creating a political sphere that will be more responsive to the needs of development.

To achieve these results, it is necessary to guarantee academic pluralism and create mechanisms to transform technical debates into *social* ones. This is the reason it is so important to facilitate interaction between academic groups and different social organizations and to disseminate the resulting debates through the mass media.

The third implication is that the strengthening of technocratic entities and autonomous centres of economic power must be accompanied by appropriate political control. One essential element in this respect is to strengthen the capacity of the units of political control to exercise this function properly. A priority issue in this regard is the development of technical support groups and think tanks for parliaments, political parties, trade unions and popular organizations, as well as for entrepreneurial organizations. Without such entities, there cannot be an appropriate dialogue with the technical sectors of governments and central banks. This is one of the priorities of a democratic agenda to which little attention has been paid.

The contributions of the recent literature on the "economics of politics" can help us better understand how political institutions comply with these principles, thus helping to improve the relationship between ideological debates, political programmes, decision-making processes and public policies. Accordingly, they contribute to an understanding of the virtues and limits of the institutions developed for overcoming the main government failures, especially with regard to ensuring the primacy of general versus specific interests, and the interests of the electorate over those of the elected, as well as the effective capacity to translate preferences into public decisions and policies. The analyses of the functioning of parties, of electoral institutions, of rules for the expression of specific interests (*lobbying*), of countervailing institutional setups and of rules that define the relationship between powers and decision-making processes are some of the critical themes in this context (Persson and Tabellini, 2002). On this subject, and in particular, on its relation to economic policies, much more research is needed (in this context, see IDB, 2000: Chap. 4).

Brief Notes on Globalization and Democracy

The tension between the principle of equality and the protection of property rights has acquired a new dimension in the present phase of globalization. The normative "levelling of the playing field" (homogenization) generated by globalization has given a new impetus to the defence of property rights and, more especially to the extension, in this area, of the rules of the game of the industrial world. This has been reflected in a number of treaties relating to protection of investment as well as in a generalization of the rules regarding the protection of intellectual property rights.

In a world where opportunities for development are unequally distributed, this normative homogenization has been accompanied by increasing distributive tensions (UNCTAD, 1997; UNDP, 1999; Bourguignon and Morrison, 2002; Cornia, 2004). Alternative explanations of these tensions continue to be the subject of heated debate. Perhaps the most appropriate explanation lies in the adverse distributive effects of market reforms (or of at least some of them) and the simultaneous weakening of the institutions of social protection, as well as the increasing reluctance and difficulties of governments to offer effective instruments of social protection (Cornia, 2004). Another explanation is the increasing asymmetry between the international mobility of some factors of production (capital and highly skilled labour) and the restricted mobility of others (low-skilled labour), which generates adverse distributive effects against the latter (Rodrik, 1997). Increase in income differentials according to the relative demand for skilled labour is the third explanation, and the one that generates perhaps the broadest consensus among analysts.

It must be remembered, however, in the face of these trends, that the present phase of globalization is a multidimensional phenomenon that has also included a global extension of common ethical principles and international objectives of a social character, which have been upheld in declarations and international conventions on human rights as well as in the declarations and action plans of the United Nations conferences and summits, including the Millennium Summit (United Nations, 2000), which have generated what can be called the United Nations development agenda. These processes and this agenda are rooted, furthermore, in the history of struggle by international civil society to ensure human rights, social equity, gender equality, environmental protection and, more recently, globalization of solidarity and the "right to be different" (cultural diversity).

This "globalization of values", as ECLAC (2001) has called it, has helped the spread of democratic regimes and a broader vision of citizenship across the world. The coincidence of this process with the liberalization of market forces has, however, generated tensions without creating mechanisms for their attenuation. The basic reason for this is that the globalization process, while promoting democracy and setting internationally agreed social goals and targets, has eroded the capacity of action of governments to meet these targets; it has reduced the "policy space", to express this problem in the terms that have become common since the Eleventh United Nations Conference on Trade and Development (UNCTAD XI), held in São Paulo in 2004. Globalization has left the complex task of maintaining social cohesion in the hands of the nation-states, but with less room for manoeuvre to realize it. Moreover, as a result of normative homogenization and the burden of conditionality in international financial assistance, the scope for diversity required by democracy has been reduced.

As has become evident in recent controversies on international financial instability, these dilemmas are only finally resolved by strengthening global governance. But current trends do not point in this direction. There are, on the one hand, problems of representation of developing countries in international economic decision making, which were been recognized at the Monterrey International Conference on Financing for Development (United Nations, 2002). On the other hand, there are no processes that would create opportunities for directly consulting citizens on economic decisions of a global character—that is to say, for going beyond the representation of citizens through their governments. Furthermore, independently of these problems, there are no strong forces at work for strengthening global economic governance.

The absence of a true internationalization of politics is, in this sense, the main paradox characterizing the current globalization process. In other words, the simultaneous accentuation of democratic forces and distributive tensions has not been accompanied by any effective strengthening of political institutions that may permit the reduction of tension between the two. In fact, although there are incipient spaces of global citizenship associated with the struggle of international civil society, their capacity to transform reality continues to depend on their incidence on national political processes.

This has profound implications for the international order. It implies, first of all, that it is necessary to create democratic spaces of a supranational character. This process will inevitably be slow, however—as reflected, for example, by the most advanced supranational process in the world, the European Union (EU). For this reason, and while the expressions of political citizenship continue to be essentially national in character, the promotion of democracy as a universal value acquires meaning today only if national representation and participation processes are allowed to determine economic and social development strategies, and if they are able to exercise an effective mediation of the tensions created by the globalization process. This means, in turn, that the *international order must be profoundly respectful of diversity*, within the limits of interdependence. It also implies that an essential function of international organizations is to support national strategies that may contribute to reducing, through political citizenship, the profound tensions existing today between the principle of equality and the functioning of the globalized markets.

The Demands for Economic and Social Rights and International Assistance

In the human rights framework that underlies this chapter, the building of a social agenda is identified with the acknowledgement that each member of the society is a citizen and, therefore, is a depository of rights. The international scope of declarations and conventions on human rights as well as the United Nations development agenda that has evolved from the global conferences and summits can, therefore, be considered as a basis for a definition of a concept of global citizenship, albeit and incipient one.

In this area, however, there has not been a full transition from national to international institutions. In actual fact, respect for human rights and the accountability for meeting internationally agreed social goals continue to be essentially national responsibilities. On the other hand, the application of these obligations is limited to the state and does not explicitly cover other social agents. Lastly, there are as yet no clear incentives for the enforcement of these rights and commitments, nor are there methods to guarantee their application in each nation-state.

One essential activity in this field relates to the production, dissemination and analysis of information regarding the situation of economic, social and cultural rights—and to the provision of "goods of social value" through which the former are expressed—as well to the compliance with goals and targets set in global summits. These periodic evaluations ought to be subject to debate in representative national forums, with the active participation of parliaments and civil society. A process of this kind will contribute to the creation of a culture of accountability for international commitments whose effectiveness depends on their ability to bring about necessary adjustments in public policies. In this manner, accountability in all of these fields will contribute to a much clearer *political demand* for international commitments. Accordingly, the mechanisms designed for the follow-up to the United Nations Millennium Development Goals, and the political visibility of these goals, represent significant progress. It would be important, therefore, to build upon this experience and create broader mechanisms of accountability, which may then eventually lead to an integral evaluation covering not only respect for declarations and conventions on human rights but also for other sets of internationally agreed social rights (the fundamental principles and rights of work agreed upon in the International Labour Organization (ILO), and the rights of children, women and ethnic groups) and the goals and targets agreed to in world summits that belong to the United Nations development agenda, with which they are closely related.

In some cases, this political demand could gradually lead to a *judicial demand* for economic and social rights, both in national and in relevant international courts. Europe has been the only place in the world where this step has been taken. In all cases, as stated before, present and future commitments and the consequent political demands for them must be in consonance with the degree of development of the countries concerned, and especially with their capacity to attain goals which could effectively benefit all citizens, while avoiding both political voluntarism and populism, and facile macroeconomics.

It is also important to acknowledge that the responsibility for the full application of social rights and goals transcends state borders. That is why some international organizations have undertaken new initiatives, including the dissemination of the concept of corporate social responsibility. One such concrete example is the United Nations Global Compact, through which subscribing enterprises commit themselves to promote respect for human rights in their sphere of activity, to comply with basic labour rights, to protect the environment and to fight corruption. Another example is the guidelines for multinational companies prepared by the Organization for Economic Cooperation and Development (OECD) in 2001. These processes have been accompanied by strictly private initiatives from both business sectors and social movements.[9] These principles of and commitments to corporate social responsibility have become subject to regular follow up by different organizations. It is worth adding, however, that significant controversy still persists between those (mainly nongovernmental organizations) who advocate schemes of corporate social responsibility of a compulsory character and business organizations who prefer voluntary frameworks of "best practices" which will spread through emulation.

On the other hand, the marked inequalities and asymmetries of the global order indicate that an essential element in the realization of rights and goals at the world level in the social area is official development assistance (ODA). ODA ought to be made available in conformity with the commitments set at the United Nations (to grant official assistance equivalent to 0.7 per cent of the gross domestic income of developed countries) and with the basic criteria shared by the international community, which were clearly spelled out at the Monterrey conference: assigning priority to the fight against poverty and "ownership" of the strategies and policies of economic and social development by the countries that adopt them (United Nations, 2002). From this perspective, development cooperation must be conceived as a simultaneous support to poverty eradication and to the construction of democracy, in accordance with a rights-based approach.

A complementary approach lies in the explicit acknowledgement that globalization will not achieve the aim of contributing to the convergence of the development levels of different countries if it is not accompanied by resource flows explicitly intended for this purpose. The EU represents an international process in which these principles have crystallized through their policy of "social cohesion". It is symptomatic of the political philosophy underlying these agreements that the deepening of economic integration during the last decade of the twentieth century was accompanied by a strengthening of the policy regarding cohesion (Marín, 1999). There is, however, no other process of this type outside the European context. That is why, as argued by some analysts, it would be desirable to extend this practice to other integration processes (see, for example, Bustillo and Ocampo, 2004, in relation to an eventual free trade area of the Americas).

Conditionality in International Financial Assistance

The analysis of international resources leads us to the debate on the conditionality attached to international financial assistance and the relationship of such conditionality with national processes of participation and political representation. The conclusions of recent debates emphatically indicate that conditionality is not an effective, or at least is an insufficient, means to fulfil those objectives that the international community wants to tie to financial assistance. If there is no true "ownership" of policies (in other words, if they do not enjoy strong domestic support), it is unlikely they will be sustained. Furthermore, ownership is essential for institution-building, which is now widely acknowledged as one of the key factors for the success of development policies.

The particular meaning of this principle, however, has been the subject of great controversy and has in practice been ignored in many cases. There have even been attempts to "force" on recipient countries the "ownership" of policies that donors and international organizations consider appropriate (Helleiner, 2000; Stiglitz, 2002). In any case, the principle of "ownership" establishes the basic rule for the donors: their role is not to replace but to support national processes of participation and political representation. This has led to the acceptance of "ownership" as a central theme of ODA (OECD/DAC, 1996) and of IMF and

World Bank programmes (Köhler and Wolfensohn, 2000; World Bank, 1998; IMF, 2001). The Paris Declaration on Aid Effectiveness of 2005 has recently raised this principle to the level of a basic criterion for ODA.

A full application of this principle requires a clear understanding of the way conditionality operates in reducing, eliminating or distorting the "ownership" of national policies. The mechanism is not—or at least not always, or not mainly—a plain and simple imposition of policies by the donors. In actual fact, four additional channels are decisive: (i) the terms under which financing is available severely restrict countries' options; (ii) in a crisis situation, possible support from donors and international financial institutions affects discussions within the government, increasing the negotiating power of groups more inclined towards the points of view of the donors; (iii) technical support that institutions provide to countries affects domestic discussions, and (iv) participation of representatives from these institutions also influences these debates.

In this manner, for "ownership" of policies to become consistent with international financial assistance, two additional conditions must be met: (i) a strict ban must be established against any form of conditionality that goes beyond the factors *directly* affecting the objectives of the programme being financed;[10] and (ii) countries must have at their disposal alternative packages of reform and adjustment, and international institutions must be available to supply such alternative support whenever countries ask for it, with the same technical rigor as is the case for traditional reform programmes. The composition of the international financial institutions' technical teams must therefore represent the heterogeneous approaches to macroeconomic and structural adjustment, and/or these institutions must be ready to tap organizations and economists who think differently to help them design alternative programmes. This implies, furthermore, that "ownership" can only be promoted through an effective pluralist discussion of the virtues of alternative macroeconomic and structural reform packages (Stiglitz, 1999).

On the other hand, the inclusion of social criteria in designing the programmes of international financial institutions, especially their emphasis on poverty reduction as an explicit objective of international cooperation, represents a significant improvement in these programmes. It is essential, however, that this should not lead to new forms of conditionality or to the promotion of a particular approach to social programmes in the developing world. In particular, the inclusion of social issues in macroeconomic and structural adjustment programmes cannot be limited to designing adequate social safety nets for social sectors affected by macroeconomic crises or structural adjustment, the issue that has received greatest attention. In fact, the compensatory approach of the social programmes has been seriously questioned (United Nations, 2001).

Rather, as has been argued throughout this chapter, it should lead to mainstreaming social objectives in the very design of macroeconomic policies and structural reforms.

CONCLUSION

The citizens' rights framework that serves as the stepping stone of this chapter bears a great resemblance to other contemporary visions of development. The concept of "human development" (UNDP, 1994), "development as freedom" (Sen, 1999) and the integral character of development (ECLAC, 2001) are various expressions of this perspective, but it has profound roots in the debates on development. As we have indicated, during the last two decades, it has been manifested mainly in the form of a gradual dissemination of global ideas and values like human rights, sustainable development, gender equality, and respect for ethnic and cultural diversity. Global values and, above all, human rights, in their dual dimension of civil and political rights, on the one hand, and economic, social and cultural rights, on the other, must be considered as the ethical framework for the formulation of development policies and for any political order.

The consequences of this new perspective are deeper than what most economists are ready to accept. Following Polanyi (1957), this basically means that the economic system must be subordinated to broader social objectives. This affirmation underscores the need to confront the powerful centrifugal forces that characterize the private sphere today. Thus, in many (developing and industrialized) countries, people are losing their sense of belonging to their society, their identification with collective objectives and their bonds of solidarity. This underscores the importance of "creating society", of a broadening awareness of the social responsibility of individuals and groups, based on initiatives which could come from the state as well as civil society. Accordingly, as we have argued, the domain of "the public" must be seen as the meeting point of collective interests more than as synonymous with the activities of the state. This means that the domain of "the public" belongs to the society, not to the state, which, while being the principal actor, is only one of the tools used by society to attain its collective development.

Another implication of this point of view is that economic and social institutions must be subjected to democratic political choice. This implies that there is no such thing as a unique or optimum design for a "market economy". As has been noted by a number of authors, there are different "varieties of capitalism" and it is not clear that any one form is superior to the others in every way—not only in relation to dynamism and economic stability but to distribution of income and social cohesion. Controversies over the virtues of different economic institutions indicate that economists are profoundly immersed in ideological debates, which can and must be resolved in the democratic arena. In that context, the role of international cooperation, of national and international technocracies—and, incidentally, of international markets—is neither to promote nor, even less so, to dictate a dominant model of economic and social organization.

NOTES

[1] This is the central message of UNDP (2004) on democracy in Latin America, itself based on O'Donnell (2002).

[2] This is the term suggested by Arturo O'Connel in commenting on a prior version of this chapter.

[3] On this aspect, see the new classical texts of Musgrave (1959) and Atkinson and Stiglitz (1980), as well as a more recent essay by Rodrik (2001).

[4] This is a redefinition of the concept of "merit goods" or "merit wants" used by Musgrave (1959).

[5] These are the preferred themes of the new institutional literature relating to the functioning of governments, but they have a long tradition in the literature relating to public choice on the use of new institutional approaches.

[6] Transparency implies, on the one hand, inclusion of all the items of expenditure within public budgets, including those of a contingent nature or those that result from the multiple tax benefits typically contemplated in tax legislation and, on the other hand, public awareness of such budgets, their execution and evaluation.

[7] The controversy over assigning right of private ownership to sources of water is a case in question.

[8] For a defence of this point of view, see Ramos (1991) and Ocampo (1992).

[9] Relevant initiatives include the Dow Jones Sustainability Index, the International Certification on Environmental Management ISO14001 and the Corporative Accountability Index, promoted by the British firm, Business and the Community, and associated with the Financial Times Stock Exchange Index.

[10] In this regard, one difficulty encountered in discussions and decisions of the IMF aimed at streamlining conditionality, is the fact that, although the IMF concentrates on macroeconomic and financial matters, it is also involved with the institutional and structural aspects that are supposedly related to them. Such a broad definition was responsible for increasing the scope of conditionality during recent decades.

REFERENCES

Albert, Michel (1991). *Capitalisme contre capitalisme.* Éditions du Seuil, Paris.
Alesina, Alberto, and Edward L. Glaeser (2004). *Fighting Poverty in the US and Europe: A World of Difference.* Oxford University Press, New York.
Atkinson, Anthony B. (1999). *The Economic Consequences of Rolling Back the Welfare State.* Munich Lectures in Economics, MIT Press, Cambridge, MA.

Atkinson, Anthony B., and Joseph Stiglitz (1980). *Lectures on Public Economics*. McGraw-Hill, New York.

Birdsall, Nancy, Augusto de la Torre and Rachel Menezes (2001). *Washington Contentious: Economic Policies for Social Equity in Latin America*. Carnegie Endowment for International Peace and Inter-American Dialogue, Washington, DC.

Bobbio, Norberto (1990). *Liberalism and Democracy*. Verso Press, London.

Borja, Jordi (2002). Ciudadanía y globalización. *Reforma y Democracia* 22, February: 117–46.

Bourguignon, François, and Christian Morrison (2002). The Size Distribution of Income Among World Citizens: 1820–1990. *American Economic Review* 92 (4): 727–44.

Bustillo, Inés, and José Antonio Ocampo (2004). Asymmetries and Cooperation in the FTAA. In Antoni Estevadeordal, Dani Rodrik, Alan M. Taylor, and Andrés Velasco (eds). *Integrating the Americas: FTAA and Beyond*. The David Rockefeller Center Series on Latin American Studies, Harvard University Press, Cambridge.

Cornia, Giovanni Andrea (ed.) (2004). *Inequality, Growth, and Poverty in an Era of Liberalization and Globalization*. Oxford University Press, Oxford, for United Nations University World Institute for Development Economics Research (UNU-WIDER), Helsinki.

De Ferranti, David, Guillermo E. Perry, Francisco Ferreira, Michale Walton (2004). *Inequality in Latin America: Breaking with History?* World Bank Latin American and Caribbean Studies. World Bank, Washington, DC.

Domínguez, Jorge I., and Susan Kaufman Purcell (1999). Political Evolution in the Hemisphere. In Albert Fishlow and James Jones (eds). *The United States and the Americas: A Twenty-first Century View*. W.W. Norton & Co., New York, for The American Assembly, Columbia University, New York: 137–73.

Dornbusch, Rudiger, and Sebastián Edwards (1989). *The Macroeconomics of Populism in Latin America*. The University of Chicago Press, Chicago.

ECLAC (1990). *Changing Production Patterns with Social Equity. The Prime Task of Latin American and Caribbean Development in the 1990s*. ECLAC Book No. 25, Economic Commission for Latin America and the Caribbean, Santiago.

ECLAC (1998). *The Fiscal Covenant: Strengths, weaknesses, challenges*. Economic Commission for Latin America and the Caribbean, Santiago.

ECLAC (2001). *Equity, Development and Citizenship*. Abridged edition. ECLAC Book No. 62, Economic Commission for Latin America and the Caribbean, Santiago.

ECLAC (2004). *Social Panorama of Latin America, 2002–2003*. Economic Commission for Latin America and the Caribbean, Santiago.

Ffrench-Davis, Ricardo (2000). *Reforming the Reforms in Latin America: Macroeconomics, Trade, Finance*, Macmillan, London, and St Martin's Press, New York.

Helleiner, Gerald (2000). External Conditionality, Local Ownership and Development. In Jim Freedman (ed.). *Transforming Development*. University of Toronto Press, Toronto: 82–97.

IDB (2000). *Development Beyond Economics: Economic and Social Progress in Latin America Report, 2000*. Inter-American Development Bank, Washington, DC.

IMF (2001). *Conditionality in Fund-Supported Programs: Policy Issues*. Policy Development and Review Department, February, International Monetary Fund, Washington, DC.

Köhler, Horst, and James D. Wolfensohn (2000). The IMF and the World Bank Group: An Enhanced Partnership for Sustainable Growth and Poverty Reduction. September, International Monetary Fund and World Bank, Washington, DC.

Kuczynski, Pedro-Pablo, and John Williamson (eds) (2003). *After the Washington Consensus: Restarting Growth and Reform in Latin America*. Institute for International Economics, Washington, DC.

Latinobarómetro (2004). Informe-Resumen Latinobarómetro 2004: Una década de mediciones. Processed: www.latinobarometro.org

Marfán, Manuel (2005). Fiscal Policy Efficacy and Private Deficits: A Macroeconomic Approach.

In José Antonio Ocampo (ed.). *Beyond Reforms: Structural Dynamics and Macroeconomic Vulnerability.* Stanford University Press, Stanford, CA, for World Bank, Washington, DC, and Economic Commission for Latin America and the Caribbean, Santiago: 161–88.

Marín, Manuel (1999). Integración y cohesión: la experiencia europea. Document prepared for the VI Meeting of The Montevideo Circle, 12 and 13 November, Santo Domingo, Dominican Republic.

Mkandawire, Thandika (2001). Social Policy in a Development Context. Processed, UNRISD, Geneva.

Moulián, Tomás (2001). *Socialismo del siglo XXI: La quinta vía.* Editorial LOM, Santiago.

Musgrave, Richard A. (1959). *The Theory of Public Finance.* McGraw-Hill, Tokyo.

North, Douglass C. (1990). *Institutions, Institutional Change and Economic Performance.* Cambridge University Press, New York.

Ocampo, José Antonio (1992). Reforma del Estado y desarrollo económico y social en Colombia. *Análisis Político* (Bogotá) 17, September–December: 3–37.

Ocampo, José Antonio (2002). Rethinking the Development Agenda. *Cambridge Journal of Economics* 26 (3), May.

Ocampo, José Antonio (2005). A Broad View of Macroeconomic Stability. UN/DESA Working Paper No. 1, October, Department of Economic and Social Affairs, United Nations, New York.

OECD/DAC (1996). *Development Co-operation Report.* Development Assistance Committee, Organization for Economic Co-operation and Development, Paris.

O'Donnell, Guillermo (2002). Notes on the State of Democracy in Latin America. Paper prepared for the project 'The State of Democracy in Latin America', United Nations Development Program (UNDP), New York.

Palme, Joakim (2000). Reevaluación del Estado de bienestar en los países nórdicos. In H. Muñoz (comp.). *Globalización XXI: América Latina y los desafíos del nuevo milenio.* Aguilar Chilena de Ediciones, Santiago.

Persson, Torsten, and Guido Tabellini (2002). *Political Economics: Explaining Economic Policy.* Zeuthen Lecture Book Series, The MIT Press, Cambridge, MA.

Polanyi, Karl (1957). *The Great Transformation: The Political and Economic Origins of Our Time.* Beacon Press, Boston.

Ramos, Joseph (1991). *Más allá de la economía: más acá de la utopía.* Corporación de Estudios para Latinoamérica (CIEPLAN), Santiago.

Rodrik, Dani (1997). *Has Globalization Gone Too Far?* Institute of International Economics, Washington, DC.

Rodrik, Dani (1999). *The New Global Economy and the Developing Countries: Making Openness Work.* Policy Essay No. 24, Overseas Development Council, Washington, DC.

Rodrik, Dani (2001). Development Strategies for the 21st Century. In Boris Pleskovic and Nicholas Stern (eds). *Annual World Bank Conference on Development Economics, 2000.* World Bank, Washington, DC: 85–108.

Ros, Jaime (2000). *Development Theory and the Economics of Growth.* University of Michigan Press, Ann Arbor, MI.

Sen, Amartya (1999). *Development as Freedom.* Alfred A. Knopf, New York.

Stiglitz, Joseph (1999). The World Bank at the Millennium. *Economic Journal* 109 (458), November: F577–F597.

Stiglitz, Joseph (2002). *Globalization and Its Discontents.* W.W. Norton, New York.

United Nations (2000). *Millennium Declaration.* Millennium Summit, 6–8 September, General Assembly, United Nations, New York.

United Nations (2001). *Social Dimensions of Macroeconomic Policy.* Report of the Executive Committee on Economic and Social Affairs (EC-ESA) of the United Nations, New York.

United Nations (2002). *The Monterrey Consensus.* International Conference on Financing for Development, March, Monterrey, México (www.un.org).

UNCTAD (1997). *1997 Trade and Development Report.* United Nations Conference on Trade and Development, Geneva.

UNDP (1994). *Human Development Report, 1994.* United Nations Development Program, New York.

UNDP (1999). *Human Development Report, 1999.* United Nations Development Program, New York.

UNDP (2004). *Democracy in Latin America: Towards a Democracy of Citizens.* United Nations Development Program, New York.

World Bank (1998). *Assessing Aid.* World Bank Policy Research Report, Oxford University Press, New York.

World Bank (2005). *World Development Report, 2006: Equity and Development.* World Bank, Washington, DC.

2
Dynamic Links between the Economy and Human Development

GUSTAV RANIS and FRANCES STEWART[1]

Human development (HD) is increasingly viewed as the ultimate objective of development in place of economic growth (EG). Yet, the links between HD and EG remain of critical importance since EG would appear to be a foremost contributor to sustained progress in HD. Moreover, not only are improvements in HD the fundamental development goal, but HD is itself an important contributor to EG over time. Hence, it is important to explore the two-way links between HD and EG. The aim of this chapter is to examine these relationships and to draw policy implications from the analysis.

HD has been defined as 'a process of enlarging people's choices' (UNDP, 1990: 10). This definition is, of course, very broad, and includes non-material aspects such as the many dimensions of political, cultural and social freedoms. In this chapter, however, we shall take a reductionist approach and focus exclusively on two important aspects—people's health and their education.

Clearly, there exist strong connections between EG and HD. On the one hand, EG provides the resources to permit sustained improvements in HD. On the other, HD improvements raise the capacities of economic agents who make the critical contributions to EG. Each of these relationships has often been acknowledged separately—for example, the way in which EG affects HD forms part of the basic needs literature, while the impact of improved labour quality on economic growth has been widely explored in the human capital literature. Yet, the two strands have seldom been combined within one dynamic analytical framework. It is important to understand the full implications of this two-way linkage in terms of both analysis and policy. The two-way linkage can be explored both analytically and through empirical investigation of the chains and their links.

In this chapter, we first identify the major links which make up the two chains between EG and HD. We then present some empirical cross-country evidence on these links. The third section develops a typology of country cases, some representing the mutual reinforcement between HD and EG and some demonstrating asymmetric performance; this is followed by an investigation of the movement of countries from one situation to another over time. The final section briefly reflects on the implications for policy.

The Two Chains

We concentrate on two causal chains, one leading from EG to HD (Chain A), the other from HD to EG (Chain B). The two chains are pictured in Figure 2.1.

Chain A: From EG to HD

Gross national product (GNP) contributes to HD through household and government activity, community organizations and non-governmental organizations (NGOs). The same level of GNP can lead to very different HD performances depending on the allocation of GNP to various groups and to distribution within each category.

The propensity of households to spend their income on items which contribute most directly to the promotion of HD, e.g., food, potable water, education and health, varies depending on the level and distribution of income across households, as well as on who controls the allocation of expenditure within households. In general, as the incomes of the poor rise, the proportion of income spent on HD increases (Behrman, 1993, 1996). This means that higher and more equally distributed growth is likely to enhance HD expenditure, as is shown by much empirical evidence. For example, one estimate suggests that if the distribution of income in Brazil was as equal as that in Malaysia, school enrolments among poor children would be 40 per cent higher (Birdsall, Ross and Sabot, 1995). There is also substantial evidence that greater female control over household expenditure increases HD allocations. In Côte d'Ivoire, for instance, an increase in women's share of household cash income was associated with significantly higher spending on food and reduced spending on alcohol and tobacco (Hoddinott and Haddad, 1991).

Turning to government—both central and local—the allocation of resources for improving HD is a function of total public sector expenditure, how much of that expenditure flows to the HD sectors, and the way in which it is allocated within these sectors. This can be expressed in the form of three ratios (UNDP, 1991)—the public expenditure ratio, defined as the proportion of GNP spent by the various levels of government; the social allocation ratio, defined as the proportion of total government expenditure devoted to the HD sectors; and finally, the priority ratio, defined as the proportion of total HD sector expenditure allocated to priorities within these sectors. To clarify, within HD

FIGURE 2.1
Human Development (HD) progress

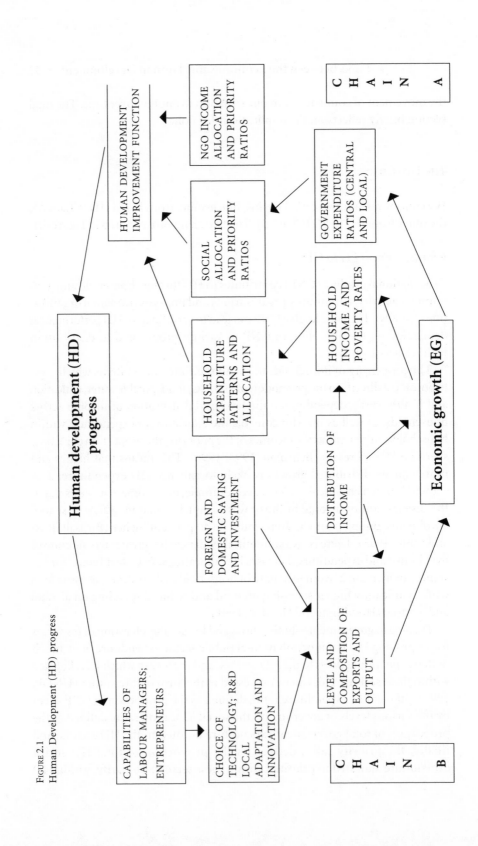

sectors, those expenditures which are clearly much more productive than others in terms of achieving advances in HD are defined as 'priorities': for example, basic education, especially at an early stage of development, is generally recognized to have had a larger impact on HD than tertiary education. The precise definition of what constitutes a priority will, however, inevitably vary according to a country's stage of development, rendering this third ratio more arbitrary than the other two. Very large variations in each of these ratios exist across countries, which means that the same level of GNP may be associated with very different levels of government spending on HD priorities (UNDP, 1991: chap. 3, 1996: chap. 3). There is evidence that local government, ceteris paribus, tends to favour HD allocations relative to central government (see Klugman, 1994; Habibi and others, 2003; Ranis and Stewart, 1994).

The significance of public expenditure choices for improving HD is illustrated by a comparison between Kenya and Malawi. In the 1980s, a similar proportion of national income went to public expenditure (27 per cent in Kenya; 30 per cent in Malawi), but Kenya had a significantly higher social allocation ratio (47 per cent, compared to 35 per cent) and priority ratio (34 per cent, compared to 14 per cent), so that the proportion of gross domestic product (GDP) going directly to HD-improving priorities in Kenya was over three times that of Malawi (5.1 per cent, compared to 1.5 per cent) (UNDP, 1996: 71).[2]

Finally, NGO or other civil society activity is typically heavily oriented towards HD objectives (e.g., projects generating income for the poor and spending on schools, nutrition and health). Although in most contexts, NGOs play a supplemental or even marginal role, in a few countries (e.g., the Bangladesh Rural Advancement Committee (BRAC) and the 'Comedores Populares' in Peru), they appear to represent a major source of HD enhancement (Riddell and others, 1995).

A further important link in Chain A is the effectiveness of these expenditures in raising HD levels, represented here by the 'Human Development Improvement Function' (HDIF). An example of one important input into this production function is female education, which abundant empirical evidence has shown to improve infant survival and nutrition (Rosenzweig and Schultz, 1982; Behrman and Wolfe, 1987a, 1987b; Barrera, 1990). Other research, on Ghana, has demonstrated that, in rural areas, the provision of basic health services improves child health and increases survival significantly, while the evidence is less clear for urban services (Lavy and others, 1995).

It is evident from this discussion of the various links in the EG-HD chain that, in general, we expect important causal connections to exist between the economy and HD achievements, but that these connections are *not automatic*: the strength of the links in Chain A varies in line with a large range of factors, including the structure of the economy, the distribution of income and the policy choices made.

Chain B: From HD to EG

Turning to Chain B, from HD to EG, in addition to being ends in themselves, higher levels of HD affect the economy by enhancing people's capacities and, consequently, their creativity and productivity. Ample evidence suggests that as people become healthier, better nourished and educated, they contribute more to economic growth through higher labour productivity, improved technology, attracting more foreign capital, and higher exports. This, of course, does not detract from the intrinsic value of improving the lives of those who cannot find employment because of disability or age, for example.

Numerous studies indicate that increases in earnings are associated with additional years of education, with the rate of return varying with the level of education (Behrman, 1990a, 1990b, 1990c, 1995a; Behrman and Deolalikar, 1988; King and Hill, 1993; Psacharopolous, 1994; Schultz, 1988, 1993a, 1993b; Strauss and Thomas, 1995). Analysis of the clothing and engineering industries in Sri Lanka showed that the skill and education levels of workers and entrepreneurs were positively related to the rate of technical change in the firm (Deraniyagala, 1995). Moreover, in agriculture, evidence suggests positive effects of education on productivity among farmers using modern technologies (Schultz, 1975; Welch, 1970; Rosenzweig, 1995; Foster and Rosenzweig, 1994; Behrman, Rosenzweig and Vashishtha, 1995). In Thailand, farmers with four or more years of schooling were three times more likely to adopt fertilizer and other modern inputs than less educated farmers (Birdsall, 1993).

These effects are embodied in growth theories. The Solow model views human capital as an important input, while the 'new growth theories' endogenize technical progress, incorporating education as well as research and development (R&D). According to Lucas (1988), for example, the higher the level of education of the workforce, the higher the overall productivity of capital because the more educated are more likely to innovate, thereby affecting everyone's productivity. A complementary view is that technical progress depends on the level of R&D in the economy. Here again, education plays a key role, both in contributing to R&D and via interactive learning (Roemer, 1990; Grossman and Helpman, 1991).

There is also a positive feedback from improved education to greater income equality. As education becomes more broadly based, people with a low income are better able to seek out economic opportunities which improves income distribution over time. For example, a study of the relationship between schooling, income inequality and poverty in eighteen countries of Latin America in the 1980s concluded that 'clearly education is the variable with the strongest impact on income equality' (Psacharopolous and others, 1992: 48).[3] Improved income distribution, in turn, has been found to be positively associated with EG (Alesina and Rodrik, 1994; Alesina and Perotti, 1994; Persson and Tabellini, 1994; Birdsall, Ross and Sabot, 1995), although the empirical basis for this appears rather fragile.[4]

Improved health and nutrition have also been shown to have direct effects on labour productivity, especially among poorer individuals (Behrman, 1993, 1996). For example, calorie increases have been widely shown to raise productivity, including among farmers in Sierra Leone, sugar cane workers in Guatemala and road construction workers in Kenya (Cornia and Stewart, 1995; Strauss, 1986; Immink and Viteri, 1981; Wolgemuth and others, 1982). A longitudinal study of a sample of children in Chile concluded that providing nutritional supplements to children to prevent malnutrition would generate benefits in terms of additional productivity six to eight times the cost of the intervention (Selowsky and Taylor, 1973). At the aggregate level also, health has been shown to be an important input into EG (Bloom, Canning and Sevilla, 2004).

Education and health alone, of course, cannot transform an economy. The quantity and quality of investment, domestic and foreign, together with the overall policy environment, form other important determinants of economic performance. Yet, the level of human development has a bearing on these factors too.

As in Chain A, the strength of the various links in Chain B varies considerably, and there is no *automatic* connection between an improved level of HD and increases in per capita GNP. It is not enough to create a larger pool of educated people; there must also exist opportunities for them to be productively employed, or this might simply increase the number of educated unemployed. Other factors which affect the rate of growth, and consequently, the strength of this chain, are the level of investment (supported by both domestic and foreign savings) and the overall policy setting. Higher levels of HD are also relevant here—they attract more foreign direct investment (FDI), induce more exports and contribute to improvements in technology and policy.

EMPIRICAL FINDINGS ON THE LINKS IN THE CHAINS

In previous work, we have explored some of the relationships in the two chains empirically, using data from 69 developing countries, applying ordinary least squares (OLS) methods, though for some variables we have a smaller number

TABLE 2.1
Chain A regressions: from EG to change in HD (measure of change in HD is IMSR, 1960–2001)

Variable	(1)	(2)	(3)	(4)	(5)	(6)	(7)	(8)
GDP per capita, 1960 x10^6	4.84	4.60	4.63	30.8	22.8	3.65	-7.13	-4.61
	(1.45)	(1.33)	(1.33)	(1.21)	(1.21)	(1.14)	(0.32)	(0.21)
GDP per capita growth rate, 1960–1980 x 10	1.06**	0.99**	1.01*	1.30	0.59	1.09*	-1.31	-1.22
	(2.07)	(1.85)	(1.85)	(1.64)	(0.94)	(1.97)	(1.58)	(1.50)
Gross primary enrolment rate, 1960 x 1000	1.08*	–	0.60	–	–	–	–	0.86
	(1.77)		(0.29)					(1.06)
Gross female primary enrolment rate, 1960 x 1000	–	1.04*	0.50	2.76***	1.07	2.21***	0.96	–
		(1.73)	(0.26)	(3.14)	(1.46)	(3.24)		
Gini coefficient, average over 1960–2001 x 1000	–	–	–		0.20	–		–
				(1.83)	(0.09)			
Poverty headcount, average over 1985–2001 x 1000	–	–	–	–	–	–	-3.83***	-3.73***
							(2.93)	(2.85)
Public expenditure on education (percentage of GDP), 1980–1990 x 100	–	–	–	–	–	1.21***	–	–
						(2.80)		
Public expenditure on health (percentage of GNP), 1960 x 100	–	–	–	–	–	6.13**	–	–
						(2.65)		

(contd)

TABLE 2.1 (contd)

Variable	(1)	(2)	(3)	(4)	(5)	(6)	(7)	(8)
Middle East dummy	0.32***	0.33***	0.33***	–	0.34***	0.41***	0.28***	0.28***
	(6.02)	(6.08)	(5.70)		(4.96)	(7.53)	(4.21)	(4.20)
Asia dummy	0.25***	0.25***	0.25***	–	0.28***	0.34***	0.19***	0.19***
	(6.01)	(6.12)	(5.84)		(5.64)	(7.30)	(3.98)	(3.93)
Latin America dummy	0.24***	0.24***	0.24***	–	0.25***	0.31***	0.26***	0.27***
	(6.10)	(5.65)	(5.60)		(5.15)	(6.86)	(5.02)	(5.29)
Intercept	0.35***	0.36***	0.35***	0.61***	0.33***	0.10	0.58***	0.57***
	(10.62)	(12.84)	(8.47)	(5.07)	(3.19)	(1.56)	(7.20)	(6.52)
Number of observations	67	66	66	55	55	43	49	50
R-squared	0.72	0.72	0.72	0.44	0.73	0.83	0.74	0.74

Notes: Figures in parentheses are absolute t-statistics. Omitted region is Africa. * indicates significance at the 10% level, ** at the 5% level and *** at the 1% level. Note that the gross female primary enrolment rate and ratio of female-to-male primary enrolment rate are highly correlated (0.76).

TABLE 2.2
Chain B regressions: from HD to EG (measure of EG is GDP per capita growth, 1960–2001)

Variable	(1)	(2)	(3)	(4)	(5)	(6)	(7)	(8)	(9)
Log GDP per capita, 1960 x 10	-2.80***	-2.64***	-3.32***	-1.54	-2.33**	-2.86***	-2.91***	-2.63***	-2.96***
	(3.42)	(3.04)	(3.80)	(1.62)	(2.38)	(3.43)	(3.66)	(3.27)	(3.81)
Literacy rate, 1970-1975 x100	1.95***	–	1.29**	0.98**	–	–	0.95	–	–
	(4.88)		(2.25)	(2.12)			(1.61)		
Literacy shortfall reduction, 1970–1980	–	–	–	–	–	–	4.97**	4.21***	1.94
							(2.22)	(2.74)	(1.53)
Log life expectancy, 1960	–	2.67***	1.43	–	1.81***	2.27***	–	–	–
		(4.31)	(1.59)		(2.93)	(3.71)			
Life expectancy shortfall reduction, 1960–1980	–	–	–	–	–	2.21***	–	–	–
						(2.71)			
Gross domestic investment (percentage of GDP), average over 1960–2001 x 100	–	–	–	5.81***	5.57***	–	–	5.04***	2.80**
				(3.71)	(4.36)			(3.60)	(2.39)
Exports (% of GDP), average over 1960–2001 x 1000	–	–	–	–	–	–	–	3.76	1.80
								(1.14)	(0.42)
Gini coefficient, average over 1960–2001 x 1000	–	–	–	-1.61	3.46	–	–	–	–
				(0.18)	(0.41)				
Poverty headcount, average over 1985–2001 x 1000	–	–	–	–	–	–	–	–	-16.4***
									(4.94)

(contd)

TABLE 2.2 (contd)

Variable	(1)	(2)	(3)	(4)	(5)	(6)	(7)	(8)	(9)
Middle East dummy	0.65***	0.17	0.48*	0.25	0.05	-0.06	0.57**	0.29	0.21
	(2.64)	(0.68)	(1.84)	(0.80)	(0.19)	(0.25)	(2.40)	(1.30)	(1.00)
Asia dummy	0.66***	0.63***	0.59***	0.46**	0.45**	0.40*	0.63***	0.56***	0.42***
	(3.41)	(3.06)	(2.95)	(2.25)	(2.33)	(1.86)	(3.36)	(3.37)	(3.14)
Latin America dummy	-0.12	-0.21	-0.22	-0.13	-0.15	-0.30	0.03	0.28	0.36**
	(0.61)	(0.94)	(1.02)	(0.62)	(0.77)	(1.43)	(0.13)	(1.62)	(2.40)
Intercept	1.19***	-8.18***	-3.62	-0.14	-6.28***	-6.89***	1.19***	0.40	1.89***
	(2.71)	(4.01)	(1.18)	(0.23)	(3.07)	(3.44)	(2.80)	(0.80)	(3.77)
Number of observations	67	69	67	55	57	69	67	67	50
R-squared	0.52	0.48	0.54	0.64	0.67	0.54	0.56	0.66	0.79

Notes: Figures in parentheses are absolute t-statistics. For region, the base group is Africa.
* indicates significance at the 10% level, ** at the 5% level and *** at the 1% level.
Note that the log of life expectancy and the poverty headcount are highly correlated (-0.59) and that the poverty headcount and the gross female primary enrolment rate are correlated (-0.51). Also, the literacy rate and the literacy shortfall reduction are highly correlated (0.83).
Source: World Development Indicators database (2003) and, on public expenditure on health, Human Development Report (2001).

of observations because of lack of data (Boozer and others, 2004). Because of the two-way causation, we used lags of the original variables to reduce the simultaneity bias.[5]

For Chain A (see Table 2.1), the variable chosen to measure human development progress was Infant Mortality Shortfall Reduction (IMSR),[6] 1960–2001. This was selected because the infant mortality rate is relatively accurate in measuring changes over time and is also correlated with other indicators, such as adult literacy and life expectancy. GDP per capita growth proved significant in most runs, as did female primary enrolment rates. Highly significant (at the 5 per cent or 1 per cent level) were social expenditure ratios, specifically public expenditure on health and education as a percentage of GDP. Income distribution, as summarized by the average value of the Gini coefficient between 1960 and 2001, proved significant, and with the expected sign, at the 10 per cent level in one of the runs, while the average poverty headcount during 1985–2001 was highly significant (at the 1 per cent level), and with the expected sign, whenever included. In other words, for every 1 per cent reduction in the poverty rate, the infant mortality shortfall reduction decreases by 3.8 per cent. HD progress was also positively related to gross female primary enrolment, showing the importance of female literacy in the HDIF. We did not have data to investigate the impact of the female contribution to household income. The regional dummies proved almost universally highly significant. Had we left them out, as indeed we did in one run, other variables would probably have gained in significance; however, given their role of capturing omitted variables (see the difference in the R-squares), we might have placed undue confidence in intercountry homogeneity among a large array of very different Third World countries.

For Chain B (see Table 2.2), the variable chosen to measure EG was GDP per capita growth during 1960–2001. We also included log GDP per capita 1960 in all equations in order to test for convergence, which was strongly confirmed in virtually all cases. GDP per capita growth was significantly related to HD improvement (at the 5 per cent or 1 per cent level) in virtually all cases, using the literacy rate and literacy shortfall reduction between 1970 and 1980 as indicators of HD. The very same result was obtained when we substituted 1960 life expectancy or life expectancy shortfall reduction between 1960 and 1980 as indicators of the level and progress in human development.

Moving on to the more conventional inputs in this production function, we found the gross domestic investment rate over the entire 1960–2001 period to be highly significant, mostly at the 1 per cent level. The export ratio, a proxy for competitiveness, proved insignificant, however. In future work, an effort should be made to obtain some indicator of technological capability, such as R&D,

patenting or FDI inflows, as an input into the production function generating per capita income growth.

As is well known, both economic and political economy arguments have been advanced, linking a more equal distribution of income to higher rates of growth. However, the average Gini coefficient over the 1960–2001 period did not prove significant. Nevertheless, when we substituted the average poverty headcount ratio, the result was surprisingly strong and highly significant at the 1 per cent level (see equation 9).

In summary, in exploring the two chains, we found significantly positive effects of EG on HD and of HD on EG. In other words, our empirical findings confirm the two-way causal connection between EG and HD by way of many, if not all, of those links that data constraints permitted us to consider. For Chain A, in addition to the positive impact of economic growth, HD improvement was larger the higher the social expenditure ratio, the higher female education enrolments, the better the distribution of income and the lower the poverty levels. For Chain B, as well as the positive impact of HD on growth, the relationship between HD and EG was stronger the higher the investment rate.

Our results also indicate that the two chains can deliver good results in a variety of ways by relying on the strength of particular links in the chains, thereby making up for the weakness of other links. For example, a country can achieve good HD progress by good EG, even in the face of an only moderately good distribution of income, as long as poverty rates are falling and the social expenditure ratio is high, as in Malaysia. Other countries have attained good HD progress with poor growth and poor distribution, but with high social expenditure and high female enrolment rates (e.g., Jamaica). In fact, research on individual countries shows that among those countries most successful with HD, each one them had high female/male enrolment ratios and relatively high social allocation ratios (Ranis and Stewart, 2000).

VIRTUOUS AND VICIOUS CYCLES AND LOPSIDED DEVELOPMENT

The existence of two chains linking HD and EG is thus strongly supported both by our framework, drawing on micro and macro studies in the literature, and by our own empirical results. This means that an economy may be on a mutually reinforcing upward spiral, with high levels of HD leading to high EG and high EG, in turn, further promoting HD. Conversely, weak HD may result in low EG and, consequently, poor progress towards HD improvement. The strength of the links in the two chains influences the extent of mutual reinforcement between HD and EG in either direction, i.e., positively or negatively.

Consequently, country performance can be usefully classified into four categories, *virtuous*, *vicious* and two types of *lopsidedness*, i.e., lopsided with relatively strong HD/weak EG (called 'HD-lopsided') and lopsided with relatively weak HD/strong EG ('EG-lopsided'). In the virtuous cycle case, good HD enhances EG, which, in turn, promotes HD, and so on. In the vicious cycle case, poor performance on HD tends to lead to poor EG performance, which in turn depresses HD achievements, and so on. The stronger the linkages in the two chains described above, the more pronounced the cycle of EG and HD, in either a positive or negative direction.

Where some linkages are weak, cases of lopsided development may occur. On the one hand, good EG may not bring about large improvements in HD if, for example, there are weak linkages, such as a low social allocation ratio; on the other hand, good HD performance may not generate good EG if there is a dearth of complementary resources because of low investment rates. Such cases of lopsided development are unlikely to persist. Either the weak partner in the cycle eventually acts as a brake on the other partner, leading to a vicious cycle case; or, if the linkages are strengthened, possibly by policy change, a virtuous cycle may result.

One way of classifying countries into the four categories was to compare their performance on HD and EG (1960–2001) with the average performance of all developing countries (see Figure 2.2). The vertical and horizontal grid lines represent the average performance for all developing countries for the period, with countries weighted by their populations in 2001. Most developing countries appear as either virtuous (NE quadrant), or vicious (SW quadrant); a

FIGURE 2.2
HD and EG performance, 1960–2001

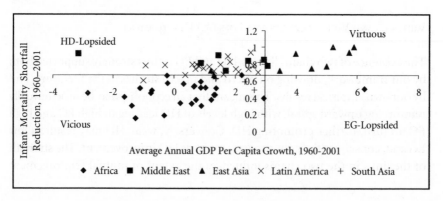

significant number show an HD-lopsided pattern, and only one an EG-lopsided one. A strong regional pattern emerges, with East Asia heavily represented in the virtuous cycle quadrant. The majority of countries in the vicious cycle quadrant are from sub-Saharan Africa, and there are a significant number from Latin America. Latin America is also strongly represented in the HD-lopsided quadrant, the one EG-lopsided country being from Africa.

The important issue for policy purposes, of course, is how a country may move towards the virtuous cycle. Much can be learned about this by looking at the ways in which countries changed their location over time (Table 2.3). Examining the movements of countries over the four decades between 1960 and 2001, we find that only two countries remained in the virtuous category throughout—the Republic of Korea and Singapore, which had highly successfully social and economic policies over the whole forty-year period. These countries combined a strong state, committed to advancing HD, with intelligent economic interventions, making good use of market forces. Four countries succeeded in moving from the HD-lopsided to the virtuous category—China from the 1960s to the 1970s; Viet Nam from the 1980s to the 1990s; Malaysia from the 1980s to the 1990s; and Chile from the 1980s to the 1990s. In the case of China and Viet Nam, the communist regimes had placed great emphasis on HD, resulting in HD-lopsided performance. In both countries, economic growth accelerated following economic reforms and a virtuous cycle was obtained. Malaysia had a virtuous performance in the 1960s, lapsed in the 1970s and then resumed good growth and HD in the 1980s and 1990s. High social expenditures explain the good HD performance, while economic growth was supported by a high investment rate. Chile suffered from depressed growth in the 1970s and 1980s as the Pinochet regime introduced very tough stabilization policies and radical economic reforms, but in the 1990s economic growth resumed.

Other countries moved from the virtuous category into the HD-lopsided category, often in response to particular short-term economic difficulties, such as the debt crisis of the 1980s, which affected many of the Latin American countries, and the 1997 East Asian financial crisis. The impact of the adjustment and debt crisis is shown, for example, in Brazil, Ecuador, Colombia, Costa Rica, the Dominican Republic, Jamaica and Uruguay, all of which moved from the virtuous quadrant to the HD-lopsided between the 1970s and the 1980s. The negative impact on economic growth of the East Asian crisis is shown by Thailand's fall from a virtuous cycle to HD-lopsided between the 1980s and 1990s. Indonesia started as a virtuous case (the 1960s), then had two decades of EG-lopsidedness and ended in the vicious cycle category owing to the impact of the financial crisis and political instability.

There was a strong tendency for countries in the vicious cycle to remain

TABLE 2.3
Virtuous, vicious and lopsided performance, 1960–2001

	1960–1970	1970–1980	1980–1990	1990–2001
Africa				
Benin	Vicious	Vicious	Vicious	Vicious
Botswana	Virtuous	Virtuous	Virtuous	HD-lopsided
Burkina Faso	Vicious	Vicious	Vicious	Vicious
Burundi	EG-lopsided	Vicious	Vicious	Vicious
Cameroon	Vicious	EG-lopsided	Vicious	Vicious
Central African Republic	Vicious	Vicious	Vicious	Vicious
Chad	Vicious	Vicious	Vicious	Vicious
Congo, Rep. of	Virtuous	Virtuous	Vicious	Vicious
Côte d'Ivoire	EG-lopsided	Vicious	Vicious	Vicious
Dem. Rep. of the Congo	Vicious	Vicious	Vicious	Vicious
Ethiopia	–	–	Vicious	Vicious
Gabon	EG-lopsided	EG-lopsided	Vicious	Vicious
Gambia	–	Vicious	Vicious	Vicious
Ghana	HD-lopsided	Vicious	Vicious	Vicious
Guinea-Bissau	–	Vicious	Vicious	Vicious
Kenya	HD-lopsided	Virtuous	HD-lopsided	HD-lopsided
Lesotho	EG-lopsided	EG-lopsided	Vicious	Vicious
Madagascar	Vicious	Vicious	Vicious	Vicious
Malawi	EG-lopsided	EG-Lopsided	Vicious	Vicious
Mali	–	Vicious	Vicious	Vicious
Mauritania	EG-lopsided	Vicious	Vicious	Vicious
Mauritius	–	–	Virtuous	HD-lopsided
Mozambique	–	–	Vicious	EG-lopsided
Namibia	–	–	Vicious	Vicious
Niger	Vicious	Vicious	Vicious	Vicious
Nigeria	EG-lopsided	Vicious	Vicious	Vicious
Rwanda	Vicious	Vicious	Vicious	Vicious
Senegal	Vicious	Vicious	Vicious	Vicious
Sierra Leone	EG-lopsided	Vicious	Vicious	Vicious
South Africa	Virtuous	HD-lopsided	HD-lopsided	HD-lopsided
Sudan	Vicious	Vicious	Vicious	EG-lopsided
Togo	EG-lopsided	Vicious	Vicious	Vicious
Zambia	HD-lopsided	Vicious	Vicious	Vicious
Zimbabwe	Virtuous	HD-lopsided	HD-lopsided	HD-lopsided

(contd)

Table 2.3 (contd)

	1960–1970	1970–1980	1980–1990	1990–2001
Middle East				
Algeria	Vicious	EG-lopsided	Vicious	HD-lopsided
Egypt	EG-lopsided	EG-lopsided	Vicious	Vicious
Iran, Islamic Rep. of	–	Vicious	Vicious	HD-lopsided
Jordan	–	–	HD-lopsided	HD-lopsided
Kuwait	HD-lopsided	HD-lopsided	HD-lopsided	HD-lopsided
Morocco	EG-lopsided	EG-lopsided	Vicious	Vicious
Oman	EG-lopsided	Vicious	Virtuous	–
Saudi Arabia	EG-lopsided	EG-lopsided	HD-lopsided	HD-lopsided
Syrian Arab Republic	Virtuous	Virtuous	HD-lopsided	HD-lopsided
Tunisia	EG-lopsided	EG-lopsided	HD-lopsided	HD-lopsided
Turkey	–	Vicious	Vicious	HD-lopsided
United Arab Emirates	–	HD-lopsided	HD-lopsided	HD-lopsided
East Asia				
China	HD-lopsided	Virtuous	Virtuous	Virtuous
Hong Kong SAR	Virtuous	Virtuous	Virtuous	HD-lopsided
Indonesia	Virtuous	EG-lopsided	EG-lopsided	HD-lopsided
Lao PDR	–	–	Vicious	Vicious
Malaysia	Virtuous	Virtuous	HD-lopsided	Virtuous
Mongolia	–	–	Vicious	Vicious
Papua New Guinea	EG-lopsided	Vicious	HD-lopsided	Vicious
Philippines	Virtuous	Virtuous	HD-lopsided	HD-lopsided
Republic of Korea	Virtuous	Virtuous	Virtuous	Virtuous
Singapore	Virtuous	Virtuous	Virtuous	Virtuous
Thailand	Virtuous	Virtuous	Virtuous	HD-lopsided
Viet Nam	–	–	HD-lopsided	Virtuous
Latin America				
Argentina	Virtuous	HD-lopsided	HD-lopsided	HD-lopsided
Bolivia	Vicious	Vicious	Vicious	Vicious
Brazil	Virtuous	Virtuous	HD-lopsided	HD-lopsided
Chile	Virtuous	HD-lopsided	HD-lopsided	Virtuous
Colombia	Virtuous	Virtuous	HD-lopsided	HD-lopsided
Costa Rica	Virtuous	Virtuous	HD-lopsided	HD-lopsided
Dominican Republic	Virtuous	Virtuous	HD-lopsided	Virtuous
Ecuador	HD-lopsided	Virtuous	HD-lopsided	HD-lopsided
El Salvador	Virtuous	Vicious	Vicious	HD-lopsided

(contd)

TABLE 2.3 *(contd)*

	1960–1970	*1970–1980*	*1980–1990*	*1990–2001*
Guatemala	Virtuous	EG-lopsided	Vicious	HD-lopsided
Haiti	Vicious	EG-lopsided	Vicious	Vicious
Honduras	Vicious	Vicious	HD-lopsided	HD-lopsided
Jamaica	Virtuous	HD-lopsided	HD-lopsided	HD-lopsided
Mexico	Virtuous	Virtuous	HD-lopsided	HD-lopsided
Nicaragua	Virtuous	HD-lopsided	Vicious	HD-lopsided
Panama	Virtuous	HD-lopsided	HD-lopsided	HD-lopsided
Paraguay	Virtuous	Virtuous	HD-lopsided	HD-lopsided
Peru	Virtuous	Vicious	HD-lopsided	HD-lopsided
Trinidad and Tobago	Virtuous	Virtuous	HD-lopsided	HD-lopsided
Uruguay	HD-lopsided	Virtuous	HD-lopsided	HD-lopsided
Venezuela (Bolivarian Rep. of)	HD-lopsided	HD-lopsided	HD-lopsided	HD-lopsided
South Asia				
Bangladesh	Vicious	Vicious	Vicious	Vicious
India	Vicious	Vicious	EG-lopsided	Vicious
Nepal	Vicious	Vicious	Vicious	Vicious
Pakistan	EG-lopsided	Vicious	Vicious	Vicious
Sri Lanka	Virtuous	Virtuous	HD-lopsided	HD-lopsided

Notes: All classifications of countries into quadrants are based on performance relative to population weighted developing world averages.
Source: World Development Indicators database (2003).

there. Altogether, twelve countries stayed in the vicious cycle throughout the four decades—nine from Africa, two (Bangladesh and Nepal) from Asia, as well as Bolivia in Latin America; only six exited, five into the HD-lopsided category (one only temporarily), and one into the EG-lopsided cagtegory. Almost all the countries leaving the vicious category had suffered civil wars which had ended or lessened in impact—e.g., El Salvador, Nicaragua, Guatemala, Papua New Guinea and the Sudan.

Lopsidedness, as expected, proved generally unstable. As noted, some countries succeeded in moving from the HD-lopsided category into the virtuous category. Just two countries remained in the HD-lopsided category throughout—Kuwait and Venezuela, both countries which could sustain HD with large expenditures financed by oil revenues. No country remained in the EG-lopsided category. EG-lopsided countries almost invariably fell into the vicious category. This was a pattern followed by sixteen countries, many of them in Africa, which succeeded in first achieving relatively high economic growth despite poor HD for a period following independence, after which growth lapsed. No country succeeded in moving from EG-lopsided to virtuous.

These findings clearly have some strong implications for policy sequencing. They show the need for balance in promoting HD and EG because it is very difficult to sustain one without the other—indeed, it seems to be impossible in the case of EG. Moreover, of greatest importance, the findings imply that it is not possible to reach the ideal of a virtuous cycle by first generating improved EG while neglecting HD, since any EG attained in this way will not be sustained.

CONCLUSIONS AND POLICY IMPLICATIONS

Our investigation into the determinants of HD progress and EG has clearly demonstrated the importance of the two-way relationship between them. The empirical work confirmed the significance of a number of links in the two chains—including income distribution, the social expenditure ratio and female education in Chain A, and the investment ratio in Chain B, in addition to the important inputs of EG and HD, respectively. Moreover, we have found that, even in the presence of some weak links in a chain, it is possible to achieve good progress by particularly strong performance in other links.

However, our most important conclusion concerns sequencing. Because of the strong two-way relationship between EG and HD, one has to promote *both* to sustain progress in either. Economic growth, which is an important input into HD improvement, is itself not sustainable without improvement in HD. The investigation of country changes over time has strong implications for the phasing of policies. Economic policy has tended to focus priority on getting the economic fundamentals 'right' as a necessary precondition for economic growth, arguing that HD improvement must await such economic growth—as in the classic 'Washington Consensus', for example. In sharp contrast, our findings contradict the view that HD improvement may be postponed until economic resource expansion makes it affordable. If HD improvement is postponed in this way, EG itself will not be sustained.

NOTES

[1] This chapter draws heavily on previous work by the authors and others: see Ranis, Stewart and Ramirez 2000; Ranis and Stewart 2000; Boozer and others 2003. We are grateful for comments on an earlier draft from José Antonio Ocampo and discussants at the New York meeting in March 2005.

[2] These calculations adopt a narrow definition of social priority expenditure, including pre-primary and first level education plus primary health care only.

[3] De Gregorio and Lee (1999: Abstract) find that 'education factors—higher attainment and

more equal distribution of education—play a significant role in making income distribution more equal'.

[4] The growth/inequality nexus has been challenged by Liu, Squire and Zou (1998) who find a negative relationship, while Barro (1999) and Deininger and Olinto (2000) argue that the relationship is non-linear and a positive relationship holds only for poor countries.

[5] Lagged values are reasonable candidates as instruments since the correlation between the residuals in the two periods analysed is not substantial.

[6] Shortfall reduction is measured relative to ceiling levels of countries at current maximum achievement, i.e., 3/1000 for infant mortality; and 85 years of age for life expectancy.

REFERENCES

Alesina, A., and R. Perotti (1994). The Political Economy of Growth: A Critical Survey of the Recent Literature. *The World Bank Economic Review* 8 (3): 351–371.

Alesina, A., and Dani Rodrik (1994). Distributive Politics and Economic Growth. *Quarterly Journal of Economics*, 109 (2): 465–490.

Barrera, A. (1990). The Role of Maternal Schooling and Its Interactions with Public Health Programs in Child Health Production. *Journal of Development Economics* 32: 69–91.

Barro, R.J. (1999). Determinants of Democracy. *Journal of Political Economy* 107 (6): S158–S183.

Behrman, J.R., and Barbara L. Wolfe (1987a). Investments in schooling in two generations in pre-revolutionary Nicaragua: the roles of family background and school supply. *Journal of Development Economics*, 27: 395–419.

Behrman, J.R., and Barbara L. Wolfe (1987b). How Does Mother's Schooling Affect the Family's Health, Nutrition, Medical Care Usage and Household Sanitation? *Journal of Econometrics* 36 (1–2): 185–204.

Behrman, J.R. (1990a). *Human Resource Led Development: Review of Issues and Development.* ARTEP/ILO, New Delhi.

Behrman, J.R. (1990b). The Action of Human Resources and Poverty on One Another: What We Have Yet to Learn. Living Standards Measurement Study (LSMS) Working Paper No. 74, World Bank, Washington DC.

Behrman, J.R. (1990c). Women's Schooling and Nonmarket Productivity: A Survey and A Reappraisal. Processed, University of Pennsylvania, Philadelphia, PA.

Behrman, J.R. (1993). The Economic Rationale for Investing in Nutrition in Developing Countries. *World Development* 21 (11): 1749–1771.

Behrman, J.R. (1995). The Impact of Distributive Policies, Governmental Expenditure Patterns and Decentralization on Human Resources. Processed, University of Pennsylvania, Philadelphia.

Behrman, J.R. (1996). Impact of Health and Nutrition on Education. *World Bank Research Observer* 11(1): 23–37.

Behrman, J.R., and A.B. Deolalikar (1988). Health and Nutrition. In H.B. Chenery and T.N. Srinivasan (eds). *Handbook of Development Economics*, vol. 1. North Holland, Amsterdam: 631–711.

Behrman, J.R., M.R. Rosenzweig and P. Vashishtha (1995). Location-Specific Technical Change, Human Capital and Local Economic Development: The Indian Green Revolution Experience. In H. Siebert (ed.). *Locational Competition in the World Economy.* Kiel Institute of World Economics, Kiel: 111–135.

Birdsall, Nancy (1993). Social Development is Economic Development. Policy Research Working Paper No. 1123, World Bank, Washington, DC.

Birdsall, Nancy, D. Ross and R. Sabot (1995). Inequality and Growth Reconsidered: Lessons from East Asia. *World Bank Economic Review* 9 (3): 477–508.

Boozer, M., Gustav Ranis, Frances Stewart and T. Suri (2004). Paths to Success: the Relationship between Human Development and Economic Growth. Economic Growth Center Discussion Paper, Yale University, New Haven.

Bloom, D., D. Canning and J. Sevilla (2004). The Effect of Health on Economic Growth: a Production Function Approach. *World Development*, 32 (1): 1–13.

Cornia, G.A., and Frances Stewart (1995). Two Errors of Targeting. In Frances Stewart *Adjustment and Poverty: Options and Choices*. Routledge, London: 82–107.

De Gregorio, José, and Jong-Wha Lee (1999). Education and Income Distribution: New Evidence from Cross-country Data. Documentos de Trabajo No. 55, Centro de Economía Aplicada, Universidad de Chile, Santiago.

Deininger, K., and P. Olinto (2000). Asset Inequality, Inequality and Growth. Processed, World Bank, Washington, DC.

Deraniyagala, Sorali (1995). Technical Change and Efficiency in Sri Lanka's Manufacturing Industry. D. Phil. thesis, Oxford University.

Fei, J.C.H., Gustav Ranis and Frances Stewart (1985). Towards Viable Balanced Growth Strategies: A Locational Perspective. Paper prepared for UNIDO, Vienna.

Foster, A.D., and M.R. Rosenzweig (1994). Technical Change and Human Resources and Investments: Consequences of the Green Revolution. Processed, University of Pennsylvania, Philadelphia, PA.

Grossman, G.M., and Ethan Helpman (1991). *Innovation and Growth in the Global Economy*. MIT Press, Cambridge.

Habibi, N., C. Huang, D. Miranda, V. Murillo, Gustav Ranis, M. Sarkar and Frances Stewart (2003). Decentralization and Human Development in Argentina. *Journal of Human Development* 4 (1): 73–101.

Hoddinott, J., and L. Haddad (1991). Household Expenditures, Child Anthropometric Status and the Intrahousehold Division of Income: Evidence from the Cote d'Ivoire. Discussion Paper No. 155, Research Program in Development Studies, Woodrow Wilson School, Princeton University.

Immink, M., and F. Viterri (1981). Energy Intake and Productivity of Guatemalan Sugarcane Cutters: An Empirical Test of the Efficiency Wage Hypothesis. *Journal of Development Economics*, 9 (2): 273–287.

ILO (1977). *Basic Needs a One World Problem*. International Labour Office, Geneva.

King, E.M., and M.A. Hill (eds) (1993). *Women's Education in Developing Countries: Barriers, Benefits, and Policies*. Johns Hopkins University Press, Baltimore, published for the World Bank, Washington, DC.

Klugman, J. (1994). *Decentralization: A Survey of Literature from a Human Development Perspective*. United Nations Development Programme, New York.

Lavy, V., J. Strauss, D. Thomas and P. de Vreyer (1995). The Impact of the Quality of Health Care on Children's Nutrition and Survival in Ghana. Living Standards Measurement Study (LSMS) Working Paper No. 106, World Bank, Washington, DC.

Liu, H., Lyn Squire and H. Zou (1995). Explaining International and Intertemporal Variations in Income Inequality. Processed, World Bank, Washington DC.

Lucas, R.E. (1988). On the Mechanics of Economic Development. *Journal of Monetary Economics* 22 (1): 3–42.

Persson, T., and G. Tabellini (1994). Is Inequality Harmful for Growth? *American Economic Review* 84 (3): 600–621.

Psacharopolous, G., S. Morley, A. Fiszbein, H. Lee and B. Wood (1992). *Poverty and Income Distribution in Latin America: The Story of the 1980s*. World Bank, Washington, DC.

Psacharopolous, G. (1994). Returns to Investment in Education: A Global Update. *World Development* 22 (9): 1325–1343.

Ranis, Gustav, Frances Stewart and A. Ramirez (2000). Economic Growth and Human Development. *World Development* 28 (2): 197–219.

Ranis, Gustav, and Frances Stewart (2000). Strategies for Success in Human Development. *Journal of Human Development* 1 (1): 49–69.

Ranis, Gustav, and Frances Stewart (1994). Decentralisation in Indonesia. *Bulletin of Indonesian Economic Studies* 30 (3): 41–72.

Riddell, R., M. Robinson, J. de Coninck, A. Muir and S. White (1995). *Non-governmental Organizations and Rural Poverty Alleviation.* Oxford University Press, New York.

Romer, P.M. (1990). Endogenous Technological Change. *Journal of Political Economy* 98: S71–S102.

Rosenzweig, M.R., and T.P. Schultz (1982). Market Opportunities, Genetic Endowments, and Intrafamily Resource Distribution: Child Survival in Rural India. *American Economic Review,* 72: 803–815.

Rosenzweig, M.R. (1995). Why Are There Returns in Schooling? *American Economic Review* 85 (2): 153–158.

Schultz, T.W. (1975). The Value of the Ability to Deal with Disequilibria. *Journal of Economic Literature,* 13 (3): 827–46.

Schultz, T.P. (1988). Education Investments and Returns. In Hollis Chenery and T.N. Srinivasan (eds). *Handbook of Development Economics.* North Holland, Amsterdam: 544–630.

Schultz, T.P. (1993a). Returns to Women's Education. In E.M. King and M.A. Hill (eds). *Women's Education in Developing Countries: Barriers, Benefits, and Policies.* Johns Hopkins University Press, Baltimore, published for the World Bank, Washington, DC: 51–100

Schultz, T.P. (1993b). Investments in the Schooling and Health of Women and Men: Quantities and Returns. *Journal of Human Resources* 28: 694–734.

Selowsky, M., and L. Taylor (1973). The Economics of Malnourished Children: An Example of Disinvestment in Human Capital. *Economic Development and Cultural Change* 22: 17–30.

Sen, A.K. (1984). Rights and Capabilities. In A.K. Sen (ed.). *Resources, Values, and Development.* Harvard University Press, Cambridge, MA: 307–324.

Strauss, J. (1986). Does Better Nutrition Raise Farm Productivity? *Journal of Political Economy* 94 (2): 297–320.

Strauss, J., and D. Thomas (1995). Human Resources: Empirical Modeling of Household and Family Decisions. In J.R. Behrman and T.N. Srinivasan (eds). *Handbook of Development Economics,* vol. 3. North Holland, Amsterdam: 1883–2023.

Streeten, Paul, S.J. Burki, Mahbub ul Haq, N. Hicks and Frances Stewart (1981). *First Things First: Meeting Basic Needs in the Developing Countries.* Oxford University Press, New York.

UNDP. *Human Development Report. Various years.* Oxford University Press, New York.

Welch, F. (1970). Education in Production. *Journal of Political Economy,* 78 (1): 35–39.

Wolgemuth, J.C., M.C. Latham, A. Hall, A. Chesher and D.W. Crompton (1982). Worker productivity and the nutritional status of Kenyan road construction laborers. *American Journal of Clinical Nutrition* 36: 68–78.

3
Policy Reform and Income Distribution[1]

GIOVANNI ANDREA CORNIA

BROAD TRENDS IN INCOME INEQUALITY

Domestic income inequality declined steadily between the early nineteenth century and the mid-1970s (Bourguignon and Morisson, 2002). Until the 1950s, this decline was mainly evident in today's advanced nations and in the socialist countries of Europe; between the 1950s and early 1970s, however, it spread to several developing countries—such as the Asian tigers, China and India—which introduced programmes of land reform, educational expansion, public health and income redistribution after achieving independence.

In spite of such declines, income inequality was still very high in most developing countries in the 1970s, mainly because of the interplay of the 'traditional causes of inequality'—including high land concentration, unequal access to education and other public services, selective access to credit, the dominance of the mining or plantation sector, and the urban bias of public policy, which allowed city-based elites to capture a disproportionate share of economic opportunities. Racial and gender discrimination were also important for inequality, and all this was rooted in social systems in which the poor and the lower-middle class had limited ability to organize, influence policy and defend their interests.

From the mid-1970s, income inequality started turning upwards in the Organization for Economic Cooperation and Development (OECD) countries (Smeeding, 2002) and in Latin America (Szekely, 2003). The 1990s witnessed a sharp rise in income polarization in the economies in transition (Milanovic, 1998). Meanwhile, in China, inequality rose slowly from 1978 to 1985, after which it rose faster (Riskin, 2003). A trend reversal also took place in the Asian tigers (Jomo, 2004), India (Deaton and Drèze, 2002) and other South Asian nations (Pal, Sengupta and Ghosh, 2004), albeit later, less markedly and from lower initial inequality levels. The limited data available for sub-Saharan Africa suggest that, following structural adjustment, the urban-rural income gap was reduced by a process of 'equalizing downward' (as in Côte d'Ivoire), though intra-urban inequality rose, while intrarural inequality rose in countries characterized by high land concentration such as Kenya, or where recovery was peasant-based, but failed to reach remote areas, as in Zambia. Meanwhile, income inequality improved in countries characterized by a peasant agriculture rebounding from years of civil strife, such as Mozambique and Uganda (McCulloch, Baulch and Cherel-Robson, 2000; Bigsten, 2000). Data limitations do not allow any conclusion for the Middle East and North African (MENA) region, though the fragmentary evidence available seems to point to substantially stable income inequality.

As a result, over the last 25 years, income inequality appears to have risen to various extents and with different effects in 70 per cent of the countries with inequality data, representing 80 per cent of the world population and gross domestic product (GDP) (Cornia with Kiiski, 2001; Cornia (ed.), 2004).[2] Except for Africa and MENA, these countries accounted for 84 to 98 per cent of the population and for 82 to 98 per cent of the GDP-PPP of their respective regions. Inequality was found to have risen in 48 countries, to have remained constant in 16, and to have declined in nine. There were notable exceptions to the dominant trend of growing inequality—for example, France, Germany, Malaysia and Jamaica—but these did not reverse the general trend.[3]

The observed increase in Gini coefficients in the 53 (out of the 73 tested) nations exhibiting growing inequality was moderate (more than 5 points) or high (5–10 points) in about thirty-five countries. Increases of 10–20 points were recorded in fourteen countries, and increases of more than 20 points in three States of the former Soviet Union. While inequality rises of 3–5 points from low initial levels may spur economic growth, large increases (as in the former Union of Soviet Socialist Republics (USSR)) or moderate increases from already high levels (as in Latin America) probably negatively affect poverty alleviation and economic growth.

The recent rise in income inequality cannot be attributed to a worsening of the traditional causes of inequality mentioned above. While high land concentration remains a major cause of rural and overall inequality, such changes cannot, as a rule, explain income inequality trends over the last two decades. Indeed, the weight of agriculture in total output and employment fell everywhere, and highly inequitable land rents declined, as a share of both GDP and agricultural output. Likewise, while countries well endowed with mineral resources are known to have high income and asset inequality, this 'curse of natural resources' hardly explains the increase in inequality over the last two decades, as the 'rent/GDP ratio' systematically declined in most mining or plantation economies from the late 1970s. Third, the apparent 'urban bias' in a more globalized world (Eastwood and Lipton, 2000) has increased in post-1984 China, Thailand and Indonesia, but has declined in Latin America and parts of Africa. Finally, worsening inequality in education is unlikely to offer a general explanation for the recent deterioration in the distribution of income.

In fact, while more unequal access to education has contributed to greater income inequality during the last two decades in Latin America, this does not seem to have been the case in other regions (Checchi, 2004).

The recent rise in inequality could also be due to 'new non-policy factors' such as skill-biased technical change, shifts in labour market participation, demographic effects and rising migrant remittances. Space limitations do not allow a careful review of these hypotheses. While these factors do affect the distribution of income in specific situations, none of them generally explains the deterioration over the last twenty years in distinctly different types of countries.

One reason why these explanations are either incomplete or misplaced is the mounting evidence that the recent increase in inequality has been associated with a rise in the 'capital share' of total income, and corresponding falls in the 'labour share' and the 'transfer share'. This shift was caused by the effects of liberalization and globalization policies that weakened labour institutions, raised interest rates and interest spreads, led to insider privatization as well as rising asset concentration and rents in the financial and real estate sector, reduced progressive redistribution via the budget, and exacerbated regional disparities.

In a number of cases, the rise in capital share was very pronounced. In the United Kingdom of Great Britain and Northern Ireland, for instance, the income share of the top one per cent of the population (with 60 per cent from capital income) rose over 1979–2001 from 21 to 34 per cent, suggesting that the capital share rose by at least 8 percentage points (Atkinson, 2003). Likewise, in South Africa, the share of profits, rents and other property incomes rose from 18 to 30 per cent of total income from 1981 to 2000. In the case of India, Banerjee and Piketty (2001) show that the share of total income accruing to the top one per cent of income earners in the late 1990s increased from 4 per cent to almost 11 per cent. Thus, though such data are still fragmentary, the evidence suggests the distribution changes of the last two decades might be associated with a shift in factor shares, rising spatial inequality and greater wage differentials unexplained by human capital theory. Scattered, but growing, evidence in this regard is available for countries as different as Argentina, Canada, Chile, Japan, Mexico, the Russian Federation, Thailand, Turkey, United States, Uzbekistan and Venezuela.

Thus, while the traditional causes of inequality still contribute to social polarization, there is mounting evidence that—contrary to the predictions of mainstream theory—recent policy changes, associated with domestic liberalization and globalization, have often been associated with rising income inequality, as will be explored in greater detail in the next section. Thus, understanding the relationship between policy reform and income inequality is essential for any effort at reducing poverty over the medium term, as in the case of the Millennium Development Goals (MDGs). This is all the more true in view of the possible interaction between the old 'structural' causes of inequality and the new 'policy-related' ones.

This chapter reviews the changes in within-country income inequality that have accompanied the recent liberalization of the domestic economy and external transactions. It argues that the conclusions of standard theory about the ex ante distributive impact of policy reform often collide with a substantial body of empirical evidence indicating that inequality rose following liberalization and globalization. Finally, the chapter explores the causes of the discrepancy between theoretical predictions and observed inequality trends for each major policy change by emphasizing the impact on inequality of poorly sequenced macroeconomic policies, incomplete markets, weak institutions, asymmetric information, widespread protectionism and structural rigidities.

EXTERNAL LIBERALIZATION AND INEQUALITY

Trade Liberalization

The Hecksher-Ohlin (HO) theorem predicts that trade liberalization will lead to greater specialization and a rise in national income in all participating countries, following a more rational global allocation of production inspired by the principle of comparative advantage. In labour-abundant countries, trade liberalization is expected to switch production from inefficient capital-intensive import substitutes to efficient labour-intensive exports. In turn, the Stolper-Samuelson (SS) corollary to the HO theorem posits that such shifts will lead to convergence in the prices of goods exchanged and in factor remunerations. Because of this, domestic inequality is expected to decline in countries endowed with an abundant labour supply and to rise in those with an abundant endowment of capital, as the demand and remuneration for the latter (unequally distributed) will increase, while the demand and remuneration for labour (distributed more equitably) will fall.

However, the empirical evidence of the impact of trade liberalization on inequality is mixed and does not always support the conclusions of HO-SS model. Several studies point to the equalizing effect of free trade. In the nineteenth century, trade liberalization raised domestic inequality in rich New World countries, but reduced it in the poor Old World countries. Likewise, in an analysis of thirty-five small developing countries, Bourguignon and Morisson (1989) conclude that the removal of trade protection in manufacturing reduced the income share of the richest 20 per cent of the population and raised that of the bottom 60 per cent. Wood (1994) arrives at a similar conclusion for East Asian exporters of labour-intensive manufactured goods.

An equally important body of literature points to the opposite conclusions for a broad range of countries. For instance, wage inequality was found to have increased in six out of seven Latin American countries that had liberalized trade, as well as in the Philippines and Eastern Europe (Lindert and Williamson, 2001). An analysis of 38 developing countries for the years 1965–1992 found that trade liberalization benefited the richest 40 per cent, while negatively affecting the bottom 40 per cent, who were hurt by greater fluctuations in the terms of trade following the opening of the economy (Lundberg and Squire, 1999). Savvides (1999) showed that the most open developing countries experienced a rise in inequality between the 1980s and the early 1990s, and a positive correlation between trade protection and the income share of the poorest quintile.

How can one explain these conflicting findings and the frequent discrepancies between empirical results and theoretical predictions? To start with, it must be underscored that the HO-SS theorem holds under very restrictive assumptions concerning trade between two countries producing two goods with two factors (capital and labour), using the same technology that remains constant over time. The model also assumes no economies of scale, efficient factor markets (characterized by free factor mobility and full employment of all factors), balanced trade and symmetric trade liberalization by all trading partners. Yet, in the real world, trade takes place in a multi-country, multi-factor and multi-goods context, in which most of the above assumptions do not hold. Indeed, a formal extension of the HO-SS model shows that the predicted efficiency and equity outcomes may not be obtained if some basic assumptions are relaxed. Alternative explanations of why inequality may rise after trade liberalization are provided below.

Changing relative endowments of countries participating in multi-country, multi-factor and multi-goods trade
The limitations of the 2x2x2 HO model are most obvious when considering the case of trade among countries whose relative comparative advantages evolve over time because of changing trade policy decisions by some other country. Country A, for instance, may have a comparative advantage in terms of unskilled labour in relation to country B, but not to country C, which has yet to liberalize its trade regime. Thus, a decision to liberalize exports by the latter may have distributional consequences for A. In particular, the prediction that A will experience a reduction in inequality due to greater trade with B is unlikely to be fulfilled as its labour intensive exports will be displaced by those of C. It may

even be the case that because of C's decision to liberalize trade, A will specialize in the production of goods with medium-high skill and capital content, with the effect of worsening its wage distribution. This is what happened in the 1990s, when entry into the world market of labour-intensive manufactures by several low-wage Asian economies affected the exports and comparative advantage of middle-income countries in Latin America, Eastern Europe and South-East Asia.

Mexico's experience from 1985 to 1990 is another well documented case of this type of situation (Alarcon and McKinley, 1998). In Chile, Costa Rica and Colombia, increasing openness raised inequality, owing to the contraction of high-skill import-substituting sectors (replaced by imports from developed economies), the expansion of the semi-skilled sectors (including agriculture) and the contraction of low-skill intensive sectors due to rising imports from low-income countries (Wood, 1995).

Liberalization in countries specializing in the export of primary commodities

The primary commodities sector has been subjected to considerable price shocks—because of both sudden variations in global demand and the 'fallacy of composition' problem caused by the growing number of suppliers entering saturated markets. Over the past two decades, these price shocks have reduced the trade/GDP ratio in most commodity-producing countries despite liberalization of their trade regimes (Birdsall and Hamoudi, 2002). These price collapses reduced their export receipts and import capacity, leading to declines in employment and earnings in the import-substituting sector (usually not fully compensated by growth of the export sector) and worsening income distribution.

Trade liberalization in countries with unequal distribution of the abundant factor

The standard HO-SS model also fails in the case of countries exporting primary commodities produced by means of an unequally distributed abundant factor. While an increase in land-intensive agricultural exports may reduce inequality in countries with egalitarian agrarian structures, it could actually raise inequality in countries dominated by latifundia. Due to the labour surplus prevalent in the rural labour market, it is unlikely that increased demand for agricultural workers will raise the subsistence wage in line with or faster than the increased export receipts.

Trade liberalization and the import of skill-enhancing
investment goods
One assumption of the HO-SS model is that production technologies utilized by the trading countries are not affected by trade itself. Yet, trade liberalization can increase access to previously restricted technologies or raise imports of capital-intensive investment goods by relaxing foreign exchange constraints. With capital-skilled labour complementarities, this 'skill-enhancing trade' may increase demand for and wages of skilled workers and reduce those of unskilled workers.

Asymmetric trade liberalization and protectionism
among trading partners
Another assumption of the basic trade model is that trade liberalization occurs in all trading partners. However, in the case of 'low-tech' African and Asian exporters, trade liberalization has led to unsatisfactory export growth, not only because of weak domestic conditions, but also because of persistent protectionism in OECD countries. Furthermore, OECD countries have not abandoned the policy—forbidden under World Trade Organization rules—of subsidizing entire sectors of agriculture and exporting their products at prices below their production costs. Thus, in most cases, unilateral liberalization, combined with restrictive trade practices by trading partners, can raise inequality and poverty in low-tech exporters, as employment and incomes in the previously protected sectors decline while jobs and wages in the export sector stagnate.

Factor immobility
In a liberalized trade regime, it is essential that workers are able to move from the declining import-substituting sector to the expanding export sector. Yet, structural rigidities and governance problems may hamper the reallocation of resources towards the export sector because of restrictions on internal migration (as in Uzbekistan), lack of infrastructure and/or housing where the tradable sector is located (as in some sub-Saharan countries), labour laws limiting the transfer of workers across industries (as in India), shortage of retraining programmes to reskill the workers made redundant in the formerly protected sector (as in transitional economies), lack of social safety nets to assist redundant workers until they find new employment (as in China), narrow credit markets and lack of new investments to absorb labour moving to the tradable sector. For these reasons, trade liberalization can lead to a fall in employment and earnings in the import-substituting sector without generating a corresponding rise in jobs and wages in the export-oriented sector. The impact on inequality is unclear, while the impact on poverty is unfavourable.

In a detailed study of the impact of trade liberalization in India, Topalova (2004) found that rural districts with the highest density of industries exposed to liberalization experienced the sharpest increase in the incidence of poverty owing to limited factor mobility across regions and industries. Topalova suggests that the impact of trade liberalization was particularly pronounced in the Indian States where rigid labour laws hampered the reallocation of labour across industries. However, the limited spatial mobility of rural labourers most adversely affected by liberalization suggests that other factors stand in the way of effective factor mobility.

Trade reorientation following capital account liberalization

The interaction between trade and capital account liberalization is another explanation that has received little attention. Sudden inflows of foreign capital can result in the appreciation and increasing instability of the exchange rate, shifting the composition of domestic demand towards cheap imports and away from domestic products, while rendering exports less competitive (Taylor, 2000). All this leads to the cancelling out the supposed positive effects of trade liberalization, as it encourages the restructuring of production via a reduction in formal employment and wages and greater reliance on outsourcing, that is to say, measures that reduce the absorption of unskilled labour and increase wage inequality.

Liberalization of Foreign Direct Investment

The predictions of economic theory about the distributive impact of foreign direct investment (FDI) are similar to those of international trade. In low-wage labour-abundant countries, 'greenfield FDI' accelerates capital accumulation and raises the demand for and (under certain conditions) the wage rate of unskilled workers. FDI may also offer better employment conditions and higher wages to all workers, regardless of their skill level, than the informal or even formal domestic sectors. The distributive impact of 'brownfield FDI' is less straightforward, as the possible long-term gains in efficiency have to be weighed against short-term retrenchments in employment that may cause an adverse distributive impact.

Evaluations of wages and employment conditions in firms controlled by transnational corporations (TNCs) and export processing zones provide mixed results about the impact of FDI. Te Velde and Morrissey (2002) found that FDI raised wages of different skill levels in four of the five East Asian countries analysed. In Mexico, in contrast, the increase in wages due to FDI was significantly lower for the unskilled than for the skilled workers (Alarcon and McKinley, 1996).

Sectoral composition of FDI

The theoretical advantages of FDI are most often observed in labour-intensive manufacturing branches such as textile, apparel, food processing, furniture, toys, beverages and assembly operations but are less evident in capital-intensive manufacturing and in the utility and mining sectors. In the latter sectors, production requires a lot of capital, little unskilled labour and some skilled workers. This reduces the demand for and wages of unskilled labour. In the resource sector, the volatility of commodity prices and employment conditions reduces the incentives to invest in education, negatively affecting the long-term distribution of income. Income inequality in the mining sector is usually very high as the ownership of mines is typically highly concentrated, with mining rents captured by the élite without much effort.

FDI in these sectors is, therefore, likely to raise inequality, through both the labour market and political economy mechanisms. In addition, when FDI involves mergers-and-acquisitions, the immediate effect is labour shedding following firm restructuring and consolidations among firms, with probable net job losses (Baldwin, 1995). While this might improve the microeconomic efficiency of firms over the medium term, the immediate effect is likely to be inequitable.

The overall distributive effect of FDI thus depends on its composition. Evidence shows that while the ratio of the combined stock of FDI rose from 19.2 per cent of world GDP in 1990 to 34.0 per cent in 2000, the sectoral composition of new FDI has shifted towards utilities, finance and trade-related services and away from mining and manufacturing. A big share of FDI is increasingly taking the shape of cross-border mergers and acquisitions, rather than greenfield projects—a trend that merely entails the transfer of existing jobs from domestic to foreign owners.

Substitution effect and 'business stealing'

Even when greenfield FDI is directed to the labour-intensive sector, its net effect on employment and income distribution has to take into account its various impacts on the local economy. This is especially important when output is sold on local markets that used to be supplied by domestic firms, which face the risk of being displaced by FDI, leading to job losses in the labour-intensive informal sector. As the latter is likely to have lower labour productivity and higher employment coefficients per unit of output than foreign firms, a full displacement of their output tends to worsen the distribution of income.

North–south plant relocation and skill-biased technical change

A further refinement of the basic model involves the technology that a multi-national seeking lower wages is likely to transfer to a developing country. While such technology may be considered to be of low-skill intensity for an advanced nation, it might be relatively skill-intensive in a developing country hosting the FDI. For instance, the outsourcing of production from the United States to the maquiladora sector in Mexico raised demand for unskilled labour in the United States (and so contributed to the rise in the skilled/unskilled wage gap) and simultaneously increased demand for what is considered skilled labour in Mexico, thus raising wage and overall income inequality in both countries (Feenstra and Hanson, 1997). New evidence from China and India suggests that FDI is becoming increasingly skill-biased in countries well endowed with cheap, literate and well trained labour.

Regional distribution of FDI and spatial inequality

One of the possible adverse effects of FDI is the increase in spatial inequality. This depends on the industrial policy of the host country that often tries to locate the FDI in more developed and accessible areas. In China, for instance, the FDI policy pursued by the local authorities between 1978 and the mid-1980s deliberately favoured the southern coastal provinces by granting special tax and duty exemptions besides relaxing labour laws. Such FDI-preferential policies were extended to the whole of China only after 1992. However, foreign investors continue to enjoy greater incentives in the coastal areas. For instance, the average 'preferential policy index'—computed by Demurger and others (2002) for 1996–1999—was 3.0 for the three main metropolises, 2.4 for typical coastal areas and only 1.3 for the central and north-western provinces. In many cases, however, the spatially inequitable effects of FDI may have been largely endogenous, as foreign investments are attracted by economies of scope and agglomeration as well as externalities existing in comparatively advanced areas. There is evidence that FDI naturally flows to areas well endowed with public infrastructure, transport facilities and industrial services, despite higher wages.

Systemic effects in a world of mobile capital and immobile labour

The mobility of capital and immobility of labour may generate strong competition among developing countries simultaneously attempting to attract FDI. These countries may thus engage in a 'race to the bottom', in which all of them make concessions to the multinational companies in terms of taxation, subsidies, labour and social security legislation, minimum wages and so on that may affect the distribution of private/public consumption and the welfare of workers. While wages in the multinational sector tend to be higher than in local firms, these wage and employment benefits may only be felt by the employees concerned. In the countries bypassed by FDI, the ex-ante concessions made to attract them may generate temporary or permanent costs unmatched by benefits.

Capital Account Liberalization

Mainstream theory maintains that capital account liberalization raises investment, employment, labour productivity and growth in countries with low capital accumulation, but with high rates of return on investments and an abundant supply of cheap labour. This raises employment and—possibly—wages in countries receiving these funds, with favourable effects for equity. In addition, the liberalization of portfolio flows permits the diversification of the financial assets of domestic investors, leading to a balancing of the risk profile of their portfolios, thus favourably affecting the national savings rate. Finally, capital account opening is supposed to exert a 'disciplining effect' on domestic policies in the fiscal and monetary areas, contributing to macroeconomic stability and credibility. Yet, empirical evidence points to widespread deterioration in income inequality following both inflows and outflows of funds, as documented for a large number of episodes in the 1990s. Possible explanations for this discrepancy include:

Appreciation of the real exchange rate due to large inflows
Large inflows of funds relative to domestic assets generally cause appreciation of the real exchange rate that reduces employment in the tradable sector, shifts resources from the tradable to the non-tradable sector and encourages subcontracting and wage cuts in the tradable sector to preserve or raise profit margins (Taylor, 2000). Countries can attempt to control exchange rate appreciation via costly sterilization of inflows or regulation, but both measures only work up to a point.

Intersectoral allocation of portfolio flows
Portfolio flows do not directly benefit the poor, as they tend to be invested in finance, insurance and real estate (FIRE) activities that have high short-term rates of return and a perceived low risk profile, while employing medium-to-highly skilled workers whose wages rise together with the skilled/unskilled wage differential. In addition, the credit boom associated with the inflow hardly

reduces credit market segmentation between those who can collateralize their loans and those who cannot, for lack of guarantees. During financial crises, credit allocation becomes particularly skewed as de-capitalized banks may reduce their lending and restrict allocation to preferred borrowers (large firms, for example). Given the proliferation and greater labour-intensity of small and medium-sized enterprises (SMEs) in developing economies, such 'credit starvation' can have serious poverty and inequality consequences.

Sudden capital outflows and financial instability
Capital account liberalization also increases the frequency of destabilizing financial crises with real effects. Left to themselves, deregulated financial systems do not perform well, owing to incomplete information, markets and contracts, herd behaviour, panics, weak supervision and asset price speculation. Indeed, as noted in a recent International Monetary Fund (IMF) paper (Prasad and others, 2003), there is no evidence that international capital flows accelerate the rate of growth in recipient countries, while there is clear evidence that they raise the instability of private consumption, with clear short and long term effects on poverty, as people in developing countries have poorer access to financial markets and cannot smoothen their consumption streams over time.

The empirical evidence suggests that the distributional impacts of financial crises have generally been negative, particularly in countries with weak labour institutions and social safety nets. Galbraith and Lu (1999) found that financial crises raised inequality in 73 per cent of cases in Latin America and 62 per cent of cases in Asia, while no impact was evident in Finland, Norway and Spain. Similarly, Diwan (1999) found that the share of labour income contracted markedly and irreversibly in the wake of financial crises. Some analyses have shown that during the first phase of such crises, income inequality may fall as the comparatively better paid workers of the FIRE sector are the first to be affected. However, the medium-term impact on inequality—transmitted by way of differential employment, wage and price effects—affects the lower deciles especially hard (Levinshon, Berry and Friedman, 1999).

Bailouts of the banking system
Large financial crises induce a medium-term worsening of inequality because of the huge costs of their resolution through recapitalization of the banking sector, bailouts for depositors and debt relief for borrowers with public money, new taxes or foregone progressive expenditures, that is to say, measures that entail redistribution from the poor to the rich in the financial sector. The average cost of bailouts in emerging economies was 14.7 per cent of the GDP of the countries affected (Halac and Schmuckler, 2003). In addition, only a few pri-

vileged participants received most of these transfers, particularly large, foreign and more informed depositors as well as borrowers. The transfers go from poorer to richer households, with clearly inequitable effects.

Limited Migrant Flow Liberalization

One irony of policy reform over the last two decades has been the limited liberalization of migrant flows between developing and transitional countries on the one hand and developed countries on the other. While migration in the period from 1870–1914 was largely State-sponsored, controlled and assisted, the same cannot be said of migration today, with restricted legal immigration and growing illegal and semi-legal immigration. Illegal migration is inefficient as it imposes large costs on migrants, enriches organized crime, increases expenditure for repression and deportation, and depresses the wages of illegal migrants. A more open migration policy would reduce income inequality among countries and—under certain conditions—within countries.

The efficiency and equity gains deriving from the current migration policy differ considerably from those observed from 1870 to 1914. During that period, sixty million mostly unskilled people migrated from the European periphery to the New World. The inequality impact of such migration broadly conformed to the predictions of standard theory. The wage and income gap between the countries of the Old and New World were substantially reduced, as globalization increased the relative demand for and the remuneration of the abundant factors and reduced those of the scarce factors. Mass migration from the periphery of Europe to the New World explained most (some 80 per cent) of the drop in the New World-Old World wage gap between 1870 and 1914 (Williamson, 1996; Andersen, 1999).

Globalization also caused a rise in within-country inequality in the rich countries of the New World and a fall in the poor ones of the Old World (Anderson, 1999). In the United Kingdom, Ireland and Sweden, the ratio of unskilled wages to farm rents per acre rose following a drop in the supply of unskilled labour due to migration, growing labour demand in the export-led manufacturing sector and a fall in the prices of agricultural products due to cheap imports. The opposite effects were observed in the New World. While migration drove up unskilled wages and drove down the rental-wage ratio in the Old World, they caused the opposite effect in the New World. In addition, as migrants were mostly unskilled, migration caused a reduction in the skilled-unskilled wage differential in the Old World, but raised the same ratio in the New World. In turn, the flow of European investments to the New World partially offset the local fall in unskilled wages, as they moderated the decline in returns to a growing supply of unskilled labour, and so retarded the rise in wage inequality, while having the opposite effects in the Old World countries that exported capital.

Domestic Financial Liberalization

Domestic financial liberalization inspired by the 'financial de-repression hypothesis' was one of the first policies to be introduced in developing countries from the mid- to late 1970s on. The theoretical arguments in support of this policy are that it leads to financial deepening, greater competition, private credit expansion and the creation of bond and stock markets, that is to say, measures that raise the savings, investment and employment rates by increasing financial intermediation, with likely positive effects on the distribution of income. Yet, the empirical evidence points to favourable effects in the OECD and a few developing countries but to negative ones in most low-income nations. How can this contradiction between theory and empirical evidence be explained?

Policy sequencing problems: financial liberalization in the presence of large budget deficits

In many cases, financial deregulation was introduced in the presence of large budget deficits that could no longer be financed by forcing commercial banks to absorb government debt at artificially low interest rates. To finance their deficit, governments were obliged to create domestic bond markets in which to sell large amounts of treasury bills. Because of the lack of credibility and the considerable volume of bond issues, interest rates often rose markedly in both nominal and real terms, with the increase being quickly transmitted to the rest of the financial sector. This shifted the distribution of income in favour of lenders, who generally belonged to high income groups, and against borrowers, who belonged to the low-to-medium income groups.

Failure to create competition in the domestic financial sector

Contrary to expectations, liberalization and privatization failed—especially in the 1980s—to increase competition in the financial sector. While the balance sheets of banks improved, the industry was transformed from a public to a private oligopoly in most cases, as signalled by highly inequitable rises in real rates and spreads after liberalization. Even the entry of foreign banks did not raise competition, as these banks concentrated on the few low-risk customers while neglecting most potential small borrowers. All this meant that the actual credit expansion was much lower than expected, and that the poor continued to be excluded from the formal credit market.

Weak regulatory capacity, financial instability and mounting banking crises

Financial liberalization was introduced without prior strengthening of the regulatory and supervisory capacities of the central bank and other public institutions. In several cases, the requirements for opening new banks were relaxed. In Latvia, a bank could be established in the early 1990s with only US$ 20,000. In Nigeria, domestic financial liberalization coincided with the resignation of some central bank staff who moved to the private sector to open new—and difficult to regulate—non-bank financial institutions. In sum, financial deregulation led to a highly inequitable increase in financial instability in many cases, as reflected by the rise in the frequency and severity of financial crises in recent years.

Discrimination against SMEs

While repressed financial systems may have allocated credit highly inefficiently, the distributive effects of financial liberalization were often regressive, for example, with the elimination of directed (and often subsidized) credit to small and medium-sized enterprises and to agriculture. The typically anti-rural bias of these reforms and risk-minimization by bank branches reduced the volume of credit to the agricultural sector. For instance, financial reforms in China lowered the number of rural credit cooperatives from over 58,000 in 1995 to 41,000 in 2001 (Pal, Sengupta and Ghosh, 2004). In India, financial liberalization eased the lending norms requiring national banks to assign a certain share of total credit to agriculture and to SMEs. As a result, most banks avoided lending to small farmers and small industries perceived to be less creditworthy, though evidence shows that this perception was groundless (Pal, Sengupta and Ghosh, 2004). The resulting credit crunch deprived the relatively poor of credit for investing in their business. Except in countries with vibrant private credit markets, the closure of rural bank branches and abolition of dedicated credit lines forced small entrepreneurs and peasants into the clutches of often usurious informal moneylenders.

United States high interest rate policy

In many countries, the financial sector was deregulated between 1982 and 1993, that is to say, a period during which the United States Federal Reserve followed a policy of high interest rates. Such liberalization and the IMF demand for large increases in interest rates in adjusting countries fuelled a worldwide rise in real interest rates to well above the secular trend of 2 to 3 per cent. As a result, several governments entered a vicious circle in which rate increases augmented the cost of debt servicing, which further pushed the budget deficit and indebtedness level upwards. In a number of middle-income and industrialized countries with large stocks of debt, this policy raised the cost of public debt servicing to almost 15 per cent of GDP (UNCTAD, 1997). The net effect of all of this was regressive, as tax incidence is broadly proportional, while ownership of financial assets is highly concentrated in developing countries. Thus, financial deregulation appears to have raised the rate of return to financial assets and the share of GDP accruing to non-wage incomes, and to have redistributed labour income to holders of state bonds via the budget.

Labour Market Liberalization

Neoclassical labour theory suggests that the liberalization of wage formation is likely to raise both employment (as enterprises are more willing to hire workers at lower wages) and wage dispersion (as workers with more human capital receive higher wages than in the past). The net distributive impact of these mutually offsetting effects is indeterminate as it depends on their relative significance. A second prediction of neoclassical theory applied to dualistic labour markets is that the abolition of minimum wage and other regulations in the formal sector raises employment and reduces the formal-informal sector wage gap, a beneficial outcome in countries with a small labour élite employed in a capital-intensive sector and a large low-wage informal sector.

Yet, with the exception of some East Asian countries, evidence over the last two decades points to an excess of negative over positive effects. For instance, liberalization of the labour market in Latin America was accompanied by slow employment creation, growing informalization, an erosion of minimum wages and greater overall wage inequality. Behrman, Birdsall and Székely (2000), for instance, show that wage differentials rose in 18 Latin American countries after liberalization of the labour market. Similar patterns were observed in some OECD and transitional countries and, lately, in the Republic of Korea, a recent OECD member. In Eastern Europe, the fall of minimum wages relative to the average wage correlated closely with the rise in earnings inequality (Cornia, 1996). In contrast, earnings concentration did not increase in a few OECD and other countries that have preserved collective bargaining institutions and adequate minimum wage levels. Some possible explanations for this gap between theory and trends follow.

Adverse effects of changes in labour institutions
The abolition of minimum wages might not stimulate labour demand, as the labour demand curve can be inelastic in a particular range, while the wage decline increases poverty and inequality. While weakening trade unions may reduce labour market rigidities, a low rate of unionization may also adversely affect social cohesion, incentives and industrial relations.

Erosion of the 'reference norm' and the rise of the P90/P10 ratio
Mounting wage inequality following liberalization was also found to be associated with a rapid surge in the highest wages, rather than with falls in the bottom wages, a fact unexplained by human capital theory, but possibly related to the expansion of the finance, insurance and real estate (FIRE) sectors and to changes in social norms for the remuneration of highly skilled people. For instance, recent increases in wage inequality in the United States and the United Kingdom might be explained by the spread of 'winner takes all' remuneration packages for top professionals and greater recourse to stock options for executive compensation.

Labour market liberalization with open trade and capital accounts
In Latin America and the former Soviet bloc, the liberalization of labour markets coincided with the opening up of foreign trade and capital movements. As noted earlier, these changes on the export front led to wage compression and the shift of labour, either to the high-wage non-tradable FIRE sector or to low-wage informal subcontracting, increasing wage inequality.

Tax Reforms

Tax reforms have been introduced over the last two decades to reduce trade taxes, in order to promote a more efficient international allocation of resources and to simplify unnecessarily complex and inefficient tax regimes characterized by a large number of taxes, deductions and exemptions. In addition, the progressiveness of wealth and other direct tax rates was reduced to minimize 'efficiency costs' (that is to say, reduced labour supply due to high tax rates) and stimulate supply responses. At the same time, greater emphasis was placed on 'horizontal equity' (that is to say, loss of equity and revenue due to numerous tax exemptions and evasion) by eliminating exemptions and improving collection. Under this new regime, the loss of revenue—caused by the elimination of trade taxes and the reduction in direct taxes on corporations—was to be compensated for by broadening the tax base through the reduction of exemptions and the introduction of value-added tax (VAT).

Although the impact of these reforms varied from country to country, the general trend has been towards lower yields and more regressiveness. In an analysis of whether tax changes contributed to the rise in income inequality over the previous fifteen years, Atkinson (2000) notes that the direct tax schedule became less progressive in all six OECD countries, although this was offset in part by broadening the tax base in three of them. A comprehensive study of tax reforms since the mid-1970s for developing countries by Chu, Davoodi and Gupta (2000) points to an average drop of one percentage point in the tax/GDP ratio between the 1980s and the 1990s (as opposed to a rise of 1.6 percentage points between the 1970s and 1980s) and a decline in the share of direct taxes and a fall in overall tax progressiveness, all of which correlate with rising inequality. In Latin America, Morley (2000) notes that tax changes shifted the burden of taxation away from the wealthy to the middle and lower classes. Similar evidence is available for Pakistan, where following tax reform, the tax burden on the poor increased by 7.4 per cent between 1987–1998 and 1997–1998, while the burden on the richest households declined by 15.9 per cent (Pal, Sengupta and Ghosh, 2004). What explains these trends that at least partly contradict the predictions of the tax theory summarized above? No detailed analysis is available, but the following hypotheses can be plausibly advanced:

Elimination of trade taxes
In many countries, trade liberalization led to considerable losses in comparatively easy-to-collect import duties and export taxes. In most cases, the decline in revenue from trade taxes was not compensated for by increased revenue generation from other taxes. In India, the reduction of import duties following trade liberalization led to a permanent reduction of the revenue/GDP ratio by almost two percentage points. The revenue decline was compensated for by reducing subsidies on agricultural inputs, rural credit and food subsidies.

Limited impact of tax broadening
The broadening of the tax base (via reduced exemptions and greater efforts in tax collection) had limited effects in terms of revenue generation and horizontal equity, possibly because of institutional weaknesses and political economic factors. In these circumstances, the expected negative effect of the reduced progressiveness of direct taxation prevailed.

Dominance of non-graduated VAT
In many countries, indirect taxes now generate the greatest share of total revenue. When applied at a unified rate to all transactions, such taxes are regressive in impact, while lower indirect tax rates for inferior goods may help preserve the

progressiveness of the tax structure. However, the differential rates approach was seldom applied.

Overall Impact of the Liberalization–Globalization Package

Mainstream theory claims that the overall policy reform package—made up of policy components generally expected to have progressive effects—will have a progressive impact on inequality. However, the few available studies on the impact of the packages provide a different picture. In an analysis of eighteen Latin American countries during the period from 1980 to 1998, Behrman, Birdsall and Székely (2000) found that the reform packages significantly increased wage differentials in the short term, though this regressive effect declined over time. They also found that the strongest impacts were due to domestic financial reform, capital account liberalization and tax reform. On balance, trade openness had no effect on the wage spread.

Székely (2003), who analysed the impact of policy reform on inequality in nineteen Latin American countries over the period 1977–2000, found that while trade reform did not affect the income share of the bottom three deciles, financial liberalization reduced them significantly. Taxation, labour market and privatization reforms did not appear to impact the income share of the poor. For Székely, the inequitable impact of financial and other liberalizations was clear, while greater trade openness appeared to reduce inequality.

In a review of twenty-one reform episodes in eighteen countries during the previous two decades (Taylor, 2000), income inequality was found to have risen in thirteen cases, remained constant in six and improved in two. Virtually without exception, wage differentials by skill level rose following trade and financial liberalization as a result of the reduction of modern sector employment, rises in productivity and wage concentration by skill within the modern sector, reallocation of excess labour to the low-paying non-tradable sector (informal services and traditional agriculture) and greater inequality within the non-tradable sector. Looking at the impact of liberalization in thirty-two developing and transitional economies for 1980–1995, Cornia with Kiiski (2001) found that while the reform packages had regressive effects overall, the effect was more pronounced in the economies of the former Soviet bloc than in countries with high initial levels of inequality.

Although the above studies do not trace the causal linkages between liberalization and globalization on the one hand and income distribution on the other, the limited evidence reviewed above and other evidence (for example, Atkinson and Brandolini, 2003) suggest that the overall liberalization package may lead to increased domestic income inequality, especially in economies with weak domestic institutions. Among the factors contributing to this increase are the incomplete switching of resources from the non-tradable to the tradable sector, leading to a fall in modern-sector employment, rising wage differentials within the modern sector, bloating of the informal sector, a lower wage share and a higher capital share linked to increasing banking and financial instability as well as labour market and tax changes. Of the six components of the liberalization package, capital account liberalization appears to have the strong-est regressive effect, followed by domestic financial liberalization, labour market deregulation and tax reform. The equity effects of privatization and trade liberalization appear to vary, with progressive effects in some countries and regressive ones in others.

CONCLUSION

The theoretical models used to promote neoliberal policy reforms are often unable to predict the inequality impact of internal and external liberalization, as they are based on simplistic and highly restrictive assumptions that do not take into account the complexity of the impact of institutional weaknesses, structural rigidities, incomplete markets, asymmetric information, persistent protectionism and the liberalization of trade, finance and labour markets in the real world.

Thus, while some neo-liberal policies can generate positive effects in countries with strong markets and institutions, favourably placed in world markets, and benefiting from FDI in labour-intensive manufacturing and egalitarian privatization, their premature and poorly-sequenced implementation under conditions of asymmetric trade liberalization, incomplete markets, weak institutions, structural rigidities and a dependent position on the world market may generate adverse distributive and growth outcomes. Under these conditions, developing countries should adopt a flexible policy approach and seek greater policy space to experiment with different more gradualist approaches. This requires that the costs and benefits of a policy proposal be assessed in advance and that liberal reforms be postponed in toto or in part until domestic and international conditions ensure reasonable success in implementing them. In some cases, more time may be required to attend to existing problems before liberalization should proceed.

Even under more favourable conditions, developing countries should post-pone sine die the liberalization of portfolio flows and reconsider the dominant approach to tax reform, as both policies tend to generate regressive effects, and should therefore be avoided rather than postponed. Finally, the international community should vigorously pursue policies ignored in the neo-liberal package in order to improve the distribution of income in both developing and developed countries. Such policies include lessening restrictions on 'regulated migration', stronger global macroeconomic coordination among the major countries to stabilize exchange rates among the principal currencies, and establishment of international safety nets to assist 'innocent bystander' countries that have to deal with the negative effects of international financial crises.

NOTES

[1] The following draws on the second half of Cornia (2004).

[2] Cornia with Kiiski (2001) carried out an empirical test on the trend changes in income inequality based on the November 1998 version of the World Income Inequality Database of the World Institute for Development Economics Research (WIDER) using 770 reliable Gini coefficients for seventy-three countries (thirty-four developing, twenty-three transitional and sixteen OECD countries) accounting for 80 and 91 per cent of the world population, and GDP-PPP (purchasing power parity), spanning the period from the mid-1950s to the mid-1990s.

[3] Up until 7 or 8 years ago, many analyses (Li, Squire and Zou, 1998) suggested that inequality indices had remained relatively stable over time. As noted, this is no longer the prevailing view in the literature, as new data and analyses point to a fairly general increase in domestic income inequality.

REFERENCES

Alarcon, Diana, and Terry McKinley (1998). "Increasing Wage Inequality Accompanies Trade Liberalization in Mexico". In Albert Berry (ed.). *Poverty, Economic Reform, and Income Distribution in Latin America*. Lynne Rienner, Boulder: 137–154.

Anderson, Edward (1999). "Globalization and Inequality in Historical Perspective". Background paper for the *Human Development Report 1999*. UNDP, New York.

Atkinson, Anthony (2000). "Increased Income Inequality in OECD Countries and the Redistributive Impact of the Government Budget". Working Paper No. 202, World Institute for Development Economics Research, United Nations University (UNU/WIDER), Helsinki.

Atkinson, Anthony, and Andrea Brandolini (2003). "The Panel-of-Country Approach to Explaining Income Inequality: An Interdisciplinary Agenda". Processed, Nuffield College, Oxford University, Oxford.

Banerji, Ajit, and Thomas Piketty (2001). "Are the Rich Growing Richer: Evidence from Indian Tax Data". Processed, MIT, Cambridge, MA and CEPREMAP, Paris. Available at: http://www.worldbank.org/indiapovertyworkshop.

Behrman, Jere, Nancy Birdsall and Miguel Székely (2000). "Economic Reform, and Wage Differentials in Latin America". Working Paper of the Research Department no. 435, Inter-American Development Bank, Washington, DC.

Bigsten, Arne (2000). "Globalization and Income Inequality in Uganda". Paper presented at the Conference on 'Poverty and Inequality in Developing Countries: A Policy Dialogue on the Effects of Globalization', 30 November–1 December, OECD Development Centre, Paris.

Birdsall, Nancy, and Amar Hamoudi (2002). "Commodity Dependence, Trade and Growth: When 'Openness' Is Not Enough". Working Paper No. 7, Center for Global Development, Washington, DC.

Bourguignon, Francois, and Christian Morisson (1990). "Income Distribution, Development and Foreign Trade". *European Economic Review* 34: 1113–1132.

Bourguignon, Francois, and Christian Morisson (2002). "Inequality among World Citizens". *American Economic Review* 92 (4): 727–744.

Checchi, Daniele (2004). "Does Educational Achievement Help Explain Income Inequality?". In G.A. Cornia (ed.). *Inequality, Growth and Poverty in an Era of Liberalization and Globalization*. Oxford University Press, Oxford: 81–111.

Chu, Ke-young, Hamid Davoodi and Sanjeev Gupta (2000). "Income Distribution and Tax and Government Social Spending Policies in Developing Countries". Working Paper No. 214, World Institute for Development Economics Research, United Nations University, (UNU/WIDER), Helsinki.

Cornia, Giovanni Andrea (1996). "Transition and Income Distribution: Theory, Evidence and Initial Interpretation". Research in Progress No. 1, World Institute for Development Economics Research, United Nations University (UNU/WIDER), Helsinki.

Cornia, Giovanni Andrea (2004). "Changes in the Distribution of Income over the Last Two Decades: Extent, Sources and Possible Causes". *Rivista Italiana degli Economisti* 9 (3), December.

Cornia, Giovanni Andrea (ed.) (2004). *Inequality, Growth and Poverty in an Era of Liberalization and Globalization*. Oxford University Press, Oxford.

Cornia, Giovanni Andrea, with Sampsa Kiiski (2001). "Trends in Income Distribution in the Post World War II Period: Evidence and Interpretation". Discussion Paper No. 2001/89, World Institute for Development Economics Research, United Nations University (UNU/WIDER), Helsinki.

Deaton, Angus, and Jean Drèze (2002). "Poverty and Inequality in India: A Re-examination". Working Paper No. 107, Centre for Development Economics, Delhi School of Economics, Delhi. Available at: http://www.cdedse.org/pdf/work107.pdf

Demurger, Silvie, and others (2002). "Geography, Economic Policy and Regional Development in China". *Asian Economic Papers* 1 (1): 146–197.

Diwan, Ishac (1999). "Labour Shares and Financial Crises". Processed, World Bank, Washington, DC.

Eastwood, Robert, and Michael Lipton (2000). "Rural-Urban Dimension of Inequality Change". Working Paper No. 200, World Institute for Development Economics Research, United Nations University (UNU/WIDER), Helsinki.

Feenstra, Robert C., and Gordon H. Hanson (1997). "Foreign Direct Investment and Relative Wages: Evidence from Mexico's Maquiladoras". *Journal of International Economics* 42: 371–93.

Galbraith, James, and Jiaqing Lu (1999). "Inequality and Financial Crises: Some Early Findings". UTIP Working Paper No. 9, LBJ School of Public Affairs, University of Texas at Austin.

Halac, Marina, and Sergio Schmuckler (2003). "Distributional Effects of Crises: The Role of Financial Transfers". Processed, World Bank, Washington, DC.

Jomo, K.S. (2004). "Growth with Equity in East Asia?". Paper prepared for the International Forum for 'Social Development, Equity, Inequalities and Interdependence', United Nations, New York, 5–6 October.

Levinshon, James, Steven Berry and Jed Friedman (1999). "Impacts of the Indonesian Economic Crisis: Price Changes and the Poor". Processed, University of Michigan, Ann Arbor.

Li, Honhyi, Lyn Squire and Heng-fu Zou (1998). "Explaining International and Intertemporal Variations in Income Inequality". *Economic Journal* 108 (446): 26–43.

Lindert, Peter, and Jeffrey Williamson (2001). "Does Globalization Make the World More Unequal?". Paper presented at the NBER Conference on 'Globalization in Historical Perspective', Santa Barbara, California, May 3–6.

McCulloch, Neil, Bob Baulch and Milasoa Cherel-Robson (2000). "Globalization, Poverty and

Inequality in Zambia". Paper presented at the Conference on 'Poverty and Inequality in Developing Countries: A Policy Dialogue on the Effects of Globalization', OECD Development Centre, Paris, 30 November–1 December.

Milanovic, Branko (1998). *Income, Inequality, and Poverty during the Transition from Planned to Market Economy*. World Bank, Washington, DC.

Morley, Samuel (2000). "Distribution and Growth in Latin America in an Era of Structural Reform". Paper presented at the Conference on 'Poverty and Inequality in Developing Countries: A Policy Dialogue on the Effects of Globalization', OECD Development Centre, Paris, 30 November–1 December.

Pal, Parthapratim, Ranja Sengupta and Jayati Ghosh (2004). "Inequality in China and South Asia: A Survey of Recent Trends". Paper prepared for the 'International Forum for Social Development, Equity, Inequalities and Interdependence', United Nations, New York, 5–6 October.

Prasad, Eshwar, and others (2003). "Effects of Financial Globalization on Developing Countries: Some Empirical Evidence". Occasional Paper No. 220, International Monetary Fund, Washington, DC.

Riskin, Carl (2003). "Pro-Poor Macro Policies in China". Paper prepared for the UNDP Workshop on 'The Macroeconomics of Poverty Reduction', Kathmandu, 4–6 January.

Savvides, Andreas (1998). "Trade Policy and Income Inequality: New Evidence". *Economic Letters* 61 (3): 365–372.

Smeeding, Timothy (2002). "Globalization, Inequality and the Rich Countries of the G-20: Evidence from the Luxemburg Income Study (LIS)". Paper prepared for the G-20 Meeting on 'Globalization, Living Standards and Inequality: Recent Progress and Continuing Challenges', Sydney, May 26–28.

Székely, Miguel (2003). "The 1990s in Latin America: Another Decade of Persistent Inequality but with Somewhat Lower Poverty". *Journal of Applied Economics* 6 (2): 317–339.

Taylor, Lance (2000). "External Liberalization, Economic Performance and Distribution in Latin America and Elsewhere". Working Paper No. 215, World Institute for Development Economics Research, United Nations University (UNU/WIDER), Helsinki.

Te Velde, Dirk Willelm, and Oliver Morissey (2002). "Foreign Direct Investments, Skills and Wage Inequality". Processed, Overseas Development Institute, London.

Topalova, Petia (2004). "Factor Immobility and Regional Impact of Trade Liberalization: Evidence on Poverty and Inequality from India". Processed, Department of Economics, Massachusetts Institute of Technology, Cambridge, MA.

UNCTAD (1997). *Trade and Development Report*. United Nations Conference on Trade and Development, Geneva.

Williamson, Jeffrey (1996). "Globalization and Inequality Then and Now: the Late 19th and Late 20th Centuries Compared". NBER Working Paper Series No. 5491, National Bureau of Economic Research, Cambridge, MA.

Wood, Adrian (1994). *North-South Trade, Employment and Inequality*. Clarendon Press, Oxford.

Wood, Adrian (1995). "Does Trade Reduce Wage Inequality in Developing Countries?" Paper presented at the conference 'The Third World after the Cold War: Ideology, Economic Development and Politics', Queen Elizabeth House, Oxford, July 5–8.

4

Trade and Employment:
Stylized Facts and Research Findings[1]

BERNARD HOEKMAN and L. ALAN WINTERS

This chapter presents a brief survey of the impact of international trade and trade reform on employment. It focuses mainly on empirical studies that have sought to establish the labour implications of greater trade and trade liberalization. As is revealed by the long bibliography at the end of this chapter—which represents only a selection from the literature—a huge amount of research has been undertaken on the subject of the relationship between trade, wages and employment. In addition, there are numerous excellent literature surveys, many of which review the underlying theory, empirical strategies, methodology and techniques in some depth.[2] Thus, we make no attempt to be comprehensive, and those seeking a more rigorous and detailed discussion of specific papers should refer to these surveys and the papers themselves. Our emphasis is on the broad themes of the literature, with a view to deriving some stylized facts and a list of possible research questions. To keep the chapter within reasonable bounds, we do not discuss labour economics-oriented literature on labour market institutions, regulation and distortions, the design and effectiveness of possible instruments to facilitate the movement of workers across sectors or employers within sectors or issues related to the relationship between trade openness and income distribution.[3]

As noted by Goldberg and Pavcnik (2004), empirical research to date has offered no conclusive evidence on the effects of trade liberalization on employment and wages. In part, this is because it is hard to obtain a good measure of trade policy, even for Organization for Economic Cooperation and Development (OECD) countries, since action is mostly on non-tariff barriers (NTBs), for which time series data are notoriously difficult to obtain. The weakness in the openness measures that confound the literature on trade and growth are equally problematic here. More fundamentally, trade policy is endogenous—among other things, labour market concerns are one determinant of trade policy, and the factors affecting policy may affect the formation of wages. Moreover, it is increasingly recognized that trade is a channel for technology diffusion and adoption, both directly (e.g., through imports of capital goods) and indirectly (e.g., by creating pressure to innovate) (Wood, 1994, 1995; Richardson, 1995; Thoenig and Verdier, 2003).[4] Therefore, there are numerous problems of endogeneity and simultaneity to be overcome before we can be confident that we understand the processes involved.

The rest of this chapter comprises seven parts. The first six consider the literature on the effects of trade or trade liberalization on aggregate employment, economy-wide wages, sectoral employment, heterogeneity and imperfect competition, productivity and institutions, and political economy. The final section collects some stylized facts and proposes a few priorities for future research.

Setting the methodological problems aside, the literature on trade and labour markets (wages and employment) concentrates on the implications for relative rewards for and employment of different "types" of labour, as differentiated either by skill (education, etc.) or by industry or sector of employment. The focus is on the incidence of greater trade or trade liberalization episodes. In the case of developed countries, attention centres mainly on the effects of greater openness, as measured by trade-to-gross domestic product (GDP) ratios or import penetration. Here, the question of interest is generally whether "wages are set in Beijing" (Freeman, 1995). In the case of developing countries, the same question arises—what happens to the relative wage of unskilled labour (is China setting wages globally?)—but there is also a greater interest in tracing the employment effects of reforms. Because developing countries have dramatically reformed their trade regimes, the literature on these countries can focus on analyzing episodes of deep trade liberalization where the source of the shock can be clearly identified in time. This greatly facilitates the attribution of effects to trade, making the developing country-based literature more informative and robust in terms of its conclusions.

AGGREGATE EMPLOYMENT

Although the main impact of trade policy reforms and greater openness will generally be on the distribution of employment across sectors and the relative returns to different types of labour (factors), we will start with the headline issue of total employment. In neoclassical models of the economy, long-run levels of employment and unemployment are determined by macroeconomic variables and labour market related institutions, rather than trade and trade policy. In line with this view, therefore, trade policy reforms per se—i.e., policies aiming to increase integration—should not have a long-term impact on employment levels, although they may, of course, be accompanied by labour and other market reforms.

Neoclassical economists recognize that, in the shorter run, the level of economic activity may be influenced both by macroeconomic policy and shocks (money supply, interest rates, fiscal policy, etc.) as well as by trade shocks or major changes in trade policy, but they argue that, in the long run, the labour market will clear in the absence of distortions, the equilibrium wage being determined by the intersection of demand and supply. The role of labour market institutions in determining this supply and demand is well established, and most analyses of trade reform take as given the long-run level of employment and consider its allocation across sectors. This is essentially the often criticized 'full employment' assumption of trade theorists. It is more properly termed an 'exogenous employment' assumption, which merely asserts that in the long run, employment returns to its initial level.

The structuralist school, on the other hand, rejects Say's Law that demand expands to absorb supply—see, for example, Ocampo and Taylor (1998). It postulates that trade and trade policy shocks can affect employment permanently by creating or destroying jobs with little or no adjustment in the sectors of the economy not directly affected by the shock or by any induced growth.

In large part, this difference in approach reflects the specific simplifications associated with different modelling strategies, which in turn stem from different perceptions about which time period to denote. Neoclassical theory may proceed *as if* adjustment to general equilibrium is instantaneous but does not seriously advance that view as a fact. It merely asserts that the important phenomena surrounding trade liberalization are the long-run developmental ones. Structuralism, on the other hand, focuses on short time periods where full adjustment has not occurred, and serves to remind us that, certainly for those affected, the adjustment path can be sufficiently long and painful to dominate their view of a policy reform.

Structuralists do not seriously advance the view that adjustment *never* occurs—otherwise, think of all the predictions that would be made for unemployed candle-makers, farmers, blacksmiths and railway engineers in Europe. Moreover, we would not have observed the structural changes of the last few decades in the developing countries that have advanced into global manufacturing markets as they have begun to trade more. Realistic policy-making should pay due regard to both time horizons: while we believe that one should certainly pay attention to adjustment periods—see, for example, Winters (2002) or Winters, McCulloch and McKay (2004)—we also believe that a long-run focus is necessary for development, and this entails adjustment.

Both theorists and empiricists have explored the long-run connection between trade policy and employment, albeit not in any great depth. Among the theorists, Stephen Matusz explores the connection by embedding theories of efficiency wages and job search into trade models. Matusz (1994) finds that, in the presence of wage rigidities, trade liberalization could either raise or lower employment. Matusz (1996) argues that, in a world of monopolistic competition, if firms pay efficiency wages, trade liberalization will increase employment (the efficiency premium being smaller) and thus has greater benefits than in a competitive model. Davidson, Martin and Matusz (1999) bring search into the trade model and find that unemployment can go either way after a liberalization. These are complex models with complex and ambiguous results, but at least they admit the possibility that trade reform could have adverse long-run consequences for employment.

Turning to the empirical evidence, however, there is no support for such a view. Marquez and Pages-Serra (1998) suggest that firm-level declines in employment per unit of output (increased efficiency) are offset by increases in firm size or numbers. IADB (2004), in a review of household data for ten countries, suggest that trade liberalization increased employment but left unemployment unchanged—i.e., it increased participation.

In a macroeconomic study, Kee and Hoon (2005) show that increasing openness lay behind much or all of the dramatic decline in the natural rate of unemployment in Singapore. Between 1966 and 2000, during which period the openness ratio—(X+M)/GDP—increased from 224 per cent to 298 per cent, the relative prices of export goods increased, and there was a rapid accumulation of capital in the export sector. Both phenomena increased the marginal product of labour (and hence, wages) in terms of non-tradables and expanded overall employment fourfold (as population doubled). The direct effects of the accumulation were larger than those of relative prices, although the latter, which is the natural consequence of trade liberalization, is probably the exogenous driver variable. Kee and Hoon show their results are robust whether either or both are exogenous or endogenous.[5]

Rodrik (1995), on the other hand, argues that the investment booms in the Republic of Korea (South Korea) and Taiwan Province of China were exogenous (government-led) and that these induced export growth, the price changes being too small to produce such strong export growth themselves. Even if this is true, however, openness was still a critical component of the policy mix, for without openness, the importing of capital goods (and, subsequently, intermediates) would have been impossible, as would have been the huge growth of exportables' output, since without access to world markets with huge potential demand, the expansion would have induced strongly declining prices.

These cases demonstrate strong macroeconomic links between trade policy and aggregate employment. Openness may or may not be sufficient to drive up employment, but, particularly in small and medium-sized economies, if booming sectors do not have access to supplies of inputs from abroad and to the large world market with its high elasticities of demand, their growth is almost bound to be curtailed very quickly.[6] The potential employment creation following greater trade integration can be significant. Thus, in the case of Madagascar, employment in the textiles export industry grew from 47,000 to some 200,000 between 1997 and 2001, with workers earning a 40 per cent premium over the average income earned in the informal sector (Nicita, 2004).

In fact, even giant economies benefit from large overseas markets. China's initial take-off was fuelled by agricultural reform, but kept running on manufactured exports, usually from export processing zones (EPZs). India had a fiscal boom in the late 1980s, but kept growing in the 1990s by way of further reforms in which trade figured strongly. To trade openness, Kee and Hoon (2005) add the benefits of openness to foreign direct investment (FDI), which introduces technology and forward and backward linkages.

Many studies indicate that absorptive capacity in the host country is crucial for obtaining significant spill-over benefits from trade or FDI. For example, using data from industrialized countries to 69 developing countries, Borenzstein and others (1998) tested the effect of FDI on growth in host countries and found that FDI contributes *more* to domestic growth than domestic investment, but this happens only when the host country has a minimum threshold stock of human capital.

Similarly, Keller (1996) argues that access to foreign technologies alone does not increase growth rates of developing countries and shows that if a country's absorptive capacity (measured by its stock of human capital) remains unchanged, a switch to outward orientation may not lead to a higher growth rate. The ability of local firms to absorb new technologies is a determinant of whether better access to trade as well as the labour turnover associated with greater competition are means of technology diffusion—in turn an important channel for growth. This suggests that a priority for any country is to pursue general policies that are complementary, such as education, efficient infrastructure and measures to reduce entry barriers for local firms into new activities. The latter is important for a number of reasons, including employment creation. To the extent that prevailing policies (e.g., taxes, restricted access to finance, etc.) discourage such investments, they should be reformed to encourage more innovation. The same is true of restrictive labour market regulation—see, for example, Besley and Burgess (2004) and Bolaky and Freund (2004).

Some commentators—e.g., Ocampo (1994)—worry that liberalization induces an increase in the marginal propensity to import, which in turn causes a tightening of foreign-exchange constraints that curtail growth at an earlier phase in the business cycle than in less open economies. This, they argue, reduces long-run growth prospects. This view is essentially a Keynesian one, whereby demand, in this case domestic demand, is the driver of growth. It ignores the potential supply-side benefits of a liberal trade regime and also the fact that the more rapid emergence of current-account constraints may lead governments to rely less on domestic demand stimuli to induce growth in favour of pursuing more stable macroeconomic regimes, which experience has long suggested lie behind sustained expansions. It is also worth noting that even in Keynesian terms, it is not inevitable that raising the average propensity to import (i.e., increasing openness) inevitably raises the marginal propensity; but in this case, exchange-rate depreciation offers an antidote. It has long been understood that successful trade liberalizations typically require real deprecia- tions—e.g., Thomas and Nash (1991)—which also have political economy benefits in terms of sustaining support for reforms, as they reduce the pressure of imports on domestic competing sectors.

The employment story is rather different when we turn to the short-run or adjustment period following trade liberalization, the period that structuralist models focus on. The churning induced by reform could clearly reduce employ- ment temporarily, as could, conceivably, a Keynesian shock emanating from increased import competition. In Chile, for instance, Edwards and Edwards (1996) find a positive association between the degree of liberalization a sector experienced and the extent of subsequent layoffs; the sectors experiencing the greatest liberalization were also the ones where unemployment was of the longest duration. (We will return to sectoral evidence later.)

Overall, however, there is surprisingly little evidence on the nature and extent of transitional unemployment in developing countries, at least in part owing to the difficulties of measuring or even defining the phenomenon in dualistic economies. A multi-country study of trade liberalization before 1985 (Papageorgiou, Michaely and Choksi, 1991) argued that experiences varied from case to case, but that, on the whole, transitional unemployment was quite small. In a survey of more than fifty studies of the adjustment costs of trade liberalization in the manufacturing sector, mostly in industrialized economies, Matusz and Tarr (1999) argue that the adjustment costs associated with tran- sitional unemployment are not high and that unemployment duration is gen- erally quite short.

Indeed, in some cases, employment appears to increase more or less instantly—as, for example, Harrison and Revenga (1998) report for Costa Rica, Peru and Uruguay. In their non-random sample, developing countries tended to show increasing employment after trade reform, while former centrally plan- ned countries in transition to a market economy showed the opposite. The problem of attribution is immense with respect to the countries in transition, however, since so much else was happening at the same time. It should also be noted that most studies of trade and employment refer to manufacturing employment, with little indication of whether their results can be generalized to apply to agriculture or services, or indeed, to any area outside the formal sector. This is a major shortcoming, at least as much conceptual as it is practical.

It makes no sense to equate meaningful work with formal employment, particularly in poor economies, where most employment is informal, even in manufacturing, and even formal jobs offer little in the way of effective social protection or improved safety provisions. Firms and/or workers may consciously prefer informality (Maloney, 2004), especially if there were tax or regulatory advantages involved, including that of remaining below the sights of corrupt officialdom. There is a concern that trade liberalization is associated with a great degree of informality. This is disputed—see below—but even where it is true, one needs to develop one's argument a great deal further before one can conclude that liberalization has reduced overall welfare emanating from work.

A further unknown is whether those laid off following trade liberalization are disproportionately poor. In developed countries, Kletzer (2004) suggests that this is so, but for developing countries, we are far from certain. Enterprise surveys report the responses of firms to trade liberalization but typically give little information on the characteristics of their employees, while household surveys, which do provide this information, cannot easily be matched to enterprises. The latter do, however, generally suggest that, in many low-income countries, very few of the poorest are employees in the formal manufacturing sector.

Evidence is available on the relationship between public sector job loss and poverty. Although this job loss is not a consequence of trade liberalization, it does deal with transitional unemployment resulting from a shock to the formal sector and may thus also inform us about the effects of trade liberalization. In fact, it probably offers an upper bound for the costs of liberalization, because public sector employees are frequently the ones with the greatest insulation from market forces and the largest rents. Thus, for example, in Ecuador, employees dismissed from the central bank earned, on average, only 55 per cent of their previous salary 15 months later (Rama and MacIsaac, 1999). In Ghana, Younger (1996) finds that most laid off civil servants were able to find new work, albeit at substantially lower income levels; nonetheless, the income levels and incidence of poverty among their households after job loss were not substantially different from the average for the whole country.

It is likely that the more protected the sector originally, the greater the adjustment costs, and the greater the shock. In local labour markets, large losses of employment can have (negative) multiplier effects on income, and markets can become dysfunctional when even normal turnover ceases as incumbents dare not resign for fear of not finding a new job. Thus, major reforms—e.g., economic transition or concentrated reforms, such as closing the only plant in a town—seem likely to generate larger and longer-lived transitional losses through unemployment than more diffuse reforms. Rama and Scott (1999) analyse the effects of retrenching the only plant in a series of one-plant towns in Kazakhstan. They estimate that for a reduction in the employment in the plant equal to 1 per cent of the local labour force, labour income in the town falls by 1.5 per cent. This is essentially a Keynesian multiplier effect. The hysteresis of the labour market would serve to deepen and prolong it further.

ECONOMY-WIDE WAGE RATES

In this section, we pursue an economy-wide analysis, but allow for the existence of several classes of labour, each of which is mobile across sectors. Assuming fixed employment of these labour forces, the research question relates to wages.

Most of the international economics literature on trade and employment or wages is based on general equilibrium analysis. In this regard, it differs from the labour economics approach, which tends to relate to partial equilibrium, focusing on labour demand and supply and the functioning of the labour market, with an emphasis on institutional factors such as minimum wages, existence of unions, incentives to pay efficiency wages, and so forth. In the labour economics literature, unemployment is generally endogenous, whereas much of the trade literature assumes full employment or imposes an exogenous constraint, such as a fixed minimum wage. It also differs from the trade literature by explicitly considering immigration in its analysis, whereas such mobility is assumed to be impossible in most trade analyses. Indeed, trade studies often assume that trade in goods and factors of production are substitutes, in that under a set of restrictive assumptions, free trade in goods is predicted to equalize the factor prices across countries.[7]

The "standard" prediction from endowment-based theories of comparative advantage (Heckscher-Ohlin) is that the distributional impacts of trade and trade liberalization operate through the effects of changes in the relative price of tradable goods as a result of liberalization or other changes that allow or expand trade. The basic result is that, once labour adjustment across industries has occurred, wage impacts depend only on the change in product prices induced by greater trade. The argument is as follows. Since OECD countries have a more educated and skilled labour force, they should specialize in products that use such factors relatively intensively. The relative prices of goods that use less skilled labour more intensively should fall as trade is liberalized (and those of skilled goods increase), which in turn should reduce the relative wages of the factors used in producing these goods domestically. At the same time, as unskilled labour-intensive activities are downsized and relative wages fall, there should be an expansion in the demand for such labour in all parts of the economy. Conversely, developing countries should specialize in goods that use less skilled labour more intensively, and liberalization should thus boost unskilled wages.

Embarrassingly, neither the product price effects nor the economy-wide expansion in unskilled labour intensity are observed in the data, suggesting that the observed rise in skill premia in OECD countries is not mainly due to cheaper unskilled-labour-intensive imports (trade). Lawrence and Slaughter (1993), Sachs and Shatz (1994), Robbins (1996), Desjonqueres, Machin and van Reenan (1999) and many others—using different methodologies "inspired" by the Heckscher-Ohlin type model—all find that trade has little explanatory effect on changes in labour demand or relative wages across industries.

The same is true of the early papers that estimate the demand for labour, a labour cost function or decompose the sources of employment change into domestic demand, trade and productivity elements. They, too, generally found that trade factors played only a minor role in job loss and/or wage inequality, productivity growth being the main factor displacing labour in the short run. Thus, for example, Freeman and Katz (1991), Katz and Murphy (1992), Revenga (1992), Bernard and Jensen (1995) and Berman, Bound, and Griliches (1994, 1998)—all of them heavily cited papers—conclude that skill-biased technical change (SBTC) accounts for the lion's share (e.g., on the basis of a strong positive association between research and development (R&D) expenditures and computerization, and a rise in the relative return to skilled labour).[8] Thus, despite different methodologies, the labour and trade literatures have been in substantial agreement on the effect of trade on wages and employment: i.e., skill-biased technical change dominates.[9]

This does not mean, however, that trade can be completely ignored as a source of wage inequality within developed or developing countries. Researchers focusing on the labour content of trade (so-called factor content studies) obtained some of the largest estimates of the effects of imports on wages (e.g., Murphy and Welch, 1991; Wood, 1994). The analysis in these papers centres on the growth in the "effective" unskilled labour force that is implied by the greater imports of unskilled-labour-intensive products from developing countries. That is, estimates are made of the labour being displaced by a given amount of imports.

The premise of these papers—best explained and argued in Wood (1994,

1995)—is that greater trade with developing countries will adversely affect the low-wage workers in industrialized nations by "effectively" expanding the stock of unskilled labour, thus lowering wages. The extent to which this "expansion" occurs is measured by the unskilled labour content embodied in the imports. Wood (1994, 1995) concludes that, with some "reasonable" assumptions, this can be quite significant. The assumptions, in addition to the standard Heckscher-Ohlin ones, are that many imports from developing countries are non-competing (i.e., are much more labour-intensive than developed country varieties ostensibly in the same sectors) and that much of the SBTC has been induced by the competitive effects of trade.[10] Note, however, that as the same relative declines in unskilled labour returns are observed in developing countries, SBTC remains an important part of the equation even in these frameworks.

SECTORAL EMPLOYMENT

Empirical approaches to assessing the impact of trade on sectoral employment are similar to those used to investigate the effects on relative wages. They include input-output based methodologies; regression-based methods that involve an estimation of labour demand or production functions; and Computable General Equilibrium (CGE)-based numerical methods, the latter often being used for ex ante assessments. Most of the literature on labour reallocation is based on country case studies; there are few cross-country empirical analyses of trade reforms—a recent example discussed below is Wacziarg and Wallack (2004). Many authors investigate the sectoral employment effects of OECD countries' trade with developing countries, calculating the jobs "created" and "lost" through exports and imports. Given the small share of developing countries in OECD trade, the general finding that net employment effects are small is not surprising. A number of studies find the effect to be positive—this is, in part, a reflection of the expansion of export-oriented activities, discussed further below.

An early paper by Grossman (1987) found that job (or earnings) losses in nine unskilled-labour-intensive United States manufacturing sectors due to import competition were very small, with the exception of consumer electronics (e.g., radios, televisions), where employment was estimated to be some 70 per cent lower than it would have been in the absence of import competition. Freeman and Katz (1991), Gaston and Trefler (1997) and Revenga (1992) are other early studies that conclude that trade does have effects on labour market outcomes—as measured by intersectoral changes in employment—but that domestic factors (e.g, demand for skilled labour and SBTC) were much more important drivers of job losses in the developed countries studied (primarily the United States and Canada). In general, little impact of trade policy changes was observed on wages.

More recent work has suggested more mixed conclusions regarding the impact of trade and trade reforms on sectoral employment in developed countries. Kletzer (2000) find a relationship between trade and job displacement in sectors identified as import sensitive but not for other sectors. Conversely, Dewatripont, Sapir and Sekkat (1999) find essentially no effect of developing country trade on European labour markets. The evidence from plant-level panel data for OECD economies is also not uniform. Some studies find increased trade exposure is associated with more labour churning and, sometimes, negative net effects on employment.

Much of the work on developed countries has focused on the impact of exchange-rate changes as opposed to trade reforms, the former being a more important source of changes in the terms of trade. Klein, Schuh and Triest (2003) use establishment-level panel data to analyse how the pattern of gross job flows in the United States is affected by the path of the real exchange rate. They find that changes in the trend of the real exchange rate affect allocation but not net employment, whereas cyclical variations of the real exchange rate induce changes in net employment, mainly through job destruction. In follow-on work, Klein, Schuh and Triest (2004) studied the joint impact of trade liberalization (the North American Free Trade Agreement (NAFTA)) and real exchange-rate changes in the United States. The way in which the reduction in tariffs impacted on job flows is similar to the effect of a trend appreciation of the currency. Other studies of this genre focusing on the United States include Gourinchas (1999a, 1999b), Goldberg and Campa (1998), Goldberg and Tracy (2001) and Revenga (1997).

Gourinchas examines the exchange-rate response of gross job flows at the 4-digit level over time and finds that appreciations are associated with substantial job churning, while periods of depreciation do not display such reallocation. Goldberg and Campa (1998) conclude that exchange-rate movements have a minor effect on employment and that job destruction is not substantially affected. Goldberg and Tracy (2001) offer an explanation for the finding that industry wages are significantly more responsive to exchange-rate changes than is industry employment. They find that the main mechanism for exchange-rate effects on wages occurs through job turnover and the strong consequences this has for the wages of workers undergoing such job transitions. Workers who remain with the same employer experience little if any wage impacts from exchange-rate shocks. In addition, they find that the least educated workers— who also have the most frequent job changes—shoulder the largest adjustments resulting from exchange-rate changes.

Insofar as currency appreciation affects the probability of job losses, whereas depreciation does not, differential effects may depend on whether industries or firms are exporters or import-competing. Losses from appreciation are more likely to be concentrated in import-competing sectors. Revenga (1992) finds that, in the United States, import-competing industries reduce employment overall during currency appreciations. All of these results suggest asymmetrical effects in the United States between appreciations and depreciations. This probably reflects a persistent pressure towards job reductions in tradables (due, perhaps, to technology or competition), with the exchange rate acting as a trigger for inevitable adjustments.

Using French firm-level data, Gourinchas (1999b) also finds that exchange-rate appreciations reduce net employment growth because of lower job creation and increased job destruction. Bentivogli and Pagano (1999) find rather limited, but diverging, effects of exchange-rate changes on job flows for a number of European countries. This may reflect differences in labour market institutions. Hence, Burgess and Knetter (1998) find that in countries with the most rigid labour institutions, such as Germany and Japan, employment is not sensitive to exchange rates, while in other countries, appreciation is associated with reductions in employment.

Studies on developing countries have tended to be much more explicitly motivated by trade reforms. An early discussion of trade and employment can be found in Krueger (1983), who argued that developing country trade liberalization should boost labour-intensive output and increase employment. Her case studies showed that developing countries' manufactured exports were, indeed, labour-intensive, but that the employment effects of liberal trade policies were generally rather muted. Calling for more research, she tentatively concluded that this was because of other distortions in factor markets.

More recent exercises have had more liberalizations and better data to consider and, although they show mixed results, the general tendency is that effects are still minor. For example, Rama (1994), applying a model of monopolistic competition to a panel of 39 sectors in Uruguay over the period 1979–1986, found a significant positive relationship between protection and employment in manufacturing, but no significant effects on real wages. Reducing the protection rate within a sector by 1 per cent led to an employment reduction of between 0.4 and 0.5 per cent within the same year. Harrison and Hanson (1999) suggest that one implication is that, during the years concerned, the labour market in Uruguay was fairly competitive, with significant employment reallocation between sectors after the reforms.

Revenga (1994), using plant-level data for Mexico, found no reduction in overall firm-level employment following reductions in tariff levels, whereas reductions in quotas were significant, but had a relatively weak impact on output and employment: a reduction in quota coverage from 90 per cent to 10 per cent of output was associated with a 4–6 per cent reduction in output and, in turn, a 2–3 per cent decline in employment. Tariff reductions did appear to affect wages, however, because, Revenga concludes, tariff liberalization eroded rents and thus had no effect on employment and output decisions. Similarly, minor employment effects elsewhere in Latin America are reported by, for example, Marquez and Pages-Serra (1998), for Latin America and the Caribbean in general, Levinsohn (1999), for Chile, and Moreira and Najberg (2000) for Brazil.

Milner and Wright (1998) explore industry-level data on Mauritius and find a slightly more encouraging response to liberalization. After an initially adverse wage effect, they find fairly strong long-run growth in wages and employment in the exportables sector (mainly with regard to female labour producing clothes). Surprisingly, however, they also find growth in the import-competing sector, which they attribute to Mauritius' overall strong economic performance. In fact, Mauritius opened up via export promotion rather than import liberalization and, according to Subramanian (2001), it owes its success to its institutions rather than to its trade policy. Hence, it is doubtful that its case is typical.

Case studies of developing countries in Roberts and Tybout (1996) also show that industry exit and entry (one indicator of intersectoral reallocation of labour) generally do not increase with import competition after controlling for demand shocks. This suggests that sectoral structure does not depend much on trade policy. Roberts and Tybout (1997) finds that more plants were exiting than were entering manufacturing in Chile during 1979–1982, despite the growth in productivity. The size of entrants tended to be larger than those exiting, however, so the overall impact on employment is unclear (Goldberg and Pavcnik, 2004). Overall, the research summarized above suggests that trade reforms induce limited reallocation of factors across manufacturing industries and that much of the reallocation may be associated more with export sectors attracting investment (including FDI entry) than with substantial downsizing of import-competing sectors of the economy.

Wacziarg and Wallack (2004) is a recent cross-country study of the effects of trade reform episodes on labour across a number of developing countries. They conclude that the presumption that reforms will result in labour reallocation is not supported by the available data. Liberalization episodes are followed by a *reduction* in the extent of intersectoral labour shifts at the economy-wide 1-digit level of disaggregation. Liberalization has a weak positive effect at the 3-digit level, but it is small in magnitude and not robust. There is no evidence of trade-induced structural change at the more disaggregated 4-digit industry level. Wacziarg and Wallack note that other—complementary—policies will be of importance. Other reforms, such as domestic deregulation and privatization, are found to have greater effects on intersectoral labour movements than trade reform in isolation. Their conclusion is, however, that claims that trade liberalization generally leads to the absolute decline of entire sectors (broadly defined) are not supported by the data.

These findings are consistent with earlier case studies of liberalization episodes. For example, the 19 studies collected in Papageorgiou, Michaely and Choksi (1991) did not reveal large employment or reallocation effects following trade reforms. An exception was Chile, where liberalization had a significant effect on employment in manufacturing, with export sectors expanding and import-competing sectors contracting—and net employment increasing.

HETEROGENEITY AND IMPERFECT COMPETITION

The results of Wacziarg and Wallack (2004) are also consistent with more recent findings for developed countries. Thus, using the United States Census of Manufactures, Bernard and others (2003) conclude that liberalization had a significant impact on aggregate trade, but that it was not accompanied by sectoral reallocations. Although Wacziarg & Wallack and other similar findings appear to discount large-scale *intersectoral* movements of labour, they do not preclude significant *intrasectoral* effects. Indeed, microeconometric analyses using firm-level data find significant turnover of firms within industries. The implication is that intrasectoral firm heterogeneity may be more important for the effects of trade liberalization than intersectoral differences.

While there is a majority-held view that SBTC explains the lion's share of the observed reduction in the relative return to low-skilled labour—as well as increases in unemployment in countries where wages are rigid (e.g., in Germany (Heitger and Stehn, 2003))—the factor-content studies noted above established a presumption that labour market outcomes are affected by international trade, although the channels through which this occurs are unclear (Greenaway and Nelson, 2001; Francois, 2004).[11] Recent papers increasingly conclude that the threat of competition drives enterprises to improve productivity and that output quality is likely to have an important role in determining labour market effects.

The simple Heckscher-Ohlin prediction that trade results in a redistribution of employment away from import substituting and towards export-oriented production assumes a world of homogenous firms and products, and inter-industry specialization and trade. In practice, most trade is of the intra-industry type, reflecting trade in intermediates or exchange of differentiated products between countries with very similar factor endowments. The Heckscher-Ohlin-Samuelson (HOS) prediction of intersectoral reallocation is partly driven by the assumption of homogeneity among producers within the same sector (Haltiwanger and others, 2004).

In principle, given that much trade involves the intra-industry trade of differentiated products, one might expect that much of the job and wage impacts of trade would also be intra-industry in nature (Jansen and Turrini, 2004). Although comparative advantage forces are likely to continue to imply that increased imports are associated with employment reductions and exports with increases, as noted by Greenaway, Hine and Wright (1999), this is not necessarily the case. First, output changes—positive or negative—occur within the same (similar) industry, so that the focus needs to be on establishing how trade impacts differently across industries depending on differences among them in the type of exposure they have to trade and the changes that have occurred. Firm-level heterogeneity will play an important role in driving job losses or creation within sectors. Second, there will be scope for reducing price-cost margins (mark-ups, rents, etc.) as well as opportunities to exploit economies of scale and to innovate (by upgrading quality, differentiating products, etc.).

Formal models have been developed recently explicitly incorporating firm-level heterogeneity. Melitz (2003) assumes that producers have heterogeneous productivity levels and models intra-industry reallocations among firms as a response to greater foreign competition. The latter leads to changes in the relative performance of firms (assumed to be monopolistically competitive), the result of intra-industry reallocations towards more productive firms. Eaton and Kortum (2002) obtain similar results in a different model. These models help provide a theoretical foundation for the empirical literature that finds that opening up trade improves the productivity of firms (Roberts and Tybout, Bernard and Jensen, among others).

Greenaway, Hine and Wright (1999) investigate the effects of trade on employment in the United Kingdom of Great Britain and Northern Ireland using a dynamic labour demand framework for a panel of 167 disaggregated manufacturing industries, motivated by the observation that most United Kingdom trade is intra-industry. They find that increases in trade volumes, both in terms of imports and exports, cause reductions in the level of derived labour demand. After disaggregating by origin of imports they find stronger effects related to trade with the European Union (EU) and the United States than to trade with East Asia. Given that much of this trade is intra-industry, they interpret this finding as evidence that trade affects x-inefficiency, with the strongest competition for United Kingdom manufacturers coming from producers in the EU and the United States. Freeman and Revenga (1999) report a similar result, Gaston and Trefler (1997) found significant employment responses to import competition in some sectors in Canada, and Gourinchas (1999a, 1999b) found a significant effect of exchange-rate fluctuations on movements of jobs across and within sectors in France, using firm-level job creation and destruction data. In the case of the United States, Bernard and Jensen (1999b) find that intra-industry reallocations to higher productivity exporters explain up to 20 per cent of productivity growth in United States manufacturing. For developing countries, Aw, Chung and Roberts (2000), among others, find that exposure to trade forces the exit of the least efficient producers in South Korea and Taiwan, while Pavcnik (2002) finds that market share reallocations contributed significantly to productivity growth following trade liberalization in Chile.

Exports, Intermediates, FDI and Global Production Sharing

Research focusing on the differential role of exports as opposed to imports as a source of effects on the labour market concludes that exports tend to positively affect labour employed in the sectors concerned, whereas imports affect it negatively. Thus, Davidson and Matusz (2003) find higher sectoral net exports to be associated with less job destruction and more job creation. Harrison and Hanson (1999) find that trade reforms result in employment expansion in export sectors and firms in Mexico, and Milner and Wright (1998) find the same for Mauritius. None of this is surprising of course, but it is important to bear in mind that greater imports have to be paid for, thus requiring and inducing output and employment in export sectors. What is more interesting is the relative effects on different types of labour.

Exporters in an industry tend to be more productive than non-exporting plants. This finding is by now very well established—e.g., Clerides, Lach and Tybout (1998), Bernard and Jensen (1999a) and Aw, Chung and Roberts (2000). One reason is that there are generally large sunk costs associated with contesting an export market (see Roberts and Tybout, 1997; Bernard and Jensen, 1999b). Hallward-Driemeier, Iarossi and Sokoloff (2002) find that in a sample of East Asian countries, both firms with foreign ownership and firms that export are significantly more productive, the productivity gap being larger the less developed the local market. Using a firm-level dataset to explore the sources of the greater productivity of exporting firms, they argue that it is in aiming for export markets that firms make decisions that raise productivity. It is not simply that more productive firms self-select into exporting, but that firms that explicitly target export markets consistently make different decisions regarding investment, training, technology and the selection of inputs, and thus raise their productivity. Hence, the "exporter selection" process is not necessarily driven by exogenous shocks, such as trade reforms, but reflects investments made by firms in anticipation of accessing foreign markets.

Feenstra and Hanson (1997), among others, have analysed the effects of FDI and outsourcing, recognizing that trade increasingly entails slicing up the value chain. (The counterpart to outsourcing is often inward FDI in developing countries). Feenstra and Hanson (1997) focus on the effects of relocating manufacturing activities to developing countries—United States FDI in Mexico—on the demand for skilled non-production and unskilled labour in Mexico. For nine industries located across multiple regions in Mexico they find that the relative demand for skilled labour is positively correlated with the change in the number of foreign affiliate assembly plants, and that FDI increases the wage share of non-production workers relative to unskilled labour. The reason is that the techniques used by foreign investors, while less skill intensive in terms of home country endowments, are relatively skill intensive in terms of Mexico's labour endowment.

Feenstra and Hanson (1999) introduce computer use as a measure of technical change and find that outsourcing plays a significant role in generating wage inequality, although they stress that this conclusion depends significantly on pass-through assumptions. They conclude that technical change explains about 35 per cent of the change in the skill premium, while outsourcing explains another 15 per cent. In subsequent work, Feenstra, Hanson and Swenson (2000) use production under the Offshore Assembly Provision of the United States tariff schedule as a measure of outsourcing. They find that outsourced production is intensive in unskilled labour relative to production in the United States, and that outsourcing is a function of the relative cost of production in the United States. The implication is that such outsourcing of part of the production chain reduces the relative demand for unskilled labour.[12]

Labour Market Institutions, Market Structure and Political Economy

As we noted above, Revenga (1997) suggests that the small labour market response found in developing countries such as Mexico and Morocco may reflect restrictive labour market regulation. However, Harrison and Hanson (1999) argue that labour market imperfections do not explain the limited reallocation effects observed in the developing countries for which micro-empirical work has been done. Citing Currie and Harrison (1997), who showed that many firms adjusted to trade reform by reducing profit margins and raising productivity rather than laying off workers, they suggest that imperfect product markets may be a more relevant factor underlying the limited impacts of trade liberalization on labour markets that have been observed.

Goldberg and Pavcnik (2005) focus on a short- to medium-run framework where the industry affiliation of workers is assumed to affect the way in which trade policy affects wages, as is the case, for example, in the specific factors model of trade. This differs from the focus above, and from much of the earlier empirical research, where the investigation centres on how trade policy affects wages by altering the economy-wide returns to a specific worker characteristic (usually defined by skill level as measured by education). Goldberg and Pavcnik investigate the relationship between trade liberalization in Colombia and industry wage premiums. Controlling for unobserved time-invariant industry characteristics through fixed effects (interpreted as reflecting the prevailing mix of political economy forces), workers in protected sectors earn more than workers with similar observable characteristics in unprotected sectors. This positive relationship persists when they instrument for tariff changes. Their results could be explained by an immobility of labour across sectors, for what-ever reason, or by the existence of industry rents that are reduced by trade liberalization, which might basically be the same phenomenon. Their findings reinforce the earlier analysis that trade reforms could increase wage inequalities in developing countries, tariff reductions being proportionately larger in sectors employing a high fraction of less-skilled workers, and loss of rents thus affecting such workers disproportionately.

Overall, as noted by Rama (2003), these studies suggest there was substantial rent sharing between protected enterprises and their workers. The removal of trade barriers erodes these rents, and the incidence of the loss is shared between the two factors, the precise shares depending on country-specific variables that remain indeterminate. Whatever the underlying reasons, the results point to the importance of both a good understanding of the institutional environment and the need to incorporate political economy considerations into the analysis.

A number of other papers have sought out the effect of trade liberalization on industry wage premia. Pavcnik and others (2004) suggest that for Brazil there is no relationship, despite a fairly major trade reform in the early 1990s. Feliciano (2001) also fails to find a significant relationship for Mexico, while, as noted above, Revenga (1997) finds a positive link. The same was true for India: while Mishra and Kumar (2005) suggest that premia are inversely related to tariffs—i.e., sectors with the greatest liberalization have the largest increases in wages—Vasudeva-Dutta (2004), using different data, finds the opposite. The Mishra-Kumar result, which parallels Gaston and Trefler's (1994) on the United States, is said to spring either from a general Stolpher-Samuelson result, whereby unskilled workers benefit from liberalization and happen to have been most protected prior to liberalization, or from an exaggerated productivity response to liberalization, whereby sectors with larger tariff cuts make larger productivity improvements and share them with labour.

Goldberg and Pavcnik (2005) control for the political economy determinants of tariff protection that may also affect industry wage premiums independently, inducing a spurious correlation between industry protection and wages. In a related paper, Attanasio, Goldberg and Pavcnik (2004) examine the response of sectoral employment shares to trade liberalization. Here again, notwithstanding large-scale trade reforms, sectors that experienced large reductions in nominal protection were not found to have been seriously affected in that sectoral employment shares remained stable between the pre-and post-reform period. Regressions of changes in sectoral employment shares on tariff changes fail to detect any relationship between trade liberalization and sectoral employment—i.e., findings similar to Revenga (1997), Currie and Harrison (1997) and Wacziarg and Wallack (2004), for instance. As the authors note, this is surprising given, for example, the existence of a large informal sector in Colombia that does not comply with labour market regulation and thus provides an additional margin of adjustment.

One possible explanation for this is that labour is more mobile across the formal and informal sectors than across industries. However, Goldberg and Pavcnik (2005) fail to find any significant differences between the two sectors. In a related paper, Goldberg and Pavcnik (2003) find that, while the share of informal workers increased in Colombia in the aftermath of the trade reforms, that increase is entirely accounted for by within-industry changes from the formal to the informal sector, rather than between industry shifts of informal workers. To summarize, it appears that trade liberalization had a significant impact on relative wages in Colombia, but not on intersectoral reallocation of labour. Whether this impact reflects industry rents or constraints on labour mobility—or other factors—remains to be determined. Goldberg and Pavcnik consider both hypotheses to be plausible.

STYLIZED FACTS AND RESEARCH AGENDA

This section attempts to consolidate our survey by noting some stylized facts as well as some lacunae that future research should fill. Recent research has offered some support for the conclusion that there is a greater role for trade in explaining labour outcomes than was suggested in the 1990s literature. This is in part a reflection of the changing nature of the globalization process—involving more trade in intermediates and services—but it is also, and more importantly, a result of the recognition that trade is both a direct and indirect channel for technological upgrading. Developing country liberalization episodes offer the best prospects of identifying trade effects as trade liberalization is discrete and often significant.

The "core" stylized facts that have both informed and emerged from research on the impact of trade on workers include the following:

- There has been a significant increase in the relative reward for skilled labour. This wage premium has been accompanied by increases in the ratio of skilled-to-unskilled employment in *all* sectors, not just those that use skilled labour intensively. Thus, unskilled labour has seen its relative remuneration fall generally. Moreover, the skill premium has risen in *both* developing and OECD countries, and rising inequality between the skilled and unskilled has become a global phenomenon;[13]
- At the same time, there has not been a large decline in the relative price of goods that use low-skilled labour relatively intensively. This is noteworthy from a trade theory perspective, as this goods price channel is the most obvious one through which greater trade and foreign competition should affect labour outcomes for those that are most dependent on production of competing goods;
- The implication of the foregoing is that trade and trade reforms can only explain a small fraction of the general increase in wage inequality observed in both developed and developing countries. The majority view in the literature is that SBTC is the primary culprit (Acemoglu, 2002);
- Whether the impacts of more open trade operate more or less through wages as opposed to employment depends significantly on labour market institutions, the efficiency of capital markets and social policies. The fact that the United States market has a more flexible labour market and a more efficient financial sector than most European countries helps to explain why wages bear a higher brunt of shocks in the United States than in the EU;
- In developing countries, it also appears that wage responses are greater than impacts on employment. Thus, a number of papers have found that trade liberalization decreased the industry wage premiums in those sectors that experienced the largest tariff reductions. This has been interpreted to be suggestive of labour market rigidities and related distortions in developing countries that prevent labour reallocation in the short-to-medium run. However, it is also consistent with a dissipation of industry rents, which may in turn have been supported by the stance in trade policy;

- In general, the magnitude of globalization effects of greater trade in OECD countries on wages and inequality are small. Similarly, the recent literature analyzing the effects of trade reforms in developing countries on industry wages are also generally small. Thus, despite the large trade liberalizations undertaken in many Latin American countries during the 1980s and 1990s, most of the research to date has found no evidence of large-scale reallocation of workers across sectors;

- Instead, the brunt of the impact appears to be concentrated within sectors. Thus, studies using plant- or firm-level data conclude that a major impact of trade reforms is natural selection among firms and reductions in x-inefficiency: less efficient firms in a sector are forced to downsize, improve efficiency or exit, with more productive firms expanding their market shares. Overall, total factor productivity increases more in industries that liberalize more;

- Correspondingly, the direct effects of trade reform on aggregate employment are muted. Different models imply different predictions for the long run, the neoclassical 'no change' model being the frequently held view. The evidence is varied: it does not suggest long-run adverse effects and in some cases suggests long-run employment gains as accessing international markets with their high elasticities of demand permits expansion and accumulation in successful sectors without encountering large declines in prices. In the short run, Keynesian employment responses and/or adjustment strains can be adverse, but they are generally not very large relative to total employment. These responses and strains are large, of course, to those who lose their jobs.

Turning to future research priorities, we would identify the following questions:

- *Who/what is protected?* Some of the micro-econometric research to date suggests that the most heavily protected sectors in many developing countries are sectors that employ a high proportion of unskilled workers who earn low wages. A corollary is that trade liberalization, especially when accompanied with investment liberalization and inward FDI, has a negative impact on unskilled workers in the short and medium run—be it in the form of lower wages and/or unemployment. An enigma highlighted by Harrison and Hanson (1999) is why these countries find it optimal to protect low-skill intensive sectors when this is their abundant factor.[14] However, this finding may also be a function of the set of countries that have been analysed, which in turn have been limited by the availability of firm-level datasets. In fact, there is also evidence that countries tend to protect more capital or skill-intensive products. From the conclusions arrived at in the numerical literature on trade and poverty it arises that the poor would benefit from trade reforms because the structure of protection is biased against goods they consume and produce—for example, Hertel and Winters (2005). Clearly the need for a pertinent comprehensive dataset is pressing;

• *Actual/potential impact of trade liberalization on wages.* The high levels of aggregation used in household surveys—2- or 3-digit ISIC (International Standard Industrial Classification of All Economic Activities)— may not be fine enough to detect worker reallocation across firms within the same industry in response to trade liberalization. This leads Goldberg and Pavcnik (2004) to call for empirical firm/plant-level studies that explore the income distributional effects of trade reforms by analyzing the impacts of reform on firms belonging to the same 3- or 4-digit ISIC sector, as reflected, for example, in the compositional changes of their output (quality upgrading or other forms of greater differentiation of their production). Information on productivity-adjusted labour costs would help identify sectors or firms that may be confronted with more serious adjustment costs after reforms. These exercises could also be augmented with information on additional operating costs related to the "quality" of the business environment of the sort generated by the World Bank's Investment Climate Research Program (World Bank, 2005a) and *Doing Business* (World Bank, 2005b);

• *Intersectoral mobility, entry/exit across sectors.* Borjas and Ramey (1995) found that the effect of trade on the labour market depended on the market structure of industries. Barriers to entry and exit will clearly have a bearing on labour market responses to further trade and investment liberalization. Capital and financial market distortions or inefficiencies will affect the ability of firms to expand or enter. These variables may be more important than the labour market. To a large extent such factors have already been studied, but not perhaps from a labour market adjustment perspective;

• *Beyond manufacturing.* The manufacturing sectors are the focus of the lion's share of research on the effects of trade on employment and wages, in both developing and developed countries. Most employment in both categories of countries is, however, in other sectors. In OECD countries services account for more than 70 per cent of turnover and employment, whereas agriculture and the informal and public sectors account for most of the employment in developing countries, especially the poorer among them. To a significant extent, services have become "tradable", be it through cross-border exchange and telecom networks (the internet, etc.) or through international factor mobility (e.g., FDI, labour movement). Adjustment to agricultural price shocks and competition may be quite different from the type of adjustment that occurs in manufacturing, giving rise to greater intersectoral reallocations of labour with associated differences in social costs and implications;

· *Formal versus informal sector and responses to trade reform.* There is little evidence that trade reforms are associated with an increase in informal employment and a worsening of working conditions. To the extent that one finds such evidence, it seems to be relevant in settings characterized by severe labour market rigidities. A good understanding of labour market institutions and their interactions with trade policy would seem to be essential for understanding the likely effects of trade liberalization on employment. In this regard, one has to recognize that informality may be a rational choice for workers as well as for firms, not a consolation prize for those who cannot enter the formal sector. But this goes beyond labour market regulation: the tax system, access to credit, and so forth will also have potentially major effects on the ability of small entrepreneurial firms to move from the informal to the formal sector to take advantage of opportunities that emerge after reforms. An interesting question that has not been studied in depth is the extent to which the limited post-reform sectoral reallocations observed in many developing countries are related to (dis)incentives to grow and/or enter into new markets;

· *Aggregate effects of trade opening in developing countries.* What happens to countries that start off with large-scale unemployment or under-employment? The cases of East Asian countries have been much studied and debated, and clearly trade openness has played an important role in the changes observed in the structure of these economies over the last 40 years. The same was true of OECD countries in the past. This is a reflection of the process of economic development and growth. Few studies exist, however, that analyse the longer-term effects of trade opening on the reduction of underemployment in the informal and rural sectors, as distinct from (or in conjunction with) other policies pursued by governments;

· *International labour mobility.* Migration, temporary or permanent, has not been discussed in this chapter, but it is clearly an important issue in determining both labour market effects and responses to reforms in developing countries. International movement of people is not just an employment or labour market issue but is a potential channel for technology transfer and may have complementary effects on trade and FDI flows.

The recent experience of India in developing a software and related services industry in Bangalore illustrates that effects and payoffs from such movements are both complex to assess ex ante and may take quite some time to materialize, but they can be large. A policy challenge for developing countries is to facilitate temporary movement abroad and to encourage returnees to undertake local research and business development. The research challenge is to better understand the policies that will both facilitate and maximize the expected benefits from such movement.

NOTES

[1] This chapter was written while Hoekman was a visiting professor at the Groupe d'Economie Mondiale, Institut d'Etudes Politiques, Paris. An earlier version of the chapter, by Hoekman alone, was presented on January 30, 2005 at the IDRC/ECES expert group meeting on trade and employment, Egyptian Centre for Economic Studies, Cairo. We are grateful to Ahmed Galal, José Antonio Ocampo and participants in the UN DESA Development Forum on "Integrating economic and social policies to achieve the UN Development Agenda", New York, 14–15 March, 2005, for comments on a previous draft.

[2] Surveys include Baldwin (1995), Cline (1997), Slaughter (1998), Johnson and Stafford (1999), Greenaway and Nelson (2001), Acemoglu (2002), Feenstra and Hanson (2004) and Goldberg and Pavcnik (2004).

[3] Income distributional effects extend, of course, beyond wages and employment to include the prices of produced outputs, non-wage income, transfers and income from assets and consumption prices—see, for example, Winters, McCulloch and McKay (2004).

[4] For example, Abraham and Brock (2003) find that trade has induced changes in technology in the EU; Morrison Paul and Siegel (2001) conclude that there is an indirect effect of trade on labour through greater incentives to adopt information technologies (computerization).

[5] Fields (2001) similarly argues that all four East Asian tigers show enhanced employment as their openness-induced growth progressed

[6] The elasticity of demand for exports is typically high even if foreign markets are restricted by tariffs. Tariffs cut sales, but not necessarily sensitivity to price changes.

[7] Lemieux (2003) is a recent investigation of whether the average wages for different classes of workers defined on the basis of their skills (education and experience) and other characteristics (gender in particular) in Canada and the United States have converged over the last two decades. He notes that aside from the restrictive conditions needed for factor price equalization to be observed, it is not very reasonable to expect national wages to be identical across countries if they are not equalized across regions of the same country (where labour and capital mobility should be much more powerful in equalizing factor prices). Using regional wage dispersion in Canada and the United States as a benchmark for assessing "how different" the wage structures in the two countries are, and controlling for national and regional differences in worker characteristics, he concludes that there has been *divergence* between the wage structures in Canada and the United States over the last 20 years.

[8] As discussed below, this literature suffers from problems of endogeneity. Thus, growth in imports may stimulate faster productivity growth. Trade-induced productivity growth may result from the pro-competitive impact of trade on x-efficiency; reduced rents and employment of unionized labour, or relocation abroad of (unskilled) labour-intensive stages of the value chain. There is substantial evidence that firms improve productivity following greater competition

from imports. Greenaway, Hine and Wright (1999), using an industry production function approach, find this to be important in the United Kingdom, as do Bernard and Jensen (1995) for the United States.

[9] See Acemoglu (2002) for an in-depth survey of the literature on (the determinants of) skill-biased technical change over the last 60 years.

[10] The magnitude of the labour demand elasticities, input-output coefficients, etc., used by researchers in these exercises is important. Sachs and Shatz (1994, 1998), for example, use a factor content approach to find much lower effects than Wood.

[11] Neary (2001) notes that it is not clear how compelling the SBTC finding is in explaining the stylized facts. He argues that in a competitive HOS type setting, it should disproportionately benefit the unskilled labour-intensive (import-competing) sector and reduce the skill premium, and this has not been observed. While detrimental to unskilled workers, SBTC should benefit sectors that employ such labour intensively, lowering their costs and thus their prices, and this has also not been observed. Moreover, it cannot be argued that SBTC is only important in skill-intensive sectors, as the skilled-to-unskilled employment ratios have risen in *all* sectors. The solution he offers is to consider the issue in an imperfectly competitive model where trade liberalization encourages both exporting and import-competing firms to invest and raise their productivity. Insofar as such investment requires relatively more skilled labour, trade openness raises the demand for skilled labour in *both* exporting and importing countries, independent of wages or changes in import volumes. He stresses that any change which intensifies the degree of competition in international markets—including technological progress itself—is likely to manifest itself in more intense competition. Thus, empirically disentangling the effects of trade and technology will always be difficult.

[12] Brainard, Lael and Riker (1997) find evidence of substitution between labour at home and labour abroad, the substitution being much higher between affiliates in countries at similar levels of development.

[13] This rising inequality is in the sense of falling relative returns to labour market participation for unskilled workers; it does not mean these workers are worse off in an absolute sense. As noted by Bourguignon and Morrison (2002), the global distribution of income in terms of absolute poverty numbers has been improving rapidly in recent decades.

[14] Explanations could include political economy (along the lines of Anderson, 1992) or the fact that it ignores that countries such as China are even more unskilled-labour abundant than the developing countries on which research has centred (e.g., Morocco, Mexico, Chile, Colombia)—see Wood (1997).

REFERENCES

Abraham, F., and E. Brock (2003). Sectoral Employment Effects of Trade and Productivity in Europe. *Applied Economics* 35: 223–235.

Acemoglu, Daron (2002). Technical Change, Inequality, and the Labour Market. *Journal of Economic Literature* 40: 7–72.

Attanasio, O., P. Goldberg and N. Pavcnik (2004). Trade Reforms and Wage Inequality in Colombia. *Journal of Development Economics* 74: 331–366.

Aw, B.Y., D. Chung and M. Roberts (2000). Productivity and Turnover in the Export Market: Micro-level Evidence from the Republic of Korea and Taiwan (China). *World Bank Economic Review* 14: 65–90.

Baldwin, Robert E. (1995). The Effect of Trade and Foreign Direct Investment on Employment and Relative Wages. *OECD Economic Studies* 23: 7–54.

Bentivogli, C., and P. Pagano (1999). Trade, Job Destruction and Job Creation in European Manufacturing. *Open Economies Review* 78 (1): 165–184.

Berman, Eli, John Bound, and Zvi Griliches (1994). Changes in the Demand for Skilled Labour within U.S. Manufacturing: Evidence from the Annual Survey of Manufactures. *Quarterly Journal of Economics* 104: 367–398.

Berman, Eli, John Bound and Stephen Machin (1998). Implications of Skill-Biased Technological Change: International Evidence. *Quarterly Journal of Economics* 113: 1245–1280.

Bernard, A., J. Eaton, J. Jensen and S. Kortum (2003). Plants and Productivity in International Trade. *American Economic Review* 93 (4): 1268–1290.

Bernard, A., and J. Jensen (1995). Exporters, Jobs, and Wages in U.S. Manufacturing: 1976–1987. *Brookings Papers on Economic Activity, Microeconomics Annual.* Brookings Institution, Washington, D.C.

Bernard, A., and J. Jensen (1997). Exporters, Skill Upgrading and the Wage Gap. *Journal of International Economics* 42: 3–31.

Bernard, A., and J. Jensen (1999a). Exceptional Exporter Performance: Cause, Effect or Both. *Journal of International Economics* 47 (1): 1–38.

Bernard, A., and J. Jensen (1999b). Exporting and Productivity. NBER Working Paper No. 7135, National Bureau of Economic Research, Cambridge, MA.

Besley, T., and R. Burgess (2004). Can Labour Market Regulation Hinder Economic Performance? Evidence from India. *Quarterly Journal of Economics* 119 (1): 91–134.

Bolaky, Bineswaree, and Caroline Freund (2004). Trade, Regulations, and Growth. World Bank Policy Research Working Paper 3255, Washington, D.C.

Borensztein, E., J. De Gregorio and J-W. Lee (1998). How Does Foreign Direct Investment Affect Economic Growth? *Journal of International Economics* 45: 115–135.

Borjas, G.J., and V.A. Ramey (1995). Foreign Competition, Market Power, and Wage Inequality. *Quarterly Journal of Economics* 110: 1075–1110.

Bourguignon, Francois, and Christian Morrison (2002). Inequality among the World Citizens: 1820–1992. *American Economic Review* 92 (4): 727–744.

Brainard, S. Lael, and David A. Riker (1997). Are U.S. Multinationals Exporting U.S. Jobs? NBER Working Paper No. 5958, National Bureau of Economic Research, Cambridge, MA.

Burgess, S., and M. Knetter (1998). An International Comparison of Employment Adjustment to Exchange Rate Fluctuations. *Review of International Economics* 6 (1): 151–163.

Clerides, S., S. Lach and J. Tybout (1998). Is Learning by Exporting Important? Micro-dynamic Evidence from Colombia, Mexico, and Morocco. *Quarterly Journal of Economics* 113 (3): 903–960.

Cline, William (1997). *Trade and Income Distribution.* Institute for International Economics, Washington, DC.

Currie, Janet, and Ann Harrison (1997). Sharing the Costs: The Impact of Trade Reform on Capital and Labour in Morocco. *Journal of Labour Economics* 15 (3): S44–S71.

Davidson, C., L. Martin and S. Matusz (1999). Trade and Search Generated Unemployment. *Journal of International Economics* 48: 271–299.

Davidson, C., and S. Matusz (2003). Trade and Turnover: Theory and Evidence. Processed, Michigan State University, East Lansing, MI. At http://www.msu.edu/~davidso4.

Desjonqueres, T., S. Machin and J. van Reenan (1999). Another Nail in the Coffin? Or Can the Trade Based Explanation of Changing Skill Structures be Resurrected? *Scandinavian Journal of Economics* 101: 533–554.

Dewatripont, Mathias, André Sapir and Khalik Sekkat (1999). Labour Market Effects of Trade with LDCs in Europe. In M. Dewatripont, A. Sapir and K. Sekkat (eds). *Trade and Jobs in Europe: Much Ado About Nothing?* Oxford University Press, Oxford: 60–78.

Eaton, J., and S. Kortum (2002). Technology, Geography and Trade. *Econometrica* 70 (5): 1741–1795.

Edwards, Sebastian, and A. Cox Edwards (1996). Trade Liberalization and Unemployment: Policy Issues and Evidence from Chile. *Cuadernos de Economia* 33: 227–250.

Feenstra, Robert C., and Gordon H. Hanson (1997). Foreign Direct Investment and Relative Wages: Evidence from Mexico's Maquiladoras. *Journal of International Economics* 42 (3–4), May: 371–393.

Feenstra, Robert C., and Gordon H. Hanson (1999). Productivity Measurement and the Impact of Trade and Technology on Wages: Estimates for the U.S., 1972–1990. *Quarterly Journal of Economics* 114: 907–940.

Feenstra, Robert C., and Gordon H. Hanson (2004). Global Production and Inequality: A Survey of Trade and Wages. In E. Kwan Choi and James Harrigan (eds.). *Handbook of International Economics.* Basil Blackwell, Oxford: 146–185.

Feenstra, Robert C., Gordon H. Hanson and Deborah Swenson (2000). Offshore Assembly from the United States: Production Characteristics of the 9802 Program. In Robert Feenstra (ed.). *The Impact of International Trade on Wages.* University of Chicago Press, Chicago: 85–122

Fields, G.S. (2001). *Distribution and Development: A New Look at the Developing World.* Russell Sage Foundation, New York and MIT Press, Cambridge, MA.

Francois, J. (2004). Assessing the Impact of Trade Policy on Labour Markets and Production. Discussion Paper No. 58, Tinbergen Institute, Rotterdam.

Freeman, Richard B. (1995). Are Your Wages Set in Beijing? *Journal of Economic Perspectives* 9, Summer: 15–32.

Freeman, Richard, and Lawrence Katz (1991). Industrial Wage and Employment Determination in an Open Economy. In J. Abowd and R. Freeman (eds). *Immigration, Trade, and Labour Markets.* University of Chicago Press, Chicago: 235–259.

Freeman, Richard, and Ana Revenga (1999). How Much Has LDC Trade Affected Western Job Markets? In Mathias Dewatripont, André Sapir and Khalid Sekkat (eds). *Trade and Jobs in Europe: Much Ado About Nothing?* Oxford University Press, Oxford: 8–32.

Gaston, Noel, and Daniel Trefler (1997). The Labour Market Consequences of the Canada-U.S. Free Trade Agreement. *Canadian Journal of Economics* 30: 18–41.

Goldberg, Linda, and Jose Campa (1998). Employment versus Wage Adjustment and the US Dollar, NBER Working Paper No. 6749, National Bureau of Economic Research, Cambridge, MA.

Goldberg, Linda, and Joseph Tracy. 2001. Exchange Rates and Wages. Staff Report No. 116, Federal Reserve Board of New York.

Goldberg, P., and N. Pavcnik (2003). The Response of the Informal Sector to Trade Liberalization. *Journal of Development Economics* 72: 463–496.

Goldberg, P., and N. Pavcnik (2004). Trade, Inequality, and Poverty: What Do We Know? Evidence from Recent Trade Liberalization Episodes in Developing Countries. NBER Working Paper No. 10593, National Bureau of Economic Research, Cambridge, MA.

Goldberg, P., and N. Pavcnik (2005). Trade, Wages, and the Political Economy of Trade Protection: Evidence from the Colombian Trade Reforms. *Journal of International Economics* 66: 75–105.

Gourinchas, P.O. (1999a). Exchange Rates Do Matter: French Job Reallocation and Exchange Rate Turbulence, 1984–1992. *European Economic Review* 43: 1279–1316.

Gourinchas, P.O. (1999b). Exchange Rates and Jobs: What Do We Learn from Job Flows? *NBER Macroeconomics Annual 1998.* MIT Press, Cambridge, MA: 153–207.

Greenaway, D., R.C. Hine and P.W. Wright (1999). An Empirical Assessment of the Impact of Trade on Employment in the United Kingdom. *European Journal of Political Economy* 15: 485–500.

Greenaway, David, and Doug Nelson (2001). Introduction and Overview. In D. Greenaway and D. Nelson (eds). *Globalization and Labour Markets.* Edward Elgar, London.

Greenaway, David, Richard Upward and Peter Wright (2000). Sectoral Adjustment and Labour Market Flows. *Oxford Review of Economic Policy* 16: 57–75.

Grossman, Gene (1987). The Employment and Wage Effects of Import Competition in the US. *Journal of International Economic Integration* 2: 1–23.

Hallward-Driermayer, M., G. Iarossi and K. Sokoloff (2002). Exports and Manufacturing Productivity in East Asia: A Comparative Analysis with Firm-level Data. NBER Working Paper No. 8894, National Bureau of Economic Research, Cambridge, MA.

Haltiwanger, John, A. Kugler, M. Kugler, A. Micco and C. Pagés (2004). Effects of Tariffs and Real Exchange Rates on Job Reallocation: Evidence from Latin America. *Journal of Policy Reform* 7 (4): 191–208.

Hanson, G., and A. Harrison (1999). Trade and Wage Inequality in Mexico. *Industrial and Labour Relations Review* 52 (2): 271–288.

Harrison, A., and G. Hanson (1999). Who Gains from Trade Reform? Some Remaining Puzzles. *Journal of Development Economics* 59: 125–154.

Harrison, A., and A.L. Revenga (1998). Labour Markets, Foreign Investment and Trade Policy Reform. In J. Nash and W. Takacs (eds). *Trade Policy Reform: Lessons and Implications.* World Bank, Washington DC: 247–276.

Heitger, B., and J. Stehn (2003). Trade, Technical Change and Labour Market Adjustment. *World Economy* 26 (10): 1481–1501.

IADB (2004). *Good Jobs Wanted: Labour Markets in Latin America.* Inter-American Development Bank, Washington, DC.

Jansen, Marion, and Alessandro Turrini (2004). Job Creation, Job Destruction, and the International Division of Labour. *Review of International Economics* 12 (3): 476–494.

Johnson, George, and Frank Stafford (1999). The Labour Market Implications of International Trade. In O. Ashenfelter and D. Card (eds). *Handbook of Labour Economics* Vol. 3B. North Holland, Amsterdam: Chapter 34.

Katz, Lawrence, and Kevin Murphy (1992). Changes in Relative Wages, 1963–1987: Supply and Demand Factors. *Quarterly Journal of Economics* 107: 35–78.

Kee, Hiau Looi, and Hian Teck Hoon (2005). Trade, Capital Accumulation and Structural Unemployment: An Empirical Study of the Singapore Economy. *Journal of Development Economics* 77: 125–152.

Keller, Wolfgang (1996). Absorptive Capacity: On the Creation and Acquisition of Technology in Development. *Journal of Development Economics* 49: 199–227.

Klein, M., S. Schuh, and R. Triest (2003). Job Creation, Job Destruction, and the Real Exchange Rate. *Journal of International Economics* 59 (2): 239–265.

Kletzer, Lori G. (2000). Trade and Job Loss in U.S. Manufacturing, 1979–1994. In Robert C. Feenstra (ed.). *The Impact of International Trade on Wages.* University of Chicago Press, Chicago: 349–393.

Kletzer, Lori G. (2004). Trade-related Job Loss and Wage Insurance: A Synthetic Review. *Review of International Economics* 12 (5): 724–748.

Lawrence, Robert, and Matthew Slaughter (1993). Trade and US Wages: Giant Sucking Sound or Small Hiccup?. *Brookings Papers on Economic Activity* 2: 161–210.

Lemieux, Thomas (2003). Trade Liberalization and the Labour Market. Processed, University of British Columbia, Vancouver, BC.

Levinsohn, J. (1999). Employment Responses to International Liberalization in Chile. *Journal of International Economics* 47: 321–344.

Maloney, W.F. (2004). Informality Revisited. *World Development* 32 (7): 1159–1178.

Marquez, Gustavo, and Carmen Pages-Serra (1998). Structural Reform and Labour Market Performance in Latin America and the Caribbean During the 90's: Much Ado About Nothing? Processed, Inter-American Development Bank, Washington, DC.

Matusz, Steven (1996). International Trade, the Division of Labour, and Unemployment. *International Economic Review* 37: 71–84.

Matusz, S.J., and D. Tarr (1999). Adjusting to Trade Policy Reform. Policy Research Working Paper No. 2142, World Bank, Washington, DC.

McMulloch, N., B. Baluch and M. Cherel-Robson (2001). Poverty, Inequality and Growth in Zambia during the 1990s. Discussion Paper No. 2001/123, UNU-WIDER, Helsinki.

Melitz, M. (2003). The Impact of Trade on Intra-industry Reallocations and Aggregate Industry Productivity. *Econometrica* 71: 1696–1725.

Moreira, Mauricio, and S. Najberg (2000). Trade Liberalization in Brazil: Creating or Exporting Jobs? *Journal of Development Studies* 36 (3): 78–99.

Murphy, Kevin, and Finis Welch (1991). The Role of International Trade in Wage Differentials. In Marvin Kosters (ed.). *Workers and Their Wages: Changing Patterns in the US*. American Enterprise Institute, Washington, DC: 39–69.

Neary, J. Peter (2001). Competition, Trade and Wages. Processed, University College, Dublin.

Nicita, Alessandro (2004). Export-led-growth, Pro-poor or Not? A Case Study of Madagascar's Textile and Apparel Industry. Processed, University of Sussex, December. At http://www.sussex.ac.uk/Units/PRU/tradelib_firms_Nicita.pdf.

Ocampo, J.A. (2004). Latin America's Growth and Equity Frustrations during Structural Reforms. *Journal of Economic Perspectives* 18 (2): 67–88.

Ocampo, J.A., and Lance Taylor (1998). Trade Liberalization in Developing Economies: Modest Benefits but Problems with Productivity Growth, Macro Prices, and Income Distribution. *The Economic Journal* 108 (450): 1523–1546.

Papageorgiou, D., M. Michaely, A. Choksi (eds) (1991). *Liberalizing Foreign Trade*. 7 volumes. Basil Blackwell, Oxford, for the World Bank, Washington, DC.

Pavcnik, N. (2002). Trade Liberalization, Exit and Productivity Improvements: Evidence from Chilean Plants. *Review of Economic Studies* 69 (1): 245–276.

Pavcnik, N. (2003). What Explains Skill Upgrading in Less Developed Countries? *Journal of Development Economics* 71: 311–328.

Pavcnik, N., A. Blom, P. Goldberg and N. Schady (2004). Trade Liberalization and Industry Wage Structure: Evidence from Brazil. *The World Bank Economic Review* 18 (3): 319–344.

Rama, Martín (1994). The Labor Market and Trade Reform in Manufacturing. In M. Connolly and J. de Melo (eds). *The Effects of Protectionism on a Small Country: The Case of Uruguay*. World Bank Regional and Sectoral Studies, Washington, DC: 108–123.

Rama, Martín (2003). Globalization and Labour Markets. *World Bank Research Observer* 18 (2): 159–186.

Rama, Martin, and D. MacIsaac (1999). Earnings and Welfare after Downsizing: Central Bank Employees in Ecuador. *World Bank Economic Review* 13: 89–116.

Rama, Martín, and K. Scott (1999). Labour Earnings in One-company Towns: Theory and Evidence from Kazakhstan. *World Bank Economic Review* 13: 185–209.

Revenga, Ana L. (1992). Exporting Jobs? The Impact of Import Competition on Employment and Wages in U.S. Manufacturing. *Quarterly Journal of Economics* 107: 255–284.

Revenga, Ana L. (1997). Employment and Wage Effects of Trade Liberalization: The Case of Mexican Manufacturing. *Journal of Labour Economics* 15 (3): S20–S43.

Richardson, J. David (1995). Income Inequality and Trade: How to Think, What to Conclude. *Journal of Economic Perspectives* 9: 33–55.

Robbins, D. (1996). HOS Hits Facts: Facts Win. Evidence on Trade and Wages in the Developing World. Processed, Harvard Institute for International Development, Cambridge, MA.

Roberts, Mark, and James Tybout (1996). The Decision to Export in Colombia: An Empirical Model of Entry with Sunk Costs. *American Economic Review* 87 (4): 545–564.

Roberts, Mark, and James Tybout (1997). Producer Turnover and Productivity Growth in Developing Countries. *World Bank Research Observer* 12 (1): 1–18.

Rodrik, Dani (1995). Getting Interventions Right: How South Korea and Taiwan Grew Rich. *Economic Policy* 20: 53–97.

Sachs, Jeffrey D., and Howard J. Shatz (1994). Trade and Jobs in U.S. Manufacturing. *Brookings Papers on Economic Activity* 1: 1–84.

Sachs, Jeffrey D., and Howard J. Shatz (1998). International Trade and Wage Inequality: Some New Results. In Susan M. Collins (ed.). *Imports, Exports, and the American Worker.* Brookings Institution Press, Washington, DC: 215–256.

Slaughter, M.J. (1998). International Trade and Labour-market Outcomes: Results, Questions, and Policy Options. *Economic Journal* 108: 1452–1462.

Subramanian, Arvind (2001). Mauritius: A Case Study. *Finance & Development* 38: 22–25.

Thoenig, M., and T. Verdier (2003). A Theory of Defensive Skill-based Innovation and Globalization. *American Economic Review* 93: 709–728.

Thomas, Vinod, J. Nash and Sebastian Edwards (1991). *Best Practices in Trade Policy Reform.* Oxford University Press, New York.

Vasudeva-Dutta, Puja (2004). Trade Liberalization and the Indian Labour Markets. Processed, University of Sussex, Brighton.

Wacziarg, Romain, and Jessica Seddon Wallack (2004). Trade Liberalization and Intersectoral Labour Movements. *Journal of International Economics* 64: 411–439.

Winters, L.A. (2002). Trade, Trade Policy and Poverty: What are the Links? *The World Economy* 25 (9): 1339–1367.

Winters, L.A., N. McCulloch and A. McKay (2004). Trade Liberalization and Poverty: The Evidence So Far. *Journal of Economic Literature* 42: 72–115.

Wood, Adrian (1994). *North-South Trade, Employment and Inequality: Changing Fortunes in a Skill-Driven World.* Clarendon Press, Oxford.

Wood, Adrian (1995). How Trade Hurt Unskilled Workers. *Journal of Economic Perspectives* 9 (3), Summer: 15–32.

Wood, Adrian (1997). Openness and Wage Inequality in Developing Countries: The Latin American Challenge to East Asian Conventional Wisdom. *World Bank Economic Review* 11 (1): 33–58.

World Bank (2005a). *World Development Report, 2005: Investment Climate.* Oxford University Press, New York, for World Bank, Washington, DC.

World Bank (2005b). *Doing Business.* World Bank, Washington, DC.

Younger, Stephan (1996). Labour Market Consequences of Retrenchment for Civil Servants in Ghana. In David E. Sahn (ed.). *Economic Reform and the Poor in Africa.* Oxford University Press, New York.

5
Trade Liberalization and Employment

EDDY LEE

Trade liberalization, loosely defined as a move towards freer trade through the reduction of tariff and other barriers, is generally perceived as the major driving force behind globalization. Rapidly increasing flows of goods and services across national borders have been the most visible aspect of the increasing integration of the global economy in recent decades. However, this has also been one of the most contentious aspects of globalization. Critics of trade liberalization have blamed it for a host of ills, such as rising unemployment and wage inequality in the advanced countries; increased exploitation of workers in developing countries and a "race to the bottom" with respect to employment conditions and labour standards; the de-industrialization and marginalization of low-income countries; increasing poverty and global inequality; and degradation of the environment. These views have spread in spite of the fact that the benefits of freer trade, in terms of improved allocation of resources and consequent gains in productive efficiency and economic growth, are a basic tenet of mainstream economic analysis.

In this context, the impact of trade liberalization on employment is of particular significance. The level of employment is a key determinant of overall economic welfare, especially in developing countries where systems of social protection are weak. In particular, the impact of trade liberalization on the level and structure of employment determines, to a large extent, its impact on poverty, wage and income distribution and the quality of employment. These latter variables are clearly among the central points of contention in the debate over trade liberalization.

Viewed within the standard theoretical framework, trade liberalization is presumed to be unambiguously good for developing countries since they are labour-abundant. Freer trade will not only increase efficiency and growth but will simultaneously increase employment opportunities and wages for their most abundant resource, unskilled labour. This would also have the additional favourable effect of reducing wage and income inequality since the unskilled are among the lowest paid in the labour market.

From this standpoint, there should be no question that trade liberalization is beneficial in terms of its growth, employment and distributional implications.

Translated into policy terms, this would mean that unilateral trade liberalization would always be a preferable policy option to import substitution or protection. Moreover, strong advocates of trade liberalization have extended this to the proposition that the sooner and more extensively trade is liberalized the greater the benefits will be.

There are, however, important theoretical reservations to this position (see, in particular, Winters, 2000). Most of these arise from the fact that the above propositions rest on the assumption that there is perfect competition and that there are only constant returns to scale in production. This is clearly at odds with the real world where, especially in developing countries, market imperfections are common and where many branches of industrial production are characterized by economies of scale. Therefore, "in the presence of certain market failures, such as positive production externalities in import-competing sectors, the long-run levels of GDP (measured at world prices) can be higher with trade restrictions than without" (Rodriguez and Rodrik, 1999). This was the underlying basis for the long-standing infant industry argument that initial protection be granted to potentially competitive industries to enable them to overcome barriers to start-up and hence to learn by doing.

More recent developments in growth and trade theory have also provided additional arguments for protection. Endogenous growth theories suggest that "trade restrictions may also be associated with higher rates of growth of output whenever the restrictions promote technologically more dynamic sectors over others" (Rodriguez and Rodrik, 1999). Apart from reaping the benefits of economies of scale, positive externalities may also be generated by an increase in the stock of knowledge through these means. This is similar to the older arguments for import substitution based on the view that increasing returns and cross-firm externalities are ubiquitous in manufacturing and that protection to promote industrialization is justified on these grounds. This is often accompanied by the argument that industrialization is a precondition for later export success. From this perspective, trade liberalization is often deplored on the grounds that it sometimes leads to de-industrialization. "New trade theory" also makes the case that strategic trade policies can raise welfare under some circumstances. By supporting its firms to gain entry into sectors of production where world demand can support only a few oligopolistic firms (e.g., aircraft production), a country can capture significant benefits for the national economy.

It has also been pointed out that standard trade theory also assumes that resources (including labour) are always fully employed and that trade will always be balanced (Ocampo and Taylor, 1998). These assumptions rarely apply in the real world (vide the high levels of unemployment prevailing in

many countries). In these circumstances, in contrast to the comfortable predictions of smooth and costless adjustment in standard theory, trade liberalization
can impose heavy adjustment costs in the form of a contraction in output, high
unemployment and wide trade deficits. Another stand of the literature also
argues that adjustment costs may be high where there is monopolistic or
imperfect competition, factor immobility and wage and price rigidity.

TRADE LIBERALIZATION AND ITS MEASUREMENT

Before proceeding to examine the empirical evidence, it is necessary to review
a few issues relating to the concept of trade liberalization and its measurement.
Relatively little attention has been paid in the current literature to the crucial
distinction between trade liberalization per se and the general effects of an
increase in trade, from whatever cause, on growth and employment. This has
been a source of confusion that should be removed. Conceptually, trade liberalization is often defined in terms of the bias in the incentive structure between
exports and imports (Greenaway, Morgan and Wright, 1998). The free trade
position is one where incentives are neutral between exports and imports.
Trade liberalization could thus be achieved by either the reduction of tariffs or
of any anti-export bias through other means (e.g., the introduction or raising
export subsidies). Another element of trade liberalization is the replacement of
an instrument of trade control by another that would distort the incentive
structure less. A common example of this is when quantitative restrictions on
trade are replaced by a tariff. In practice there are several ways in which the
extent of trade liberalization can be measured, but there are problems with
each of these. One measure usually adopted is that of relying on announced
changes in policy such as a reduction in tariffs or the removal of quantitative
restrictions. This, however, must be checked against actual performance and
the possibility for instrument substitution, i.e., changes in other policies that
may negate the intended effects of the announced policy changes. A second
measure is based on a direct estimate of the change in the bias in the trade
regime as reflected in changes in relative prices. This, however, often runs up
against problems of weighting and aggregating price changes. A third measure
is to use multiple criteria such as tariff changes and changes in relative prices,
but this too faces the same problems of weighting and aggregation.

It is also important to note briefly a few methodological problems that are
commonly encountered in studies of trade liberalization. A particularly challenging problem is that of separating out the effects of trade liberalization from
those of other policy shifts, macroeconomic crises and other externally-

generated shocks that may occur at the same time. Another is that of the counter-factual (or the alternative scenario that is assumed would have prevailed in the absence of trade liberalization) that is used to establish the effects of trade liberalization. This counterfactual is often assumed to be a situation where pre-existing policies would have prevailed. This may not be appropriate since trade liberalization often occurs after an economic crisis and, in these circum-stances, pre-existing polices are no longer viable.

EMPIRICAL EVIDENCE ON TRADE LIBERALIZATION AND EMPLOYMENT

There has been considerable liberalization of trade in the post-Second World War era. This has been particularly pronounced since the 1980s. Over 100 countries across the world have adopted some measure of trade liberalization, such as the reduction of tariffs, quantitative restrictions and other non-tariff barriers to trade. As a result, average levels of tariffs and other barriers to trade have fallen significantly in the majority of countries in the world. These trade liberalization measures have often been accompanied by the liberalization of policies towards foreign direct investment as well as wider liberalization meas-ures, such as the removal of controls over domestic investment, deregulation of domestic product and labour markets, privatization and both internal and external financial liberalization.

These other accompanying liberalization measures make it especially difficult to distinguish the consequences of trade liberalization from the effects of other policies. It is often difficult to disentangle the effects of trade policies per se from those of other measures of liberalization that occurred contem-poraneously. It is also important to note that there were important differences among countries in the initial degree of protection at which liberalization was initiated, in the macroeconomic circumstances that surrounded the initiation and the implementation of trade liberalization programmes, in the extent of liberalization that was undertaken, in the pace and sequencing of trade liberalization measures, and in the relationship between trade and other liberal-ization measures. This makes it inherently difficult to arrive at general con-clusions about the effects of trade liberalization.

It is, thus, difficult to draw any firm conclusions on the impact of trade liberalization simply on the basis of associations between changes in trade on the one hand and growth and employment performance on the other. The first problem is one of establishing causality between trade liberalization and growth and employment performance. An increase in exports and the trade-to-GDP ratio cannot automatically be attributed to the effects of trade liberalization, as other factors are involved. The growth in exports and the trade-to-GDP ratio could be the result of higher growth achieved through a successful development strategy or favourable external market conditions. This is especially so since export growth is typically a major component of overall growth and the two are strongly correlated. Yet, as we shall see below, this has not deterred various proponents of trade liberalization from using such an approach to establish their case.

Multi-Country Studies

A prominent case in point are two studies, Dollar (1992) and Sachs and Warner (1995), that have been highly influential in forming the widely accepted view that countries with lower policy-induced barriers to trade experience faster growth, once other relevant country characteristics are controlled. Both of these studies are based on a cross-section analysis for a large number of countries regarding the relationship between an index of "openness" of the economy and growth performance. The Dollar study claimed that for a sample of 95 countries over the period between 1976 and 1985, growth was negatively correlated with each of the two indices of openness used. The first index was a measure of real exchange rate distortion while the other was an index of real exchange rate variability. The rationale for the use of these indices was that the more open an economy, the lower the extent of exchange rate distortion and the less the variability in the exchange rate. The Sachs and Warner study arrives at a similar conclusion on the relationship between the degree of openness and growth. The study is a cross-section analysis of a large sample of 70 countries. Countries were classified as either "open" or "closed" based on five criteria—the level of average tariffs, the coverage of non-tariff barriers, whether or not it had a socialist economic system, whether or not it had a State monopoly of major exports, and the level of the black market premium.

The findings of both these studies have been seriously questioned by a convincing critique (Rodriguez and Rodrik, 1999) which centres on the fact that the indicators of "openness" used are seriously flawed. They are not reliable measures of trade barriers and are also highly correlated with other sources of poor economic performance. That being the case, the proposition that trade liberalization by itself leads to higher growth remains unproven.

Another recent attempt to revive the issue is the paper by Dollar and Kraay (2001). This paper identifies a group of countries, the "post-1980 globalizers" that have seen large increases in trade and significant declines in tariffs over the past 20 years and claims that "their growth rates have accelerated from the 1970s to the 1980s to the 1990s, even as growth in the rich countries and the rest of the developing world has declined". The paper also claims that "since there is little systematic evidence of a relationship between changes in trade volumes (or any other globalization measure we consider) and changes in the income share of the poorest, the increase in growth rates that accompanies expanded trade leads to proportionate increases in incomes of the poor". The paper is, however, more convincing on the effects of trade expansion on growth than on the effects of trade policy. As pointed out by Rodrik (2001), the paper is also flawed by applying an "arbitrary set of selection criteria to their sample of countries". In particular, they "combine a policy measure (tariff averages) with an outcome (import/GDP) measure in selecting countries. This is conceptually inappropriate, as policy makers do not directly control the level of trade ... the tools at the disposal of governments are tariff and non-tariff barriers, not import or export levels". This is significant because the countries in the sample that implemented the deepest trade liberalization, as opposed to those who experienced the greatest trade expansion, did not perform well in terms of the rate of economic growth achieved. Similarly, it was inappropriate to attribute the higher growth in India and China to trade liberalization. In these countries, "the main trade reforms took place about a decade after the onset of higher growth. Moreover, these countries' trade restrictions remain among the highest in the world".

A recent review of the empirical evidence on the effects of trade liberalization (Greenaway, Morgan and Wright, 1998) also comes to a more nuanced conclusion than the earlier Dollar or Sachs and Warner studies. This review concludes that trade liberalization has resulted in both an increase and a decline in the growth rate depending on country circumstances. Many countries were observed to have experienced an investment slump after trade liberalization, suggesting that a "J-curve" effect is at work. This suggests that there are at least short-run costs of adjustment after trade liberalization. Trade liberalization has also tended to be associated with an increase in current account deficits in spite of an increase in exports. These mixed results indicate that the impact of trade liberalization is not uniform but, on the contrary, is strongly influenced by factors such as the nature of the liberalization programme, the extent of pre-existing distortions in the trade regime and the flexibility of markets.

There have been relatively few cross-section studies that focus directly on the impact of trade liberalization on employment. A major World Bank study (Papageorgiou, Choksi and Michaely, 1990) dating back to 1990 attempted to demonstrate the benefits of substantial trade liberalization. Based on the examination of 36 distinct episodes of trade liberalization in 19 countries, it offered very reassuring conclusions about the benefits of trade liberalization. Among its conclusions were the views that "even in the short run liberalization went hand in hand with faster rather than slower growth" and that "trade liberal-ization did not as a rule raise unemployment even in individual sectors of the economy such as manufacturing and agriculture". It explains the latter outcome in terms of the fact that a slowdown in manufacturing growth was compensated by a rise in agricultural growth and employment as a result of trade liberalization. It also claimed that this increase in agricultural growth, together with the fact that there was an increase in labour-intensive exports, increased the demand for labour overall and hence led to an improvement in income distribution.

These results have, however, been challenged. Greenaway (1993) and Collier (1993) have questioned these findings primarily on methodological grounds. More recently, Agenor and Aizenman (1996) have pointed out that these studies provide only limited evidence on changes in employment in non-manufac-turing production activities or changes in the aggregate unemployment rate. These problems are compounded by methodological shortcomings in the case studies. That being the case, the sanguine conclusions about the employment effects of trade liberalization are not sustainable.

A recent World Bank study on globalization (Dollar and Collier, 2001) takes a less sanguine view of the employment effects of trade liberalization than some of the World Bank's earlier studies. While reiterating the benefits of trade liberalization for both employment and wages over the long run, the study recognizes that there are significant transitional problems that need to be faced. It notes that the skill premium, and hence wage inequality, has risen in several countries in the aftermath of trade liberalization. It also notes that "a series of case studies on the effects of trade liberalization shows a considerable dispersion of the net impact on employment". More significantly, it highlights the problems that "small declines in employment may hide substantial job churning" and that "some of the important losers from globalization will be formal sector workers in protected industries".

A series of International Labour Organization (ILO) case studies on China, India, Malaysia, Mexico and Brazil focused on the effects of the growth of trade on employment and wages in manufacturing industries.[1] The countries chosen for study had all experienced rapid growth in trade in the past two decades and were among the leading group of developing countries that had benefited most from the growth in world trade. The studies focused on the manufacturing sec-tor because it had spearheaded trade growth and had felt the effects of trade expansion most strongly. In the three Asian emerging economies studied, trade growth had a generally favourable effect on employment and wages in manu-facturing. Apart from stimulating output growth, trade growth has had the effect of increasing the employment intensity of manufacturing output. More-over, unskilled (or low-skilled) workers have benefited more than skilled workers because employment growth has been faster in export-oriented industries, which mainly employ low-skilled workers, than in other industries. It also appears that employment in import-competing industries continued to increase in spite of increased import competition. Real wages of unskilled workers have risen whenever surplus labour has become insignificant, but they have not declined even where surplus labour remains significant. Real wages of skilled workers have generally risen. Thus, wage inequality has improved in some situations but has worsened in others. In contrast to what was the case in the Asian countries, the favourable effects of trade growth on employment and wages were not observed in Latin American countries, such as Brazil and Mexico. In these countries, employment in manufacturing has either not risen appreciably or has fallen. Real wages of unskilled workers have tended to decline, and the wage differential between skilled and unskilled workers has increased rather sharply. The studies suggest that these trends may be attributable to unfavourable initial conditions (e.g., extremely unequal distribution of assets), problems of macroeconomic management and overdependence on external resources, but more work is required to develop adequate insights.

The sharply contrasting employment effects between countries suggest that country-specific and contingent factors are important, and the value of any broad generalization on the link between trade liberalization and employment is therefore undermined. This suggests that it would be more fruitful to look at country-specific studies in the search for answers.

Country Studies

The view in favour of country-specific studies is supported by the divergent results that have been revealed by recent country studies that examine the relationship between trade liberalization and employment. A study on Mexico (Ravenga, 1994) found that in the period between 1984 and 1990 a 10 per cent reduction in tariff levels was associated with a 2 to 3 per cent reduction in employment. The wage differential between skilled and unskilled workers also widened. The study also argues that the absence of large aggregate employment effects was due to wage flexibility; wages had declined significantly throughout the adjustment period. A study of Brazil (Mesquita and Najberg, 2000) found that the trade liberalization at the beginning of the 1990s had a slight negative short-term impact on employment: it found that between 1990 and 1997 there was a 32.4 per cent drop in employment in capital-intensive industries and a 13.3 per cent decline in the labour-intensive industries. This decline in employment could note be attributed solely to trade liberalization since the trade reforms were carried out in a macroeconomic environment that was marked by high inflation and recessionary conditions. Among the explanations that it offers for the decline in employment are a sharp increase in productivity in the capital-intensive industries and poor export performance in the labour-intensive industries. In Chile (Levinsohn, 1999), the trade liberalization of the 1970s coincided with severe macroeconomic shocks. The effects of these shocks on employment far outweighed those associated with the trade liberalization. The combined effect of these two factors resulted in an 8 per cent decline in net manufacturing employment between 1979 and 1986. An interesting feature of this study is that, in addition to looking at net changes in employment levels, it also attempts to estimate job creation and destruction using firm-level data. This suggests that about a quarter of all workers in manufacturing changed jobs in this period, indicating that there was a far greater extent of labour-market adjustment than what was suggested by looking only at industry-level figures on the net change in employment. The study also stresses the importance of looking at the impact of trade liberalization on the size structure of enterprises. In the case of Chile, it is important to note, however, that after 1986, employment performance improved significantly although concern was still being expressed in the late 1990s that "a relatively large number of jobs being created include little or no employment or social protection and the situation appears to be worsening" (Torres, 2001).

There were also mixed results emerging from three studies of trade liberalization in African countries. In Zimbabwe (Rattso and Torvik, 1998), it was found that the drastic trade liberalization implemented in the early 1990s resulted in a contraction in output and employment that was accompanied by a sharp increase in imports and a rising trade deficit. The study argues that the contraction in output was associated with de-industrialization, a development that may also have had unfavourable effects on the future growth potential of the economy. Real wages also fell in the wake of trade liberalization. In contrast, a study on Mauritius (Milner and Wright, 1998) found far more favourable outcomes from trade liberalization. The reduction in protection for local firms that had been implemented during the period 1985–1987 led to the expected rise in employment in export industries but no contraction in employment in the industries producing importables. The latter was due to an increase in the supply of female labour (which eased the labour supply constraint) and strong overall growth in the economy. In Morocco (Currie and Harrison, 1997), the substantial trade liberalization implemented during 1984–1990 did not have very strong employment effects. The average level of import penetration increased only slightly due to a contraction in domestic demand and the devaluation of the currency. A 21 per cent decline in tariff protection in "high impact" industries led to a 6 per cent decline in employment. At the same time, a 24 per cent decline in tariffs in the export-oriented sectors led to only a 1.7 per cent decline in employment.

It is notable that most of these studies focus on employment in the manufacturing or the organized sector of the economy. Little is said about employment in the rural or urban informal sectors. Yet, this is where the major part of employment occurs in low-income countries and where the majority of the poor earn their livelihoods. The impact of trade liberalization on employment in the rural and urban informal sectors is thus important from the standpoint of overall welfare and poverty reduction.

There are several reasons for the relative neglect of these sectors. One basic reason is the paucity of data on employment and other economic variables in these sectors. Another is that the primary impact of trade liberalization has been on the manufacturing and other organized sectors of the economy. Much of the economic activity in the urban informal sector and in subsistence agriculture consists of non-tradables. The impact of trade liberalization on employment is thus largely indirect, occurring through changes in relative prices and in the probability of obtaining employment in the organized sector. In addition, there is considerable heterogeneity in the employment profiles of individuals and households within these sectors. They vary greatly in terms of their endowments of assets and in their labour activity profile. This implies that the impact of trade liberalization on employment will also vary greatly according to these differences in initial conditions, making the analysis very complex. Variations in the institutional context in which different groups of producers find themselves compound the problem, since these differences affect the nature and extent of the impact of trade liberalization. Here again, therefore, there is a need for context-specific analyses that do not allow for easy generalizations.

A particular concern that has surfaced over the impact of trade liberalization on workers and producers outside the organized sector is that of their possible exclusion from the benefits of that liberalization. From a labour market perspective, the concern is that, even where trade liberalization results in a rapid increase in employment opportunities (e.g., in the labour-intensive manufacturing sector), illiterate or poorly educated workers from the rural and urban informal sectors would be unable to benefit from these new opportunities. The reason for this is that even unskilled jobs in the organized sectors require at least a primary education that these workers do not have. There is similar concern over the ability of micro and small farms and enterprises to overcome the handicaps they face in terms of access to credit and knowledge of market opportunities and product standards in order to benefit from new opportunities created by trade liberalization.

Wage Inequality

There has also been a very pronounced interest in the issue of the impact of trade liberalization on wage inequality. A special issue of the *Journal of International Economics* (2001) explored several channels through which trade could affect wage inequality, other than the standard one of Hecksher-Ohlin and Stolper-Samuelson. The first of these is that "trade liberalization can affect the relative bargaining power of labour versus capital. For example, if trade liberalization increases the elasticity of demand for labour, it would reduce the bargaining position of workers and therefore wages" (Feenstra, 2001). Of related interest is the argument advanced in another article on the impact of increased mobility of capital. It argues that this will have even stronger effects than trade liberalization in weakening the bargaining position of labour. It notes that "a subsidy for workers financed by a tax on capital income is the obvious remedy for redistributing the gains from international capital mobility" (Rodrik and van Ypersele, 2001: 58), but this requires tax coordination at the international level, since tax competition becomes a greater problem with higher capital mobility.

A second channel through which trade is thought to affect wage inequality is the increased role of outsourcing and the relocation of labour-intensive (and low-skilled) parts of production processes from advanced to developing countries. This shedding of relatively labour-intensive production in the advanced economies is likely to shift demand to skilled workers and increase their relative wages. There is evidence that outsourcing has increased but its impact on wage inequality in the advanced countries has yet to be clearly established (Hummels, Ishii and Yi 2001; Feenstra and Hanson, 1997[2]). In the case of developing countries, it has also been argued that participation in the production chains created through outsourcing has been a factor contributing to a rise in wage inequality. The basic reasoning here is that, given the large gap in skill levels between advanced and developing countries, the low-skill jobs transferred from the former constitute relatively skilled jobs (e.g., requiring a high school education) in a developing country. There is some empirical verification of this in the case of Mexico (Feenstra and Hanson, 1997[3]). A related argument is that skill-biased technological change in the industrialized countries is being transmitted to developing countries through increasing trade and foreign direct investment flows. There is some fragmentary evidence that this may actually be occurring (Berman and Machin, 2004).

A third channel through which trade liberalization can affect wage inequality is through strengthening incentives to produce for export markets. It has been argued that, in order to compete successfully in export markets, firms have to invest in more sophisticated and relatively more skill-intensive machinery, hence pushing up the demand for skills (Feenstra, 2001[4]). However, there has been very little empirical testing of this hypothesis so far.

All of this new work on the links between trade liberalization and wage inequality has been inspired by the need to explain why, contrary to the predictions of the Hecksher-Ohlin and Stolper-Samuelson framework, wage inequality has increased after trade liberalization in several countries. But it should be noted that this has been a phenomenon that has been largely confined to several Latin American countries, in sharp contrast to the experience in Asia. It remains an open question as to what has accounted for this difference.

POLICY ISSUES

Nothing in the foregoing negates the proposition that there are gains from trade and that there are costs associated with protectionism. The issue is not whether countries should try to benefit from freer trade but how this should be achieved. What the preceding discussion has tried to suggest is that there is no basis for a blanket prescription of "big bang" trade liberalization that is applicable to all countries. The relationship between trade liberalization and growth and employment is likely to be "a contingent one, dependent on a host of countries and external characteristics" (Rodriguez and Rodrik, 1999). Differences in country circumstances (such as the level of development or whether a country has comparative advantage in primary commodities or manufactures) are likely to warrant different strategies of trade liberalization.

The international economic environment is also an important determinant of the extent to which developing countries can derive benefits from trade liberalization. Higher and more balanced growth in the global economy will obviously provide a more conducive environment for trade liberalization than the current situation of uneven growth coupled with huge macroeconomic and trade imbalances. Similarly, greater market access for both the agricultural and non-agricultural exports of developing countries is crucial for enabling them to benefit from trade liberalization. This will also significantly mitigate the danger of the 'fallacy of composition' effect inherent in simultaneous trade liberalization by all developing countries. Without higher growth and greater market access, trade liberalization runs the risk of becoming a zero-sum game that continues to marginalize many low-income countries. In this context, there is also a clear need for greater international assistance to the least developed countries to strengthen their capacity to benefit from trade liberalization. There is thus a challenging agenda for change in international policies that needs to be urgently addressed.

This aside, it is also important to note that in terms of national policies the choice is not a simple "either/or" between protection and free trade. The options also include intermediate positions that may make good economic sense in particular circumstances (see Lee and Vivarelli, 2004, especially chapters 4, 5 and 13). This point emerges quite forcefully in the context of the literature on the reasons behind the East Asian economic miracle. Free traders have interpreted this experience as one that epitomizes the virtues of trade liberalization. They have highlighted the trade liberalization in these countries as being the key to the successful export-led industrialization that transformed these economies. But there is persuasive literature that points out that this is an oversimplification. These countries did not undertake "big bang" trade liberalization, but moved towards a more neutral trade regime through selective export-promotion policies. The trade policies were also embedded in a coherent home-grown development strategy within which the State played a central role in mobilizing domestic investment and in influencing its allocation. Prior import-substitution to develop a manufacturing base was also held to have been a precondition for the later success in achieving a rapid increase in manufacturing exports.

The implications of such selective government intervention for trade policies does, however, depend on whether the capacity to implement the East Asian type of strategy exists in other developing countries. The successful implementation of an interventionist strategy of promoting infant industries and "picking winners" in industrial policy requires a strong State and an efficient administration, conditions that are not widely met in developing countries. To this extent therefore such a strategy may not be widely replicable even if underlying economic circumstances make it potentially feasible. Nonetheless, even without opting for a more interventionist strategy, countries can still choose to exercise more discretion over the timing of trade liberalization measures, the initial extent of the liberalization, the pace of implementation, and whether or not other liberalization measures should be implemented simultaneously. For example, on the latter point, some observers have pointed out the dangers inherent in implementing trade and capital account liberalization simultaneously.

More generally, trade liberalization needs to be embedded within a coherent set of macroeconomic, structural and social policies in order to be successful. It needs to be accompanied by complementary policies, such as the maintenance of an appropriate real exchange rate and macroeconomic stability; an institutional environment conducive to the growth of entrepreneurship and productive investment; effective institutions and policies for social protection; well-functioning and appropriately regulated labour, product and financial markets; and measures to enhance the capacity of poor producers and workers in the rural and urban informal sectors to benefit from trade liberalization. This is a clear example of the importance of ensuring coherence between economic and social policies.

The efforts of developing countries to benefit from the liberalization of world trade thus require essential support from the right national economic and social policies and institutions. Without such support, the potential gains from trade liberalization and other economic reforms will be thwarted by obstacles such as barriers to entry into newly competitive activities, market failures and other limitations on factor mobility. In addition, the gains that are realized are also likely to be unevenly distributed because of the lack of an even playing field for all economic agents. A particular challenge is that of equipping poor producers and workers in the rural and urban informal sectors with the means to share in the benefits of the trade liberalization.

An obvious priority is in the area of education and training policies. Low levels of education and skills in the labour force are a basic barrier to industrial development, even in many labour-intensive industries. Greater effort to achieve universal primary education and skill-development programmes that are responsive to changes in labour demand are therefore required in the least developed countries. Similarly, in the emerging market economies the expansion of secondary and tertiary education with an emphasis on meeting the demand for new technical skills will be an important instrument to counteract the tendency towards a widening of wage differentials between skilled and unskilled workers in the aftermath of trade liberalization that has been observed in several countries.

Another important area for action is to increase the employment intensity of growth. Since the majority of the labour force in low-income countries is still employed in agriculture, measures to stimulate agricultural exports will obviously be important. These will comprise measures to remove any policy discrimination against the agricultural sector as well as programmes to provide small agricultural producers with the necessary credit, extension services and marketing assistance to enable them to take advantage of new export opportunities. Such measures are also likely to have a positive impact on the reduction of poverty. Policies and programmes to develop a dynamic small enterprise sector that is linked to export markets are also likely to raise employment growth and improve the distribution of income. This is due to the high labour intensity of this sector and the predominance of poorer workers within it. Policy changes to remove biases against small enterprises, to provide incentives for subcontracting from small firms and to increase the provision of information and marketing assistance to small firms will be highly beneficial.

Active labour market policies to facilitate adjustment to changes in the structure of production brought about by trade liberalization will also need to be emphasized. Measures to provide retraining for displaced workers, job search assistance and other measures to facilitate labour mobility will be important in this connection. The effectiveness of such programmes is also likely to be greatly enhanced by the strengthening of social dialogue on economic reform programmes and of worker-management cooperation in handling restructuring at the enterprise level. Social dialogue aimed at reaching consensus on reforms that improve the functioning of labour markets while preserving essential protection for workers will also be important.

Finally, the strengthening of social protection will be essential for mobilizing broad popular support for trade liberalization and other economic reforms. Providing adequate income support for displaced workers is a necessary complement to active labour market and poverty-reduction policies. More generally, trade liberalization and other economic reform programmes must have due regard for their likely social impact. Every effort needs to be made to minimize their social cost through measures such as an ex ante analysis of their social impact. In particular, the impact of price changes on the poor, of the possible destruction of markets important to poor producers, and of changes in the demand for labour need to be given serious attention in policy design.

NOTES

[1] These and other studies on "globalization and employment policy" are available from www.ilo.org/public/english/employment/strat/global/index.htm

[2] This argues that taking outsourcing into account would significantly increase the role attributable to trade in the explanation of rising wage inequality in the advanced countries.

[3] This study presents evidence that the sharp increase in foreign investment in Mexico's northern border region contributed significantly to the rising demand for skills, and hence, the rise in wage inequality.

[4] See also Robbins (2003) and Arbache (2001) for reviews of the literature on this issue.

REFERENCES

Agenor, P., and J. Aizenman (1996). Trade liberalization and unemployment. *Journal of International Trade and Economic Development* 5 (3): 265–286.

Arbache, J.S. (2001). Trade and Evidence. Processed, Instituto de Pesquisa Economica Aplicada (IPEA), Rio de Janeiro, December.

Berman, Eli, and Stephen Machin (2004). Globalization, Skill-biased Technological Change and Labour Demand. In Eddy Lee and Marco Vivarelli (eds). *Understanding Globalization, Employment and Poverty Reduction.* Palgrave Macmillan, Houndmills.

Collier, Paul (1993). Higgledy-piggledy liberalization. *The World Economy* 16: 503–512.

Currie, J., and A. Harrison (1997). Sharing the costs: The impact of trade reform on capital and labor in Morocco. *Journal of Labour Economics* 15 (3ii), July: S44–S72.

Dollar, David (1992). Outward-oriented developing economies really do grow more rapidly: Evidence from 95 LDCs, 1976–85. *Economic Development and Cultural Change* 40 (3): 523–544.

Dollar, David, and Paul Collier (2001). *Globalization, growth and poverty: Building an inclusive world.* Oxford University Press, New York, for World Bank, Washington, DC.

Dollar, David, and Aart Kraay (2001). Trade, Growth, and Poverty. Policy Research Department Working Paper No. 2615, World Bank, Washington, DC.

Feenstra, Robert C., and Gordon H. Hanson (1997). Foreign direct investment and relative wages: Evidence from Mexico's maquiladoras. *Journal of International Economics* 42: 371–393.

Feenstra, Robert C. (2001). Introduction. *Journal of International Economics* 54: 1–3.

Feenstra, Robert C., and Gordon H. Hanson (2001). Global production sharing and rising wage inequality. A survey of trade and wages. NBER Working Paper No. 8372, July, National Bureau of Economic Research, Cambridge, MA.

Greenaway, D. (1993). Liberalizing foreign trade through rose-tinted glasses. *Economic Journal* 103: 208–223.

Greenaway, D., W. Morgan and P. Wright (1998). Trade reform, adjustment and growth: What does the evidence tell us? *Economic Journal* 108 (450), September: 1547–1561.

Hummels, David, Jun Ishii and Kei-Mu Yi (2001). The nature and growth of vertical specialization in world trade. *Journal of International Economics* 54: 75–96.

Journal of International Economics, 54 (2001).

Levinsohn, J. (1999). Employment responses to international liberalization in Chile. *Journal of International Economies* 47: 321–344.

Mesquita, M., and S. Najberg (2000). Trade liberalization in Brazil: Creating or exporting jobs?. *Journal of Development Studies* 30 (3), February: 78–100.

Milner, C., and P. Wright (1998). Modelling labour market adjustment to trade liberalization in an industrializing economy. *Economic Journal* 108, March: 509–528.

Ocampo, J.A., and Lance Taylor (1998). Trade liberalization in developing economies: Modest benefits but problems with productivity growth, macro prices, and income distribution. *Economic Journal* 108 (450), September: 1523–1546.

Papageorgiou, D., A. Choksi and M. Michaely (1990). *Liberalization of foreign trade in developing countries: The lessons of experience.* World Bank, Washington, DC.

Rattso, J., and R. Torvik (1998). Zimbabwean trade liberalization: Ex post evaluation. *Cambridge Journal of Economics* 22: 325–346.

Ravenga, A. (1994). *Employment and wage effects of trade liberalization: The case of Mexican manufacturing.* World Bank, Washington, DC.

Robbins, D.J. (2003). The impact of trade liberalization upon inequality in developing countries: a review of theory and evidence. Processed, International Policy Group, Policy Integration Department, International Labour Office, Geneva.

Rodriguez, Francisco, and Dani Rodrik (1999). Trade policy and economic growth: A skeptic's guide to the cross-national evidence. NBER Working Paper No. 7081, April, National Bureau of Economic Research, Cambridge, MA.

Rodrik, Dani (2001). Comments on 'Trade, Growth, and Poverty' by D. Dollar and A. Kraay. Processed, Kennedy School of Government, Harvard University, Cambridge, MA.

Rodrik, Dani, and Tanguy van Ypersele (2001). Capital mobility, distributive conflict and international tax coordination. *Journal of International Economics* 54: 57–73.

Sachs, Jeffrey, and Andrew Warner (1995). Economic reform and the process of global integration. *Brookings Papers on Economic Activity* 1: 1–118.

Torres, R. (2001). *Towards a socially sustainable world economy: An analysis of the social pillars of globalization.* International Labour Office, Geneva.

Winters, L. Alan (2000). Trade and Poverty: Is there a connection? In *Trade, Income Disparity and Poverty.* Special Study No. 5, World Trade Organization, Geneva.

6
International Capital Flows, Financial Stability and Growth

GRACIELA L. KAMINSKY[1]

The explosion of capital flows to emerging markets in the early and mid-1990s and their reversal following the crises in Asia, Latin America and the transition economies have reignited a heated debate on the benefits and drawbacks of financial globalization. Many have argued that globalization has gone too far and that international capital markets have become extremely erratic, with "excessive" booms and busts in capital flows triggering bubbles and financial crises and magnifying the business cycle. In contrast, the traditional view asserts that international capital markets enhance growth and productivity by allowing capital to flow to its most attractive destination.

Even if international capital flows do not trigger excess volatility in domestic financial markets, it is still true that large capital inflows can spark off inflation in the presence of a fixed exchange-rate regime. Moreover, transitory capital inflows may distort relative prices, with the domestic economy losing competitiveness as a result of the appreciation of the real exchange rate. Therefore, it is no wonder that policy makers have used a variety of tools to manage these flows, especially flows of the "hot money" type.

This chapter re-examines the evidence on the characteristics of international capital flows since 1970 and summarizes some of the findings of the research conducted in the 1990s on the effects of globalization. It first presents a brief history of international capital flows to emerging markets, paying particular attention to the volatility of bank lending and portfolio flows. Second, the chapter reviews the literature on the behaviour of mutual funds specializing in emerging markets as well as the lending behaviour of European, Japanese and United States banks to emerging markets around the time of the Mexican, Thai and Russian crises. The results suggest that episodes of surge in capital inflows do, in fact, end abruptly—whether owing to home-grown problems or contagion from abroad. Third, the chapter reviews the evidence on the short- and long-run effects of financial deregulation on financial and real cycles. Interestingly, the stylized evidence suggests that although financial liberalization may trigger excessive booms and busts in the short-run, financial markets tend to stabilize and growth accelerates in the long run. This section also examines briefly the linkages between globalization and institutional reform. Fourth, the chapter reviews the literature on managing international capital flows. The conclusion summarizes what we know about financial globalization and examines policy options.

A Brief History of Capital Flows

The 1970s witnessed a remarkable boom of capital flows to emerging economies. The dramatic surge in international capital flows was triggered by the oil shock in 1973–1974, the growth of the Eurodollar market and the remarkable increase in bank lending during 1979–1981. Latin America was the main recipient of this heavy capital inflow, with capital flows to the region peaking at US$44 billion in 1981 (see Figure 6.1). Overall, capital inflows to this region, which mostly took the form of syndicated bank loans (see Figure 6.2), reached about 6 per cent of the region's gross domestic product (GDP). The pace of international lending came to an abrupt end in 1982 with the hike in world real interest rates to levels not seen since the 1930s. Suddenly, emerging countries became the pariahs of international capital markets and they were not only excluded from voluntary capital markets but also forced to run current-account surpluses to repay their foreign debts.

By the late 1980s, there was a revival of international lending. While flows to Latin America made a tremendous comeback, capital inflows to Asia also surged, with capital flows increasing tenfold from their averages in the early 1980s. This time, however, the composition of capital flows changed, bank lending having been replaced by foreign direct investment (FDI) and portfolio investment. Bank lending to both Asia and Latin America declined from 70 per cent of net private capital flows in the 1970s to about 20 per cent in the 1990s. While FDI constituted the largest share of capital flow to Asia and Latin America, portfolio investment (bonds and equity) also increased substantially, accounting for up to 40 per cent of total capital flows in the mid-1990s. In absolute terms, bond and equity flows to Asia (excluding those counted as FDI) increased to US$27 billion in 1993 while those to Latin American peaked at US$69 billion in 1994.

As in the 1980s, booms in the 1990s were followed by capital flow reversals. The first reversal occurred in the immediate aftermath of Mexico's currency crisis in December 1994. However, for most countries, capital flows resumed within a year and returned to their peak values soon thereafter. In the aftermath of that crisis, capital flows to Asian economies were essentially not affected, the

FIGURE 6.1

Private capital flows to emerging markets (billions of U.S. dollars)

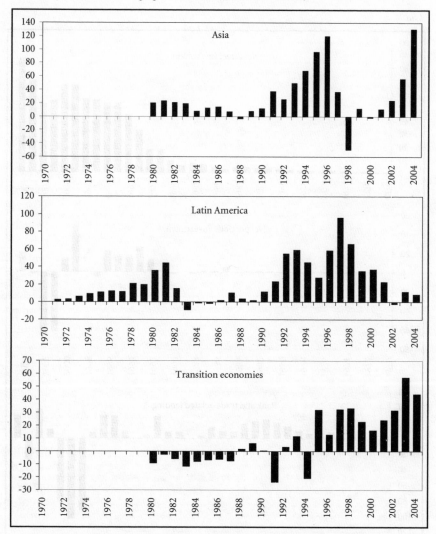

Note: The countries comprising Asia are Bangladesh, China, Hong Kong, India, Indonesia, Malaysia, Pakistan, the Philippines, Singapore, South Korea, Taiwan, Thailand and Viet Nam. The countries comprising Latin America are Argentina, Brazil, Chile, Colombia, the Dominican Republic, Ecuador, Guatemala, Mexico, Peru, Uruguay and Venezuela. The countries comprising the transition economies are Albania, Armenia, Azerbaijan, Belarus, Bosnia and Herzegovina, Bulgaria, Croatia, the Czech Republic, Estonia, Georgia, Hungary, Kazakhstan, Kyrgyzstan, Latvia, Lithuania, Macedonia, Moldova, Mongolia, Poland, Romania, Russia, Serbia and Montenegro, Slovakia, Slovenia, Tajikistan, Turkmenistan, Ukraine and Uzbekistan.

Source: World Economic Outlook 2005.

FIGURE 6.2
Composition of private capital flows to emerging markets (billions of U.S. dollars)

Asia

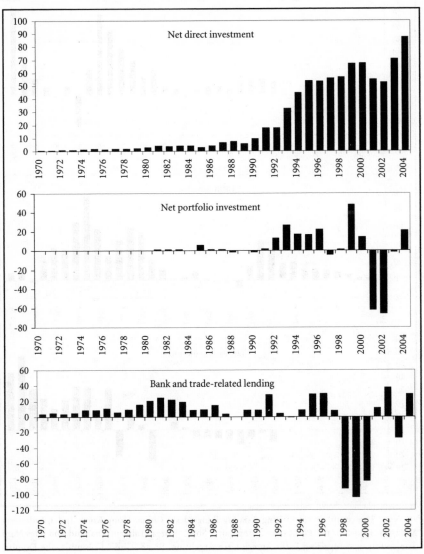

(contd)

Figure 6.2 *(contd)*

Latin America

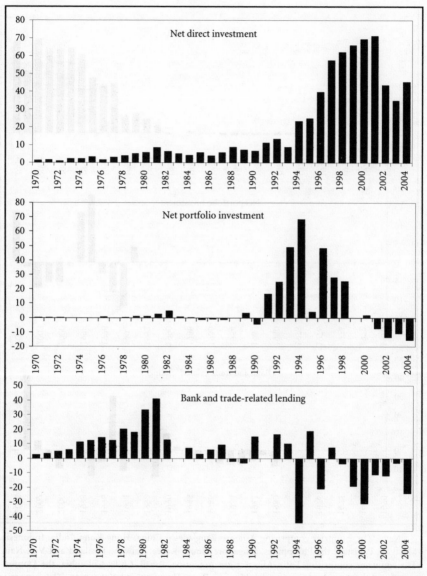

(contd)

FIGURE 6.2 *(contd)*

Transition economies

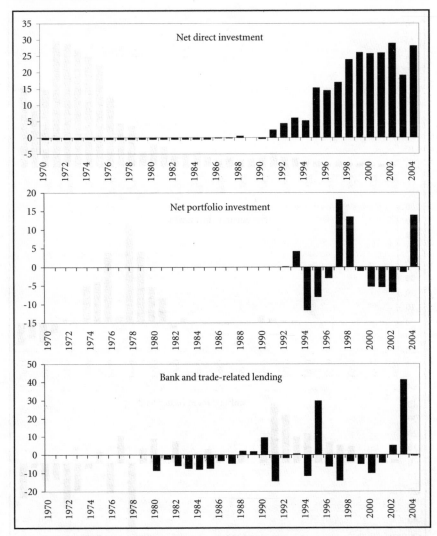

Notes: The countries comprising Asia are Bangladesh, China, Hong Kong, India, Indonesia, Malaysia, Pakistan, the Philippines, Singapore, South Korea, Taiwan, Thailand and Viet Nam. The countries comprising Latin America are Argentina, Brazil, Chile, Colombia, the Domini-can Republic, Ecuador, Guatemala, Mexico, Peru, Uruguay and Venezuela. The countries comprising the transition economies are Albania, Armenia, Azerbaijan, Belarus, Bosnia and Herzegovina, Bulgaria, Croatia, the Czech Republic, Estonia, Georgia, Hungary, Kazakhstan, Kyrgyzstan, Latvia, Lithuania, Macedonia, Moldova, Mongolia, Poland, Romania, Russia, Serbia and Montenegro, Slovakia, Slovenia, Tajikistan, Turkmenistan, Ukraine and Uzbekistan.

Source: World Economic Outlook 2005.

crisis being confined to a small number of Latin American countries. The second, more severe reversal came in 1997 during the Asian crisis. This reversal was later aggravated by the Russian default in August 1998 and the Brazilian crisis in 1998–1999. This time, the collapse in capital flows was more pronounced and sustained. The reversal was similar in magnitude to the one witnessed after the debt crisis, with total capital flows to Latin America declining by about 31 per cent in 1998 and declining further by 47 per cent in 1999. The sudden stop in capital flows to Asia was more pronounced, with total capital flows declining from an inflow of US$120 billion in 1996 to an outflow of US$50 billion in 1998. The reversal of short-term portfolio flows to Asia (bonds, equities and bank lending) was equally as severe, with flows declining from an inflow of US$52 billion in 1996 to an outflow of US$92 billion in 1998. In Latin America, short-term capital flows declined from an approximate inflow of US$30 billion in 1996 to an approximate outflow of US$31 billion in 2000.[2]

The evidence from transition economies is similar to that of Asia and Latin America. In the mid 1990s, capital flows boomed, peaking at US$33 billion in 1998. Portfolio bond and equity flows and bank lending suffered a significant reversal in the late 1990s, with private capital flows declining to US$16 billion. Capital flows to all emerging markets resumed only in 2003 following the decline in interest rates in industrial countries.

The Behaviour of Mutual Funds

The booms and busts in international capital flows have brought international investors to the limelight. International investors are often seen as the main culprits of financial market instability and have even been the subject of attacks by government officials. Many have argued that, more often than not, international investors panic and withdraw funds from countries with sound fundamentals. Assessing the behaviour of international investors has been a daunting task because data on international investors' portfolios is almost non-existent. Only recently has a novel databank on mutual fund portfolios provided by Emerging Market Funds Research, Inc. become available for research. This databank covers the positions of nearly 1,400 international emerging market equity fund, with an average position of about US$120 billion in 1996. It includes United States registered and offshore funds as well as funds registered in Luxembourg, the United Kingdom of Great Britain and Northern Ireland, Ireland, the Cayman Islands, Canada and Switzerland. Both open- and closed-end funds are also included in this dataset, which starts at 1995. Kaminsky, Lyons and Schmukler (2002) and Borenzstein and Gelos (2003) have used this dataset to study the behaviour of funds specializing in emerging markets. In particular, they examine whether domestic fragility is at the heart of portfolio decisions by mutual fund managers or whether mutual funds just herd together.

Kaminsky, Lyons and Schmukler describe the evolution of mutual funds in Asia, Latin America and transition economies and then examine the determinants of mutual fund flows to these regions. Their findings are presented in Figures 6.3 and 6.4 and in Table 6.1. Figure 6.3 shows the average quarterly net flows to these regions from 1995 to 1999. Mutual fund flows to emerging markets peaked in the second quarter of 1997, reaching about US$8 billion. Overall, booms in mutual fund flows were followed by reversals. Reversals were not persistent after the Tequila crisis. Outflows from Latin America reached about US$4 billion in 1995, but mutual funds increased their positions in Latin America by about US$2 billion in the first half of 1996. The Tequila crisis did not have any spillovers in Asia or in transition economies. In fact, flows to Asia ballooned to almost US$11 billion in 1996, while flows to transition economies remained stable throughout 1995–1996. The picture changed after the Asian crisis. This time, mutual funds pulled out not only from Asia but also from Latin America, with net outflows in the latter region reaching about US$1 billion in the six months following the collapse of the Thai baht. Mutual fund withdrawals took a turn for the worse in 1998, reaching about US$4 billion in Asia and also in Latin America, with substantial outflows from transition economies after the Russian crisis.

Figure 6.4 assesses the problem of the sudden stops in times of financial turmoil. It reports the average quarterly flows (as a percentage of the mutual funds' initial positions) to countries in Asia and Latin America, as well as to transition economies in the two quarters following three crises. The top panel looks at the aftermath of the Mexican devaluation in December 1994, the middle panel examines the aftermath of the collapse of the Thai baht in July 1997, and the bottom panel studies the aftermath of the Russian devaluation and moratorium in August 1998. To capture the magnitude of the sudden-stop syndrome, this figure reports total flows relative to average flows (also as percentages of their initial positions) during the whole sample (1995–1999). For example, following the Mexican devaluation, mutual funds sold about 5 per cent of their Brazilian positions (relative to their average quarterly buying/ selling from 1995 to 1999). Thus, as shown in the first panel in Figure 6.3, Brazil experienced unusual withdrawals of about 5 per cent in the aftermath of the Mexican devaluation. As shown in the last panel, Malaysia was the country most affected in the aftermath of the Russian crisis, with abnormal outflows of approximately 30 per cent.

The extent of the mutual fund sudden stop in the aftermath of the three

FIGURE 6.3
Mutual funds: quarterly flows to emerging countries (billions of U.S. dollars)

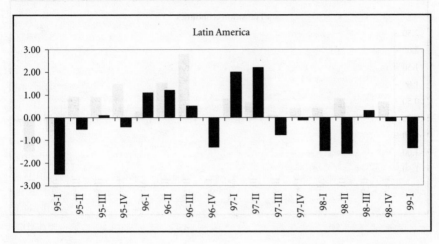

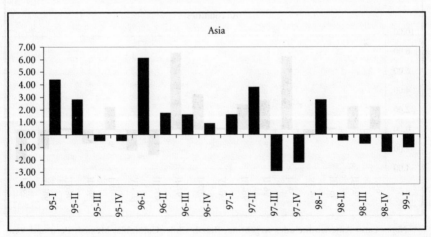

(contd)

FIGURE 6.3 *(contd)*

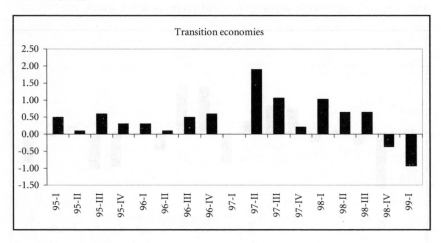

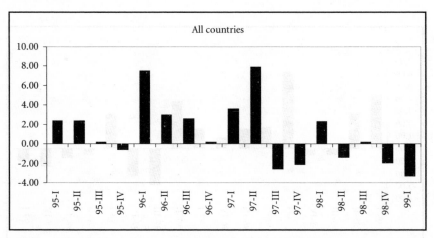

Notes: Latin America includes Argentina, Brazil, Chile, Colombia, Mexico, Peru and Venezuela. Asia includes China, Hong Kong, India, Indonesia, Malaysia, Pakistan, the Philippines, Singapore, South Korea, Sri Lanka, Taiwan and Thailand. Transition economies include Armenia, Azerbaijan, Belarus, the Czech Republic, Georgia, Hungary, Kazakhstan, Kyrgyzstan, Moldova, Poland, Russia, Slovakia, Tajikistan, Turkmenistan, Ukraine and Uzbekistan.

Source: Kaminsky, Lyons and Schmukler (2002).

FIGURE 6.4
Mutual fund flows: global spillovers

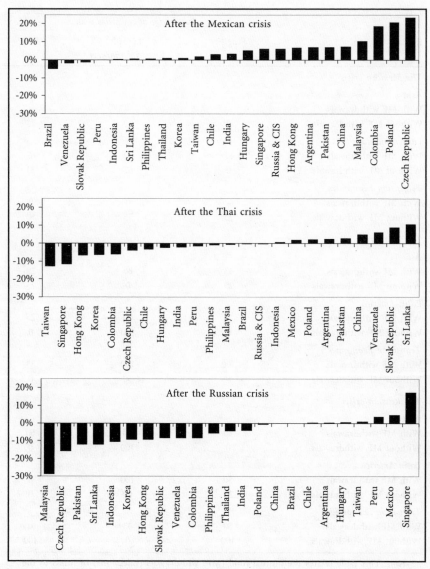

Notes: The Mexican crisis began in late December of 1994, the Thai crisis in July 1997 and the Russian crisis in August 1998. Mutual fund flows are the average net buying/selling (as a percentage of the end of the preceeding quarter holdings) in the two quarters following the outbreak of the crisis, relative to the sample average.
Source: Kaminsky, Lyons and Schmukler (2002).

TABLE 6.1
The behavior of mutual funds during crises

Region	Percentage of countries with		
	Fragility	Liquid financial markets	Risk
The Mexican crisis			
Asia			
With MF withdrawals	–	–	–
Without MF withdrawals	0	42	25
Latin America			
With MF withdrawals	67	33	67
Without MF withdrawals	0	67	33
Transition Economies			
With MF withdrawals	–	0	0
Without MF withdrawals	33	75	50
The Thai crisis			
Asia			
With MF withdrawals	43	86	29
Without MF withdrawals	25	0	25
Latin America			
With MF withdrawals	75	50	25
Without MF withdrawals	0	100	0
Transition Economies			
With MF withdrawals	100	100	33
Without MF withdrawals	0	50	0
The Russian crisis			
Asia			
With MF withdrawals	40	40	60
Without MF withdrawals	0	100	0
Latin America			
With MF withdrawals	50	100	0
Without MF withdrawals	20	60	0
Transition Economies			
With MF withdrawals	50	33	0
Without MF withdrawals	100	0	100

Note: This table relates the mutual fund (MF) withdrawals (injections) of funds to the emerging markets shown in figure 4 with indicators of fragility, liquidity of financial markets, and economic and political risk in those economies.

– denotes no data available.

Source: Kaminsky, Lyons and Schmukler (2002)

crises was substantially different. The so-called Tequila Crisis was circumscribed to Latin America. Moreover, "abnormal" mutual fund withdrawals in the aftermath of the collapse of the Mexican peso were confined to a handful of Latin American countries, with only Brazil and the Bolivarian Republic of Venezuela—besides the crisis country, Mexico—suffering average withdrawals of 5 and 2 per cent, respectively, in the two quarters following the devaluation. In contrast, mutual funds increased their exposure to Asian countries and transition economies, with (above-trend) flows oscillating around 4 per cent for Asia and 11 per cent for the transition economies.

The aftermath of the collapse of the Thai baht presents a different picture of the international mutual funds industry. It is in this episode that we first observe signs of a more general retrenchment of mutual funds in emerging markets. Mutual fund flows to Asian economies were well below trend in the two quarters following the collapse of the Thai baht. Only flows to China, Pakistan and Sri Lanka were above average. Interestingly, after the collapse of the Thai baht, we observe substantial withdrawals from Hong Kong, Singapore and Taiwan, with average quarterly withdrawals oscillating at about 12 per cent above average in the case of Singapore and Taiwan and about 7 per cent for Hong Kong. The retrenchment this time also affected Latin America and the transition economies, with withdrawals reaching about 6 per cent for Colombia and 4 per cent for the Czech Republic during the two quarters following the outbreak of the Thai crisis. Colombia, the Czech Republic, Chile, Hungary and Peru were the countries most affected in this episode, with sales averaging about 3 per cent above average.

The flight away from emerging markets became more pronounced during the Russian crisis, with about half of the countries in the sample experiencing abnormal sales of about 10 per cent or even larger. In some cases, withdrawals were massive. For example, average mutual funds sales (relative to trend) in Malaysia reached 30 per cent while those in the Czech Republic were in the order of 16 per cent. Some Latin American countries were also dramatically affected in the aftermath of the Russian collapse. For example, Colombia and Venezuela suffered average quarterly outflows of about 8 per cent. Mutual funds investments in Mexico and Peru were the only ones that did not suffer following the worldwide turmoil triggered by the Russian default. In fact, inflows to Mexico were 5 per cent above the average observed in the 1995–1999 period.

Table 6.1 examines in detail why some countries were severely affected by mutual fund withdrawals while others were left unscathed. Three factors are examined: economic fragility, liquidity of financial markets[3] and economic and political risk. Fragility is captured using the probabilities of crises (Kaminsky, 1998) that measure the likelihood of crises conditional on eighteen indicators reflecting macroeconomic vulnerabilities in each country. These indicators provide information about fiscal and monetary imbalances, financial and real vulnerabilities, current-account and capital-account problems and world factors.

Fiscal deficits and monetary imbalances are captured by means of two indicators: fiscal deficit/GDP ratio and excess M1 real balances (supply of money relative to money demand). Current-account problems are captured by four indicators: exports, imports, real exchange rates (deviations from equilibrium) and terms of trade. Capital-account problems (debt problems) are captured by two indicators: foreign-exchange reserves of the central bank, and the foreign debt/exports and short-term debt/foreign-exchange reserves ratios. Real vulnerability is captured by two indicators: output and real interest rates. Financial vulnerability is captured by six indicators: domestic credit/GDP ratio, M2/reserves ratio, deposits, M2 multiplier, stock prices and an index of banking crises. Finally, world factors are captured by one indicator: the world interest rate. A country is classified as fragile if the probability of a crisis is higher than 50 per cent; otherwise it is considered healthy.

Liquidity is captured by means of four indicators. The first one—the volume traded in the stock market—provides an overall measure of the size and depth of the stock market. The second one—the share of the mutual funds portfolio in each country at the onset of the crisis—is related to mutual funds liquidity in each country, since investors cannot sell in countries in which they have basically no exposure. These first two indicators provide two different pictures of liquidity of financial markets. The third indicator dates the time when firms in emerging markets start to trade in mature and more liquid financial markets. The fourth indicator captures the ability of investors to rapidly change their portfolio in a particular country. In particular, this last indicator evaluates the extent of restrictions to capital mobility in each country. Restrictions could add "sand in the wheels" of capital markets and thus curtail liquidity.[4]

Finally, the risk indicator captures both political and economic uncertainty. The political risk indicator captures uncertainty due to expected changes of authorities or future policy actions. It also identifies widespread social unrest. The risk indicator also captures economic risk, such as imposition of restrictions to capital mobility in response to crises. A country is classified as risky when there is at least either political or economic risk.

Table 6.1 shows the characteristics of countries that suffer abnormal withdrawals and injections in the aftermath of the three crises.[5] The table groups the countries into three regions: Asia, Latin America and transition economies. As shown in the first column, countries with fragile economies constitute the bulk of the countries that suffer withdrawals. For example, during the Mexican crisis, Latin America was the only region that suffered withdrawals. Interestingly, 67 per cent of the countries that suffered withdrawals in this episode were also countries with deteriorated fundamentals. Again, during the Thai crisis, at least 75 per cent of the countries that suffered withdrawals in the transition economies group and Latin America were countries with economic vulnerabilities. Similarly, 43 per cent of the Asian countries affected by abnormal withdrawals also had deteriorated economies. For example, Korea, Colombia, the Czech Republic and Chile suffered huge withdrawals in the aftermath of the Thai crisis—the Czech Republic and Korea were the two most vulnerable countries during the Asian crisis (Thailand ranked fourth) in the sample of 25 countries, while Colombia ranked sixth. In contrast, countries that did not experience mutual fund withdrawals were less fragile in general (see Goldstein, Kaminsky and Reinhart 2001).

However, domestic fragilities were not the only explanation of the sudden-stop syndrome. For example, China did not even suffer a mild hiccup in the midst of the Asian crisis even when devaluation fears were widespread among investors and the vulnerability of its financial system was widely known. In contrast, Singapore, Taiwan and Hong Kong—countries with the most liquid financial markets in the region—suffered pronounced capital-flow reversals even when their economies looked far healthier than that of China. Overall, 86 per cent of the countries in the Asia-Pacific region that suffered withdrawals were countries with quite liquid financial markets. In contrast, all the countries in that region unaffected by the Thai crisis had illiquid financial markets.

Finally, risk also had an important role, with 40 per cent of the countries most affected by withdrawals also experiencing political and economic risk. For example, in 1994, in the midst of the banking crisis, Venezuela abandoned convertibility. Far from discouraging capital outflows, the implementation of restrictions to capital mobility seems to have also contributed to the fire sales of Venezuelan assets. Malaysia suffered substantial losses in the aftermath of the Russian crisis when it introduced outright controls on capital outflows. Interestingly, the withdrawals may have been triggered by the increased risk—perceived or real—associated with the country.

Borenzstein and Gelos (2003) provide complementary results that help characterize the behaviour of mutual funds in emerging markets. The authors examine whether mutual funds follow herding strategies using Lakonishok, Shleifer and Vishny's (1992) measure of herding, a measure that allows an assessment of whether funds move in the same direction more often than one would expect than if they had traded independently and randomly. Borenzstein and Gelos' results suggest that mutual funds do herd together. In particular, for a given country, the number of funds moving in the same direction was approximately 8 per cent greater than one would have expected had they acted independently. Herding is less pronounced among closed-end funds, suggesting that herding behaviour might be traceable to the behaviour of individual investors rather than that of fund managers. Finally, herding in some crisis episodes was also more pronounced. For example, at the onset of the Brazilian crisis, herding on Brazilian assets increased to 15 per cent.

The Behaviour of Banks

As shown earlier, bank-related lending has been quite volatile in the last three decades. This section examines the role of European, Japanese and United States banks in spreading the crises of the 1990s. The Bank for International Settlements (BIS) Consolidated Banking Statistics are used to examine the role of the three international banking clusters. In particular, international claims of reporting BIS banks in emerging economies, including both total cross-border claims and local claims in foreign currency booked by foreign offices, are studied. The difference between total cross-border claims and international claims is quite wide for countries with highly dollarized economies and with an important presence of foreign banks, such as Latin American countries.

As shown in Figure 6.5, bank flows poured into Asia throughout most of the 1990s and accelerated following the Mexican crisis. Bank loans to emerging Asia expanded by 89 per cent from June 1994 to June 1997. Part of the rise in lending was due to the European banks' goal of achieving a higher profile in emerging markets, particularly in Korea. Much of the lending boom, especially in the case of Thailand, Indonesia and Korea, was due to a rapid expansion in credit from Japanese banks. Faced with a slumping economy and little domestic loan demand, Japanese banks increasingly looked overseas to the rapidly growing economies of Southeast Asia as potential borrowers. United States bank lending to Asia was modest before the crisis. By June 1997, the United States banks' positions in emerging Asia had only reached US$32 billion and only accounted for 20 per cent of all United States bank lending to developing countries. In contrast, by the onset of the Thai crisis, Japanese banks had exposure to Asia four times as much as United States banks (US$124 billion). European bank lending to emerging Asia was also significant and, by the onset of the Thai crisis, the exposure of European banks to Asia surpassed that of Japanese banks, reaching US$161 billion. The exposure of European banks to emerging Asia accounted for about a half of all their lending to emerging markets; Korea alone accounted for 40 per cent of their lending to the developing world.

FIGURE 6.5
Bank lending to Asia, Latin America and the transition economies (billions of US dollars)

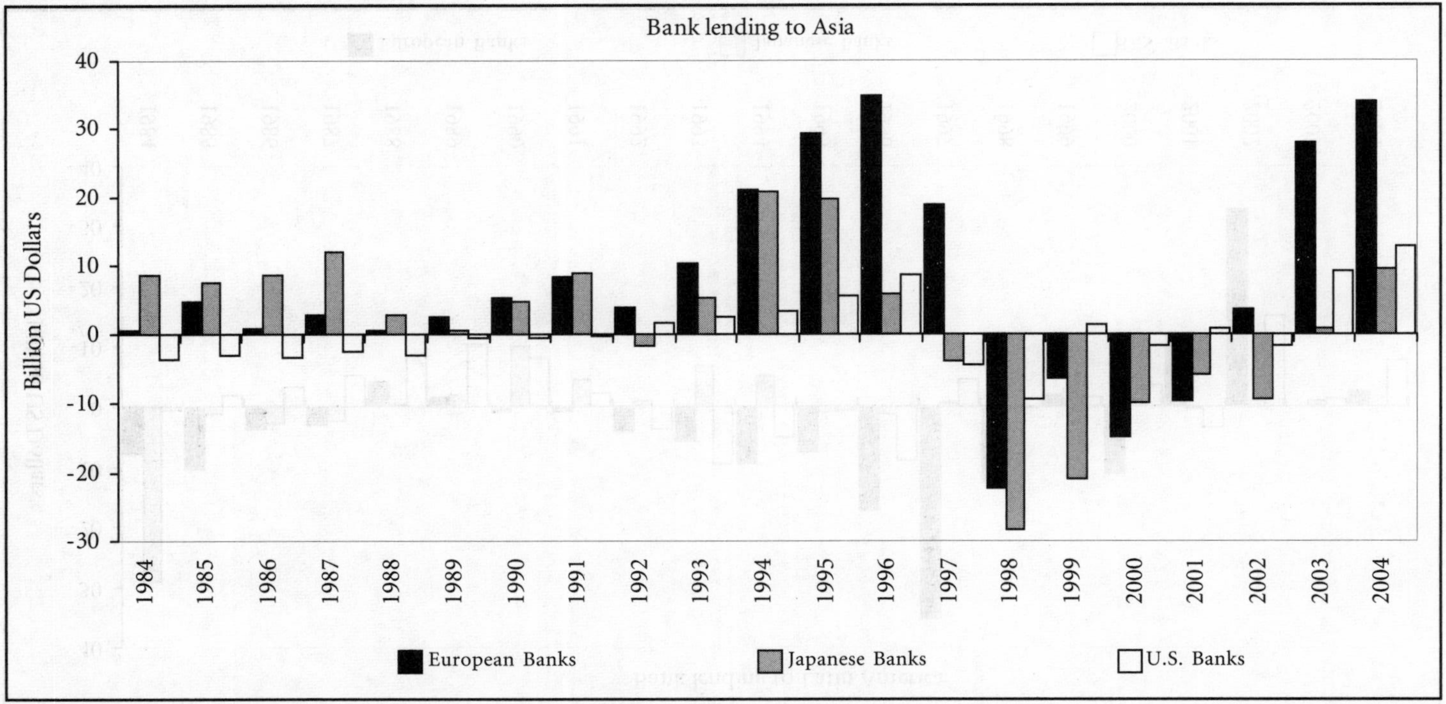

Bank lending to Asia

(contd)

FIGURE 6.5 (*contd*)

Bank lending to Latin America

Billion US Dollars

40 30 20 10 0 -10 -20 -30 -40

1984 1985 1986 1987 1988 1989 1990 1991 1992 1993 1994 1995 1996 1997 1998 1999 2000 2001 2002 2003 2004

European Banks   Japanese Banks   U.S. Banks

(*contd*)

FIGURE 6.5 (contd)

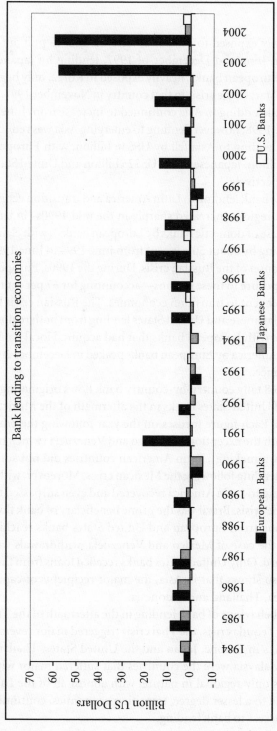

Bank lending to transition economies

Billion US Dollars

■ European Banks   ▨ Japanese Banks   □ U.S. Banks

Notes: Asia includes Afghanistan, Armenia, Azerbaijan, Bangladesh, Bhutan, British Overseas Territories, Brunei, Cambodia, China, Fiji, French Polynesia, Georgia, India, Indonesia, Kazakhstan, Kiribati, Kyrgyzstan, Laos, Macau, Malaysia, the Maldives, Mongolia, Myanmar, Nauru, Nepal, New Caledonia, North Korea, Pakistan, Papua New Guinea, the Philippines, the Solomon Islands, South Korea, Sri Lanka, Taiwan, Tajikistan, Thailand, Tonga, Turkmenistan, Tuvalu, U.S. Pacific Islands, Uzbekistan, Viet Nam, Wallis Futuna and Western Samoa. *Latin America* includes Argentina, Belize, Bolivia, Brazil, Chile, Colombia, Costa Rica, Cuba, Dominica, the Dominican Republic, Ecuador, El Salvador, the Falkland Islands, Grenada, Guatemala, Guyana, Haiti, Honduras, Jamaica, Mexico, Nicaragua, Paraguay, Peru, St. Lucia, St. Vincent, Suriname, Trinidad and Tobago, Turks and Caicos, Uruguay and Venezuela. *Transition economies* include Albania, Belarus, Bosnia and Herzegovina, Bulgaria, Croatia, Cyprus, the Czech Republic, Czechoslovakia, Estonia, the German Democratic Republic, Hungary, Latvia, Lithuania, Macedonia, Malta, Moldova, Poland, Romania, Russia, Serbia and Montenegro, Slovakia, Slovenia, the Soviet Union, Turkey and Ukraine.

Source: Bank for International Settlements.

Japanese banks, heavily exposed to Thailand, were the first to pull out of emerging Asia. Between June and December of 1997, lending by Japanese banks fell by 8 per cent. European banks, heavily exposed to Korea, only began to pull out following the start of the crisis in that country in November 1997. In net terms, European bank lending to Asia continued to increase from June to December 1997. By June 1998, however, lending to emerging Asia was reduced across the board. Bank lending to Asia fell by US$46 billion, with European banks recalling US$12 billion, Japanese banks US$25 billion and United States banks US$9 billion, respectively.

Figure 6.5 also reports bank lending to Latin America and transition economies. Exposure to these regions increased sharply in the mid 1990s (in large part driven by the purchase of domestic banks by European banks), with claims on these regions increasing by about 50 per cent from June 1994 to June 1998, immediately before the onset of the Russian crisis. During the 1990s, European banks had the largest exposure to these regions—accounting for 67 per cent to Latin America and 84 per cent to transition economies. The Russian crisis led to some withdrawals of Japanese and United States lending from both regions, but this was not the case with European banks that had acquired local banks. Total exposure to Latin America by European banks peaked in December 2000 and has not recovered since.

Figures 6.6, 6.7 and 6.8 tally country-by-country bank flows originating in European, Japanese and United States banks in the aftermath of the Mexican, Thai and Russian crises. Each figure focuses on the year following the crisis. Figure 6.6 shows that with the exception of Mexico and Venezuela (which had a banking crisis of its own making), Latin American countries did not suffer major reversals in bank lending following the Mexican crisis. Moreover, within a year of the crisis, lending to Latin America recovered and even surpassed the levels observed before the crisis. Brazil was the prime beneficiary of bank flows during 1995, with lending from European and United States banks reaching US$15 billion. Even in the case of Mexico and Venezuela, withdrawals were not made across the board. Only United States banks recalled loans from these countries. Figure 6.6 also shows that in Asia, the major recipients of capital flows in 1995 were Korea, Thailand and Indonesia.

Figure 6.7 shows the behaviour of bank lending in the aftermath of the Thai crisis. In contrast to the Tequila crisis, the Thai crisis triggered major reversals in bank flows from banks in Europe, Japan and the United States. Thailand, Korea, Indonesia and Malaysia were the countries that suffered major withdrawals. Contagion was only regional in nature, with almost all of the Latin American countries, and to a lesser degree, transition economies, continuing to have uninterrupted access to bank lending.

FIGURE 6.6
Bank flows: global spillovers after the Mexican crisis: December 1994–December 1995

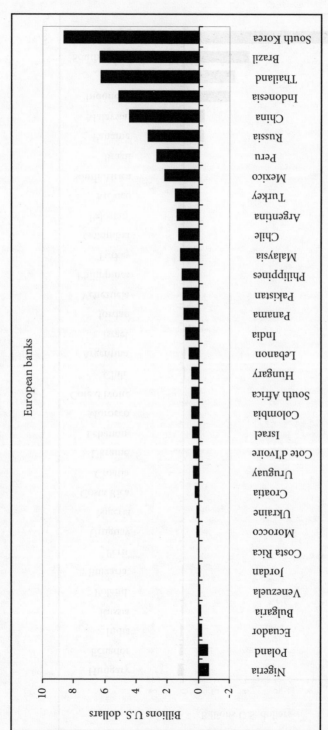

European banks

(contd)

Figure 6.6 (contd)

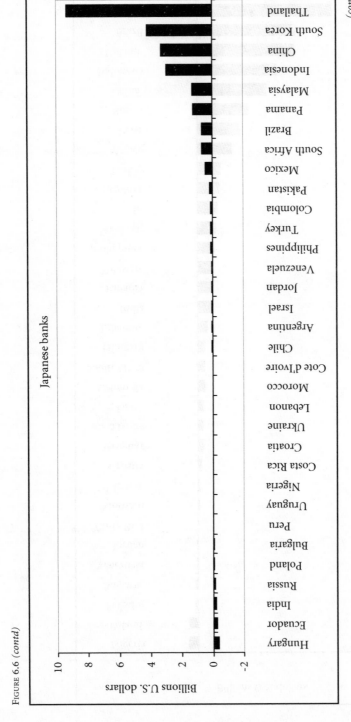

Japanese banks

Figure 6.6 *(contd)*

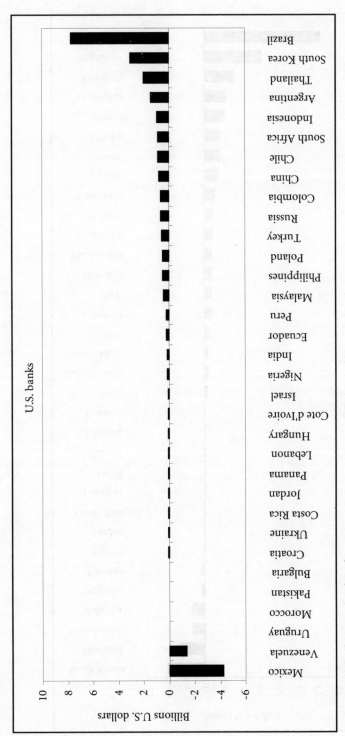

U.S. banks

Source: Bank of International Settlements.

FIGURE 6.7
Bank flows: global spillovers after the Thai crisis: June 1997–June 1998

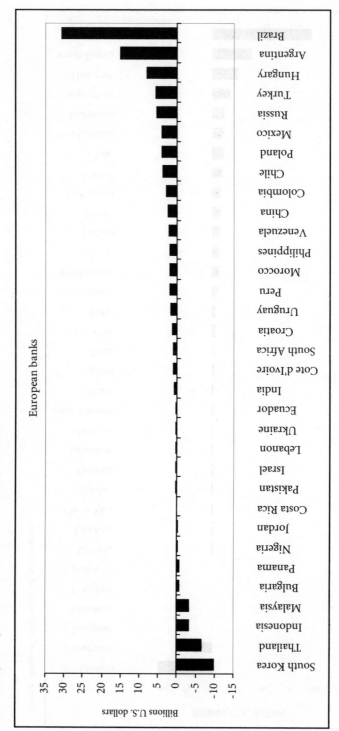

(contd)

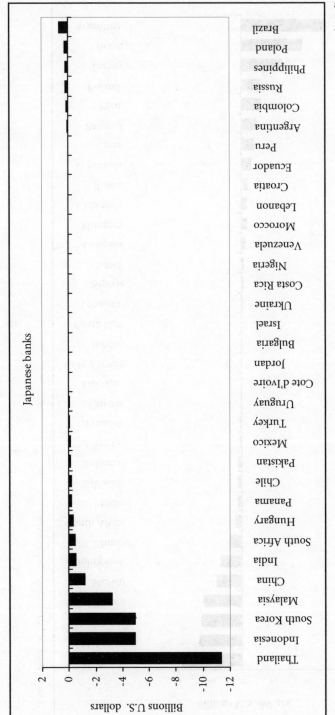

FIGURE 6.7 (contd)

(contd)

FIGURE 6.7 *(contd)*

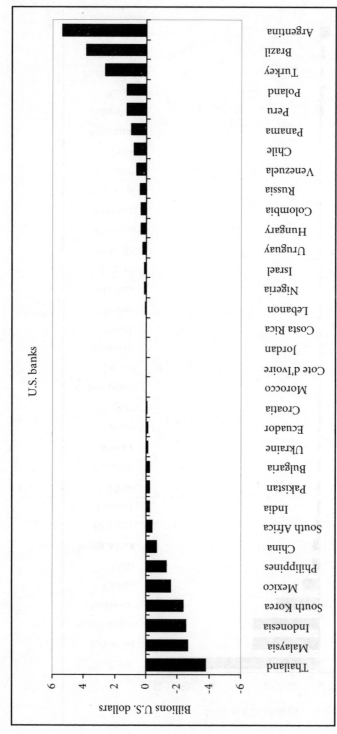

U.S. banks

Argentina
Brazil
Turkey
Poland
Peru
Panama
Chile
Venezuela
Russia
Colombia
Hungary
Uruguay
Israel
Nigeria
Lebanon
Costa Rica
Jordan
Cote d'Ivoire
Morocco
Croatia
Ecuador
Ukraine
Bulgaria
Pakistan
India
South Africa
China
Philippines
Mexico
South Korea
Indonesia
Malaysia
Thailand

Billions U.S. dollars

6 4 2 0 -2 -4 -6

Source: Bank of International Settlements.

FIGURE 6.8
Bank flows: global spillovers after the Russian crisis: June 1998–June 1999

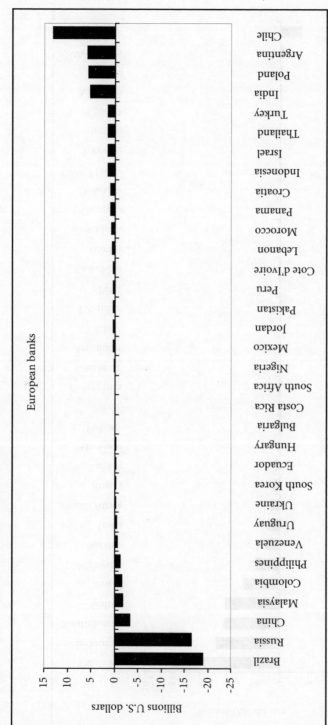

(contd)

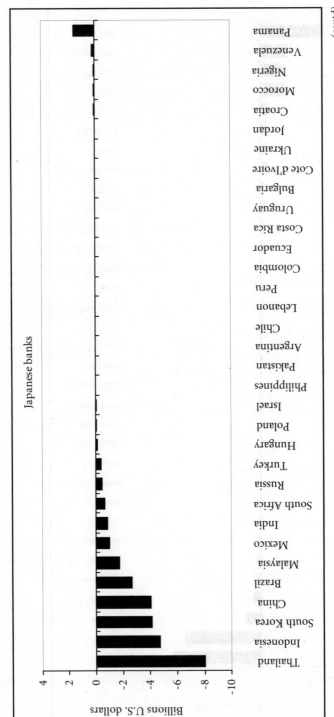

FIGURE 6.8 (contd)

(contd)

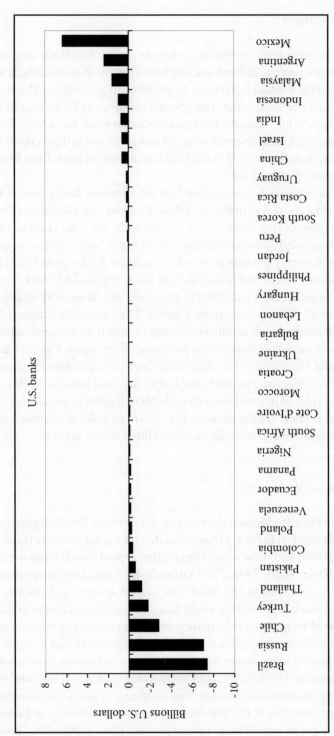

FIGURE 6.8 *(contd)*

Source: Bank of International Settlements

Figure 6.8 presents spillovers from the Russian crisis. As was the case with mutual funds, the reversal in bank lending following the Russian default was not restricted to the Russian Federation or neighbouring countries. This time, the reversal was more widespread, and affected countries as far away as Brazil and South Africa. While Japanese banks continued to recall loans from Thailand, Indonesia and Korea, reversals were not just restricted to these countries. Japanese banks, as well as United States banks, also recalled loans from Brazil, Mexico, India and South Africa.

More formal evidence below suggests that international banks were at the centre of financial contagion in the late 1990s. Kaminsky and Reinhart (2000) examine contagion during the debt crisis in 1982, the Mexican crisis in 1994 and the Asian crisis in 1997, and find that United States banks were at the core of the contagion during the debt crisis, while Japanese banks spread the Thai crisis to Indonesia, Korea and Malaysia. Van Rijckeghem and Weder (2001) examine the Tequila, Asian and Russian crises and the flows to 31 emerging countries from 17 BIS country-creditor banks. Their evidence supports the idea that the degree to which countries compete for funds from common bank lenders is a fairly robust predictor of the incidence of contagion. Finally, Caramazza, Ricci and Salgado (2000) extend earlier work on indicators of vulnerability to currency crises by examining the role of financial linkages while controlling for the roles of internal and external macroeconomic imbalances and trade spillovers. Their results indicate that financial links do matter while exchange-rate regimes and controls on capital flows do not seem to.

GLOBALIZATION AND VOLATILITY

As discussed in the introduction, the views on the effects of financial globalization have been diverse; there are those who defend capital controls (Rodrik, 1998; Stiglitz, 1999) and those who maintain that capital should be allowed to move freely (Dornbusch, 1998). The rationale for restricting international capital flows is grounded in the belief that market failures and distortions pervade capital markets around the world. One of the most frequently cited distortions is that of asymmetric information, which is rampant in international capital markets due to geographical and cultural differences that complicate the task of obtaining information. In addition, imperfections in international markets are magnified by the difficulties in enforcing contracts across borders.[6] With imperfect information, investors may overreact to shocks, withdrawing massively from countries at the first signs of economic problems, or become euphoric and pour in capital in quantities beyond those justified by "good" fundamentals. On the other hand, those who consider international capital markets to be efficient favour unrestricted capital movements. Financial liberalization is believed to improve the functioning of financial systems, increasing the availability of funds and allowing cross-country risk diversification. Moreover, it is also claimed that financial integration tends to facilitate economic growth.

This section will summarize some of the findings in the literature on the effects of globalization on financial markets and the real economy, paying particular attention to the evidence on these conflicting views. In particular, the section will focus on the short- and long-run effects of financial integration on real and financial volatility.

Financial Markets

The evidence from the crises of the 1990s suggests that crises are preceded by "excessive" capital inflows that, in turn, fuel large expansions in domestic credit and bubbles in financial markets (for example, see Sachs, Velasco, and Tornell, 1996). There is also evidence that most episodes of banking crises are preceded by financial liberalization (for example, see Kaminsky and Reinhart, 1999; Demirguc-Kunt and Detragiache, 1999). To reconcile the evidence that globalization is at the heart of financial crises with the hypothesis that international capital markets allow capital to move to its most attractive destination and promote more stable financial markets, Kaminsky and Schmukler (2003) examine the possible time-varying effects of financial liberalization on stock market price cycles.[7] Figure 6.9 reproduces some of the results in that paper. The figure shows the average amplitude of booms and crashes for fourteen emerging markets[8] during periods of repression, the short-run effects of liberalization and the long-run effects of liberalization.

The evidence in this figure seems to point to excessive cycles, with larger booms followed by larger crashes in the immediate aftermath of financial liberalization. However, liberalization does not permanently bring about more volatile financial markets. If liberalization persists, stock markets in emerging countries become more stable. One possible explanation examined in the chapter (using a variety of measures of law and order) is that financial liberalization triggers institutional reforms that make financial markets function better. Interestingly, the evidence for the fourteen emerging countries indicates that deregulation indeed preceded institutional reforms. This sequence may be due to the actions of domestic investors who, having access to international capital markets following deregulation, demand better enforcement rules to continue to invest in domestic financial markets. As suggested by Stultz (1999), the liberalization

FIGURE 6.9

Average amplitude of booms and crashes in stock prices in 14 emerging markets (in percentage points)

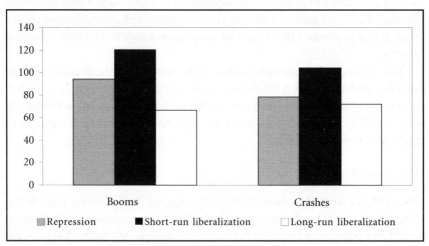

Source: Kaminsky and Schmukler (2002).

and gradual integration of emerging markets into international financial markets may help strengthen the domestic financial sector, as foreign investors generally have better skills and more information and can thus monitor management in ways that local investors cannot. Liberalization also allows firms to access mature capital markets. Firms listed on foreign stock markets are in the jurisdiction of a superior legal system with higher disclosure standards that will promote more transparency in the management of the firm and can trigger improvements in corporate governance.

Business Cycles and Growth

The evidence in the previous section is suggestive of excessive booms and busts in financial markets in developing countries following globalization but of more stable financial markets in the long run if globalization persists. This section will examine the relationship between globalization and business cycle fluctuations and growth.

First, the section presents a study of business cycle characteristics of international capital flows. Figure 6.10 shows international capital flows to emerging markets in Asia, Latin America and transition economies, as well as annual output growth rates. The panels suggest that capital flows have been pro-cyclical, with large inflows in good times and outflows during recessions. For example,

FIGURE 6.10
Private capital flows to emerging markets and GDP annual growth rates

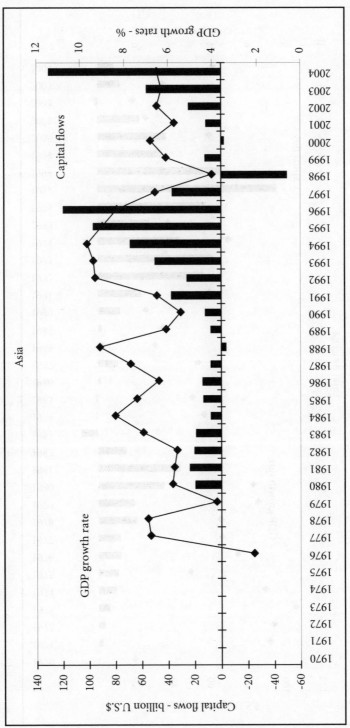

(contd)

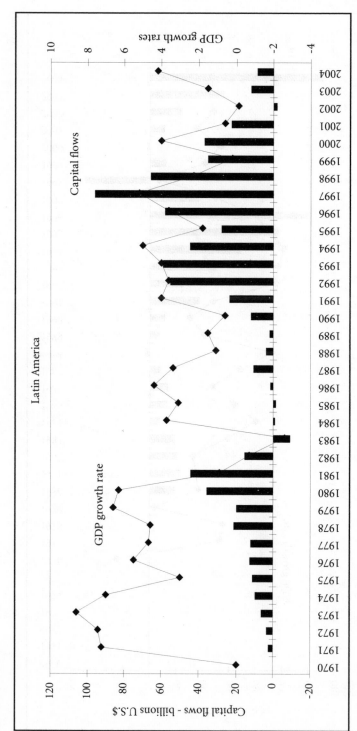

FIGURE 6.10 (*contd*)

(*contd*)

FIGURE 6.10 (*contd*)

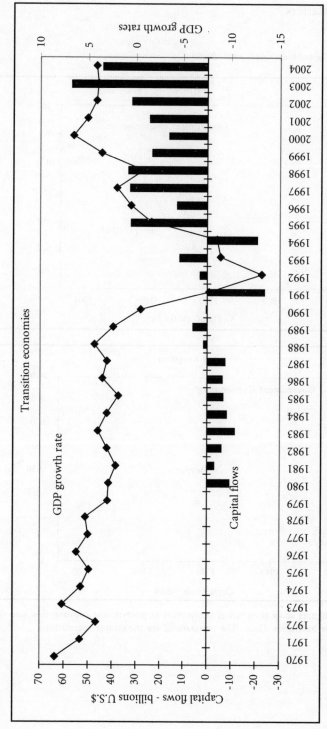

Transition economies

GDP growth rate

Capital flows

Note: The countries comprising Asia are Bangladesh, China, Hong Kong, India, Indonesia, Malaysia, Pakistan, the Philippines, Singapore, South Korea, Taiwan, Thailand and Viet Nam. The countries comprising the transition economies are Albania, Armenia, Azerbaijan, Belarus, Bosnia and Herzegovina, Bulgaria, Croatia, the Czech Republic, Estonia, Georgia, Hungary, Kazakhstan, Kyrgyzstan Latvia, Lithuania, Macedonia, Moldova, Mongolia, Poland, Romania, Russia, Serbia and Montenegro, Slovakia, Slovenia, Tajikistan, Turkmenistan, Ukraine and Uzbekistan. The countries comprising Latin America are Argentina, Brazil, Chile, Colombia, the Dominican Republic, Ecuador, Guatemala, Mexico, Peru, Uruguay and Venezuela.

Source: World Economic Outlook.

FIGURE 6.11
Fiscal polity and the business cycle, 1980–2000

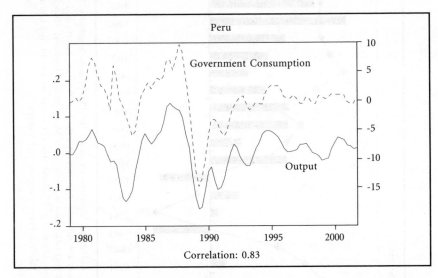

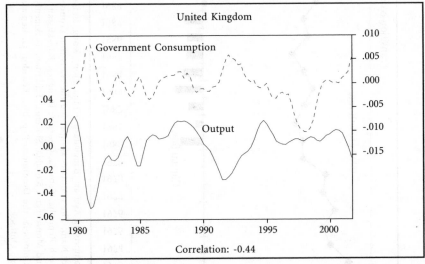

Notes: These figures show the cyclical component of government consumption and GDP obtained using the band-pass filter. The correlations are the sample correlations.

Latin America's growth rates oscillated at around 4.5 per cent in periods of capital inflows, while growth rates were about 1 per cent in periods of sudden stops. Similarly, Asia's economic activity collapsed to about 5.5 per cent after the sudden stop in capital flows in the late 1990s, after growing at an average annual growth rate of 8.5 per cent during the earlier period of large capital inflows. This evidence contrasts sharply with the prescription that international capital markets should allow countries to smooth out the effect of the business cycle. Countries seem to have lost access to international credit markets during recessions on a systematic basis.

This non-optimal behaviour of international capital flows has also been studied by Calvo and Izquierdo (2003), who observe that sudden reversals in capital flows to emerging economies lead to large real depreciations and profound downturns. Perhaps what makes these sudden reversals even more devastating is that they seem to trigger contractionary macro-policies. For example, as shown in Figure 6.11, Peru introduced austerity programs in the early 1980s and in the late 1980s in the aftermath of debt and currency crises. In contrast, the United Kingdom pursued counter-cyclical policy in the aftermath of the 1992 European Monetary System (EMS) currency crisis when the pound was allowed to float. While Peru lost access to international capital markets, the United Kingdom did not. These are not isolated cases. As reported in Kaminsky, Reinhart and Végh (2004), macro-policies tend to be pro-cyclical in developing countries while they are counter-cyclical or acyclical in industrialized countries. That is to say, macro-policies tend to smooth out the business cycle in industrial countries but magnify it in developing countries, as shown in Table

TABLE 6.2
Correlations between the cyclical components of macropolicies, real GDP, and net capital inflows

| Countries | Correlations with real GDP | | | Correlations with net capital inflows | | |
| | Fiscal policy | | Monetary policy | Fiscal policy | | Monetary policy |
	Government expenditure	Inflation tax	Lending interest rate	Government expenditure	Inflation tax	Lending interest rate
OECD	-0.13	0.16	0.23	0.03	0.04	0.19
Non-OECD	0.33	-0.15	-0.05	0.20	-0.16	-0.06

Notes: A positive (negative) correlation between government expenditure (inflation tax) and real GDP indicates pro-cyclical fiscal policy. A negative correlation between lending interest rates and real GDP indicates pro-cyclical monetary policy. A positive (negative) correlation between government expenditure (inflation tax and lending interest rates) and net capital inflows indicates that contractionary macropolicies are linked to episodes of low net capital inflows. The cyclical component of the various indicators was obtained using the HP filter.
Source: Kaminsky, Reinhart and Vegh (2004).

6.2. The left panel in Table 6.2 reports the correlation between the cyclical components of fiscal and monetary policy with the business cycle. The right panel shows the correlations of the cyclical components of fiscal and monetary policy with net capital inflows. Interestingly, the evidence suggests that international capital flows to developing countries may trigger pro-cyclical macro-policies. For example, government expenditure (inflation tax) is positively (negatively) correlated with net capital inflows, indicating that periods of capital inflows are associated with expansionary fiscal policies and periods of capital outflows with contractionary fiscal policies. While more research is needed, the stylized evidence suggests that international capital flows may trigger more volatile business cycles in emerging economies.

While this evidence points to links between financial integration and output instability over the business cycle, there is also evidence that financial integration promotes growth. A variety of authors have examined the effects of domestic and external deregulation of financial markets in emerging economies and found that they generally trigger sustainable growth in the long run. For example, Bekaert, Harvey and Lundblad (2002) examine the effects of the opening of the stock market to foreign investors on growth in a sample of about 90 developing countries and find that, overall, liberalization triggers an increase in growth by approximately one percentage point. They find that the investment to GDP ratio increases in the aftermath of liberalization and that factor productivity increases significantly as well. The authors conclude that the effects of liberalization are so strong not only because they reduce financing constraints but also because foreign investors may insist on better corporate governance thus indirectly reducing the cost of external financing.

Similarly, Galindo, Micco and Ordoñez (2002) study whether financial liberalization promotes economic growth by analyzing its effect on the cost of external financing to firms. In particular, the hypothesis is that the liberalization of domestic and external financial markets reduces the cost of external funds faced by firms by reducing the impact of problems associated with moral hazard and adverse selection. From this perspective, the impact of financial development differs according to the needs of particular firms for external funds. Firms that rely more on external funds will be more heavily impacted by financial development than those that require little capital. The results suggest that industries that depend on external finance grow almost 1 per cent faster, relative to industries with low external financing dependence, in episodes of globalization compared to episodes of repression. However, the evidence on the links between financial liberalization and growth is not conclusive. For example, Edison and others (2002), using data from 57 countries from 1980 to 2000, conclude that there is no robustly significant effect of financial integration on economic growth.[9] Similarly, Kraay (1998), using a sample of 117 countries, finds no effect of financial liberalization on growth or, at best, mixed results.

Perhaps the inability of past research to agree on the effects of financial globalization on economic growth lies in the fact that liberalization has time-varying effects on growth. Loayza and Ranciere (2002) present some evidence that suggests this might be the case. These authors estimate transitory and trend effects of financial deepening on growth using a sample of about 80 countries and find that financial deepening, which in general is closely related to financial liberalization, harms growth in the short run but leads to higher growth in the long run. These latest results are closely linked to the results in Kaminsky and Schmukler (2003) and suggest that financial liberalization triggers growth in the long run because it fuels institutional reform.

Gourinchas and Jeanne (2002) also explore this theme and distinguish two classes of benefits of financial globalization. The first category includes benefits in terms of international allocative efficiency, such as consumption smoothing in response to shocks or the possibility of accelerating domestic capital accumulation with the help of foreign capital. The second class of benefits encompasses incentives to implement good policies or reform that are generated by an open capital account. This includes imposing market discipline on domestic macroeconomic policies induced by the threat of capital flight. More broadly, it can also include incentives to reform the domestic economic system in a way that reduces unproductive activities (diversion, rent-seeking) or secures better guarantees of property rights. To examine the relative importance of the benefits of international allocative efficiency, the authors calibrate a simple neoclassical growth model of a small, open, capital-scarce economy with data on post-World War Two emerging economies. While they find that financial openness increases domestic welfare by allowing households to smooth consumption and by increasing the possibility of accelerating domestic capital accumulation, they also find that the benefits are not very large when compared to the benefits of alternative policies that reduce domestic distortions or increase domestic productivity.[10]

MANAGING INTERNATIONAL CAPITAL FLOWS

The evidence seems to suggest that in the short run, globalization triggers the bankruptcy of financial systems and protracted recessions. Even if capital inflows do not trigger excess volatility in domestic financial markets, it is still true that they trigger inflation in the presence of a fixed exchange-rate regime. Moreover, transitory capital inflows may distort relative prices, with the domestic economy losing competitiveness as a result of the appreciation of the real ex-change rate. Therefore, policy makers have used a variety of tools to manage these flows, especially those of the "hot money" type. While they have introduced capital controls in some cases, they have also resorted to sterilized intervention or have introduced fiscal austerity to help "sterilize" the expansive monetary effects of foreign-exchange purchases. Governments have also allowed more exchange-rate flexibility to avoid a burst of inflation during episodes of capital inflows, in the knowledge that if the appreciation of the real exchange rate is unavoidable, it is better that it takes place through a nominal appreciation rather than through domestic inflation.

The effects of sterilized intervention and exchange-rate policy in the presence of large capital inflow episodes have been documented extensively in Reinhart and Reinhart (1998). Emerging markets mostly peg their domestic currency, floating only in the immediate aftermath of crises (see Calvo and Reinhart, 2000). With fixed exchange-rate regimes, capital inflows trigger an accumu-lation of reserves by the central bank and an explosion of the monetary aggre-gates. To avoid inflation, monetary authorities have to sterilize the effects of the intervention in the foreign-exchange market by selling securities in the dom-estic open market. Naturally, sterilization can only be effective if domestic and foreign assets are not close substitutes. The evidence for emerging markets sug-gests that while sterilization only has short-run effects (see Reinhart and Rein-hart, 1998), many countries have resorted to sterilized intervention. For exam-ple, Colombia (during most of 1991), Indonesia (during 1991–1992) and Malaysia (during 1991–1993) implemented open market operations on a vast scale to fully sterilize capital inflows. Less strongly, but still forcefully, the cen-tral banks of Chile, Korea, Mexico, the Philippines and Thailand partly sterilized the capital inflows of the early and mid-1990s.

In most cases, domestic short-term interest rates rose when sterilization began, suggesting that policy had an impact, at least in the short run. Interest-ingly, and at odds with the central banks' initial purpose, strong sterilized inter-vention, by triggering large hikes in domestic interest rates, also triggered an increase in the volume of aggregate capital flows, mostly of the "hot money" type.[11] Another disadvantage of sterilized intervention was that the hikes in domestic interest rates also increased the cost of capital to the Government, as the central banks acquired relatively low-yield foreign-exchange reserves and issued high-yield sterilization bonds. In practice, these quasi-fiscal losses were not trivial. For example, the central bank losses associated with the sterilization effort in Colombia in 1991 reached about 0.6 per cent of GDP (see Rodriguez, 1992). Similarly, the losses in Chile due to the sterilization attempt during

1990–1992 amounted to about 1.4 per cent of GDP (see Kiguel and Leiderman, 1993).

The explosion of capital inflows to emerging markets in the early and mid-1990s were at first counterbalanced through sterilized intervention. This intervention managed to avoid nominal appreciation or a hike in inflation. As the inflows persisted and as the foreign exchange reserves continued to accumulate, however, these policies became quite costly. At this point, central banks in Asia and Latin America allowed the exchange rate to move more freely so that the real appreciation was effected through a nominal appreciation rather than through a hike in domestic inflation. As described in Reinhart and Reinhart (1998), Chile and Colombia allowed several appreciations in the midst of the capital inflow episode. For example, Chile allowed its currency to appreciate by 5 per cent in January 1992 and by 9.5 per cent in November 1994. Similarly, Colombia allowed its currency to appreciate by 5 per cent in January 1994 and by 7 per cent in November 1994. In addition to Chile and Colombia, the Czech Republic and Mexico also allowed their currencies to float somewhat more freely. All of these countries widened their exchange-rate intervention bands in the early 1990s.

CONCLUSION

The explosion of capital flows to emerging markets in the early and mid-1990s and the recent reversal following the crises around the globe have reignited a heated debate on how to manage international capital flows. Capital outflows worry policy makers, but so do capital inflows, as they may trigger bubbles in asset markets and lead to an appreciation of the domestic currency and a loss of competitiveness. Policy makers also worry that capital inflows are mostly of the "hot money" type, which is why capital controls have mostly targeted short-term capital inflows. While capital controls may work, at least in the very short run, the introduction of restrictions to capital mobility may have undesirable long-run effects. In particular, capital controls protect inefficient domestic financial institutions and thus may trigger financial vulnerabilities.[12] Capital controls may also delay improvements in corporate governance of non-financial firms because, as countries liberalize their capital accounts, domestic corporations start participating in international capital markets, mainly through cross-listing in major world stock exchanges, with higher disclosure standards and under the jurisdiction of a superior legal system. This certainly promotes more transparency in the management of the firm and can trigger improvements in corporate governance (for example, see Stultz, 1999). Thus, regulation of capital flows may not only provoke financial vulnerabilities but also lower economic growth. Policy makers have also resorted to sterilization of capital flows to regain control of monetary policy. While sterilization may provide some relief, it may also be quite costly to central banks. Moreover, the ability of Governments to control international capital flows or to sterilize them diminishes with globalization.

In conclusion, there is no optimal policy to deal with the risks of volatile international capital flows, as policies that may work in the short run may have adverse effects in the long run. Since there is evidence that currency and banking crises tend to occur in economies with deteriorated fundamentals, conservative macroeconomic policies should be at the heart of dealing with volatile capital flows. Further research should examine whether countries can deregulate financial systems without becoming vulnerable to crises. Since the costs of crises have been quite large, this last question deserves much attention.

NOTES

[1] This chapter draws on previous research with Richard Lyons, Carmen Reinhart, Sergio Schmukler and Carlos Végh. The chapter was previously circulated under the title "Volatile International Capital Flows: A Blessing or a Curse?" I would like to thank José Antonio Ocampo for his very useful comments, and Victor Cheng and Nilanjana Sarkar for their excellent research assistance.

[2] This chapter is restricted to the analysis of portfolio and bank-related flows. Still, it is important to note that in contrast to the booms and sudden stops in portfolio and bank flows, FDI to emerging markets continuously increased even in the midst of currency turmoil (in part driven by purchases of firms in distress following the crises). This led many to single out FDI as a stabilizing flow (see, for example, Reisen and Soto (2001) and Sarno and Taylor (1999)) and to support policies encouraging FDI. This reasoning has been challenged by Claessens, Dooley and Warner (1995), who emphasize that capital-flow labels are meaningless in the presence of derivatives or efforts to circumvent capital controls.

[3] Liquidity may have an important effect on investors' portfolio allocations since investors may want to avoid illiquid markets to minimize the price collapses always present when there is no ready market.

[4] To identify liquid markets, countries are ranked by region according to their volume traded and according to their share in the mutual funds portfolio at the onset of the crisis. The dummy variable related to volume traded is given a value of one if the country ranks among the top 30 per cent of most liquid countries in the region in that category, and a value of zero otherwise. Similarly, countries are classified as liquid (that is to say, the dummy variable is given a value of one) if they rank among the 30 per cent of the countries with the largest share in mutual fund portfolios for the region. A third dummy is created to capture whether emerging market firms are trading in mature financial markets: the variable is given a value of one if they do, and zero if they do not. Finally, the variable capturing restrictions to entry and exit of foreigners in the stock markets of emerging economies is given a value of one if there are no restrictions, and zero if there are. All of this information is collapsed into a liquidity variable

that is the average of the four univariate liquidity dummy variables. Thus, the general index of liquidity, the average of the four components, can have five values: 0, 1/4, 2/4, 3/4 and 1, with a value of one indicating a highly liquid market. I classify a country as having liquid financial markets when this dummy takes a value of 0.5 or higher.

[5] See Kaminsky, Lyons and Schmukler (2002) for a country-by-country detail on fragility, liquidity, risk and mutual fund withdrawals.

[6] For an excellent discussion on the effects of asymmetric information in assets markets, see Eichengreen and Mussa (1998).

[7] In order to date the episodes of financial liberalization, we construct a chronology of financial liberalization in the domestic financial sector, the capital account, and the domestic stock market. The chronology allows for episodes of partial and full liberalization.

[8] The fourteen emerging economies are Argentina, Brazil, Chile, Colombia, Hong Kong, Indonesia, Korea, Malaysia, Mexico, Peru, the Philippines, Taiwan, Thailand and Venezuela.

[9] See Prasad and others (2003) for a review of the literature on the effects of financial globalization on growth.

[10] The evidence in Arteta, Eichengreen and Wyplosz (2001) also suggests that the positive growth effects of liberalization are stronger in countries with strong institutions, as measured by standard indicators of the rule of law.

[11] See Montiel and Reinhart (1999) for a study of 15 sterilization episodes in Africa, Asia, Latin America and transition economies, and Christensen (2005) for the analysis of the sterilization policy in the Czech Republic during the capital inflow episode of the early 1990s. In both studies, the authors conclude that sterilization created a vicious circle of high interest rates, more capital inflows and the need for additional sterilization interventions.

[12] Claessens, Demirgüç-Kunt and Huizinga (1998) present evidence that liberalization of the capital account and foreign bank entry lead to improvements in banking system efficiency.

REFERENCES

Arteta, Carlos, Barry Eichengreen, and Charles Wyplosz (2001). When Does Capital Account Liberalization Help More than it Hurts? NBER Working Paper No. 8414, National Bureau of Economic Research, Cambridge, MA.

Bekaert, Geert, Campbell Harvey, and Christian Lundblad (2001). Does Financial Liberalization Spur Growth? NBER working paper No. 8245, National Bureau of Economic Research, Cambridge, MA.

Borensztein, Eduardo, and Gastón Gelos (2003). A Panic-Prone Pack? The Behaviour of Emerging Market Mutual Funds. IMF Working Paper No. 198, April, International Monetary Fund, Washington DC.

Calvo, Guillermo, Alejandro Izquierdo, and Luis Mejía (2003). On the Empirics of Sudden Stops. Processed, Inter-American Development Bank, Washington, DC, May.

Caramazza, Francesco, Luca Ricci, and Ranil Salgado (2000). Trade and Financial Contagion in Currency Crises. IMF Working Paper No. 55, International Monetary Fund, Washington DC.

Christensen, J. (2004). Capital Inflows, Sterilization, and Commercial Bank Speculation: The Case of the Czech Republic in the Mid-1990s. IMF Working Paper No. 218, International Monetary Fund, Washington DC.

Claessens, Stijn, Michael Dooley, and Andrew Warner (1995). Portfolio Capital Flows: Hot or Cold? World Bank Economic Review 9: 153–174.

Claessens, Stjin, Asli Demirgüç-Kunt, and Harry Huizinga (1998). How Does Foreign Entry Affect the Domestic Banking Sector? Processed, May, World Bank, Washington DC.

Demirguc-Kunt, Asli, and Enrica Detragiache (1999). Financial Liberalization and Financial Fragility. In *Annual World Bank Conference on Development Economics.* World Bank, Washington DC: 303–331.

Dornbusch, Rudiger (1998). Capital Controls: An Idea Whose Time is Past. In *Should the IMF Pursue Capital-Account Convertibility?.* Essays in International Finance 207, International Finance Section, Department of Economics, Princeton University, May 20–27.

Edison, Hali, Michael Klein, Luca Ricci, and Torsten Slok (2002). Capital Account Liberalization and Economic Performance: A Review of the Literature. Working Paper No. 120, International Monetary Fund, Washington DC.

Eichengreen, Barry, and Michael Mussa, with Giovanni Dell'Ariccia, Enrica Detragiache, Gian Maria Milesi-Ferretti, and Andrew Tweedie (1998). Capital Account Liberalization: Theoretical and Practical Aspects. Occasional Paper 172, International Monetary Fund, Washington, DC.

Galindo, Arturo, Alejandro Micco and Guillermo Ordoñez (2002). Financial Liberalization and Growth: Empirical Evidence. Paper presented at the Conference on 'Financial Globalization: A Blessing or a Curse', World Bank, Washington, D.C.

Goldstein, Morris, Graciela Kaminsky, and Carmen Reinhart (2000). *Assessing Financial Vulnerability: An Early Warning System for Emerging Markets.* Institute for International Economics, Washington, DC.

Gourinchas, Pierre, and Olivier Jeanne (2002). On the Benefits of Capital Account Liberalization for Emerging Economies. Processed, Princeton University, Princeton, NJ.

Kaminsky, Graciela (1998). Currency and Banking Crises: The Early Warnings of Distress. International Finance Discussion Paper No. 629, October, Board of Governors of the Federal Reserve System, Washington, DC.

Kaminsky, Graciela, and Carmen Reinhart (2000). On Crises, Contagion, and Confusion. *Journal of International Economics,* 51 (1), June: 145–168.

Kaminsky, Graciela, and Sergio Schmukler (2003). Short-Run Pain, Long-Run Gain: The Effects of Financial Liberalization. NBERWorking Paper No. 9787, June, National Bureau of Economic Research, Cambridge, MA.

Kaminsky, Graciela, Richard Lyons, and Sergio Schmukler (2002). Fragility, Liquidity, and Risk: The Behaviour of Mutual Funds During Crises. Processed, World Bank, Washington, DC.

Kaminsky, Graciela, Carmen Reinhart, and Carlos Végh (2004). When it Rains, it Pours: Procyclical Capital Flows and Macro Policies. In Mark Gertler and Kenneth S. Rogoff (eds). *NBER Macroeconomics Annual 2004.* National Bureau of Economic Research, Cambridge, MA: 11–53.

Kiguel, Miguel, and Leonardo Leiderman (1994). On the Consequences of Sterilized Intervention in Latin America: The Case of Colombia and Chile. Processed, Tel Aviv University, Tel Aviv.

Loayza, Norman, and Romaine Ranciere (2002). Financial Development, Financial Fragility, and Growth. Working Paper No. 145, Central Bank of Chile, Santiago.

Prasad, Eshwar, Kenneth Rogoff, Shang-Jin Wei, Ayhan Kose (2003). Effects of Financial Globalization on Developing Countries: Some Empirical Evidence. IMF Occasional Paper 220, International Monetary Fund, Washington, DC.

Reinhart, Carmen, and Vincent Reinhart (1998). Some Lessons for Policy Makers Dealing with the Mixed Blessing of Capital Inflows. In Miles Kahler (ed.). *Capital Flows and Financial Crises.* Council on Foreign Relations, New York: 93–127.

Reisen, Helmut, and Marcelo Soto (2001). Which Types of Capital Inflows Foster Developing-Country Growth? *International Finance* 4 (1): 1–14.

Rodrik, Dani (1998). Who Needs Capital Account Convertibility? In S. Fischer and others [eds].

Should the IMF Pursue Capital-Account Convertibility? Essays in International Finance No. 207, Department of Economics, Princeton University, May.

Sachs, Jeffrey, Aaron Tornell and Andrés Velasco (1996). Financial Crises in Emerging Markets: The Lessons from 1995. *Brookings Papers on Economic Activity, 1996:1*: 147–215.

Stiglitz, Joseph (1999). Bleak Growth for the Developing World. *International Herald Tribune,* April 10–11, p. 6.

Stultz, Rene (1999). Globalization of Equity Markets and the Cost of Capital. Processed, Dice Center, Ohio State University, Columbus.

7

The Economic and Social Effects of Financial Liberalization: A Primer for Developing Countries[1]

JAYATI GHOSH

For more than a decade now, financial liberalization in developing countries has been cited as a necessary and significant part of an economic policy package promoted by what used to be called the "Washington Consensus". Typically, financial sector liberalization in developing countries has been associated with measures that are designed to make the central bank more independent, relieve "financial repression" by freeing interest rates and allowing financial innovation, and reduce directed and subsidized credit, as well as allow greater freedom in terms of external flows of capital in various forms.

Increasingly, these policies are not imposed from outside, whether through the conditionality of multilateral lending institutions or bilateral pressure. Rather, policy makers, and especially those in finance ministries across the developing world, appear to have absorbed and internalized the idea that such measures are necessary to improve the functioning of the financial sector generally, in terms of profitability, competitiveness and intermediation, as well as to attract international capital to increase resources available for domestic investment. These ideas are usually supported by media, which caters to the elite in developing countries, to the extent that their constant reiteration also ensures that such measures have wide support among the elite and middle classes, who often have the most political voice in these countries.

Yet, the arguments in favour of financial liberalization—both theoretical and empirical—are relatively flimsy, and there are many grounds for scepticism regarding the claims made by the votaries of such measures. Indeed, there are good reasons for questioning both the extent and the pattern of the kind of financial liberalization that is promoted. In many cases, the social and economic effects have been especially adverse for the poor and for farmers and workers, who have not only suffered more precarious conditions even during a so-called "financial boom", but two have typically also been the worst affected during a financial crisis or the subsequent adjustment. It is also worth noting that the extreme forms of liberalization are neither effective nor necessary, and that a large variety of alternative measures, as well as varying degrees of liberalization, is not only possible but can also be observed in several more 'successful' developing countries.

In this context, this chapter examines various issues that are of immediate policy significance for developing countries. In the first section, the main elements of the standard pattern of financial liberalization that has become widely prevalent in developing countries are briefly described. In the second section, I consider the theoretical arguments for and against such measures. The third section contains a discussion of the political economy of such measures. The fourth section identifies the main economic and social effects of these measures, based on the actual experience of a number of emerging markets in the past one and a half decades. The final section draws some policy conclusions, and presents the case that a range of alternative strategies is still open to policy makers in developing countries.

THE NATURE OF FINANCIAL LIBERALIZATION

Financial liberalization refers to measures directed at diluting or dismantling regulatory control over the institutional structures, instruments and activities of agents in different segments of the financial sector. These measures can relate to internal or external regulations. (Chandrasekhar, 2004)

Internal financial liberalization typically includes some or all of the following measures, to varying degrees:

a) The reduction or removal of controls on the interest rates or rates of return charged by financial agents. Of course, the central bank continues to influence or administer that rate structure through adjustments of its discount rate and through its own open market operations. But deregulation typically removes interest rate ceilings and encourages competition between similarly placed financial firms aimed at attracting depositors on the one hand and enticing potential borrowers to take on debt on the other. As a result, price competition squeezes spreads and forces financial firms (including banks) to depend on volumes to ensure returns;

b) The withdrawal of the State from the activity of financial intermediation with the conversion of the "development banks" into regular banks and the privatization of the publicly owned banking system, on the grounds that their presence is not conducive to the dominance of market signals in the allocation of capital. This is usually accompanied by the decline of directed credit and the removal of requirements for special credit allocations to priority sectors, whether they be government, small-scale producers, agriculture or other sectors seen as priorities for strategic or developmental reasons;

c) The easing of conditions for the participation of both firms and investors in the stock market by diluting or doing away with listing conditions, by providing freedom in pricing of new issues, by permitting greater freedoms to intermediaries, such as brokers, and by relaxing conditions with regard to borrowing against shares and investing borrowed funds in the market;

d) The reduction in controls over the investments that can be undertaken by financial agents and, specifically, the breaking down the "Chinese wall" between banking and non-banking activities. Most regulated financial systems sought to keep separate the different segments of the financial sector such as banking, merchant banking, the mutual fund business and insurance. Agents in one segment were not permitted to invest in another for fear of conflicts of interest that could affect business practices adversely. The removal of the regulatory walls separating these sectors leads to the emergence of "universal banks" or financial supermarkets. This increases the interlinkages between and pyramiding of financial structures;

e) The expansion of the sources from and instruments through which firms or financial agents can access funds. This leads to the proliferation of instruments such as commercial paper and certificates of deposit issued in the domestic market and allows for offshore secondary market products such as ADRs (American Depository Receipts—the floating of primary issues in the United States market by firms not based in the United States) or GDRs (Global Depository Receipts);

f) The liberalization of the rules governing the kinds of financial instruments that can be issued and acquired in the system. This transforms the traditional role of the banking system's being the principal intermediary bearing risks in the system. Conventionally, banks accepted relatively small individual liabilities of short maturities that were highly liquid and involved lower income and capital risk and made large, relatively illiquid and risky investments of longer maturities. The protection afforded to the banking system and the strong regulatory constraints thereon were meant to protect its viability given the role it played. With liberalization, the focus shifts to that of generating financial assets that transfer risks to the portfolio of institutions willing to hold them;

g) The shift to a regime of voluntary adherence to statutory guidelines with regard to capital adequacy, accounting norms and related practices, with the central bank's role being limited to supervision and monitoring.

External financial liberalization typically involves changes in the exchange control regime. Typically, full convertibility for current-account transactions accompanying trade liberalization have been either prior or simultaneous reforms, which are then complemented with varying degrees of convertibility on the capital account. Capital-account liberalization measures broadly cover the following, in increasing degree of intensity, but with a wide variety of patterns of implementation:

a) Measures that allow foreign residents to hold domestic financial assets, either in the form of debt or equity. This can be associated with greater freedom for domestic firms to undertake external commercial borrowing, often without government guarantee or even supervision. It can also involve the dilution or removal of controls on the entry of new financial firms, subject to their meeting pre-specified norms with regard to capital investments. This does not necessarily increase competition, because it is usually associated with the freedom to acquire financial firms for domestic and foreign players and extends to permissions provided to foreign institutional investors, pension funds and hedge funds to invest in equity and debt markets, which often triggers a process of consolidation;

b) Measures which allow domestic residents to hold foreign financial assets. This is typically seen as a more drastic degree of liberalization, since it eases the possibility of capital flight by domestic residents in periods of crisis. However, a number of countries that receive "excessive" capital inflows that do not add to domestic investment in the net and are reflected in unnecessary accumulation of foreign-exchange reserves, have turned to such measures as a means of reducing pressure on the exchange rate;

c) Measures that allow foreign currency assets to be freely held and traded within the domestic economy (the "dollarization" of accounts). This is the most extreme form of external financial liberalization, which has been implemented only in very few countries.

THE THEORETICAL ARGUMENTS FOR FINANCIAL LIBERALIZATION

Underlying most of the arguments for financial liberalization measures are some basic monetarist postulates, namely: (i) that real economic growth is determined by the available supply of factors of production such as capital and labour and the rate of productivity growth, and changes in money supply do not have any impact on real economic activity and the growth of output; (ii) that money supply is exogenous rather than endogenous to the system and can be controlled by the monetary authorities, who can successfully pursue well-defined targets for monetary growth, and (iii) that inflation is attributable to an excessive growth of money supply relative to an exogenously given "real rate of growth of output" and can be moderated by reducing the rate of growth of money supply. These postulates can then lead to arguments for an "independent" central bank whose essential job would be to control inflation by using money market levers to control money supply and therefore the price line.

The basic difficulty with these arguments is now rather well known. There is no clearly discernible relationship between the rates of growth of money supply and of inflation on the one hand and real output growth on the other. The monetarist argument is based on the twin assumptions of full employment (or exogenously given aggregate supply conditions) and aggregate money supply determined exogenously by macro-policy. Neither of these assumptions is valid; on the contrary, there is a strong case for arguing that, in a world of financial innovation where quasi-moneys can be created, the overall liquidity in the system cannot be rigidly controlled by the monetary authorities.

Rather, the actual liquidity in the system is endogenously determined. Therefore, the real monetary variable in the hands of the Government is the interest rate, and thus, attempts to control money supply typically end up as forms of interest rate policy instead. The notion of a stable "real demand for money" function (where the demand for money is determined by the level of real economic activity) is one which gets demolished by the possibility of speculative demand for money, a feature which, if anything, is enhanced by financial sophistication and the greater uncertainties operating in today's economies.

Further, though the package of policies described above has evolved over time, often in response to the demands of increasingly omnipresent and mobile international financial interests, its origins lie in the neoclassical notion of efficient financial markets. Capital markets are seen as being competitive and informationally efficient when they ensure the availability and full utilization of information required to determine the value of assets as well as to identify the best investments. These features ensure that the return that an investor expects to get from an investment would be equal to the opportunity cost of using the funds in some other project. To the extent that the structure of financial markets—the combination of institutions, instruments and agents—approximates this ideal, the system is seen as being able to mobilize the maximum savings for investment and allocate it most efficiently.

In addition, the need to eliminate financial repression (in the McKinnon-Shaw sense) has been provided as a powerful argument in favour of financial liberalization. Repressive policies are seen to be inimical to financial deepening, in the context of the observed empirical relationship between financial deep-ening and growth. Financial repression is said to have a depressive effect on savings rates and thereby to result in capital shortages and adversely affect growth. It is also argued that financial repression tends to selectively ration out riskier projects, irrespective of their social relevance, because interest rate ceilings imply that adequate risk premiums cannot be charged.

But there is, of course, a large theoretical literature pointing out that financial markets inherently cannot be as perfect as this and, indeed, are structurally more imperfect than the markets for goods. Since information as a commodity has strong public good characteristics (non-rivalry in consumption and non-excludability in provision), this typically results in the inadequate acquisition of information even in apparently "competitive" markets. In financial markets this means that those who manage investments are, therefore, inadequately monitored, which encourages inappropriate risk-taking or even fraud that could lead to insolvency. There are many examples of market failure in financial markets resulting from asymmetric information, adverse selection, incentive-incompatibility and moral hazard, which are then aggravated because of further imperfections and the inter-linkages between financial agents.[2] These are, of course, in addition to the other more standard forms of imperfection in markets resulting, for example, from imperfect competition, oligopolies and increasing returns.

There are other problems that result because social returns differ from pri-vate returns. Projects with high social returns may not be the ones that deliver the highest profits to the bank or financial investor. Banks may be willing to increase their exposure to "sensitive sectors" like the stock and real estate mar-kets, given the higher interest that clients are willing to pay on the expectation of larger speculative profits. Besides exposing banks to the dangers of a stock or real estate market collapse, such options reduce lending to investors in manufac-turing or the agricultural sector who cannot accept extremely high interest rates. This was one of the principal reasons why Governments sought to create public sector banks and direct public and private credit to socially important sectors.

Likewise, there are reasons to question the arguments about financial repres-sion. There are reasons to believe that financial deepening (measured by the ratio of financial to real wealth) and increased financial intermediation (meas-ured by the share of financial assets of financial institutions in total financial assets) need not be, in themselves, stimuli to growth, despite myriad efforts to prove that this is true. The existence of usurious money lending in backward agriculture, which limits rather than promotes growth, is indicative of the fact that inequality of a kind inimical to growth influences the nature of a financial structure. Also, evidence suggests that financial crises are inevitably preceded by a phase of financial deepening and increased intermediation.

Further, the implicit view that savings are automatically reinvested and that any increase in savings leads automatically to an increase in investment is a pre-Keynesian argument with little relevance to demand-constrained economies with unutilized resources. Empirical studies of savings have shown that there is little relationship between national savings and real interest rates. Similarly, the developmental or social role of banking is especially relevant when lowering interest rates can increase the quality of borrowers, and it can have substantial beneficial effects if the Government is able to select the better projects and recipients of finance.

The Political Economy of Financial Liberalization

The current role of international finance is critically related to the manner in which finance capital rose to a position of dominance in the global economy and to the role that cross-border flows of capital have been playing in the process of globalization. High rates of cross-border capital flows were evident during the late nineteenth and early twentieth centuries. In the inter-war period, these capital movements became dominantly speculative in nature and were associated with very high volatility in currency markets, even among the industrial countries of the time. It was precisely this experience of currency instability and competitive devaluation that provided the impetus for the establishment of the Bretton Woods system, which was based on fixed exchange rates and stringent capital controls for the first two and a half decades.

The major industrial capitalist countries first began relaxing controls on currency movements in the late 1960s, and the move to "floating" or flexible exchange rates in the 1970s hastened the process. In that decade, there were specific developments outside the realm of finance itself that contributed to an increase in international liquidity, such as the surpluses generated by oil exporters after the oil price increases, which were largely deposited with the international banking system. This was reflected in the explosion of the Euro-currency market in the 1970s.

From the 1980s, there were other real factors that created pressures for the expansion of finance. These included the changing demographic structure in most of the advanced countries, with baby boomers reaching an age where they were emphasizing personal savings for retirement. This was accentuated by changes in the institutional structures relating to pensions, whereby in most industrial countries, public and private employers tended to fund less of the planned income after retirement, requiring more savings input from employees themselves. All this meant growing demands for more variety in the form of savings as well as higher returns, leading to the greater significance of pension funds, mutual funds and the like.

Financial liberalization in the developed countries was closely related to these developments. However, it also contributed to the generation of savings which were in excess of investment ex ante. Financial liberalization in the developed countries increased the flexibility of banking and financial institutions when creating credit and making investments, and permitted the proliferation of institutions like hedge funds which, unlike the banks, were not subject to much regulation. It also encouraged "securitization", or capital flows in the form of stocks and bonds, rather than loans, and "financial innovation", involving the creation of a range of new financial instruments or derivatives such as swaps, options and futures, virtually autonomously created by the financial system. These instruments allowed players to trade in the risks associated with an asset without trading the asset itself. Finally, it increased competition and whetted the appetite of banks to earn higher returns, thus causing them to search out new recipients for loans and investments in economic regions that were hitherto considered to be too risky.

Financial liberalization began with versions of the "big bang" in developed country markets. This was because, by the late 1960s, it became clear that old-style Keynesian policies were increasingly incapable of dealing with the secular deceleration that threatened most developed countries, especially the United States. Further, with a weakening United States economy leading to the breakdown of the Bretton Woods arrangement and the emergence of a world of floating exchange rates, pursuing Keynesian-style policies in any one country threatened a collapse of the currency. Any effort to pump-prime the system generated inflation, rendered domestic goods less competitive in world markets, widened the trade deficit and weakened the currency. The collapse of old-fashioned Keynesianism was therefore also related to the fact that it was based on the assumption of a particular type of nation State, which was no longer valid. In consequence, some other means of trying to spur growth was required, and this role was played by the easy availability of liquidity in the "international" banking system based in the developed countries.

There followed a massive increase in international liquidity, as banks and non-bank financial institutions desperately searched for means to keep their capital moving, since that had become the route to higher profits in the financial sector. There were booms in consumer credit and housing finance in the developed industrial nations. However, when those opportunities petered out, a number of developing countries were discovered as the "emerging markets" of the global financial order. Capital—in the form of debt and equity investments—began to flow into these countries, especially those that were quick to liberalize rules relating to cross-border capital flows and regulations governing the conversion of domestic into foreign currency. As a result of these developments, there was a host of new financial assets in emerging markets characterized by higher interest rates, ostensibly because of greater investment risks in these areas. The greater 'perceived risk' and higher returns associated with financial instruments in these countries provided the basis for a whole range of new derivatives that bundled these risks and offered hedges against risk in different markets, each of which promised high returns.

There are a number of features characteristic of the global financial system that have evolved in this manner. One of the most important of current significance is the growing importance of unregulated financial agents, such as the so-called hedge funds, in the system. Although hedge funds first originated immediately after the Second World War, they have grown in number and financial strength in recent times. Their investors include major international banks, which are themselves forced by rules and regulations to avoid risky transactions promising high returns, but which use the hedge funds as a front to undertake such transactions. More recently, even mutual funds and pension funds have been attracted to hedge funds because of the higher returns promised, and this is currently the fastest growing segment of the international financial sector.

Second, the current global financial system is obviously characterized by a high degree of centralization. With United States financial institutions intermediating global capital flows, the investment decisions of a few individuals in a few institutions virtually determine the nature of the "exposure" of the global financial system. Unfortunately, unregulated entities making huge profits on highly speculative investments are at the core of that system.

Further, once institutions that are free of the now-diluted regulatory system exist, even those that are more regulated become entangled in risky operations. They are entangled because they themselves have lent large sums in order to benefit from the promise of larger returns from the risky investments undertaken by the unregulated institutions. They are also entangled because the securities on which these institutions bet in a speculative manner are also securities that these banks hold as "safe investments". If changes in the environment force these funds to dump some of their holdings to clear claims that are made on them, the prices of securities the banks directly hold tend to fall, thus affecting their assets position adversely.

Entanglement takes other forms as well. With financial firms betting on interest rate differentials and exchange-rate changes at virtually the same time, the various asset markets relating to debt, securities and currency are increasingly integrated. Crises, when they occur, do not remain confined to one of these markets but quickly spread to others, unless stalled by government intervention. Finally, the rise of finance in the manner described above feeds on itself in complex ways.

This means that there are two major consequences of the new financial scenario: it is difficult to judge the actual volume and risk of the exposure of individual financial institutions; and within the financial world, there is a complex web of entanglement, where all firms are mutually exposed, but where each individual firm is exposed to differing degrees to particular financial entities. It also makes a mockery of prudential norms, such as "capital adequacy" ratios, which have supposedly become more strict over time, since it becomes difficult to actually define or measure the extent of capital once such pyramiding of assets is widely prevalent.

Further, the process of financial consolidation on this base has substantially increased the risks associated with the system. During the 1990s, the three-decade-long process of proliferation and rise to dominance of finance in the global economy reached a new phase. The international financial system was being transformed in ways that were substantially increasing systemic risk and rendering the system more crisis-prone. Central to this transformation was growing financial consolidation. This has concentrated financial activity and decision-making in a few economic organizations and also integrated areas of financial activity earlier separated from one another to ensure transparency and discourage unsound financial practices.

The proximate explanation for the wave of financial liberalization in the developing countries is that this pyramidal growth of finance, which increased the fragility of the system, was seen as an opportunity. Enhanced flows to developing countries, initially in the form of debt and subsequently in the form of debt and portfolio investments, led to two consequences. First, the notion of external vulnerability which underlay the interventionist strategies of the 1950s and 1960s no longer seemed relevant—after all, any current-account deficit could be financed, it appeared, as long as such capital inflows were assured. Second, growth was now easier to ensure without having to confront domestic vested interests, since international liquidity could be used not merely to finance current and capital expenditures but also to ease any supply-side constraints that would otherwise hamper such growth.

Until quite recently, the financial press, the international financial institutions and large sections of the academic community were uninhibitedly in favour of these tendencies. It was argued that this created an opportunity for developing countries to launch on an integrationist growth strategy, since in any case, the sums they required were seen as a small fraction of the international liquidity being created by the financial system. For western finance, emerging markets were a hedge, and for developing countries, international finance was an opportunity. A cosy relationship seemed easy to build. It appeared that all that was needed was the liberalization of finance and a monetary policy that ensured interest rates high enough to make capital inflows attractive, even after adjusting for risk.

Trade and financial liberalization in developing countries would not have been sustainable, even for short periods, had it not been for the availability of fluid finance from the financial centres of the world economy. The availability of such finance reflected the rise to dominance of finance capital in the global economy, reforms protecting and privileging its interests and the consequent role that cross-border flows of capital played in the process of globalization. It also reflected the emergence of a "financial class" within many developing countries, which became a major lobby promoting the interests of international finance in general with respect to both financial liberalization and domestic macroeconomic policies.

This virtual financial explosion in developing country markets is largely explained by the factors encouraging financial capital to move out of the developed countries. First, emerging financial markets, though volatile, offer extremely high returns in a period when the debt overhang and slow growth in the developed countries has affected financial interests adversely. That makes risk-discounted returns in the developing countries much better than in the developed. Second, privatization programs have put up for sale resources of substantial value that can be acquired relatively cheaply in a context of currency depreciation. Third, these are markets in which the pent-up demand for credit is substantial and where innovative financial instruments have not been experimented with in the past. And finally, real interest rates, and therefore financial sector returns, tend to be relatively high in developing countries undertaking adjustment programs involving monetary stringency.

The combination of debt and portfolio capital has meant that for the last three decades, at least the more developed among the developing countries have found it much easier—except, of course, when crisis strikes—to access private foreign capital flows. This is taken to imply that the rise to dominance of finance and its globalizing influence has rendered the current-account deficit in many developing countries less of a binding constraint.

But the boom obviously could not be consistent in all emerging markets. First, it became clear that none of these borrowers were in a position to meet their debt-service payments without resorting to further borrowing. This, together with the evidence of the colossal overexposure of the international banking system in many developing countries, set afoot the deceleration in the flow of liquidity that came to be called the 'debt crisis'. The banks, of course, could not pull out completely, because that would have spelt closure for many of them, as much of developing country debt would have had to be written off rather than rescheduled.

But the problem went deeper, since with the rise to dominance of finance capital relative to industrial capital in the developed nations, the financial system was awash with liquidity, but creditworthy borrowers were difficult to come by in an increasingly recessionary environment. In the event, debt was replaced with other kinds of non-debt private capital flows. Here too, however, the evidence suggests that, barring rare exceptions, periods of accelerated capital flow were followed by inevitable financial crises, when foreign investors turned wary and chose to withdraw their investments.

It is interesting to note that the enthusiasm for financial liberalization, especially of capital account transactions, appears to be unabated among developing country policy makers, despite all the evidence of greater frequency and intensity of crises in emerging markets. Indeed, the acceptance of capital-account liberalization continues, even though research from very mainstream quarters, including the International Monetary Fund (IMF), increasingly suggests that financial liberalization plays little role in increasing the investment rates of developing countries and exposes countries to many undesirable risks of volatility, deflation and crisis.[3]

In many countries, financial reforms are seen, even now, as the most essential and urgent of the "second-generation reforms" that typically follow upon the "first-generation reforms" such as trade liberalization, privatization of a range of public activities and internal deregulation of various markets. It is also clearly the case that the pressures for financial liberalization do not come only from external agencies; rather, there are internal pressures generating from the economic requirements of domestic capital, the interests of local elites and the emergence of domestic "financial classes" as described above.

THE NEGATIVE EFFECTS OF FINANCIAL LIBERALIZATION

There are some significant negative economic and social effects of financial liberalization, which are often so large that they significantly outweigh any benefits in terms of access to more capital inflows. These relate both to financial markets and to the real economy. Essentially, financial liberalization creates exposure to the following kinds of risk: a propensity to financial crises, both external and internal; a deflationary impact on real economic activity and reduced access to funds for small-scale producers, both urban and rural. This in turn has major social effects in terms of loss of employment and more volatile material conditions for most citizens.

Financial Fragility and the Propensity to Crisis

It is now widely accepted that financial liberalization has resulted in an increase in financial fragility in developing countries, making them prone to periodic financial and currency crises. These relate both to internal banking and related crises, and currency crises stemming from more open capital accounts. The origin of several crises can be traced to the shift to a more liberal and open financial regime, since this unleashes a dynamic that pushes the financial system towards a poorly regulated, oligopolistic structure, with a corresponding increase in fragility. Greater freedom to invest, including in sensitive sectors such as real estate and stock markets, ability to increase exposure to particular sectors and individual clients and increased regulatory forbearance all lead to increased instances of financial failure. In addition, as mentioned earlier, the emergence of universal banks or financial supermarkets increases both the degree of entanglement of different agents within the financial system and the domino effects of individual financial failures.

Financial markets, left to themselves, are known to be prone to failure because of the public goods characteristics of information which agents must acquire and process. They are characterized by insufficient monitoring by market participants. Individual shareholders tend to refrain from investing money and time in acquiring information about management hoping that others will do so instead and knowing that all shareholders, including themselves, benefit from the information garnered. As a result, there may be inadequate monitoring leading to risky decisions and malpractice. Financial firms wanting to reduce or avoid monitoring costs may just follow other, possibly larger, financial firms in making their investments, leading to what has been observed as the "herd instinct" characteristic of financial players. This not merely limits access to finance for some agents, but could lead to overlending to some entities, the failure of which could have systemic effects. The prevalence of informational externalities can create other problems. Malpractice in a particular bank leading to failure may trigger fears among depositors in other banks, resulting in a run on deposits there.

Disruptions may also occur because expected private returns differ from social returns in many activities. This could result in a situation where the market undertakes unnecessary risks in search of high returns. Typical examples are lending for investments in stocks or real estate. Loans to these sectors can be at extremely high interest rates because the returns in these sectors are extremely volatile and can touch extremely high levels. Since banks accept real estate or securities as collateral, borrowing to finance speculative investments in stock or real estate can spiral. This type of activity thrives because of the belief that losses, if any, can be transferred to the lender through default, and lenders are confident of government support in case of a crisis. This could feed a speculative spiral that can in time lead to a collapse of the bubble and bank failures.

Meanwhile, all too often the expected microeconomic efficiency gains are not realized. Even in the United States, bond markets play a limited role and equity markets virtually no role at all in financing corporate investment in these countries. The stock market is primarily a site to exchange risks rather than raise capital for investment. In developing countries, too, the new issues market is small or non-existent except in periods of a speculative boom, and bank lending post-liberalization privileges risky high-return investment rather than investment in the commodity-producing sectors like manufacturing and agriculture. The effects on those sectors of liberalization are indirect, as they are realized through the demand-generating effects of housing and personal finance booms, which in many circumstances also tend to increase the fragility of the system.

Another result of financial liberalization in imperfect markets is the strengthening of oligopolistic power through the association of financial intermediaries and non-financial corporations. Financial intermediaries that are a part of these conglomerates allocate credit in favour of companies belonging to the group; this is by no means a more efficient means of allocation than could have occurred under directed-credit policies of the Government.

Moreover, while financial liberalization does encourage new kinds of financial savings, total domestic savings typically do not increase in many cases, and expansion of available financial savings is often the result of and inflow of foreign capital. With deposits and loans of less than six months' duration dominating, liberalization does not necessarily result in intermediation of financial assets with long-term maturities either. And despite short booms in stock markets, there tends to be relatively little mobilization of new capital or capital for new ventures. In fact, small investors tend to withdraw from markets because of allegations of manipulation and fraud, and erstwhile areas of long-term investments supported by State intervention tend to disappear. Not surprisingly, investment performance does not usually reflect signs of improved volume or more efficient allocation either.

External financial liberalization, with associated capital inflows, only aggravates these consequences. Indeed, all the evidence on capital inflows and subsequent crises suggests that once an emerging market is "chosen" by financial markets as an attractive destination, processes are set in motion which are eventually likely to culminate in crisis. This works through the effects of a surge of capital inflows on exchange rates (unless the capital does not add to an increase in domestic investment but simply ends up adding to reserves).

An appreciating real exchange rate encourages investment in non-tradable sectors, the most obvious being real estate, and in domestic asset markets generally. At the same time, the upward movement of the currency discourages investment in tradables and therefore contributes to a process of relative decline in real economic sectors, and even deindustrialization in developing countries. Given the differential in interest rates between domestic and international markets and the lack of any prudence on the part of international lenders and investors, local agents borrow heavily abroad to directly or indirectly invest in the property and stock markets.

Thus, it was no accident that all of the emerging market economies experiencing substantial financial capital inflows also experienced property and real estate booms, as well as stock market booms, around the same time, even while the real economy may have been stagnating or even declining. These booms, in turn, generated the incomes to keep domestic demand and growth in certain sectors growing at relatively high rates. This soon resulted in signs of macroeconomic imbalance, not in the form of rising government fiscal deficits, but as a current-account deficit reflecting the consequences of debt-financed private profligacy.

However, once there is growing exposure in the form of a substantial presence of internationally mobile finance capital, any factor that spells an economic setback, however small or transient, can trigger an outflow of capital as well. And the current-account deficits that are necessarily associated with capital-account surpluses (unless there is large reserve accumulation) eventually create a pattern whereby the trend becomes perceived as an unsustainable one, in which any factor, even the most minor or apparently irrelevant one, can trigger a crisis of sudden outflows.

One very common conclusion that has been constantly repeated since the start of the Asian crisis in mid-1997 is the importance of "sound" macroeconomic policies once financial flows have been liberalized. It has been suggested that many emerging markets have faced problems because they allowed their current-account deficits to become too large, reflecting too great an excess of private domestic investment over private savings. This belated realization is a change from the earlier obsession with government fiscal deficits as the only macroeconomic imbalance worth caring about, but it still misses the basic point.

This point is that, with completely unbridled capital flows, it is no longer possible for a country to control the amount of capital inflow or outflow, and both movements can create consequences which are undesirable. If, for example, a country is suddenly chosen as a preferred site for foreign portfolio investment, it can lead to huge inflows which in turn cause the currency to appreciate, thus encouraging investment in non-tradables rather than tradables, and altering domestic relative prices and, therefore, incentives. Simultaneously, unless the inflows of capital are simply (and wastefully) stored up in the form of accumulated foreign-exchange reserves, they must necessarily be associated with current-account deficits.

Large current deficits are therefore necessary by-products of the surge in capital inflow, and that is the basic macroeconomic problem. This means that any country which does not exercise some sort of control or moderation over private capital inflows can be subject to very similar pressures. These then create the conditions for their own eventual reversal, when the current-account deficits are suddenly perceived to be too large or unsustainable. In other words, what all this means is that, once there are completely free capital flows and com-pletely open access to external borrowing by private domestic agents, there can be no "prudent" macroeconomic policy; the overall domestic balances or imbalances will change according to the behaviour of capital flows, which will themselves respond to the economic dynamics that they have set into motion.

This points to the futility of believing that capital-account convertibility accompanied by domestic prudential regulation will ensure against such boom-bust volatility in capital markets. With completely unbridled capital flows, it is no longer possible for a country to control the amount of capital inflow or outflow, and both movements can create consequences that are undesirable. Financial liberalization and the behaviour of fluid finance have therefore created a new problem which is analogous to the old "Dutch disease", with capital inflows causing an appreciation of the real exchange rate that causes changes in the real economy and therefore generates a process that is inherently unsustainable over time.

Deflation and Developmental Effects

The most forceful critique of financial liberalization relates not only to the enhanced possibility of crises, but to the argument that it has a clear bias towards deflationary macroeconomic policies and forces the State to adopt a deflationary stance to appease financial interests. (Patnaik, 2003) To begin with, the need to attract internationally mobile capital means that there are limits to the possibilities of enhancing taxation, especially on capital. Typically, prior or simultaneous trade liberalization has already reduced the indirect tax revenues of States undertaking financial liberalization, and so tax-GDP ratios often deteriorate in the wake of such liberalization. This then imposes limits on government spending, since finance capital is generally opposed to large fiscal deficits. This not only affects the possibilities for countercyclical macroeconomic stances of the State but also reduces the developmental or growth-oriented activities of the Government.

Financial interests are against deficit-financed spending by the State for a number of reasons. To start with, deficit financing is seen to increase the liquidity overhang in the system, and is therefore viewed as being potentially inflationary. Inflation is anathema to finance since it erodes the real value of financial assets. Second, since government spending is "autonomous" in character, the use of debt to finance such autonomous spending is seen as introducing into financial markets an arbitrary player not driven by the profit motive, whose activities can render interest rate differentials that determine financial profits more unpredictable. If deficit spending leads to a substantial build-up of the State's debt and interest burden, it is possible that the Government may intervene in financial markets to lower interest rates with implications for financial returns. Financial interests wanting to guard against that possibility tend to oppose deficit spending. Finally, since financial interests privilege the role of markets, the presence of the State as regulator and the interventionist activity of the State can be seen as de-legitimizing the role of finance, which is another reason why financial markets tend to prefer the reduction and control of government deficits.

These tendencies affect real investment in two ways. First, if speculative bubbles lead to financial crises, they squeeze liquidity and increase costs for current transactions and result in distress sales of assets and deflation that adversely impact on employment and living standards. Second, inasmuch as the maximum returns to productive investment in agriculture and manufacturing are limited, there is a limit to what borrowers would be willing to pay to finance such investment. Thus, despite the fact that social returns to agricultural and manufacturing investment are higher than those for stocks and real estate, and despite the contribution that such investment can make to growth and poverty alleviation, credit at the required rate may not be available.

This is why it is increasingly recognized that liberalization can dismantle the very financial structures that are crucial for economic growth. While the relationship between financial structure, financial growth and overall economic development is complex, the basic issue of financing for development is really a question of mobilizing or creating real resources. In the old development literature, finance in the sense of money or financial assets came into play only when looking at the ability of the State to tax away a part of the surplus to finance its development expenditures, and at the obstacles to deficit-financed spending, given the possible inflationary consequences if real constraints to growth were not overcome. By and large, the financial sector was seen as adjusting to the requirements of the real sector.

In the brave new world, however, when the financial sector is increasingly left unregulated or covered by a minimum of regulation, market signals determine the allocation of investible resources and therefore the demand for and the allocation of savings intermediated by financial enterprises. This can result in the problems conventionally associated with a situation where private rather than overall social returns determine the allocation of savings and investment. It aggravates the inherent tendency in markets to direct credit to non-priority and import-intensive but more profitable sectors, to concentrate investible funds in the hands of a few large players and to direct savings to already well-developed centres of economic activity.

The socially desirable role of financial intermediation therefore becomes muted. This certainly affects employment-intensive sectors such as agriculture and small-scale enterprises, where the transaction costs of lending tend to be high, the risks many and collateral not easy to ensure. The agrarian crisis in most parts of the developing world is at least partly, and often substantially, related to the decline in the access of peasant farmers to institutional finance, which is the direct result of financial liberalization. Measures which have reduced directed credit towards farmers and small producers have contributed to rising costs, greater difficulty of accessing necessary working capital for cultivation and other activities, and have reduced the economic viability of cultivation, thereby adding directly to rural distress. In India, for example, there is strong evidence that the deep crisis of the cultivating community, which has been associated with a proliferation of farmers' suicides and other evidence of distress such as mass migrations and even hunger deaths in different parts of rural India, has been related to the decline of institutional credit, which has forced farmers to turn to private moneylenders and involved them once more in interlinked transactions to their substantial detriment.

It also has a negative impact on any medium-term strategy for ensuring growth in particular sectors through directed credit, which had been the basis for the industrialization process through much of the twentieth century. In the past, in a large number of developing countries, the financial structure had been developed keeping in mind its developmental instrumentality. Financial structures were therefore created to deal with the difficulties associated with late industrial entry: capital requirements for entry in most areas were high, because technology for factory production had evolved in a capital-intensive direction from its primitive industrial revolution level; competition from established producers meant that firms had to concentrate on production for a protected domestic market or be supported with finance to survive long periods of low-capacity utilization during which they could find themselves a foothold in world markets.

Not surprisingly, therefore, most late industrializing countries created strongly regulated and even predominantly State-controlled financial markets aimed at mobilizing savings and using the intermediary function to influence the size and structure of investment. This they did through directed credit policies and differential interest rates, and the provision of investment support to the nascent industrial class in the form of equity, credit and low interest rates.

By dismantling these structures, financial liberalization destroys an important instrument that historically evolved in late industrializers to deal with the difficulties of ensuring growth through the diversification of production structures that international inequality generates. This implies that financial liberalization is likely to have depressing effects on growth through means other than just the deflationary bias it introduces into countries opting for such liberalization.

This is all the more significant because the process of financial liberalization across the globe has not generated greater net flows of capital into the developing world, as was expected by its proponents. Rather, for the past several years, the net outflows have been in the reverse direction. Even the emerging markets, which have been substantial recipients of capital inflows, have not experienced increases in aggregate investment rates as a consequence, but have built up their external reserves. This is only partly because of precautionary measures to guard against possible financial crises; it also indicates a macroeconomic situation of ex ante excess of savings over investment resulting from a deflationary macroeconomic stance. For example, East and South Asia together received US$186 billion of capital inflows in 2003, but added to their foreign-exchange reserves to the tune of US$245 billion in the same year!

The curious workings of international financial markets have contributed to international concentration, whereby developing countries (particularly those in Asia) hold their reserves in US Treasury bills and other safe securities, and thus contribute to the fact that the United States economy currently absorbs more than two thirds of the world's savings. At the same time, developing countries are losing in financial terms because of the costs of holding these reserves since, typically, the reserves are invested in very low-yielding "safe" assets while capital inflows include debt-creating flows at much higher rates of interest. This inverse and undesirable form of financial intermediation is, in fact, a direct result of the financial liberalization measures that have simultaneously created deflationary impulses and increased financial fragility across the developing world.

ALTERNATIVE STRATEGIES FOR DEVELOPING COUNTRY FINANCIAL SYSTEMS

It is evident from this discussion that complete financial liberalization—in the sense of implementing *all* of the various internal and external measures described here, is neither necessary nor desirable. In fact, such extreme measures have not been implemented by the more successful developing country industrializers. In fact, the examples of those countries that have successfully industrialized—from the nineteenth century onwards, and continuing to date—is instructive, because there are two features which are common to all of them: some degree (usually substantial) of directed credit; and some controls on cross-border capital flows.

The role played by directed credit in countries like Japan and the South Korea is well known, but it was in fact also a crucial element of the industrialization strategy in nineteenth-century Germany and in the early twentieth-century United States, among others.[4] Control over the allocation of bank credit continues to be one of the most significant ways in which the Chinese Government is able to control both the level and distribution of economic activity in the ongoing phase of rapid economic growth.

Similarly, capital controls of various sorts have been very important in allowing the economic space required for industrializing countries to influence domestic investment and reduce unintended volatility in markets. It is true that trade controls and the encouragement of a degree of import substitution has also been very necessary for late industrializers, and that too is something which is much more possible and likely when the capital account is also controlled.

The typical response to this among policy makers is that all this may be historically true, but the world has changed and such strategies are no longer possible because the forces of globalization and the new international regimes have dramatically restricted the scope for autonomous national policies. The most common argument today is that developing countries simply have no choice but to follow the path of greater external economic integration and financial liberalization.

However, this is not really true, as is evident even from the actual practices being followed in different parts of the developing world, which do not get adequate publicity. In particular, with respect to the capital account of the balance of payments, there is a wide range of possibilities and methods of regulation or direction of capital flows. There is already a large set of controls which have been used quite recently (and continue to be used in some countries) which provide good examples.[5] Capital controls of varying sorts have been used to effect in recent times by countries ranging from Chile and Colombia to Taiwan Province of China and Singapore.

There are the more obvious direct controls which regulate the actual volume of inflow or outflow in quantitative terms. These can relate to foreign direct investment (FDI) and to external borrowing by residents as well as to portfolio capital flows. In addition, these can be directed within the economy towards particular sectors or recipients through positive or negative lists. But there are also more indirect or market-based methods which have been increasingly used to regulate capital movements. Several countries have specified a minimum residence requirement (of one to three years) on portfolio capital inflows and also on FDI. Chile and Colombia had provided for a non-interest bearing reserve requirement (of between 33 per cent to as much as 48 per cent of the total inflow) to be held for one year with the central bank to ensure that the inflows were not of a speculative nature.

For portfolio capital, other specific measures are possible. In some countries, foreigners are prevented from purchasing domestic debt instruments and corporate equity. The extent of foreign portfolio investment (FPI) penetration in the domestic stock market can be regulated, with a limit on the proportion of stocks held by such foreign investors. Exit levies can be imposed that are inversely proportional to the length of the stay, meaning that capital which leaves the country sooner is subject to a higher tax. In any case, differential rates of taxation provide an important means of regulating capital flows and can be flexibly adjusted to suit different conditions and changing circumstances.

In the case of external commercial borrowing, some countries have imposed a tax on foreign loans. Others have provided fiscal incentives for domestic borrowing and investment. Domestic banking regulations can also play an important role in ensuring that private external debt does not reach undesirable proportions and in directing resources towards particular sectors.

The international financial press tends to portray such controls as rigid and as acting as disincentives to investment. But the reality is very different—experience shows that these controls can be, and have been, used flexibly and altered in response to changing circumstances. Furthermore, they have typically not acted as a disincentive to continued capital inflows of the desired variety; instead, they have ensured that such inflows actually contribute to increasing investment in socially effective ways. It is worth noting that China, which still retains the largest number and most comprehensive of controls over all forms of capital flow among all countries, has also been the largest recipient of capital inflows in the developing world.

Some capital control measures may be required not only to prevent crises and excessive changes in the exchange rate, which render the economy externally uncompetitive, but also to enable the continuation of domestic financial policies that promote sustainable industrialization. It should now be obvious that some role for directed credit is essential not only to ensure a sustained industrialization strategy but also in order to ensure that the goals of employment generation and social equity are met.

Similarly, controls over domestic financial activity and the regulatory role of the central bank need to be emphasized in order to prevent domestic financial crises and excessive cyclical volatility. Prudential controls of the kind promoted by the Bank for International Settlements are not the obvious solution, since they tend to be pro-cyclical in their effects, are too greatly determined by the context and requirements of developed countries and are insufficiently flexible for developing countries (Griffith-Jones and Ocampo, 2004).

So, there is a strong case for developing countries to ensure that their own financial systems are adequately regulated with respect to their own specific requirements, which may vary substantially, depending upon the size and nature of their economies, the extent of external integration, the relative importance of the banking system vis-à-vis the capital market, and so on. All this means that blindly following the Anglo-Saxon model of financial systems is neither necessary nor desirable; indeed, the more successful developing country industrializers have been those who have adopted much more unique and controlled financial regimes.

One pervasive myth that deserves to be shattered is that greater international trade exposure and trade dependence necessarily require greater financial integration and both internal and external financial liberalization. In fact, the most successful trading economies of the recent past have been those which have relatively more controlled financial systems. China is, of course, the best example, where a major export boom and rapid trade dependence have been associated with a financial system which allows the Government not only to systematically channel credit in desired areas, but also to use this as a major macroeconomic instrument for demand management and smoothing business cycles. The rapid expansion of Chinese enterprise does not appear to have been inhibited by such controlled credit, even in the period when mainland Chinese entrepreneurs could not directly access bank credit; neither has the growing integration of China with the world economy been hampered by the absence of any capital market worth the name. In fact, future economic historians may even find that such controlled credit was an important factor behind the rapid export-led industrialization drive.

Finally, it is worth considering the argument that more controlled financial systems encourage opacity, corruption and "crony capitalism", all of which are not only wasteful of resources but can lay the grounds for subsequent crises. This is the view of those who have, for example, blamed the East Asian financial crises of the late 1990s on such financial control-based "crony capitalism". It is, of course, no one's case that corruption is either desirable or even acceptable; however, it should nevertheless be noted that high levels of "corruption" and "crony capitalism" have had little effect on reducing the level of per capita income or retarding the rate of economic growth, as the experience of countries as far afield as Japan and the United States makes amply clear.

Further, the real solution for such problems is to encourage greater openness about the direction of finance and to increase public accountability of such financial transactions, rather than leave socially important decisions of resource allocation to the workings of private financial markets that are neither account-able nor transparent and that, in any case, are prone to various types of market failure. While corruption is an ever-present danger, it is so under all financial systems, the most deregulated and market-determined ones. Financial liberal-ization in the name of reducing corruption therefore does not reduce the possi-bility or likelihood of corruption, while it exposes the economy to myriad risks and reduces the capacity of the State to promote autonomous and sustainable development.

Clearly, therefore, if the development project is to continue at all in large parts of the world where it remains essentially partial and incomplete, some government control over the financial sector remains essential. This, in turn, means that strategies that are only concerned with the "sequencing" of liberal-ization measures are asking the wrong question. The real question should be: Which financial controls should be maintained, restored or introduced in order to ensure a viable, stable and socially desired pattern of development?

NOTES

[1] The arguments in this chapter have been deeply influenced by continuous discussions and collaborations with C.P. Chandrasekhar, Prabhat Patnaik and Abhijit Sen. I am also grateful to Jomo K.S. and the participants in the United Nations Department of Economic and Social Affairs (UN/DESA) Development Forum on 'Integrating Economic and Social Policies to Achieve the United Nations Development Agenda', held at United Nations, New York, on 14–15 March 2005 for their useful insights.

[2] The implications of these theoretical points have been usefully summarized in Stiglitz (1993).

[3] See, for example, Prasad and others (2003), Feldstein (ed.) (2003).

[4] Summary accounts of these experiences are provided in Reinert (ed.) (2004) and Chang (2002).

[5] Epstein, Grabel and Jomo (2004) outline various strategies already used by different developing countries.

REFERENCES

Akyuz, Yilmaz (2002). *Reforming the Global Financial Architecture: Issues and Proposals.* Zed Books, London.

Chandrasekhar, C.P. (2004). Financial liberalization and the macroeconomics of poverty reduction. Draft Thematic Summary on Financial Liberalization for the Asia-Pacific Programme on the Macroeconomics of Poverty Reduction, May.

Chang, Ha-Joon (2002). *Kicking Away the Ladder.* Anthem Press, London.

Feldstein, Martin (ed.) (2003). *Economic and Financial Crises in Emerging Market Economies.* University of Chicago Press, Chicago.

Ghosh, Jayati, and C.P. Chandrasekhar (eds) (2003). *Work and Well-being in the Age of Finance.* Tulika, New Delhi.

Griffith-Jones, Stephany, and Jose-Antonio Ocampo (eds) (2000). *Reforming the International Financial System.* FONDAD, The Hague.

Epstein, Gerald, Ilene Grabel and Jomo, K.S. (2004). Capital management techniques in developing countries: an assessment of experiences from the 1990s and lessons from the future. G-24 Discussion Paper No. 27, United Nations Conference for Trade and Development (UNCTAD/GDS/MDPB/G24/2004/3), Geneva.

Kregel, Jan (2004). External financing for development and international financial instability. G-24 Discussion Paper No. 32, United Nations Conference for Trade and Development (UNCTAD/GDS/MDPB/G24/2004/8), Geneva.

Reinert, Erik (ed.) (2004). *Globalisation, Economic Development and Inequality: An Alternate Perspective.* Edward Elgar, Cheltenham.

Patnaik, Prabhat (2003). The humbug of finance. In *The Retreat to Unfreedom.* Tulika, New Delhi.

Prasad, Eswar, Kenneth Rogoff, Shang-jin Wie and Ayhan Kose (2003). Effects of financial globalisation on developing countries: Some empirical evidence. IMF Occasional Paper No. 220, International Monetary Fund, Washington DC.

Stiglitz, J.E. (1993). The role of the state in financial markets. In *Proceedings of the World Bank Annual Conference on Development Economics.* World Bank, Washington, DC.

Taylor, Lance, and John Eatwell (eds) (2002). *International Capital Markets: Systems in Transition.* Oxford University Press, New York.

8

Development and Social Goals: Balancing Aid and Development to Prevent 'Welfare Colonialism'

ERIK S. REINERT

> "...just as we may avoid widespread physical desolation by rightly turning a stream near its source, so a timely dialectic in the fundamental ideas of social philosophy may spare us untold social wreckage and suffering."
> Herbert S. Foxwell, Cambridge economist, 1899.

The Millennium Development Goals (MDGs) are noble goals for a world sorely in need of urgent action to solve pressing social problems. They rest, however, upon completely new principles whose long-term effects are neither well thought through nor well understood. In this chapter, I shall attempt to explain why the MDGs do not represent good social policy in the long run.

One novelty of the MDG approach lies in the emphasis on foreign financing of domestic social and redistribution policies rather than on domestic financing by the developing countries themselves. Disaster relief, which used to be of a temporary nature, now finds a more permanent form in the MDGs. In countries where more than 50 per cent of the government budget is financed by foreign aid, huge additional resource transfers are being planned. This raises the question of the extent to which this approach will put a large number of nations permanently 'on the dole', a system similar to 'welfare colonialism', which will be discussed at the end of the chapter.

The pursuit of the MDGs may appear as if the United Nations institutions have abandoned the effort to treat the causes of poverty and have instead concentrated on attacking its symptoms. In this chapter, I shall argue that palliative economics has, to a considerable extent, taken the place of development economics. Indeed, the balance between development economics (radically changing the productive structures of poor countries) and palliative economics (easing the pains of economic misery) is key to avoiding long-term negative effects.

How We Used to Deal with Problems of Development

In less than one generation, a stark contrast has emerged between the type of economic understanding underlying the Marshall Plan, on the one hand, and the type of economic theory behind today's multilateral development discourse and the Washington institutions, on the other. The Marshall Plan grew out of recognition of the flaws of its precursor, the Morgenthau Plan. While the goal of the Morgenthau Plan was to deindustrialize Germany, the goal of the Marshall Plan was not only to reindustrialize Germany but also to establish a *cordon sanitaire* of wealthy nations along the borders of the communist bloc in Europe and Asia, from Norway to Japan. The self-enforcing mechanisms that maintain the vicious circles of a Morgenthau Plan are outlined in Figure 8.1 while the virtuous circles of a Marshall Plan are outlined in Figure 8.2.

Judging from the number of nations lifted out of poverty, this reindustrialization plan was probably the most successful development project in human history. The fundamental insight behind the Marshall Plan was that the economic activities in the countryside were qualitatively different from those in the cities. In his famous June 1947 speech at Harvard, United States Secretary of State George Marshall (later awarded the Nobel Peace Prize) stressed that "the farmer has always produced the foodstuffs to exchange with the city dweller for the other necessities of life". This division of labour, i.e., between activities with increasing returns in the cities and activities with diminishing returns in the countryside, was "at the present time…threatened with breakdown. This division of labour is the basis of modern civilization." In this way, he recognized the relevance of the cameralist and mercantilist economic policies of previous centuries.

Economists and statesmen from Antonio Serra and Alexander Hamilton to Abraham Lincoln and Friedrich List would certainly have agreed that civilization requires activities generating increasing returns. The principles behind the 'toolbox' used by nations going from poverty to wealth, through the creation of 'city activities' (Appendix 8.1), have been surprisingly consistent. Yet, many of today's problems are due to the conditionalities imposed by the Washington institutions that outlaw the use of the policy measures contained in this toolbox.

After World War II, these general principles did not produce the same success in every country. Some of the most successful countries (e.g., the Republic of Korea (South Korea)) temporarily protected new technologies for the world market, while some of the least successful ones permanently protected mature technologies, often for small home markets, by limiting competition (e.g., the small countries of Latin America). Appendix 8.2 classifies 'good' and 'bad' protectionist practices. In many countries, however, real wages were considerably

FIGURE 8.1

The mechanisms of a Morgenthau Plan: the 'vicious circle' of economic underdevelopment

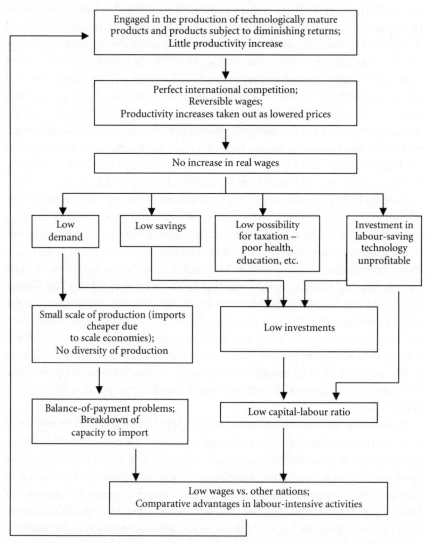

Note: It is futile to attack the system at any one point, e.g., by increasing investment when wages are still low and demand is absent. An instance of this is poor capital utilization and excess capacity in Latin American least developed countries.

Source: Reinert (1980: 41).

FIGURE 8.2
The systemic effects of a Marshall Plan: the 'virtuous circle' of economic development

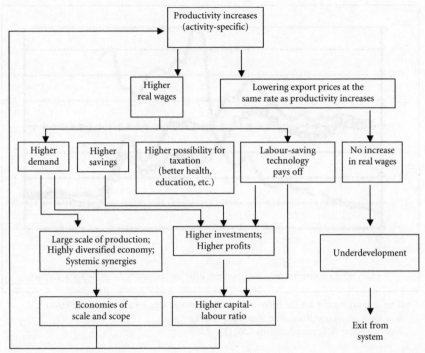

Note: In a closed system, with a constant employment rate, the only way that GNP per capita can grow is through the "virtuous circle". However, the system can be cut off at any one point, e.g., if higher demand goes to foreign goods alone, the circle will break.

Source: Reinert (1980: 39).

FIGURE 8.3
Peru: diverging trends of real wages and exports, 1960–1990

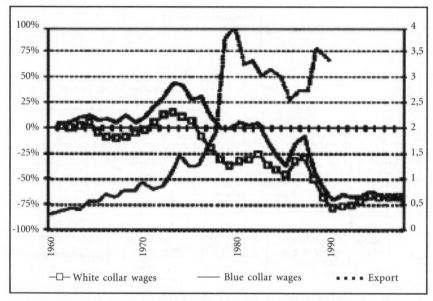

Note: Export figures are in current US dollars, thus exaggerating the visual effect.
Sources: Real wages: Roca and Simabuco (2004).
Exports: Webb & Fernández Baca (2001).

higher when this inefficient industrial sector was in place than they are today with a much weakened industrial sector (see, for example, Figure 8.3). For centuries it was understood that having an 'inefficient' industrial sector produced higher real wages than having no industrial sector at all, and that this 'inefficient' sector ought to be made more efficient rather than be closed down. Figure 8.3 suggests that we may have established a world economic order that maximizes international trade rather than international welfare.

In its simplest form, this argument is born out of the role of increasing and diminishing returns in trade theory as the starting points for virtuous and vicious circles of growth or poverty. A praxis ignoring these mechanisms may cause factor price polarization rather than factor price equalization. Serra (1613) first established increasing returns, virtuous circles and large economic diversity as necessary elements for wealth creation. This principle was used almost continuously—with brief interruptions—until it was abandoned with the emergence of the 'Washington Consensus'. Since the 1980s, 'structural adjustment' has de-industrialized many poor peripheral countries and produced falling real wages.[1] Mainstream theory has long claimed that deindustrialization does not matter. On the contrary, according to the first World Trade Organization (WTO) Director-General, Renato Ruggiero, free trade would unleash "the borderless economy's potential to equalize relations between countries and regions".

In the 1930s, maintaining the gold standard and balancing the budget were viewed as economic fundamentals which locked the world into a sub-optimal equilibrium and prevented Keynes' policies from being carried out. Similarly, having free trade as the ideological centrepiece of development policies since the debt crises of the 1980s, has locked the less industrialized countries into a suboptimal equilibrium.

Rather than continuing policies based on the most simplistic version of mainstream trade theory, the conflict between free trade and real wages in non-industrialized countries must be considered seriously. Specialization in activities with diminishing returns in the face of increasing population pressures also has serious environmental consequences (Reinert, 1996).

Poverty in many Third World and former Second World countries is not caused by transitory problems but rather by the permanent features of nations that have different economic structures. Historically, few nations had the ambition to compete with the world industrial leaders of the day. But they understood that compared to being a supplier of raw materials, the nation could massively improve its welfare by industrializing, even if the industrial structure created would end up being less efficient than that of the world leader. The logic is like that of an individual who, instead of being London's most efficient shoeshine boy, raises his income by choosing to become a mediocre lawyer.[2] Thus, when United States started industrializing, its leaders merely wanted to create a (less efficient) version of the production structure in England, a process which required tariffs. Successful industrialization under protection, however, carries the seeds of its own destruction. By the 1880s, United States economists—invoking the same arguments based on scale and technology that were used to protect industries in the United States in the 1820s—argued for free trade. The same tariff that created a manufacturing industry for a period of time was now hurting the same industry (Schoenhof, 1883). This is why Friedrich List, a prominent protectionist, was in favour of global free trade only after all countries had achieved their comparative advantage outside the diminishing returns sector (Reinert, 1998). In other words, he disagreed not over the principle of free trade as such, but rather over its timing.

If one reads Adam Smith, an icon of free trade and laissez-faire, on economic development at an early stage, one finds his views are very much in line with those of classical development economists who advocate industrialization. In his earlier work, *The Theory of Moral Sentiments* (Smith, 1759/1812), Smith argued for 'the great system of government', which is helped by adding new manufactures. Interestingly, he argued that new manufactures are not to be promoted to help suppliers or consumers but in order to improve the 'great system of government'.

It is also possible to argue that Adam Smith was a misunderstood mercantilist, who strongly supported the mercantilist policies of the past, but argued that they were no longer necessary for England. He praised the Navigation Acts protecting English manufacturing and shipping against Holland, arguing "they are as wise…as if they had all been dictated by the most deliberate wisdom" and holding them to be "perhaps, the wisest of all the commercial regulations of England" (Smith, 1776/1976: I, 486–487). All in all, Smith described a development that had become self-sustaining—a kind of snowball effect—originating in the protectionist measures of the past. Only once did Smith use the term 'invisible hand' in *The Wealth of Nations*—when it sustained the key import substitution goal of mercantilist policies, and the consumer preferred domestic to foreign industry (Smith, 1776/1976: 477). This was only possible when 'the market' took over the role previously played by protective measures, and national manufacturing no longer needed such protection.

The praxis of economic development has been to assimilate and produce less efficient 'copies' of the economic structure of wealthy nations. The key features of the economic structure of wealthy nations—a large division of labour (with a large number of different industries and professions) and a sector with increasing returns (industry and knowledge-intensive services)—were codified by economists such as Antonio Serra (1613), James Steuart (1767), Alexander Hamilton (1791) and Friedrich List (1841/1909). These principles are, at times, unlearned—as in France in the 1760s, Europe in the 1840s and the world in the 1990s.

These periods ultimately came to an end because of their great social costs, however. Physiocracy in France created shortages and scarcity of bread, contributing to the onset of the French revolution (see, for example, Kaplan, 1976). The free trade euphoria of the 1840s met its backlash in 1848, with revolutions in all large European countries except England and Russia. David Ricardo's trade theory has been proven wrong every time it is applied asymmetrically to increasing and diminishing return industries.[3] He is right, however, in saying that the 'natural' wage level is subsistence. The trade liberalization euphoria of the 1990s has increased poverty in several peripheral countries, but our response to this has also been wrong. We have been focusing too much on the symptoms—rather than the causes—of the problem.

THE PRESENT SITUATION

Standard economics tends to see development as a process largely driven by *accumulation* of investments in physical and human capital.[4] Standard economic theory underlying today's development policies is generally unable to recognize qualitative differences between economic activities. Almost none of today's failed or failing states could pass George Marshall's test for what brings about modern civilization, as they have very weak manufacturing sectors and are unable to generate the virtuous exchange between city and rural activities. They also have very little diversity in their economic base, a limited division of labour and specialize in activities subject to diminishing returns.

Historically, modern democracy began in nations where this civilizing trade between urban and rural areas had already been established, e.g., in the Italian city states. In the most successful city states—including states with a scarcity of arable land, such as Venice and the Dutch Republic—power did not lie with the landowning class. In Florence, 40 or so landowning families were banned from political life in the thirteenth century, thus enabling Schumpeterian 'cronyism' where political and economic interests 'colluded' in ways that created widespread wealth. Dependency on raw materials encouraged feudalism and colonialism, neither of which leads to political freedom. Similarly, the United States Civil War was essentially between the South, where landowners had vested interests in agriculture and cheap labour, and the North, which had with vested interests in industrialization. The history of Latin America has been, in many ways, similar to the history of the United States, except that the outcome was analogous to the South's winning the Civil War.

In the alternative economic paradigm—which could broadly be called evolutionary and historical—the process of development is driven by *assimilation*: learning from more advanced countries by 'copying' both their economic structure and their institutions.[5] Key elements in this assimilation strategy are institutions such as patent protection, scientific academies and universities. In this model, economic growth tends to be activity-specific, tied to 'clusters' of economic activities characterized by increasing returns, dynamic imperfect competition and rapid technological progress. In addition to capital, the process requires transferring and mastering skills and, above all, creating a viable market for activities with increasing returns where the absence of purchasing power and massive unemployment tend to go hand in hand. By generally using models assuming full employment, the Washington institutions avoid a key issue that locks nations in poverty—the lack of formal employment. Since sixteenth-century Holland and Venice, only nations with healthy manufacturing sectors have achieved anything close to full employment without massive rural under-employment.

The dominant economic theory today represents what Schumpeter called "the pedestrian view that it is capital *per se* that propels the capitalist engine": development is seen as largely driven by the accumulation of capital, physical or human. According to Richard Nelson, "The premise of neoclassical theory is that, if the investments are made, the acquisition and mastery of new ways of doing things is relatively easy, even automatic". More importantly, a core assumption of standard economics that is seldom acknowledged is that economic structure is irrelevant, as capital *per se* will lead to economic development, regardless of the economic structure within which investment is made. The alternative theory suggests that economic activities have very different windows of opportunity as carriers of economic growth. In other words, we have to rid ourselves of what James Buchanan calls 'the equality assumption' in economic theory, which is probably its most important, but least discussed premise.[6] The ability, at any time, to absorb innovation and knowledge—and consequently to attract investments—varies enormously from one economic activity to another.

The Problem

Viewing capital *per se* as the key to growth, loans are given to poor nations with productive/industrial structures that are unable to absorb such capital profitably. Interest payments often exceed the rate of return on investments made. 'Financing for development' may therefore take on the characteristics of a pyramid scheme, the only ones to gain being those who started the scheme and who are close to the door (see Kregel, 2004). Similarly, investments in human capital, made without corresponding changes in the productive structure to create demand for the skills acquired, will tend to promote emigration. In both cases, Gunnar Myrdal's 'perverse backwashes' of economic development will be the result: more capital—both monetary and human—will flow from the poor to the rich countries. One explanation for this lies in the type of economic structure—locked into a vicious circle with a lack of supply and demand and an absence of increasing returns—that characterizes poor nations. United States industrial policy from 1820 to 1900 is probably the best example for Third World countries to follow today until these nations are ready to benefit from international trade.

Recommendation

As with the Marshall Plan, funds must be matched by the establishment of industrial and service sectors that can absorb the physical and human investments. Diversification from raw material production is necessary to create a basis for democratic stability and increased welfare, even if the new sectors are initially unable to survive world market competition. This incipient industrialization will need special treatment of the kind afforded by the Marshall Plan and will require interpreting the Bretton Woods agreement in the same manner as in the immediate post-World War II era.

The neoclassical economists' poor understanding of how businesses operate also contributes to the problem. At the core of their economic theory of capitalism is perfect competition and equilibrium, a state which produces very little profit. Any successful and profitable business enterprise rests, almost by definition, on some kind of rent-seeking. The poverty-stricken Third World probably most closely corresponds to conditions of diminishing returns and perfect competition, while the rich countries, whose exports are produced under conditions of Schumpeterian-dynamic imperfect competition, are 'rent seekers', whose rents lead to higher wages and a higher tax base. This failure to understand development as Schumpeterian imperfect competition is at the heart of the arguments against industrial policy. Anything that causes imperfect competition tends to be seen as contributing to corruption and 'cronyism'.

Keynes saw investments as resulting from what he called 'animal spirits'. Without 'animal spirits'—the will to invest in uncertain conditions—capital is sterile, in the worlds of both Joseph Schumpeter and Karl Marx. The motivating force behind 'animal spirits' is the desire to maximize profits, thus upsetting the equilibrium of perfect competition. From a businessman's point of view, poor countries often suffer from low investments because of a lack of profitable investment opportunities, largely due to low purchasing power and high unemployment. Subsistence farmers are not profitable customers for most producers of goods and services. Tariffs can create incentives to move production to the labour markets of the poor. Historically, this has been seen as a conscious trade-off between the interests of 'man-as-a-wage-earner' and 'man-as-a-producer'. The idea that industrialization would rapidly increase employment and wages—which would more than offset the temporarily higher cost of manufactured goods—was at the core of Prebisch's import-substitution industrialization, as well as of United States economic theory around 1820 (see, for example, Raymond, 1820).

The idea that greater 'openness' would improve the lot of the poor countries is both counter-intuitive and contrary to historical experience. In many cases, the sudden 'opening' of a backward economy killed off the little manufacturing activity that existed, thus exacerbating the situation (see Reinert, 2003; 2004b). From the unification of Italy in the nineteenth century to the integration of Mongolia and Peru in the 1990s, historical experience shows that free trade between nations of very different levels of development tends to destroy the most efficient industries in the least efficient countries (the Vanek-Reinert effect). Figure 8.3 shows how the export increases that followed the opening up of the Peruvian economy were accompanied by falling real wages. In Peru, as in many other Latin American countries, real wages peaked during the period of 'inefficient' import substitution. The ports, airports, roads, power stations, schools, hospitals and service industries created by this inefficient industrial sector led by rent-seekers were *real* and could not have been created without the demand for labour and infrastructure that this sector generated.[7]

The timing of opening an economy is also crucial. Opening up an economy too late can seriously hamper growth, while opening up an economy too early will result in deindustrialization, falling wages[8] and increasing social problems. An anonymous traveller, who observed the effects of economic policy in different European countries in 1786, reached this conclusion: "Tariffs are as harmful to a country after the arts [manufacturing industry] have been established there, as they are useful to it in order to introduce them" (Anonymous, 1786: 31).

Southern Mexico experienced this destructive sequence of de-industrialization, de-agriculturalization[9] and depopulation. That large numbers of subsistence farmers should be made 'uncompetitive' by subsidized First World agriculture is a relatively new, but alarming, trend that may persist even after the subsidies are removed. In India, there are around 650 million farmers, a large proportion of whom will be as 'uncompetitive' as their Mexican colleagues if and when free trade opens up. In the poorest countries today, a trade-off exists between maximizing international trade—which is what present policies achieve—and maximizing human welfare (see Figure 8.3). This trade-off needs to be addressed in a manner different than that of merely compensating the losses of the poor countries through increased aid.

History has shown that the vicious circles of poverty and underdevelopment can be effectively attacked by changing the productive structure of poor and failing states. This entails increasing diversification away from sectors with diminishing returns (traditional raw materials and agriculture) to sectors with increasing returns (technology intensive manufacturing and services), in the process creating a complex division of labour and new social structures. In addition to breaking away from subsistence agriculture, this will create an urban market for goods, which will induce specialization and innovation, bring in new technologies and create alternative employment as well as the economic synergies that unite a nation-state. The key to coherent development is an interplay between sectors with increasing and diminishing returns in the same labour market.

Malthusian vs. Schumpeterian Cronyism

2005: A Filipino sugar producer uses his political influence to get import protection for his products.

2000: Mayor Daley of Chicago (ignoring the advice of University of Chicago economists) provides subsidies to already wealthy high-tech investors through an incubator programme.

1950s and 1960s: Swedish industrialist Marcus Wallenberg uses his close contacts with Labour Party Minister of Finance, Gunnar Sträng, to win political support to carry out his plans for the Swedish companies Volvo and Electrolux.

1877: Steel producers in the United States use their political clout to impose 100 per cent duty on steel rails (Taussig, 1897: 222).

1485: Woolworkers use their connections to King Henry VII to influence the state to give them subsidies and to impose an export duty on raw wool so as to increase raw material prices for their competitors on the Continent, thus slowly killing the wool industry elsewhere, e.g., in Florence.

The above examples all involve crony capitalism and rent-seeking behaviour that mainstream economic theory tends to abhor. A crucial difference separates the first example from the rest, however. The Filipino crony differs from the other cronies in that he gets subsidies for a raw material with diminishing returns that competes in a world market facing perfect competition. In other words, he is a Malthusian crony, leading his country down the path of diminishing returns (in spite of technological change which counteracts this). The others are Schumpeterian cronies, producing under what Schumpeter called historical increasing returns (a combination of both increasing returns and fast technological change). If we couple this with trade theory, we see that the tilted playing fields of Schumpeterian cronyism produce vastly different results than those of the Malthusian crony.

Keynes once said, "the worse the situation, the less laissez-faire works". If we insist on abandoning industrial policy because moving away from perfect competition will cause some cronies to get rich, we have totally misunderstood the nature of capitalism. After all, capitalism *is* about getting away from perfect competition.

Economic development is caused by structural changes which break the equilibrium, creating rents. Insisting on the absence of rents is insisting on a steady and stationary state. There is still a need to choose which activities to protect, however, which in turn creates cronies. Abraham Lincoln protected the steel cronies—by paying a little more for steel,[10] the United States created a huge steel industry with many high-paying jobs that also provided a base for government taxation. Economic development is about aligning the public interests of the nation with the private vested interests of the capitalists. The failure of standard economics to understand the dynamics of the business world will lead to a failure to understand the economic essence of colonialism. By preventing colonies from having their own manufacturing industries, economic activities with high growth potential and mechanization remained in the mother country, whereas activities with diminishing returns went to the colonies.

The immense transfers that accompany the MDG process will necessarily also lead to cronyism. Through this initiative, some will get wealthy, since crony-free economics only exists in neoclassical models. By opting for Schumpeterian cronyism, instead of aid-based cronyism, it will be possible for poor countries to extricate themselves from economic dependency.

We seem to have unlearned the logic behind policy tools for economic development. Patents and modern tariffs were created at about the same time, in the late 1400s. These rent-seeking institutions were created using the very same understanding of the process of economic development in order to protect knowledge (in the case of patents) and to produce in new geographic areas (in the case of tariffs). Both patents and tariffs represent legalized rent-seeking to promote goals not achievable under perfect competition.

Why are the rent-seeking and cronyism arguments not applied to patents, but only used against tariffs and other policy instruments used in poor countries? With some justification, it can be said that the wealthy countries are establishing rules that legalize constructive rent-seeking in their own countries but prohibit similar ones in the poor countries.

THE WASHINGTON CONSENSUS AND SEQUENTIAL SINGLE-ISSUE MANAGEMENT

Following the fall of the Berlin Wall, variations of neoclassical economics became the only game in town. Neoclassical economics was, however, in

Nicholas Kaldor's term, an *untested theory*. Although neoclassical theory had provided an effective ideological shield during the Cold War, no nation had ever been built on this theoretical framework. In its most extreme form, as practised around 1990, if nations 'got their prices right', economic growth would follow automatically, regardless of economic structures. By 1990, policy recommmendations were formulated around Samuelson's 'law' of factor price equalization and neglected other important theoretical contributions, including key insights by the founding father of neoclassical economics, Alfred Marshall. Marshall had not only described taxes on activities with diminishing returns in order to subsidize activities with increasing returns as being good development policy, but he had also emphasized the importance of a nation's producing in sectors where most technical progress was to be found, as well as the role of synergies (industrial districts).

In the 1990s, as the world economy failed to deliver results following trade liberalization, the search began for other explanations based on the premises of neoclassical economics. The search for a factor which would ensure factor price equalization with free trade resulted in various policy fads:

- 'getting prices right';
- 'getting property rights right';
- 'getting institutions right';
- 'getting governance right';
- 'getting competitiveness right';
- 'getting national innovation systems right';
- 'getting entrepreneurship right'.

This vision of "the borderless economy's potential to equalize relations between countries and regions" was based on erroneous theory, and instead became a nightmare in many poor countries. As economic growth is an uneven process by nature, only wise political intervention can even out factor price polarizations. Attributing poverty to a lack of entrepreneurship comes across as being particularly uninformed. In contrast to most people in wealthy countries who can make a living on their largely routine jobs, the poor of the world have to use their entrepreneurial talents every day in order to secure sustenance.

This sequence of policy fads failed to address several fundamental blind spots in neoclassical economics:

a) Its inability to register qualitative differences, including the different potentials of economic activities as contributors to economic growth;

b) Its inability to acknowledge synergies and linkages;[11] and
c) Its inability to cope with innovations and novelties, and how these are differently distributed among economic activities.

Together, these blind spots of contemporary mainstream economics prevent many poor countries from developing. China and India—probably today's most successful developing countries—have, for decades, followed the recommendations of the Marshall Plan, rather than the Washington Consensus.

While learning is a key element in development, it may also be passed on in the economy simply as falling prices to foreign consumers. The key insight by Schumpeter's student Hans Singer was that learning and technological change in the production of raw materials, particularly in the absence of a manufacturing sector, tend to lower export prices, rather than increase the standard of living in the raw material producing nation (Singer, 1950). Learning tends to create wealth for producers only when they are part of a close network, once called 'industrialism'—a dynamic system of economic activities subject to increasing productivity through technical change and a complex division of labour. The absence of increasing returns, dynamic imperfect competition and synergies in raw material-producing countries are all part of the mechanisms that perpetuate poverty.

Since the 1990s, huge resources have been increasingly employed by well-intentioned governments along the largely sterile 'mainstream' path of inquiry, without exploring alternative theoretical approaches. The best social policy, however, is to create development, but not by the rich creating subsidized reservations where the poor are kept, largely underemployed and 'underproductive'. The Indian reservations in North America are a sad example of policies that subsidize without changing productive structures. Similarly, the MDGs are far too biased towards palliative economics rather than structural change, i.e., towards treating the symptoms of poverty rather than its causes. While such policies may be needed under current critical conditions, they will remain poor social policies in the longer term unless the deeper roots of the problem are confronted.

Although malaria was endemic to Europe for centuries, present not only in the South but also in the Alpine valleys and all the way to the Kola peninsula in north-western Russia, it rid itself of the disease through industrialization and development. Advanced and intensive agriculture, irrigation systems, huge public health efforts and eradication plans enabled Europe to eradicate malaria. Europe's development over time also enabled European states to honour their debts.

Instead of embarking on a similar economic development model, Africa continues to preserve colonial economic structures, exporting raw materials and maintaining underdeveloped industrial sectors. Debt cancellation and free mosquito nets merely address the symptoms of these problems.

CREATING 'WELFARE COLONIALISM'

Current policies risk inadvertently undermining the development potential of aid with its palliative effects. What we may be creating is a system that could be described as 'welfare colonialism', a term coined to describe the economic integration of the native population in Northern Canada (Paine, 1977). The essential features of welfare colonialism are:

1) A reversal of the colonial drain of the old days, the net flow of funds going to the colony rather than to the mother country;
2) Integration of the native population in ways that radically undermine their previous livelihoods; and
3) The placing of the native population on unemployment benefits.

In Paine's view, welfare colonialism identifies welfare as the vehicle for stable 'governing at a distance' through exercise of a particularly subtle, 'non-demonstrative' and dependency-generating form of neocolonial social control that pre-empts local autonomy through 'well-intentioned' and 'generous', but ultimately 'morally wrong', policies. Welfare colonialism creates paralyzing dependencies on the 'centre' in a peripheral population, a centre exerting control through incentives that create total economic dependency, thereby preventing political mobilization and autonomy. The social conditions in which the native inhabitants of North American reservations find themselves today show us that, in their case, the final effect of massive transfer payments has been to create a dystopia, rather than a utopia.

The recent discussion on whether or not aid to Ethiopia should be cut as a sanction against the Ethiopian government illustrates the kind of dilemmas which will necessarily accompany 'welfare colonialism'. The rich countries will always be in the position to cut off aid, food and livelihood sources of poor countries if they disapprove of their national policies. As long as 'development aid' remains palliative, rather than developmental, seemingly generous and well-intentioned development aid will inevitably become powerful mechanisms by which rich countries will seek to control poor countries. Rather than promoting global democracy, such policies will lead towards global plutocracy.

We already see aid and other transfers creating passivity and disincentives to work in poor nations. Haitian observers point to family transfer payments from the United States, which create disincentives to work for a going rate of US$0.30 an hour in Haiti. A Brazilian research project on the highly laudable Zero Hunger Project, carried out at different government levels (national, state and local) for various programmes targeted to fight hunger, concludes that these projects are, to a large extent, ineffective since they treat the symptoms of poverty by distributing food or subsidizing food prices rather than by creating situations where the poor can become breadwinners (Lavinas and Garcia, 2004). These are welfare colonialism effects that result from treating the symptoms, rather than addressing the causes of poverty.

The idea of nations producing under increasing returns (industrialized nations) paying annual compensation to nations producing under constant or diminishing returns (raw material producers) is not a new one. It is a logical conclusion of standard trade theory and has been present in United States college textbooks from the 1970s.[12] Until recently, the favoured option was to industrialize the poor countries, even if it meant that their industries would not be competitive in the world market for a considerable period of time. Making free trade the linchpin of the world economic system—one to which all other considerations must yield—has made welfare colonialism appear as the only option. The alternative option of developing the poor world is presently absent because many do not wish to abolish free trade as the core of the world economic order. The long-term and cumulative effects of having this group of nations specialize in pre-industrial economic structures will be staggering, however.

In 1947, political pressure due to the spectre of communism resulted in successful development practices. The free traders in Washington had to yield to the political need for protectionist development policies encircling the communist bloc, which led to the astonishing success of the Marshall Plan in Europe and the East Asian miracle. It is perhaps a faint hope that today's terrorist threat will yield a similar situation where free trade is temporarily abandoned in order to promote development as a *political*, rather than a *social*, goal.

During the Enlightenment, civilization and democracy were understood to be products of a specific type of economic structure. The origins of this understanding can be found more than 100 years earlier; according to Francis Bacon (1620), "There is a startling difference between the life of men in the most civilized province of Europe, and in the wildest and most barbarous districts of New India. This difference comes not from the soil, not from climate, not from race, but *from the arts*". When German economist Johan Jacob Meyen stated in 1770, "It is known that a primitive people does not improve their customs and institutions, later to find useful industries, but the other way around", he expressed something which was considered common sense at the time. Nineteenth-century thinkers, from Abraham Lincoln to Karl Marx, shared the idea that civilization is created by industrialization. As Marx put it, industrialization "draws all, even the most barbarian, nations into civilization".

We ought to use our understanding of policies that have been successful in the past to solve today's challenges, while remaining firmly grounded in an understanding of the present technological and historical context. The connection between production and civilization must be understood, and the theoretical focus should shift from trade to production. Different technological developments affect different economic activities, creating huge variations in the windows of opportunity to innovate. Hence, core issues—like economies of scale, specialization, lock-in effects, the effects of diminishing returns, the *assimilation of knowledge,* and the economic structures of poor countries—should not be ignored. We should read not only Schumpeter on technical change and 'creative destruction', but also open our eyes and minds to the type of 'destructive destruction' that can be observed in the peripheral countries of the world.

EUROPE'S PRESENT PROBLEMS REFLECT THE PROBLEMS OF GLOBALIZATION

As mentioned earlier, our present failure to understand why so many countries stay poor is intimately tied to a number of blind spots that make it extremely difficult, if not impossible, to create a theory of uneven economic development. As Lionel Robbins warned us more than 50 years ago, the basic features of the neoclassical paradigm produces a *Harmonielehre*, where economic harmony is already built into the assumptions on which the theory rests. Today, this paradigm hinders, rather than helps, our understanding of the reasons behind poverty. As Thomas Kuhn (1962: 37) said, "A paradigm can, for that matter, even insulate the community from those socially important problems that are not reducible to the puzzle form, because they cannot be stated in terms of the conceptual and instrumental tools the paradigm supplies".

Any long-term solution for Africa and other poor regions will have to rest on a theory of uneven development. This theory, which allowed for successful economic policy for 500 years—from Henry VII's England in 1485 to the integration of Spain and Portugal into the European Union (EU) in 1986—is now virtually extinct. Although a complete outline of this theory and its accompanying policy measures lie beyond the scope of this chapter, some core elements can be mentioned here.

The present approach towards the poor is very much tilted in favour of *palliative economics* to ease the pains of poverty rather than to permanently eradicate it through economic development. In addition, the current approach makes it possible to continue and even extend (as in the World Trade Organization (WTO) negotiations) present practices without investigating the problems with globalization in the periphery. The same myths—based on ideology rather than experience—and the same policies are still in place. Keeping in power the same people who introduced the neoclassical shock therapy measures responsible for much of the problem has been a mistake. It virtually guarantees that we do not engage in a fundamental discussion of *what went wrong*. Instead, what is needed is a theory that explains why economic development, by its very nature, is such an uneven process. Only then can the appropriate policy measures be put in place.

The problems created by the currently dominant economic theory are not limited to the Third World countries. In the case of the EU, most developed nations have experienced increasing economic inequalities internally. The same problems are thus experienced on three levels—globally, within the EU and within most developed nations. The cause behind these developments is essentially the same: theories that worked for centuries have been abandoned. Tensions within the European Community are the result of the same economic forces that create poverty around the world. Those in the old member states of the EU feel betrayed because their welfare is being eroded, while those in the new member states feel betrayed because their welfare is not improving as fast as expected. Not surprisingly, this unexpected situation has caused many to ask what went wrong.

Although German economist Friedrich List (1789–1846) is hardly mentioned in today's economic textbooks, his economic principles not only industrialized Continental Europe in the nineteenth century, but also facilitated European integration from the early 1950s up to and including the successful integration of Spain and Portugal into the EU in 1986. It was not until the introduction of the Stability and Growth Pact that List's principles were abandoned in favour of the kind of economics that dominates the Washington Consensus. The result has been increasing unemployment and poverty in the old core countries, inflaming the debate that resulted in the rejection of the proposed new European constitution (see Reinert and Kattel, 2004).

Below are three of List's key principles, which contrasted with standard textbook economics. In order to develop Africa and other poor countries, the present neoclassical economic principles must be abandoned in favour of the old Listian principles.

- *Listian principle*: A nation first industrializes and is then gradually integrated economically into nations at the same level of development.

Neoclassical principle: Free trade is the goal *per se*, even before the required stage of industrialization is achieved. The 2004 EU enlargement was directly at variance with Listian principles. First, the former communist countries in Eastern Europe (with the exception of Hungary) suffered dramatic deindustrialization, unemployment and underemployment. These countries were then abruptly integrated into the EU, creating enormous economic and social tensions. From the point of view of Western Europe, the factor price equalization promised by international trade theory proved to be an equalization *downward*.

- *Listian principle*: The preconditions for wealth, democracy and political freedom are all the same: a diversified manufacturing sector subject to increasing returns[13] (which historically means manufacturing, but also includes knowledge-intensive services). This was the principle promoted by the first United States Secretary of the Treasury, Alexander Hamilton (1791), upon which the United States economy was built. It was rediscovered by George Marshall in 1947, as mentioned above.

Neoclassical principle: All economic activities are qualitatively alike, so what is produced does not matter. The ideology is based on 'comparative advantage', without recognizing that it is actually possible for a nation to specialize in being poor and ignorant, engage in economic activities that require little knowledge, and operate under perfect competition and diminishing returns and/or bereft of any scale economies and technological change.

- *Listian principle*: Economic welfare is a result of synergy. The thirteenth century Florentine Chancellor, Brunetto Latini (1210–1294), explained the wealth of cities as a *common weal* ('un ben comune'; see Reinert, 1999).

Neoclassical principle: "There is no such thing as society", Margaret Thatcher (1987).

As Kuhn described above, these Listian principles cannot be captured by the tools of the reigning economic paradigm. Understanding List requires the recognition of qualitative differences between economic activities, diversity, innovations, synergies and historical sequencing of processes—all of which are blind spots in standard economics.

Working with economic tools that prevent them from understanding List's points, today's mainstream economists grope for explanations of continued poverty. They return to factors that have been studied and discarded, like race and climate, and refuse to see how historical experience demonstrates that the economic structure of wealthy countries have certain characteristics that poor nations lack, e.g., increasing returns, innovation, diversity and synergies. The collapse of the first wave of globalization led economists to eugenics and racial hygiene.[14] Africans were not seen as poor because of the colonial economic structures that had been imposed on the continent, but rather because they were black. Today, the ostensibly more politically correct version of this type of theory is that Africa is poor because blacks are corrupt.

DIVERSITY AS A PRECONDITION FOR DEVELOPMENT

Another blind spot of economics is its inability to understand the importance of diversity for economic growth. Diversity is a key factor in development for a variety of reasons. First, a diversity of activities with increasing returns—maximizing the number of professions in an economy—is the basis for the synergy effects called economic development. This was the standard understanding from the 1600s (see Reinert, 2004a). Second, modern evolutionary economics point to the importance of diversity as a basis for selection between technologies, products and organizational solutions, all of which are key elements in an evolving market economy (see Nelson and Winter, 1982). Third, diversity has been an important explanation for European 'exceptionalism', where a large number of nation-states, in competition with one another, created tolerance and a demand for diversity. A scholar, whose views were not popular with a particular king or ruler, could find employment in a different nation, thus creating a greater diversity of ideas.

Fourth, religious diversity was emphasized by Johann Friedrich von Pfeiffer (1718–1787), one of the most influential German economists of the eighteenth century. While some economists believe that more rapid economic growth is promoted by some religions, rather than others,[15] Richard Tawney (1926), the famous English historian, emphasized the declining importance of religion in propelling capitalism. About 150 years earlier, Pfeiffer argued that when a diversity of 'competing' religions exists within a state, religion, as an institution, will lose much of its power over the inhabitants. The existence of alternatives will remove fear and other factors that contribute to fanaticism, and a new tolerance will open up for a desirable diversity of its population and skills (Pfeiffer, 1778).

We live in an age of great ignorance today, where established qualitative arguments exploring the process of economic development have been abandoned. The importance of diversity is just one of these arguments. The banality of today's explanations about poverty being a result of climate and corruption amply testifies to this ignorance, which is fortified by the absence of historical knowledge and of an interest in proven principles that have brought nation after nation from poverty to wealth over five centuries. As Paul Krugman has pointed out, previous economic insights tend to fade away, only to be rediscovered later. In a situation similar to the one we are in now, an enlightened group of nineteenth-century German economists caught the ear of Chancellor Bismarck and were allowed to design that country's developmental and welfare state. Similarly, just after World War II, the world understood that economic development was the result of synergies and increasing returns. Combined with the political threat of communism, this understanding made it possible to overrule the free trade ideologies in Washington and reindustrialize Europe and industrialize parts of Asia. In order to restart growth, it is necessary to reinvent this type of economic theory.

POLICY IMPLICATIONS

Aiming for Increasing Returns, Diversity and the Common Weal

From an economic point of view, the poor populations on the world periphery may be seen either in terms of *consumption* or in terms of *production*. From the consumption point of view, there are two billion people whose extremely low purchasing power causes them to live on the brink of famine and disease. One suggestion would be to give them more purchasing power through aid, and it is this suggestion that has inspired the MDGs and traditional development assistance. Since many of the victims of poverty are farmers, another normal reaction would be to make their farming more efficient.

These policies, however, go squarely against successful development policies of the past. Only the presence of manufacturing industry produces efficient agriculture. As David Hume (1767) said in his *History of England*, "Promoting husbandry...is never more effectually encouraged than by the increase of manufactures". The conscious creation of such synergies and the economic diversity that makes them possible have been mandatory 'passage points' for all nations going from poverty to wealth since the late 1400s (see Reinert and Reinert, 2005).

From a production point of view, incorporating insights from David Hume to George Marshall, we get a very different picture which shows a world suffering from a huge *underutilization of resources*, with around two billion people who are severely underemployed or unemployed, engaged in economic activities that are far from 'efficient'. This is the logic found in the original Bretton Woods agreement: poor nations are operating very far from their production possibility frontier, many resources being underutilized.

The Marshall Plan was based on the principle of fully utilizing underutilized resources to protect and create industrialization, diversity and activities with increasing returns in all the nations involved. The post-war interpretation of poverty included assigning a social cost to the underutilization of resources, e.g., unemployment that could be measured using shadow prices, and justified temporary protection to achieve both full employment and a diversified industrial structure. Today, the Washington Consensus uses models assuming full employment, assigning no social or other costs to the fact that human resources in Third World countries are hugely underemployed. Viewing *palliative economics* as the only solution is thus a natural consequence of this view.

In an expanding world economy, where many raw materials are rapidly becoming strategic commodities, the poor 'stand in the way' of access to these raw materials, not unlike the native American 'Indians' being a hindrance to the settlers' use of land. For some United States conservatives, placing the poor on 'reservations' is an option to be seriously considered. Only a decade ago, two American authors recommended the establishment of a *custodial state* in a much publicized book: "by custodial state, we have in mind a high-tech and more lavish version of the Indian reservation for some substantial minority of the nation's population, while the rest of America tries to go about its business" (Herrnstein and Murray, 1994: 526). The MDGs are uncomfortably close to combining the consumption-based view of poverty with the idea of establishing reservations where the basic needs of the poor are taken care of while the rest of the world gets along with its business.

In the original Bretton Woods agreement, unemployment and under-employment justified the protection of national economies until full employment was reached. National development plans—e.g., to industrialize a country—were legitimate reasons for tariff protection under the original Bretton Woods agreement. Similarly, today, it is necessary to temporarily let the free trade principle yield to the principles of economic development and structural change. In short, the conditionalities of the Washington institutions must be subordinated to the original Bretton Woods agreement, as interpreted during its first decades.

In order to implement such policies, we must understand that the process of catching up for very poor countries involves a trade-off between the interests of 'man-the-producer' and 'man-the-consumer'. In addition, we need to realize that static absolute efficiency may differ considerably from long-term income-maximizing efficiency. As Paul Samuelson recently said, "You need more temporary protection for the losers. My belief is that every good cause is worth some inefficiency". (*Süddeutsche Zeitung/New York Times*, 2004: 10).

At the time when England was the only nation to have industrialized, any consideration of *static efficiency* meant that no other nation ought to follow its path to industrialization. All of the nations that followed England's path to wealth did so only by sacrificing *static efficiency* in order to achieve a higher long-term *dynamic efficiency*. Industrializing the United States by targeting and protecting certain industries at that time was just as statically inefficient as protecting Africa's industries is today. The very rapid increase in real wages after the boycotts of the United States (during the Napoleonic Wars), and of South Africa and Rhodesia, testifies to the beneficial effects of protectionism, even when imposed from the outside. It is important to keep in mind, however, that—unlike many Latin American countries after World War II—it is essential to combine protection with national or regional competition. Appendix 8.2 establishes guidelines for 'good' and 'bad' protection based on historical experience.

In the poorest periphery, targeting economic diversity has to begin with economic activities that already exist. In the original spirit of Bretton Woods or Keynesian doctrine, one starting point for increasing real employment would be to identify the smallest tariffs which would maximize economic results in terms of employment and national value added, while minimizing the profitability of smuggling. For example, many poor countries import large quantities of poultry from developed countries. A small tariff on poultry could easily create much more employment and value added than the cost of the tariff. It should be kept in mind that tariffs have always played the dual role of producing revenues while creating more productive economic structures. In weak states, ports were often the only territories fully under government control, and tariffs were the easiest form of revenue to collect.

Free trade among nations at the same level of development has always been beneficial. Regional integration is, therefore, key to development. The problem, however, is that poor neighbouring countries often have little to sell to each other. In Africa, pressures from the United States and the EU, together with the spaghetti bowl of regional integration schemes (Common Market for Eastern and Southern Africa (COMESA), East African Community (EAC) Southern African Customs Union (SACU), Southern African Development Community (SADC)) and cross-membership of countries in these schemes, present difficulties for development and discourage policies promoting industrialization under local competition. The pressures to export faced by developing countries undermine, rather than advance, the Listian principle of regional integration that must precede any successful globalization. The EU presses for market access for their apples in Egypt, thereby destroying the century-old tradition of Egypt's buying apples from Lebanon. The present carving up of Africa into different economic spheres is exactly the opposite of what Africa needs, which is stronger economic integration within Africa and a certain degree of development before opening up for globalization.

A unifying characteristic of the 50 poorest countries in the world today is an almost total absence of manufacturing industries. The key insight that having an inefficient manufacturing sector produces a higher standard of living than having no manufacturing sector at all, will have to be recognized in order to transform poor into middle-income nations. Only this insight can stop the parallel race to the bottom in terms of democracy and economic welfare. After all, it was common knowledge in the eighteenth century that democracies were products of diversified economic structures, and not the other way around.

During the last two decades, the United Nations Industrial Development Organization (UNIDO) and other United Nations institutions, such as the United Nations Conference on Trade and Development (UNCTAD), the United Nations Development Programme (UNDP), the International Labour Organization (ILO), the Economic Commission for Latin American the Caribbean (ECLAC), the United Nations Research Institute for Social Development (UNRISD) and the United Nations Children's Fund (UNICEF), have been overshadowed by the aggressiveness of the Washington institutions. The United Nations institutions have virtually been bullied into silence, and the political turmoil around the 2003 UNDP report *Making Global Trade Work for People* testifies to this censorship. The report—financed by civil society foundations— was almost withdrawn because of political pressure and was only salvaged due to the intervention of these same foundations. It is indeed time for United Nations agencies to start working together in a more coordinated way in order to be heard.

In 1956, Nobel Economics Laureate Gunnar Myrdal advised Third World leaders on the subject of economic theory. Myrdal (1956: 77) stated that:

> They should be aware of the fact that very much of these theories are partly rationalizations of the dominant interest in the advanced and rapidly progressing industrial countries…it…would be pathetic if the young social scientists of the under-developed countries got caught in the predilections of the thinking in the advanced countries, which are hampering the scholars there in their efforts to be rational but would be almost deadening to the intellectual strivings of those in the under-developed countries. I would instead wish them to have the courage to throw away large structures of meaningless, irrelevant and sometimes blatantly inadequate doctrines and theoretical approaches and to start out from fresh

thinking right from their needs and their problems. This would then take them far beyond the realm of both out-moded Western liberal economics and Marxism.

APPENDIX 8.1
'Mercantilist' economic policies of the generic developmental state

Continuity of policy measures and toolkit, from England in 1485 (under Henry VII) to South Korea in the 1960s: a mandatory passage point for economic development.
... the fundamental things apply, as time goes by.
Sam, the pianist, in 'Casablanca'.

1) Recognition of wealth-creating synergies clustered around activities with increasing returns and continuous mechanization. Recognition that 'we are in the wrong business'. Conscious *targeting, support and protection* of activities generating increasing returns.
2) Granting of temporary monopolies/patents/protection to targeted activities in certain geographical areas.
3) Recognition of development as a synergetic phenomenon and, consequently, of the need for a diversified manufacturing sector, 'maximizing the division of labour' (Serra, 1613)—drawing on observations of the Dutch Republic and Venice.
4) Accumulation of empirical evidence showed that the manufacturing sector solved three policy problems endemic to the Third World: increasing national value added (GDP), increasing employment, and balance-of-payment problems.
5) Attraction of foreigners to work in targeted activities (historically, religious persecution was important).
6) Weakening of landed interests (from England under Henry VII to South Korea). (Physiocracy as a reflection of the landowners' rebellion against this policy.)
7) Tax breaks for targeted activities.
8) Cheap credit for targeted activities.
9) Export subsidies for targeted activities.
10) Strong support for the agricultural sector, in spite of its clearly being seen as incapable of independently bringing the nation out of poverty.
11) Emphasis on learning and education (United Kingdom apprentice system under Elizabeth I).
12) Patent protection for valuable knowledge (Venice from the 1490s).
13) Export taxes/bans on raw materials to make them more expensive for competing nations (starting with Henry VII in late 1400s, whose policy was very effective in severely damaging the wool industry in Medici Florence).

Source: Reinert and Reinert (2005).

APPENDIX 8.2
Two ideal types of protectionism compared

East Asian: 'good'	Latin American: 'bad'
Temporary protection of new industries/products for the world market.	Permanent protection of mature industries/products for the home market (often very small).
Very steep learning curves compared to the rest of the world.	Learning that lags behind the rest of the world.
Based on a dynamic Schumpeterian view of the world—market-driven 'creative destruction'.	Based on a more static view of the world—planned economy.
Domestic competition maintained. Core technology locally controlled.	Little domestic competition. Core technology generally imported from a broad/assembly of imported parts/'superficial' industrialization.
Massive investment in education/industrial policy created a huge demand for education. Supply of educated people matched demand from industry.	Less emphasis on education/type of industries created did not lead to huge (East Asian) demand for education. Investment in education therefore tends to feed emigration.
Meritocracy—capital, jobs and privileges distributed according to qualifications. Equality of land distribution (South Korea). Even income distribution increased home market for advanced industrial goods.	*Nepotism* in the distribution of capital, jobs and privileges. Mixed record on land distribution. Uneven income distribution restricted scale of home market and decreased competitiveness of local industry.
Profits created through dynamic 'Schumpeterian' rent-seeking.	Profits created through static rent-seeking.
Intense cooperation between producers and local suppliers. Regulation of technology transfer oriented towards maximizing knowledge transferred.	Confrontation between producers and local suppliers. Regulation of technology transfer oriented towards avoiding 'traps'.

NOTES

[1] This analysis is complicated by the fact that the wages and incomes of the self-employed as a percentage of GDP are falling in most countries, whereas wages for those working in the FIRE (finance, insurance, real state) sector are increasing. This wage/self-employed share of GDP has been close to 70 per cent in Norway and around 23 per cent in Peru.

[2] The idea that a nation upgrading its skills in the same way a person could was part of the US industrialization strategy in the 1820s (Raymond 1820).

[3] This asymmetry is the core of the argument in Frank Graham's 1923 article, a basis for Krugman's New Trade Theory.

[4] This discussion builds on Nelson (2006).

[5] Historical evidence of this practice in Europe can be found in Reinert (2004a).

[6] At core, the Enlightenment project was one of ordering the world by creating taxonomies or classification systems, of which Linnaeus's is the best known. Neoclassical economics achieves analytical precision precisely by lacking any taxonomy: everything is qualitatively alike. Therefore its conclusions, like factor price equalization, are essentially already built into its assumptions.

[7] I am grateful to Carlota Perez for having formulated this insight.

[8] Though not necessarily falling GDP per capita (see footnote 1).

[9] As imported and subsidized United States food takes over from local maize and wheat production.

[10] That the steel tariff later got as high as 100 per cent was a result of technological change and rapidly falling prices in a situation where the tariff was not based on value, but weight (dollars per ton).

[11] The slogan 'get national innovation systems right' proved to be an exception as it refers to a synergistic phenomenon. However, this does not lead very far because of the theory's inability to distinguish between different windows of opportunity, e.g., for innovation in Microsoft, under hugely increasing returns, and in a goat herding firm in Mongolia, under critically diminishing returns. In standard analysis, Schumpeterian economics tends to be added like thin icing on a thoroughly neoclassical cake.

[12] 'Thus the country which eventually specializes completely in the production of X (that is, the commodity whose production function is characterized by increasing returns to scale) might agree to make an income transfer (annually) to the other country, which agrees to specialize completely in Y (that is, the commodity whose production function is characterized by constant returns to scale)' (Chacholiades, 1978: 199). See also Reinert (1980).

[13] The works of Jane Jacobs on the role of the cities arrive at the same conclusion as List, albeit from a different starting point.

[14] Irving Fisher was both a leading economist and the leader of the eugenics movement in the United States in this period. For a discussion, see Ross (1998).

[15] Werner Sombart emphasized the role of Judaism, and Max Weber the role of Protestantism.

REFERENCES

Anonymous (1786). *Relazione di una scorsa per varie provincie d'Europa del M. M.... a Madama G.. in Parigi.* Nella Stamperia del R. Im. Monastero di S. Salvatore, Pavia.

Bacon, Francis (1620). *Novum Organum.* Joannem Billium, Typographum Regium, London.

Chacholiades, Miltiades (1978). *International Trade Theory and Policy.* McGraw-Hill, New York.

Graham, Frank (1923). Some Aspects of Protection further considered. *Quarterly Journal of Economics,* 37: 199–227.

Hamilton, Alexander (1791). *Report on the Subject of Manufactures.* Excerpt in Frank Taussig

(1921). *Selected Readings in International Trade and Tariff Problems*. Ginn & Company, Boston.

Herrnstein, Richard J., and Charles Murray (1994). *The Bell Curve: Intelligence and Class Structure in American Life*. Free Press, New York.

Hume, David (1767). *History of England. Vol. III*. Millar/Cadell, London.

Kaplan, Steven (1976). *Bread, Politics and Political Economy in the Reign of Louis XV*. Martinus Nijhoff, The Hague.

Kregel, Jan (2004). External Financing for Development and International Financial Stability. G-24 Discussion Paper No. 32, UNCTAD, Geneva.

Kuhn, Thomas (1962). *The Structure of Scientific Revolutions*. University of Chicago Press, Chicago.

Lavinas, Lena and Eduardo Henrique Garcia (2004). *Programas Sociais de Combate à Fome. O legado dos anos de estabilização econômica*. Editora UFRJ/IPEA, Coleção Economia e Sociedade, Rio de Janeiro.

List, Friedrich. (1841/1909). *The National System of Political Economy*. Longmans, London.

Myrdal, Gunnar (1956). *Development and Underdevelopment*. National Bank of Egypt, Cairo.

Nelson, Richard R., and Sydney Winter (1982). *An Evolutionary Theory of Economic Change*. Harvard University Press, Cambridge, MA.

Nelson, Richard R. (2006). Economic Development from the Perspective of Evolutionary Economic Theory. *The Other Canon Foundation and Tallinn University of Technology Working Papers in Technology Governance and Economic Dynamics* No. 1. Downlodable on http://hum.ttu.ee/tg/.

Paine, Robert (ed.) (1977). *The White Arctic. Anthropological Essays on Tutelage and Ethnicity*. Institute of Social and Economic Research, Memorial University of Newfoundland, St. Johns.

Pfeiffer, Johann Friedrich von (1778). *Vermischte Verbesserungsvorschläge und freie Gedanken*. Vol. 2. Esslinger, Frankfurt.

Raymond, Daniel (1820). *Thoughts on Political Economy*. Fielding Lucas, Baltimore.

Reinert, Erik S. (1996). Diminishing Returns and Economic Sustainability: The Dilemma of Resource-based Economies under a Free Trade Regime. In Stein Hansen, Jan Hesselberg and Helge Hveem (eds). *International Trade Regulation, National Development Strategies and the Environment: Towards Sustainable Development?* Centre for Development and the Environment, University of Oslo, Oslo: 119–150.

Reinert, Erik S. (1998). Raw Materials in the History of Economic Policy; or, Why List (the Protectionist) and Cobden (the Free Trader) Both Agreed on Free Trade in Corn. In Gary Cook (ed.). *The Economics and Politics of International Trade: Freedom and Trade, 1846–1996. Volume 2*. Routledge, London: 275–300.

Reinert, Erik S. (1999). The Role of the State in Economic Growth. *Journal of Economic Studies* 26 (4/5): 268–321.

Reinert, Erik S. (2003). Increasing Poverty in a Globalised World: Marshall Plans and Morgenthau Plans as Mechanisms of Polarisation of World Incomes. In Ha-Joon Chang (ed.). *Rethinking Development Economics*. Anthem, London: 453–478.

Reinert, Erik S. (2004a). Benchmarking Success: The Dutch Republic (1500–1750) as seen by Contemporary European Economists. In *How Rich Nations got Rich. Essays in the History of Economic Policy*. Working Paper No. 1, SUM-Centre for Development and the Environment, University of Oslo: 1–24. http://www.sum.uio.no/publications

Reinert, Erik S. (2004b). Globalisation in the Periphery as a Morgenthau Plan: The Underdevelopment of Mongolia in the 1990s. In Erik Reinert (ed.). *Globalization, Economic Development and Inequality: An Alternative Perspective*. Edward Elgar, Cheltenham: 157–214.

Reinert, Erik S., and Rainer Kattel (2004). The Qualitative Shift in European Integration: Towards Permanent Wage Pressures and a 'Latin-Americanization' of Europe? Working paper no. 17, Praxis Foundation, Estonia. http://www.praxis.ee/data/WP_17_2004.pdf.

Reinert, Erik S., and Sophus Reinert (2005). Mercantilism and Economic Development: Schumpeterian Dynamics, Institution Building and International Benchmarking. In K.S. Jomo and Erik S. Reinert (eds). *Origins of Development Economics*. Zed Books, London.

Roca, Santiago, and Luis Simabuco (2004). Natural Resources, Industrialization and Fluctuating Standards of Living in Peru, 1950–1997: A Case Study of Activity-Specific Economic Growth. In Erik S. Reinert (ed.). *Globalization, Economic Development and Inequality: An Alternative Perspective*. Edward Elgar, Cheltenham: 115–156.

Ross, Eric (1998). *The Malthus Factor: Poverty, Politics and Population in Capitalist Development*. Palgrave Macmillan, London.

Schoenhof, Jacob (1883). *The Destructive Influence of the Tariff upon Manufacture and Commerce and the Figures and Facts Relating Thereto*. New York Free Trade Club, New York.

Serra, Antonio (1613). *Breve Trattato delle Cause che Possono far Abbondare l'Oro e l'Argento dove non sono Miniere*. Lazzaro Scorriggio, Naples.

Singer, Hans W. (1950). The Distribution of Gains between Investing and Borrowing Countries. *American Economic Review* 40: 473–485.

Smith, Adam (1759/1812). *The Theory of Moral Sentiments*. In *The Works of Adam Smith. With an account of his life and writings*. 5 volumes. T. Cadell and W. Davies & Co., London.

Smith, Adam (1776/1976). *An Inquiry into the Nature and Causes of the Wealth of Nations*. University of Chicago Press, Chicago.

Steuart, James (1767). *An Inquiry into the Principles of Political Economy: being an Essay on the Science of Domestic Policy in Free Nations. In which are particularly considered population, agriculture, trade, industry, money, coin, interest, circulation, banks, exchange, public credit, and taxes*. 2 volumes, A. Millar & T. Cadell, London.

Süddeutsche Zeitung/New York Times (2004). September 20: 10.

Taussig, F.W. (1897). *The Tariff History of the United States*. Putnam's, New York.

Tawney, Richard (1926). *Religion and the Rise of Capitalism: A Historical Study*. J. Murray, London.

Webb, Richard, and Graciela Fernández Baca (2001). *Perú en Números*. Instituto Cuanto, Lima.

9
Constraints to Achieving the MDGs with Scaled-Up Aid

FRANÇOIS BOURGUIGNON and MARK SUNDBERG

The international community is preparing to embark on a grand experiment, something never attempted before. A new compact is being designed to both scale up aid and change the way it is delivered and how it is used by recipient countries. The goal is to make dramatic progress in advancing human development in the world's poorest countries. The complexity of the task is enormous; but so is the promise of improving the lives of millions of people and building a safer, more stable and more prosperous world.

The main element of this experiment is a new "mutual accountability" on the part of both the donor community and the recipient countries. It aims to overcome the dilemma at the heart of scaling up aid: whereas donors are unwilling to transfer large resources to developing countries without guarantees that credible plans and competent institutions are in place to use resources to advance the Millennium Development Goals (MDGs), developing countries need a credible guarantee of sustained support in order to build sound plans and undertake the necessary institutional strengthening. The essence of the Monterrey Consensus of 2002 is that donors and International Financial Institutions (IFIs) work together to improve the quality of aid mobilization and delivery, to improve aid predictability and stability, and to ensure that aid is aligned with national development strategies. Recipient governments must for their part have credible financial management capacity, governance and service delivery mechanisms to ensure that resources will be used effectively.

This chapter addresses the macro and structural challenges facing aid recipients and donors that lie at the heart of the Monterrey Consensus and its implicit accountabilities. How can developing countries approach macroeconomic and structural constraints that potentially prevent new aid flows from being effectively employed or that present intertemporal tradeoffs? How can labour market constraints to scaling up aid be handled? How should countries sequence aid inflows to reduce price effects that could reduce growth potential? Does aid risk undermining fiscal sustainability in otherwise stable economies? What does improving aid quality and predictability imply for developing countries embarking on the preparation of ten-year development strategies? These were all important questions during 2005, the "Year of Development", and remain so.

Several papers have been written recently on this subject (including IMF 2005a, 2005b; Heller, 2005; Foster, 2003; World Bank, 2004a, 2005d). These papers discuss the potential short-run macroeconomic issues that may arise from large increases in aid, depending on how the aid is utilized and given the different structural characteristics of the recipient country. There has been little effort, however, to systematically gauge the impact on poor countries of higher aid flows targeting the MDGS. One reason is that there is little experience with such rapidly scaled-up assistance targeting the social and development needs of developing countries. Another reason is that it requires an understanding of the complex interactions of both the macroeconomy and the underlying characteristics of the specific MDG services to which aid is being directed. Both of these factors pose special challenges to planners and economists examining these interactions.

This chapter contributes to this literature by revisiting the main macro and structural issues posed by a rapid scaling-up of aid inflows, with particular reference to typical structural features of low-income African economies. It examines both the implications of aid flows from the perspective of recipient countries and the issue of improving the external quality of aid from donors and IFIs. Following a discussion of the main policy issues, the chapter presents one modelling approach that captures some of the main macro and institutional characteristics of aid recipients, which is then applied to the case of Ethiopia. The simulations presented are aimed at helping to think through the effects of higher ODA flows, but of course models simplify reality and the actual response will always vary—there will inevitably be surprises.

The next section of the chapter reviews the main macroeconomic and structural issues posed by a rapid scaling up of external assistance. The third section briefly presents a modelling framework for examining macro and sectoral interactions surrounding scaling up to reach the MDGs. The fourth section examines the case of Ethiopia and presents the results of a simulated scaling up of aid that would be adequate for reaching the MDGs by 2015.

Constraints to Scaling Up Aid to Reach the MDGs

There are several constraints to achieving the MDGs and to external aid as an instrument for reaching the MDGs, particularly in the short run. The constraints that are frequently cited revolve around macroeconomic features of developing country markets, structural constraints to scaling up service delivery, limitations to economic policy management and issues concerning how aid itself is provided (for instance, Heller, 2005; World Bank, 2004a, 2005d). Macroeconomic issues arise from the magnitude of aid relative to the domestic economy and the impact of large externally financed public expenditures on relative prices in the economy. The potential costs of large aid inflows appreciating the local currency and undermining traded goods competitiveness (Dutch disease) is often cited.

Structural constraints to scaling up relate to skilled labour shortages, weak capital markets and potential infrastructure bottlenecks. Each of these potentially act to increase the marginal costs of increasing delivery of public services essential to achieving the MDGs—such as education, health care, water and sanitation services. The quality of governance and institutions will also influence the outcome of scaling up, presenting both risks of higher corruption or "capture" as aid flows increase as well as opportunities to strengthen anti-corruption measures and reinforce accountability mechanisms that can improve governance.

Finally, the volatility of aid flows, fragmentation of external support and the multiplicity of donor objectives independent of government development strategies can exact significant "compliance costs" associated with aid flows. These are largely outside the control of aid recipients but can impose serious costs on the capacity to manage and plan for the use of aid in recipient countries.

Each of these concerns has been discussed widely in the literature on aid effectiveness. The empirical evidence relevant to the current debate over scaling up aid is, however, quite limited for two reasons. First, there has been no historical experience with regard to increasing external support in the amounts being discussed today. Second, the mechanisms and modalities of aid are changing: aid is becoming more selective and focused on countries that demonstrate capacity and stronger performance; geopolitics are less of a force in aid allocation; and international discourse on aid modalities has come to focus on results and outcomes rather than on counting inputs alone. This has largely been in recognition of the failed aid programmes of the past.

This section discusses six factors affecting the ability of scaled-up aid flows to help developing countries achieve the MDGs. The first of these is the contribution of aid to growth. Without increasing growth rates, it will not be possible for most low-income countries to reach Goal 1 of the MDGs (MDG 1) of halving income poverty. A second factor is the macroeconomic management of large aid inflows to minimize the erosion of export competitiveness and reduced growth opportunities in the future. Third, for many countries, the second major constraint to scaling up public service delivery (after financing) is labour.

Skilled labour shortages have major implications for the timing and scope of scaling up public service delivery. Fourth, large aid inflows will require competent management of public resources and budgets, and management of the allocation of funds to meet capital and recurrent expenditures to ensure fiscal sustainability. Fifth, related to all of these is the quality of overall governance. Governance is the catalyst behind creating conditions in which not only does aid reach its intended purpose but, more generally, the business environment is such that development finance of all types can generate growth and encourage innovation. Finally, the quality of external aid also impacts on development outcomes. Aid volatility, predictability, fragmentation and alignment with the development objectives of recipients are key parameters in the effective scaling up.

Scaling Up Aid and Accelerating Growth

Accelerating growth performance is critical if scaling up aid to developing countries is to help them achieve and maintain the MDGs. Based on average growth rates over the most recent decade, many developing countries, including most in sub-Saharan Africa, are unlikely to achieve MDG 1 (the halving of income poverty from 1990 levels). Growth not only serves to both reduce poverty directly and generate jobs that will be needed to keep people permanently out of poverty, but it also generates domestic resources that will be needed to reach and sustain the non-income MDGs.

Can scaled-up aid flows help low-income countries accelerate growth performance, however? This is a complex and controversial topic. The association between aid and growth has spawned considerable debate over whether aid helps or harms the process. Cross-country regression analysis has been used in dozens of papers attempting to identify how aid and growth are related (Rajan and Subramanian, 2005a; 2005b: Clemens, Radelet and Bhavnani, 2004: Burnside and Dollar, 2000; 2004: Easterly, Levine and Roodman, 2003, to name only a few recent examples). This topic will not be explored in depth here, but there are several reasons to discount the recent analytic work that suggests that aid does not contribute to growth, or that it may even retard it.

First, there are serious methodological problems with cross-country regression analysis in dealing with aggregation and with identifying the direction of causality. Second, the purpose and uses of aid have changed historically, particularly since the end of the Cold War, and aid today is much more targeted towards good performers and less driven by geopolitical interests than was true even a decade ago (World Bank, 1998; Dollar and Levin, 2004). Moreover, aid is highly heterogeneous and serves many purposes unrelated to growth (including emergency assistance, such as the recent Tsunami relief), or indirectly related thereto (such as technical assistance). Third, much of the aid allocated to the social sectors may significantly affect growth, but only in the long run, and this is not captured by the cross-country regression work that typically examines growth over a short-term horizon. Finally, there have been major developments in aid architecture that are rapidly changing the role and parameters of aid. The Paris Declaration, discussed below, is one example, but in addition, from the recipient's side, there is a greater impetus towards ownership and country control of the aid process.

By contrast, there is considerable evidence suggesting high rates of return and aid effectiveness based on micro evidence from specific projects and applications. Well-documented cross-border efforts to eradicate water-borne diseases, or to protect and jointly manage natural resources, are frequently cited examples. In other projects, rigorously prepared impact evaluations have shown high returns to many aid-supported projects (for example, China's South-West Poverty Reduction Project and Indonesia's Kecamatan Development Project).[1]

Country case studies can also shed light on the contribution of aid to development and can allow consideration of unique circumstances and contributing factors that are lost in cross-country analysis. There is ample evidence from individual case studies of enormous waste and leakages in aid flows, particularly during the period of the Cold War, with no evidence supporting a positive growth impact in these cases. But there is also a growing case study literature providing insights into more recent experience. A recent study of aid to African countries shows that, in a group of 11 relatively "high performance" countries, high aid flows are associated with improved growth performance, although more work is needed for a clearer examination of causality (Bourguignon, Gelb and Versailles, 2005). Individual country evidence underscores the importance of country circumstances; there is no simple set of rules linking aid flows to stronger performance.

This broad conclusion—that there are no blueprints linking aid flows to growth performance and that individual country circumstances must be assessed to identify strategic priorities—is similar to the overall conclusion of the recent World Bank report on growth performance in the 1990s (see World Bank, 2005c), which reflects contributions by Rodrik (World Bank, 2005c; 2005e) and other development economists examining the lessons of development experience in the 1990s. The proposal stemming from their work is that the specific constraints to growth must be carefully analysed in each country case in order to identify where constraints are binding and, hence, where resources and policy reforms are needed to unlock innovation and realize growth potential.

The implication of this with regard to the scaling up of aid flows and the critical need to generate growth is that scaling up must be built around a thorough understanding of the binding constraints to growth, and public investment supported by aid should be directed towards addressing these constraints in order to unleash growth potential. This is, of course, extremely difficult in practice. It requires a thorough understanding of both technical constraints, in particular critical infrastructure needs and skill requirements, as well as institutional needs, key governance parameters and even demographics. Investment in human immunodeficiency virus/acquired immunodeficiency syndrome (HIV/AIDS) prevention and treatment may be one of the most important elements in improving growth performance in some African countries, as discussed in Heller, 2005.

Among the many factors that may contribute to or constrain growth, access to quality infrastructure is one for which aid has a potentially important and catalytic role to play. There is increasing evidence that infrastructure has an important role in growth performance (Estache, 2004, on Africa; World Bank, 2004b). National transport networks and telecommunications linking markets, water management and control to benefit agriculture, and availability of reliable power to manufacturing are key factors influencing opportunity, innovation and growth. As infrastructure networks are developed (roads, energy and irrigation), linking producers and consumers to national and international markets, important network effects are captured which may help generate the necessary growth. Another avenue is through the role of infrastructure investment, which helps reduce the indirect costs (affected by factors such as reliability of power, transport logistics and timing, etc.) and losses related to the business environment that depress firm productivity, as highlighted in recent work on African economies by Eiffert, Gelb and Ramachandran, 2005. A sufficient level of investment will be required to capture these gains and reach a threshold where economy-wide network effects will support higher productivity.

Infrastructure is also costly, requires large-scale investments and is vulnerable to corruption, weak management and inadequate budgeting for operations and maintenance. External aid working through governments can potentially play an important role in financing large infrastructure, and can put in place sustainable regulatory and budgetary systems. Aid to support public investment in health, education or sanitation services may also generate growth, but that is likely to be over the longer term and may not be evident until new cohorts of better-educated and healthier workers enter the work force.

Competitiveness and Real Exchange-Rate Constraints

The scaling up of aid both to meet infrastructure needs and to realize investment in basic social services in order to achieve the MDGs is estimated to require new financing flows that would double, or even quadruple, current aid levels in some cases. Aid flows could account for 20 per cent, 40 per cent or even higher shares of gross domestic product (GDP). A well-recognized risk to economic performance in the presence of large foreign aid inflows is through upward pressure on the real exchange rate and the resulting reduced competitiveness of exports and import-competing goods. The export sector is often considered likely to be the most dynamic and an important contributor to growth. Price effects that could undermine dynamic export growth potential could prove very costly to the economy over time.

The impact of aid flows on relative prices, the exchange rate and competitiveness will depend on many factors. One factor is the share of aid that is spent and the share absorbed, as highlighted in recent International Monetary Fund (IMF) case studies (IMF 2005a). The more aid that is spent, rather than accumulated as domestic reserves, and the less that is absorbed through the sale of foreign exchange to meet import demand, the greater the pressure on the exchange rate to appreciate. A second factor is the relative import intensity of aid-financed expenditures. The greater the import content of aid projects, the less impact there will be on domestic prices. A third factor is the level or surplus capacity in the economy. To the extent that supply can expand to meet new demand without placing upward pressure on domestic prices, there will be less pressure on the real exchange rate to appreciate. A fourth factor is the impact of aid expenditures on growth and productivity. The more that aid finances investment, rather than consumption, and new technologies, or enhances factor productivity and generates a positive growth dynamic, the less the pressure on domestic prices to rise and the real exchange rate to appreciate.

The impact of aid flows on competitiveness has both static, short-run effects as well as a dynamic impact on productivity and growth, with implications for how aid affects the economy over time. A large increase in aid flows that are spent and absorbed may generate problems in the short run as relative price effects dominate, but over time this situation is likely to ease if the initial jump in aid finances investments that help to accelerate growth.

The empirical literature on Dutch disease reveals a wide range of real exchange-rate responses to aid surges, ranging from significant real appreciation to real depreciation. As stressed in Bevan (2005), the extent to which aid flows are associated with the problem of real exchange-rate appreciation depends largely on the relative impact on real demand and supply across sectors. A survey of the literature on empirical studies of country-level evidence on Dutch disease from high aid inflows has generally concluded that the effects are ambiguous and depend on country-specific circumstances.

Even if scaling up aid leads to an erosion of competitiveness and a drag on growth over the medium run, it does not imply that these costs outweigh the benefits of aid. Lost growth opportunities must be weighed against the social and human development gains that aid can help to advance—improving health outcomes, education levels or access to water and sanitation. Moreover, many of these investments have a long-term impact on human capital development that may improve growth performance in the long run, but this is very difficult to measure.

In summary, the risks of Dutch disease appear to be real and potentially serious, particularly when scaling up aid, and heavy aid dependence is likely to extend over many years. There is, however, no general *a priori* case against scaling up based on competitiveness arguments. Both theory and empirical evidence suggest that the long-term interactions are highly complex, very difficult to predict and cannot be simplified into general rules. The long-run response of the economy will depend on several factors affecting the underlying productivity and growth dynamics across sectors, including the care with which domestic policy makers will handle the issue of the real exchange rate. These factors must be examined on a case-by-case basis drawing on the structural and institutional features of the economy.

Labour Markets and Absorptive Capacity

Structural features of low-income economies are likely to constrain the capacity to scale up aid. For many countries, because of skilled labour requirements for meeting the MDGs, labour markets in particular are likely to pose constraints to absorptive capacity and the pace of scaling up. Public expenditures centred on meeting the MDGs will in most cases require a major expansion of basic social services in health and education. For many low-income countries, this will place a much greater demand on the scarce pool of skilled labour that is currently available or that is expected to be trained over the coming decade. Increasing demand for large numbers of teachers, clinicians, accountants and engineers will either not be met in the short run or will need to be accommodated through drawing skilled labour from other parts of the economy (public or private sector), or through importing skilled labour. Importing labour, however, is often not an option for basic service delivery, owing to considerations of affordability and special requirements (language, cultural issues, and so forth).

Expanding the supply of basic education and health services requires increased public spending, largely on non-tradable inputs with high labour intensity but low import intensity. Constraints on skilled labour serve to bid up the skill premium in order to attract skilled labour and increase the overall labour costs of the public sector. Even in a labour-abundant economy, specific skill shortages can greatly exacerbate these pressures.

A sequenced approach to scaling up the MDG-related social services is clearly needed in order to avoid disruptive pressures and associated costs due to skill bottlenecks. Investing in the expansion of teacher and medical training capacities should precede large-scale ramping up of school and clinic construction and staffing. In other words, the sequencing of aid outlays will have a significant impact on associated costs, the optimal path being one that will allow the supply of labour to expand in tandem with increased demand for scaled-up services.

Fiscal Sustainability

Large-scale aid flows and long-term aid dependence also raise the basic issue of fiscal sustainability, as has been pointed out in a recent discussion of scaling up (Heller, 2005). There are several aspects of fiscal sustainability worth noting. The first is the relation of aid flows to indebtedness. For many low-income countries, both Highly Indebted Poor Countries (HIPC) and non-HIPC countries, national indebtedness is a significant constraint on external borrowing. For HIPC countries, borrowing constraints as a result of compliance with regulations governing the HIPC process delimit the scope for new borrowing, even on highly concessionary terms. For many low-income countries, the scale of resource transfers required to meet the MDGs makes scaling up investments with non-grant financing out of the question. The recent Gleneagles debt-relief initiative should help alleviate this situation.

Second, even with full grant financing through 2015, fiscal sustainability would remain an issue. Domestic revenue capacity is unlikely to increase rapidly enough to cover costs. Recurrent costs alone are likely to outstrip total revenues for many low-income countries. Improving domestic revenue capacity and thinking beyond the current 2015 MDG target date is essential for maintaining fiscal sustainability.

A third issue concerns the impact of aid and high *aid dependence* on fiscal behaviour, particularly as regards weakening the revenue effort. The revenue effort will decline, it is suggested, in the presence of continued aid flows, particularly if higher aid flows are associated with lower domestic revenue capacity. However, unambiguous empirical evidence of this is hard to find. Brautigam and Knack (2004) find a significant statistical relationship between higher levels of aid and a lower share of tax to GDP, although causality is difficult to establish. On the other hand, a recent examination of 11 African countries concludes that the tax effort actually increased during the 1990s, when aid flows increased (Bourguignon, Gelb and Versailles, 2005). A simple correlation between tax/GDP and aid/GDP shows that the relationship is not significantly far from zero. Selecting only highly aid-dependent countries does not alter this finding. Country-by-country analysis is needed to have a better understanding of this, in particular to clarify the relationship between prolonged aid dependence and its impact on fiscal policies, governance and institution-building.

Finally, there is the related question of public expenditure management and the capacity to manage expenditure needs across sectors in order to maintain the right balance between recurrent and capital spending and to develop systems for financing the recurrent costs necessary for long-run sustainability of scaled-up service delivery levels. This problem is common and applies to all public finance, not just to aid. But higher aid dependence is likely to intensify the fiscal planning challenge. The problem is greatly intensified in the current context since large levels of aid are needed to finance labour-intensive public services, such as schools and clinics, especially where it will take years to train adequate numbers of skilled staff. If aid levels fall for some unanticipated reason—missed disbursement triggers, cumbersome processing requirements or for political reasons—then the ability of the government to continue meeting required recurrent needs is in question. Potential costs can be large. These concerns are better understood now and are reflected in the Paris Declaration (see discussion below).

Role of Governance

There is a broad range of institutional and governance issues that generally lie at the heart of national reform programmes and Poverty Reduction Strategies. These include measures to improve public expenditure management, strengthen accountability mechanisms, reduce resource loss through "capture" and corruption, and deregulate excessive government controls. From a narrow standpoint, governance includes fiduciary standards that governments must meet in order to receive aid commitments, particularly for budget support: sound accounting procedures, budget management capacity, a well-functioning treasury system and a process for audit and oversight that provides confidence that resources are being spent where they are allocated.

More broadly, governance and institutional reforms can be thought of as measures to improve the efficiency of public resource utilization. They affect the underlying productivity of public services and aim to both directly and indirectly reduce unit costs of public service provision—through lower teacher absenteeism, reduced waiting times for public services, improved regulatory oversight and lower leakage in the use of central government resources for delivery of services to end-users. Simple reforms can sometimes yield major benefits.[2]

At the same time, there is concern that aid and extended aid dependence may also contribute to a downward spiral of worsening governance, ranging from clientelistic governments feeding on aid flows to the less obvious, but potentially costly, impact of aid that results in shifting priorities and resources towards donor preferences and away from domestic voices in the shaping national development strategies.

Clearly, governance is a vast and crucial issue, covering much more than public finance—and including the investment climate for growth and the rule of law, for instance—and is relevant to all public activities, not just those that may be aid financed. Sorting through the linkages between aid flows and governance outcomes is complex and is an important analytic issue with respect to scaling up aid flows.

Volatility and Fragmentation of Aid Flows

The costs to aid efficiency arising from multiple donor programmes, poor alignment with the recipient's development agenda and uncertainty over aid flows is well recognized, although not readily quantified. Uncertainty over the timing and levels of aid disbursements make budget planning difficult and potentially costly, as expenditures crucial to project success can be delayed or put on hold. Aid directed to the priorities of donors may not conform to the development needs and priorities of recipient countries, potentially diverting resources away from more important and higher yielding uses. Moreover, the burden of complying with multiple donor processing requirements and logistical support can place a large "compliance tax" on developing countries. In the context of low-income countries with capacity limitations, these costs are not trivial. And they become undoubtedly worse as the number of donors and magnitude of lending increases.

The 2005 Paris Declaration on Aid Effectiveness is designed to address these concerns and raise donor awareness. It calls on all donor countries to align their programmes with recipient priorities, eliminate duplication of effort and provide more predictable multi-year aid commitments. It also calls for the integration of global programmes and earmarked support into recipient countries' development programmes. Adjusting the incentives of donors and IFIs to implement this programme remains a major challenge, and only limited progress has been made to date.

Under a programme that is fully harmonized with country systems, and aligned with the recipient's development strategy, the costs to aid efficiency would essentially disappear. Aid would flow through the budget directly to support the expansion of public services and would be administered and overseen using the same standards and practices as other public resource flows. Project implementation units, if necessary, would be common across donors and IFIs. Missions and donor reporting would be minimal, except where necessary to show results and evidence of progress.

The mechanics of aid commitments, allocation and disbursement are a very long way from this standard at present, but the harmonization and alignment agenda is clearly intended to be a central element of efforts to further scale up aid and assist aid recipients with their management challenges.

In conclusion, this section has briefly reviewed the main factors affecting capacity to scale up aid flows and put aid to effective use in achieving the MDGs. It has noted the complexity of the process in terms of both macroeconomic and microeconomic aspects of aid absorption. It has also argued that both the governance environment in developing countries and the governance and design of aid flows by donors and IFIs can profoundly affect the scope for, and impact of, scaling up aid. Strategic planning for scaling up needs to bring these different elements together to consider how aid flows should be sequenced in light of absorptive capacity, which instruments and investments are likely to be most effective and which specific interventions will address the most binding constraints to development and aid effectiveness. Few modelling tools approach this set of concerns to allow both an analysis of the macroeconomic environment and consideration of more microeconomic, sector-specific constraints to scaling up. The next section describes one such approach that has been developed at the World Bank to assist in identifying scaling up scenarios.

A FRAMEWORK FOR SIMULATING SCALING UP TO ACHIEVE THE MDGS

The framework used for projecting attainment of MDG targets is known as MAMS (Maquette for MDG Simulation) and examines capacity constraints and trade-offs in achieving the MDGS. MAMS is a dynamic computable general equilibrium (CGE) model which has been extended to include a module that covers MDGs related to poverty, health, education, and water and sanitation. As noted in the introduction, the rationale for the use of a model of this type is that the pursuit of MDG strategies has strong effects throughout the economy via markets for foreign exchange, factors (especially labour) and goods and services, with feedback effects that may significantly alter the findings of more narrow sectoral analyses. For example, the amount of real health or education services that a dollar in aid can purchase may change significantly in light of changes in exchange rates, prices and wages. In addition, existing relationships between different MDGs (e.g., health and education) may influence the expansion in real services that is required—improvements in water and sanitation, for example, may reduce the expansion in health services that is required to reach health MDGs.

In the application described in the following section, the model is applied to an Ethiopian database and solved for the period 2002–2015.[3] More specifically, building on the recent literature and sector studies on health and education outcomes, MAMS considers the following MDGs:

(MDG 1) halving, between 1990 and 2015, the headcount poverty rate;

(MDG 2) achieving universal primary education (100 per cent completion rate by 2015);

(MDG 4) reducing by two-thirds, between 1990 and 2015, the under-five child mortality rate by 2015;

(MDG 5) reducing by three fourths, between 1990 and 2015, the maternal mortality rate; and

(MDG 7) reducing by half, by 2015, the number of people without access to safe water and basic sanitation.

The model allows for a relatively detailed treatment of government activities related to the MDGs. Government consumption, investment and capital stocks are disaggregated by function into four education sectors, three health sectors, sectors for water and sanitation, public infrastructure and other government activities. The major government revenue sources are taxes (direct and indirect), foreign borrowing and foreign grants. The non-government economy is represented by a single sector producing tradable and non-tradable goods and services. The primary factors of production are divided into public capital, private capital and three types of labour (unskilled, skilled and highly-skilled). GDP growth is a function of growth in the stocks of labour and capital, and productivity growth. The composition and overall growth of the labour force depends on the evolution of the education sector, whereas capital stock growth depends on investments. Productivity growth is also endogenous, depending on growth in the stock of public capital in infrastructure.

The core MDG module specifies how changes in the different MDG indicators are determined. To the extent possible, it is parameterized on the basis of detailed sector studies on Ethiopia. In the module, the government has an annual primary education budget covering teacher salaries, recurrent operations and maintenance costs, and capital investment (for example, in new classrooms). Recurrent expenditures and the capital stock in primary education together determine the supply side.[4] Demand for primary schooling and student behaviour—the population share that enrols in the first grade, graduation shares among the enrolled and the shares of the graduates that choose to continue to next grade—depend on the quality of education (student-teacher and student-capital ratios), income incentives (using current wages as a proxy, the expected relative income gain from climbing one step on the salary ladder), the under-five mortality rate (a proxy for the health status of the school population), household consumption per capita and the level of public infrastructure services.

This specification of sector demand and supply captures lags between investment and outcomes and is one strength of the approach. Based on sector studies, it can be seen that the lags between increased enrolments and outcomes at different education levels are related to the number of years required for completion, and actual completion rates.

The specification of health services draws on a World Bank health sector strategy report for Ethiopia. Improvement in under-five and maternal mortality rates (MDGs 4 and 5) are determined by the level of health services per capita (public and private services), per capita consumption and the population shares with access to improved water and sanitation services (MDG 7). The package of health services that achieves MDGs 4 and 5 also includes sufficient HIV/AIDS prevention services to halt its spread (part of MDG 6). For water and sanitation, the population shares with access to improved services are modelled as functions of per capita household consumption and provision of government water and sanitation services.

The provision of the additional government services needed to achieve the MDGs clearly requires additional resources—capital, labour and intermediate inputs—which then become unavailable to the rest of the economy. The effects of a programme depend on how it is financed—from foreign sources, domestic taxes (which reduce consumption) or domestic borrowing (which crowds out private investment). Even with 100 per cent foreign grant financing for additional services, which minimize domestic resource costs, the rest of the economy is affected through two main channels—labour markets and relative prices. Expanding the provision of health or education services increases demand for teachers, nurses and doctors, thereby reducing the number of skilled workers available in other sectors. Increased school enrolment also reduces the size of the overall labour force (since it removes a larger part of the school-age population from the labour force), though in the medium run it adds to the share of skilled labour in the labour force. Two forces drive changes in relative commodity prices. First, domestic demand switches towards MDG-related government services, which impacts on economy-wide production costs and prices. Second, increased aid flows lead to an appreciation of the real exchange rate, which is reflected in increased prices of non-traded relative to traded outputs. These manifestations of Dutch disease can bring about long-lasting changes in the structure of production, which is diverted from exports and import-competing goods.

The limitations on absorptive capacity are captured through three main channels. Two channels have just been mentioned, the labour market and changes in the real exchange rate (relative price of the domestic good at international prices). The third channel is represented by potential infrastructure bottlenecks, particularly in transport and energy. Large investments in education services, for example, will tend to reduce further absorptive capacity as skilled labour is diverted to education, as the relative price of non-tradables rises (e.g., real wages are bid up, reflecting the Dutch disease effect) and if infrastructure bottlenecks reduce the efficiency of public service delivery. Moreover, the impact will not be limited to the education sector but will affect costs throughout the economy, including other public services and the private sector.

Policy makers thus face important trade-offs: increased investment in public service delivery is essential for improved MDG outcomes but, beyond a certain point, the unit costs begin to rise along with indirect costs to other sectors. The challenge is to keep costs down while, at the same time, targeting social outcomes over time. Building absorptive capacity is clearly a central element in this process.

There are also important complementarities across spending on different MDGs—represented by cross-elasticities in our modelling framework—where progress for one MDG may contribute to progress for other MDGs. For example, progress in the provision of improved water and sanitation services has a positive impact on heath outcomes. In addition, the provision of education services (primary, secondary and higher) helps to expand the skilled workforce needed both to increase productivity of the private sector and to work in publicly funded schools and clinics.

SCALING UP AID: A COUNTRY APPLICATION

Results from the simulations using the MAMS model, calibrated for Ethiopia, suggest that the MDGs could be achieved by 2015 under certain circumstances; however, this would require large levels of grant financing and careful attention to the allocation and sequencing of investments. Although the simulations are presented for Ethiopia, they have general relevance for other low-income countries with weak capacity and large ODA requirements for reaching the MDGs.[5]

Two assumptions are particularly critical for the simulations that follow. First, all of the incremental costs of scaling up aid are treated as fully financed by foreign grants. As domestic revenues grow, they help offset total costs, but the bulk of financing is external and in grants, rather than loans. This sets aside important issues over the stability of financing and restrictions that are imposed by Ethiopia's heavy indebtedness and limitations imposed by the HIPC process. Second, constraints on governance and public expenditure management are also set aside: financing for development is managed at current levels of efficiency and the institutional or governance impact of foreign financing is set aside. The importance of these assumptions is considered below.

Based on present trends, Ethiopia is expected to fall far short of achieving most of the MDG targets by 2015, including income poverty, primary school completion and water and sanitation. Lack of financing is the single largest constraint to accelerating progress. Results from the Ethiopia MAMS model suggest that the MDGs can be reached but will require large increases in grant financing and careful sequencing of grant-financed public investment.

Figure 9.1 shows the foreign grant financing requirements under four scenarios to illustrate differences in the costing achievements of the MDGs. In all scenarios, the deficit of the public budget is covered by foreign grants. In the status quo or "base case", the different areas of government services and GDP all grow at an annual rate of about 4 per cent. This performance is similar to Ethiopia's past growth trend. Government domestic revenues are assumed to

FIGURE 9.1
Foreign grant financing (US$ per capita)

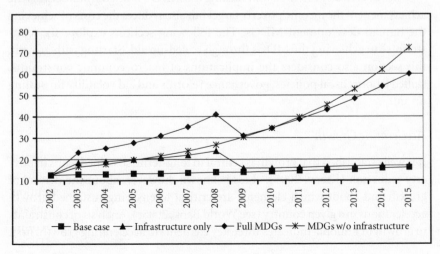

grow somewhat faster so that aid as grant financing expands at an average rate of 1.5 per cent a year, while foreign loans are assumed to remain constant.

The base scenario is contrasted with three other scenarios that include foreign grants directed towards meeting the MDGs. The first case, "full MDGs", expands foreign grant financing to reach each of the targeted MDGs—reducing income poverty along with education, health, and water and sanitation targets. The two other cases shown separate out the investment in basic national infrastructure required to boost economic growth ("infrastructure only") and investment in the five education, health, and sanitation MDGs in the model ("MDGs without infrastructure").

The achievement of both the social and income poverty MDGs by 2015 is estimated to require grant financing of around US$60 per capita by the end of the period, or approximately 40 per cent of GDP, compared with current levels in Ethiopia of just below 20 per cent. If foreign grants target only physical infrastructure to accelerate growth and income poverty reduction (excluding the other MDGs), much lower levels of grant financing are required. Over the first half of the period, financing roughly doubles to US$24 per capita at its peak in 2008 and then subsides as productivity improvements and revenue response to higher growth cut financing needs.[6]

By contrast, the scenario targeting *only the social MDGs* to the neglect of core infrastructure requires higher financing than in the full MDG scenario. Financing needs rise to US$70 per capita by the end of the period. Although the full MDG scenario includes added investment in core infrastructure, it also serves to lift total productivity, accelerate growth and boost government revenues, which together act to reduce overall aid requirements.

Growth is clearly essential for reaching the MDGs. It not only underpins the achievement of the income poverty target but also reduces the costs of achieving the human development MDGs. The following sections explore six "constraints" to achieving the MDGs through scaled-up aid. Starting with growth, this section also considers the implications of macroeconomic constraints, skilled labour, fiscal policies, governance reforms and aid volatility for scaling up aid.

Accelerating Growth

It is well established that growth is central to long-term, sustained gains in poverty reduction (Kraay, 2005).[7] Less is known, however, about the drivers of growth and about which elements are critical to ensuring sustained growth accelerations in a given country (see World Bank, 2005c). Analysis of constraints to growth in Ethiopia indicates three key elements to accelerating growth: first, focusing public investment on infrastructure to strengthen urban-rural marketing linkages; second, investing in improved water management to improve agricultural productivity; and third, improving the investment climate and strengthening security of land tenure to reduce risk facing private producers and investors (see World Bank, 2005d). The first two of these elements require investment in core infrastructure.

Core infrastructure considered key to accelerating growth in Ethiopia includes a basic transport system and the expansion of power generation and distribution, to better link the urban, peri-urban and rural economies. Large-scale investments in water management and irrigation systems are also included to help raise agricultural productivity. All of these investments help reduce the indirect costs to private investment (affected by such factors as the *reliability* of power, and transport logistics and timing) and business-related losses that depress firm productivity, as highlighted in a recent work on African economies by Eiffert, Gelb and Ramachandran (2005).

Figure 9.2 illustrates the impact of the different MDG investment scenarios on economic growth in Ethiopia. Under current trends, illustrated by the base case, poverty is forecast to decline to around 29 per cent of the population—compared with 38 per cent in 1990 (not shown)—far short of the MDG target of 19 per cent of the population. In the full MDG case, however, investment in basic infrastructure helps accelerate the growth rate relative to the base case by about 1.5 per cent annually and is critical for the halving of poverty incidence

FIGURE 9.2
MDG1—share of population living on $1 (PPP) per day or less (%)

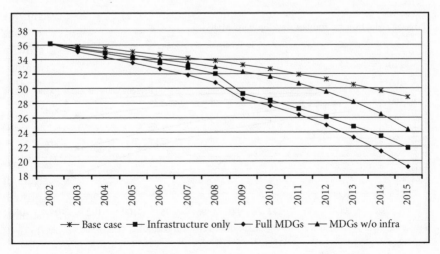

from its 1990 level of 36 per cent of the population. Growth in household consumption[8] helps drive poverty down to the MDG target of 19 per cent by 2015 (using a conservative estimate of poverty elasticity of—1 with respect to mean household consumption per capita).

Between these two scenarios are the cases where increased investment in core infrastructure is separated from investment in the human development MDGs. In the case of spending on only the MDGs independent of core infrastructure, growth is also increased, but by far less than spending on infrastructure. This occurs mainly through raising the supply of skilled labour and through increased employment generated by higher public investment.[9] Relative to the investment share, however, the contribution from basic infrastructure is much greater, reducing the poverty incidence to 22 per cent by 2015, compared with 26 per cent in the case of investments in the human development MDGs only.

The argument being presented is not that investment in infrastructure alone will suffice to accelerate growth. Indeed, investment in non-income MDGs clearly contributes to growth and poverty reduction, as Figure 9.2 illustrates. The suggestion is, however, that with adequate governance and institutions in place to regulate infrastructure, there is a need to lead with strong infrastructure investment in order to both accelerate growth and reduce the unit costs of achieving non-income MDGs. The suggestion is also that there are significant trade-offs between investing in infrastructure and social services.

Figure 9.3 illustrates the trade-offs suggested by these simulations for investing in infrastructure-targeting growth versus investment for reaching the human development MDGs. For a fixed level of real resources (expressed in present

FIGURE 9.3
Poverty reduction vs. human development MDGs

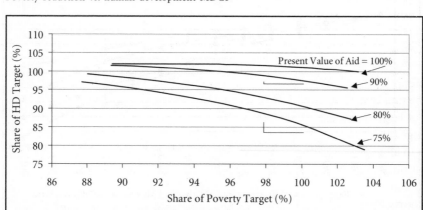

discounted terms), there are different combinations of the poverty reduction and human development targets that can be achieved. At full financing (indicated as 100 per cent), all of the targeted MDGs can be reached. Point A illustrates this level where all of the MDG targets have been reached. As can be seen, trade-off here between human development targets and growth is almost flat, i.e. there is little scope for increasing the human development indicators at the expense of growth. On the other hand, if total financing over the ten years is reduced by one fourth, the impact is pronounced. As shown, poverty reduction could be held to the level needed to achieve the MDG target (at point B) and the trade-offs would be steeper. Full achievement of the poverty target can be achieved, but only with a 15 per cent shortfall in meeting the other MDG targets. By reallocating resources from growth-oriented infrastructure to investment in social services for human development, a one per cent fall in income growth would lead to an increase in meeting the human development MDG targets by around 2.5 per cent.

These changing trade-offs are essentially due to the rapidly decreasing marginal returns to spending in human development on getting close to full completion of the MDGs. In other words, reaching the last children to send them to school, or reaching the most remote communities to improve health or to bring water, is much more expensive than when the economy is relatively far away from completion of the MDGs. As a result, giving up on non-income MDGs gives a much higher return in terms of private output and income MDGs when close to the goal—with all the aid that is needed—than when the economy is far away from the goal because of insufficient aid.

Macroeconomic Constraints and Competitiveness

As discussed above, aid flows permit a much larger trade deficit, draw resources to non-traded sectors and place upward pressure on the real exchange rate, thereby reducing competitiveness and resources flowing to traded goods and services. These concerns are well recognized.[10] As stressed in Bevan (2005), the extent to which aid flows are associated with the problem of real exchange-rate appreciation depends largely on the relative impact on demand and supply. The supply response, depending on the effects of aid on productivity across sectors, largely determines the depth and duration of adverse effects following the surge in aid.

In all of the Ethiopian scenarios, there is evidence of exchange-rate appreciation, rising real wage rates and a deterioration in the trade balance as imports expand and export performance is weakened. Figure 9.4 shows the path of real exports through 2015. Deteriorating export competitiveness (Dutch disease

FIGURE 9.4
Real exports as a share of GDP, 2002–2015

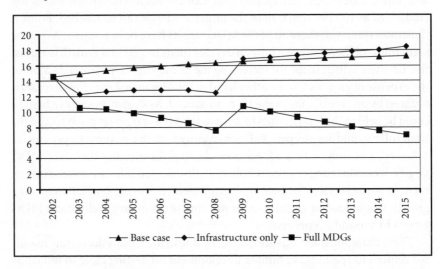

effects) is clearly a concern. Aid-induced appreciation of the exchange rate and the collapse in exports are severe. Under the full MDG scenario, exports fall from around 14 per cent of GDP to 8 per cent by 2015, and the real exchange rate appreciates by close to 20 per cent. However, the impact on real GDP growth over this period of high aid flows and public investment is quite limited.

Public spending on infrastructure and MDG services differ in their effects on the supply side and in their import intensities. Infrastructure spending has a positive but lagged impact on productivity, whereas spending on MDG services has only a very modest impact on productivity in the short run but affects supply through adding to the stock of skilled labour. Infrastructure spending initially leads to exchange-rate appreciation, until productivity improvements raise growth of GDP, household incomes and demand. The import intensity of basic infrastructure in Ethiopia is also high, reducing the adverse price impact and resource switching effects.

By contrast, investment in social services takes longer to impact on productivity and hence has less effect over the ten-year time frame for the MDGs. This places greater pressure on the real exchange rate. In the case of the use of foreign aid to support human development and forego investment in core infrastructure, the real exchange rate appreciates by about 30 per cent and dramatically reduces the exports to less than half their initial share of GDP by 2015. Appreciation of the real exchange rate (the change in relative prices of the domestic good) also reduces the purchasing power of foreign grants, requiring larger commitments to finance investment in the human development MDGs.

If export performance is taken to be a key dynamic driver for long-term economic performance, then the loss in export share could pose a long-term, and potentially serious, trade-off between scaling up aid inflows to meet the non-income MDGs and poverty reduction. The dynamic cost to foregone output could be potentially large and points to the need for careful consideration of macroeconomic policy options and policies to contain harmful effects on competitiveness.

Skilled Labour Constraints

Severe labour constraints pose a further challenge to scaling up in Ethiopia. Scaling up spending will increase demands on skilled labour in particular—physicians, nurses, teachers, engineers, etc. The case of expanding primary enrolment is illustrative. Between 2002 and 2015, around 75,000 additional teachers are needed for the system to achieve the 100 per cent completion target and to meet quality standards in education.[11] This requires investment in teacher training facilities and expansion of the number of higher education graduates to meet this target. In the short run, skilled labour can be hired from other sectors, in particular the private sector, but at the cost of both higher wages and lost output as labour exits the private sector. Accelerating this process imposes higher costs on output.

Figure 9.5 shows the path of real wages under three scenarios: the base case and the full-MDG case examined earlier, and a third case in which aid is frontloaded to accelerate the hiring of teachers and the boosting of enrolment targets.

FIGURE 9.5
Real wages of workers with secondary school education (in local currency)

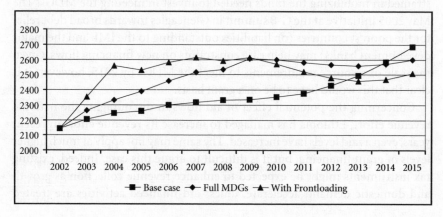

As more funds are spent on hiring skilled labour into education, real wages increase significantly to induce labour away from other uses, raising unit costs of production. Wages for skilled labour rise both in education and in the private sector, as well as elsewhere in the public sector. In the scenario in which aid outlays are frontloaded to accelerate primary education expenditures, real wages spike to levels close to 25 per cent above their starting values. By the middle of the projection period, however, the path moderates, and real wage growth not only moderates but begins to decline. This is because investment in teacher training and other secondary and higher education programmes helps expand the supply of skilled labour *with a lag*, and wage pressures begin to moderate. The appropriate sequencing of investment in teacher training, capital inputs and possible adjustment of quality standards are clearly important determinants of the labour supply and wage response.

There are plausible conditions under which the market-clearing wage for skilled labour, as suggested by the model, is not sufficient for the generation of adequate supply. Skilled labour may be attracted abroad by higher wages—a chronic problem for many developing countries—new graduates may not be of sufficient quality or there may not be adequate incentives for skilled workers to relocate to remote areas. Under these circumstances, skilled wages would have to rise more sharply in order to recruit and retain adequate teachers, gene-rating even higher costs to overcome capacity constraints.

Fiscal Constraints

Most of the potential fiscal constraints to scaling up aid discussed earlier cannot be readily illustrated in the MAMS model. All external support is assumed to be in the form of grants, for example, and public debt is not a constraint to increased financing. If this were not the case, Ethiopia would be highly con-strained in mobilizing the funds needed to invest in meeting the MDGs. The May 2005 initiative at the G-8 summit in Gleneagles towards broad debt relief for the poorest countries (on liabilities outstanding to the IMF and the major development banks) may help ease constraints on new financing flows. Given the scale of resource requirements to meet the MDGs by 2015, however, it is clear that this would have to be on a grant basis.

Concerning the potential effect of aid flows in discouraging the national revenue effort, Ethiopia has managed to increase its revenue effort in recent years, even as aid levels have increased. The same may not apply at much higher levels of grant financing, but it is difficult to argue this case. Indeed, existing tax instruments might be expected to enhance revenue collection as growth and domestic demand accelerate, unless aid-financed activities are treated differently for tax collection purposes (an issue in aid harmonization and avoidance of distortions arising from unequal treatment).

Evidence from the MAMS modelling on the ability to sustain the *recurrent* cost burden of scaling up aid suggests this is unlikely to be a major burden. Over the simulation period to 2015, the share of total incremental spending required on recurrent costs is around one third, two thirds of which is being on capital goods. Total incremental recurrent costs for education, health, water and sanitation, and infrastructure spending amount to around 5.6 per cent of GDP in 2005 and roughly double to around 10 per cent of GDP by 2015 (see Figure 9.6). As a share of total tax revenues over this period, this represents a much smaller increase, from just under 18 per cent in 2005 to about 24 per cent by 2015. The recurrent cost burden is clearly increasing, with capital maintenance costs assuming an increasing share in this regard, but there is no a priori reason to consider this an unmanageable burden.

Of greater concern is the quality of public expenditure management and the capacity of the government to adequately budget and disburse for recurrent costs in the budget. This is a challenge in all countries—including those of the Organization for Economic Cooperation and Development (OECD)—where political incentives and economic efficiency are often not well aligned. It is a particularly acute problem in low-income countries, such as Ethiopia, and requires investment in institutional strengthening and measures to insulate public expenditures from political discretion. Public expenditure management in Ethiopia is being tracked under the HIPC tracking process and has shown

Figure 9.6
Incremental recurrent and capital spending 2005–2015

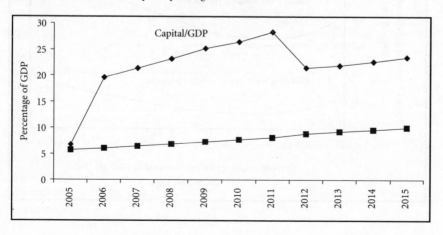

some improvement since 1999/2000, when the tracking process began, but major challenges to the quality of budget preparation and execution remain.

An additional fiscal issue that arises concerns the timing of aid disbursements to minimize the total costs of reaching the MDGs. Some argue that more resources are required up front in order to generate the push needed for escaping the "poverty traps" that afflict the poorest countries. The arguments for "frontloading" aid are difficult to validate empirically on a purely macroeconomic basis (see Kraay and Raddatz, 2005).

In MAMS, a simplistic test of the costs and benefits of investment frontloading can be seen from Figure 9.7. Consider the effect of frontloading aid, i.e., of adjusting the share of total expenditures spent in the first five-year period (2005–2010). The resulting U-shaped curve shown in Figure 9.7 shows how the present discounted value of foreign aid required to reach the MDGs changes as the share of resources spent in the first 5 years (i.e., the frontloaded share) increases from very low to high levels. The upper curve shows that, at a level of around 20 per cent, costs are minimized and then rise at an accelerating pace as capacity constraints become more binding (labour costs rise, infrastructure congestion costs increase, exchange-rate appreciation reduces the purchasing

FIGURE 9.7
Expenditure frontloading and foreign aid requirements.

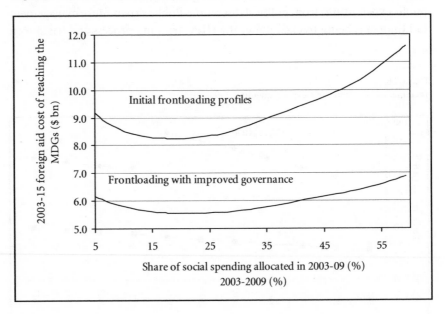

power of aid, etc.). In the extreme, at some point, with around 70 per cent frontloading, costs sharply accelerate until the MDGs cannot be achieved. Frontloading a substantial share of resources is not cost-minimizing in this case.

Governance and Institutional Reform

Foreign grant financing for scaling up services to meet the MDGs can drive *demand* for more and better services, but whether the *supply* is forthcoming depends in large measure on the quality of institutions and governance for translating external financial resources into the required goods and services. In an environment of good governance and policies, there is relatively little leakage or loss of efficiency involved in scaling up. This environment would include a healthy investment climate in which private entrepreneurs can start up business and take advantage of new opportunities.

Institutional quality and governance issues cannot be explicitly modelled in this framework, but they are key to managing many of the constraints to scaling up. Although the MAMS model does not directly address the critical question of how underlying institutional capacity and governance can be improved, it can help to illustrate the basic importance of institutional strengthening and governance vis-à-vis the costs and sustainability of scaling up. The recent Country Economic Memorandum on Ethiopia (World Bank, 2005b) identifies the investment climate as one of the main areas for strengthening in order to improve growth performance.

A heuristic illustration of the impact of governance and institutional reforms can be seen by assuming that on average the net impact of governance improvements raises cost efficiency by two per cent, compounded annually, independent of the rate of public investment. Using Figure 9.7 again to illustrate the impact of these reforms and frontloading, a new U-curve is shown to depict the cost of achieving the MDGs under different ratios of resource frontloading. The lower U-curve in Figure 9.7 suggests several effects. First, the productivity gain reduces the cost of achieving the MDGs along all points of the curve and "flattens" it, reducing the total variation in costs. The total cost of achieving the MDGs by 2015 in present value terms would fall by around one third as a result of the productivity gains derived from improved governance.

Second, the new point of cost minimization suggests greater frontloading. This may seem contrary to the expectation of less frontloading in anticipation of lower unit costs in the future. The ambiguity arises from the relative strength of two underlying effects pushing in opposite directions. The efficiency gain is like a relative price change, as the present value of expenditures in the first period falls by less than it does in the second period, shifting expenditure shares to the first period. The behavioural response, however, is to shift consumption to the second period.

One implication of this analysis is that anticipated incremental gains in underlying governance or productivity should not be a reason to delay public expenditures towards capacity-building and service delivery. Even if there are underlying efficiency gains that reduce costs over time, they do not constitute a reason to delay investment in the MDGs, but rather suggest that the same constraints to absorptive capacity—labour costs, macroeconomic constraints, infrastructure congestion—guide the investment path. Good governance is the catalyst for creating an environment in which development finance can generate growth more generally and accountability mechanisms can be built to help ensure service delivery.

The Quality of Aid and Aid Volatility

Not only the quantity of aid but the quality of aid—the way in which aid is provided—is vital to development outcomes. Aid that is tied to specific imports or import origin, or aid that is uncertain, volatile or fragmented across donors significantly reduces the value of total aid flows. Many donors also require different reporting standards and accounting, often affected outside normal budgetary channels, which impose a "compliance tax" on recipient countries.

One important element in this regard is aid volatility. Empirical work on aid volatility shows that aid flows, on which some countries depend for more than half of total government expenditures, are more volatile than fiscal revenues. Moreover, shortfalls in aid and domestic revenues tend to coincide; amplifying swings in fiscal capacity (see Bulíř and Hamann, 2003). Some argue that the scaling up of aid that is now anticipated is likely to increase aid volatility and compel countries to take further steps towards buffering against such volatility (Eiffert and Gelb, 2005).

The MAMS model is not well designed to test the implications of aid volatility for the MDG outcomes. Consider, however, two different paths for aid disbursements containing the same present discounted value of total aid. In one case, there is complete predictability and control of timing, and the government can plan and sequence outlays to maximize social and growth outcomes. In the second case, aid is expected to be constant and, over the first five years, high aid flows are maintained—then aid suddenly stops. Clearly, the second case will have worse implications. Higher aid flows for the first half of the period would have allowed more rapid progress, although with decreasing returns, but thereafter there would be a sudden shock to the system leading to the serious problems that developing countries face not infrequently: a collapse in revenues leading to politically expedient (or legal) cutbacks—typically in public investment and operations and maintenance expenditures rather than salaries and debt service obligations. Simulations can aim to estimate the cost of these two patterns. The consequences of a sudden stop in aid can be severe, adversely affecting social stability, public service delivery, institutional continuity and, of course, politics—extending well beyond factors captured in most models.

CONCLUSIONS

The constraints to scaling up aid to low-income counties and their ability to effectively absorb scaled-up aid is an issue of major concern in the debate over international financing of MDG efforts. This chapter has explored six aspects of grant financing for scaling up public service delivery, drawing on a modelling framework that brings together a macroeconomic consistency framework with country specific microeconomic issues affecting sector response to scaled-up aid efforts. Four main points arise from this analysis.

First, a focus on improving growth performance in tandem with strengthening service delivery is essential. Growth performance depends to a significant extent on improving the quality and access of households and businesses to core infrastructure services—transport, power, water and communications. Strengthening infrastructure to improve growth in low-income countries both underpins income poverty reduction and has widespread benefits for reducing the cost and foreign financing requirements for reaching human development MDGs.

Second, the macroeconomic impact of large aid flows on the competitiveness of the tradables sector (Dutch disease) can be serious, resulting in a significant decline in the share of exports in the economy. The costs to future growth depend largely on the impact of aid and policies in generating productivity growth of both traded goods and domestic goods and services. Strategic investments to boost productivity and address trade constraints are important for avoiding adverse macro effects, and the potential tradeoffs need to be carefully weighed.

Third, sequencing of investments is important for minimizing the costs of reaching the MDGs, particularly in light of skilled labour demand for scaling up service delivery and short-run labour supply limitations. Skilled labour supply can only be expanded with a lag, requiring sequencing together with investment in complementary inputs and infrastructure. Large-scale front-loading of capital and labour investments is costly as it pushes against absorptive capacity constraints, intensifies the premium on skilled wages and bids labour away from the private sector, thereby depressing growth.

Fourth, improvement in the underlying governance and institutional structures, including improvement of public expenditure management, help to secure broad productivity improvements in public service delivery and should underpin development strategies. Their cumulative effect can significantly reduce the overall costs of achieving the MDGs and secure long-term productivity gains.

Finally, this work suggests that several elements of country-specific development strategies need to be in place to ensure that large increases in aid can be effectively used to achieve the MDGs in low-income countries. Quantitative simulation research to analyse alternative strategies can capture some of these key elements and provide insights into aid effectiveness and to reaching the MDGs. Simulations can only be approximate, but can help to guide decision making.

NOTES

[1] See Ravallion and Chen, 2005, and Alatas, Guggenheim and Wong, 2005, for impact evaluations of these projects.

[2] One often-cited example is from Uganda, where a newspaper campaign to boost the ability of parents to monitor local officials' handling of school grants helped to sharply reduce losses. With greater public awareness and transparency, 'capture' or leakage of budget resources fell from 80 per cent to 20 per cent between 1995 and 2001 (Reinikka and Svensson, 2003).

[3] The model is presented in detail in Bourguignon and others, 2004; 2005: Lofgren, 2004. Preliminary applications to Ethiopia are discussed in Lofgren and Diaz-Bonilla, 2005; Sundberg and Lofgren, 2005. This remains work in progress.

[4] Private supply of education services has not been separately included since it is relatively small in Ethiopia, but it could be elaborated for countries where it is important.

[5] Presented in Bourguignon and others, 2004; 2005.

[6] Note that the 'kink' in grant financing requirements in 2008/09 corresponds to a threshold effect of initial investment in infrastructure on productivity. It is indeed reasonably assumed that there is a five-year gestation lag in the effect of infrastructure on the productivity of the private and public sectors. Financing needs are reduced when higher productivity gains kick in. A more continuous representation of this phenomenon could have been used; however, the interest of the discontinuous specification used here is to illustrate the crucial role of the productivity effect of infrastructure.

[7] Note that equity—in particular expanding opportunity and access to services for poor people—is also a fundamental policy parameter (see World Bank, 2005a) which is not explored here.

[8] Income growth is assumed to be distributionally neutral across household income groups. Ongoing work with MAMS disaggregates the economy by major sectors—agriculture, services and manufacturing—allowing greater refinement in the treatment of sector growth rates, intersectoral migration and more differentiated returns to labour.

[9] Also contributing to higher growth and consumption is the exchange-rate effect of the currency's appreciation, which helps raise average real purchasing power.

[10] Heller and Gupta, 2002, provide a clear overview of the issues and cite several country studies.

[11] This assumes a 40:1 student teacher ratio, compared to the current 75:1 ratio. Higher ratios reduce the quality of education services and may reduce demand for schooling, although some argue for lower and less costly standards.

REFERENCES

Alatas, Vivi, Scott Guggenheim, and Susan Wong (2005). An evaluation of the Kecamatan Development Project. Presentation for 'Reducing poverty on a global scale', World Bank, Washington, DC: 210–211.

Bevan, David (2005). An analytical overview of aid absorption: Recognizing and avoiding macroeconomic hazards. Paper for the Seminar on 'Foreign Aid and Macroeconomic Management', March 14–15, Maputo, Mozambique. In Peter Isard, Leslie Lipschitz, Alexandros Mourmouras, and Peter Heller (eds). Macroeconomic Management of Foreign Aid: Opportunities and Pitfalls. Forthcoming, International Monetary Fund, Washington, DC.

Bourguignon, François, Maurizio Bussolo, Luiz Pereira da Silva, Hans Timmer, and Dominique van der Mensbrugghe (2004). MAMS: Maquette for MDG simulations. Processed, March, World Bank, Washington, DC.

Bourguignon, François, Maurizio Bussolo, Caroline Diaz-Bonilla, Hans Timmer, and Dominique van der Mensbrugghe (2005). Aid, service delivery and the MDGs in an economy-wide framework. Forthcoming, Working Paper, World Bank, Washington, DC.

Bourguignon, François, Alan Gelb and Bruno Versailles (2005). Policy, aid and performance in Africa: The G11 and other country groups. Forthcoming, Working Paper, World Bank, Washington, DC.

Brautigam, Deborah, and Stephen Knack (2004). Foreign aid, institutions and governance in Sub-Saharan Africa. Economic Development and Cultural Change 52 (2): 255–286.

Bulíř, Aleš, and A. Javier Hamann (2003). Aid volatility: An empirical assessment. IMF Staff Papers 50 (1): 64–89.

Burnside, Craig, and David Dollar (2000). Aid, policies and growth. American Economic Review 90 (4): 847–868.

Burnside, Craig, and David Dollar (2004). Aid, policies and growth: Revisiting the evidence. Policy Research Working Paper No. 3251, World Bank, Washington, DC.

Clemens, Michael A., Steven Radelet and Rikhil Bhavnani (2004). Counting chickens when they hatch: The short term effect of aid on growth. Working Paper No. 44, November, Center for Global Development, Washington, DC.

Dollar, David, and Victoria Levin (2004). The increasing selectivity of foreign aid, 1984–2003. Policy Research Working Paper Series No. 3299, May, World Bank, Washington, DC.

Easterly, William, Ross Levine, and David Roodman (2003). New data, new doubts: A comment on Burnside and Dollar's 'Aid, policies, and growth'. CGD Working Paper No. 26. Centre for Global Development: Washington, DC. Published as 'Aid, Policies, and Growth: Comment'. American Economic Review 94 (3): 774–780.

Eiffert, Benn, and Alan Gelb (2005). Improving the dynamics of aid: Toward more predictable budget support. Policy Research Working Paper No. WPS3732, World Bank, Washington, DC.

Eiffert, Benn, Alan Gelb, and Vijaya Ramachandran (2005). Business environment and comparative advantage in Africa: Evidence from the investment climate data. Working Paper No. 56, February, Center for Global Development, Washington, DC.

Estache, Antonio (2004). Emerging infrastructure policy issues in developing countries: A survey of the recent economic literature. Policy Research Working Paper Series No. 3442, World Bank, Washington, DC.

Foster, Mick (2003). *The Case for Increased Aid*. Report to the Department for International Development (DfID), London.

Heller, Peter S. (2005). Pity the finance minister: Managing a substantial scaling-up of aid flows. Processed, Fiscal Affairs Department, International Monetary Fund, Washington, DC.

Heller, Peter, and Sanjeev Gupta (2002). Challenges in expanding development assistance. IMF Discussion Paper PDP/02/5, March, International Monetary Fund, Washington, DC.

International Monetary Fund (2005a). The macroeconomics of managing increased aid inflows: Experiences of low-income countries and policy implications. Processed, August, Policy Development and Review Department, International Monetary Fund, Washington, DC.

International Monetary Fund (2005b). The macroeconomic challenge of scaling up aid to low income countries. Processed, August, African Department, International Monetary Fund, Washington, DC.

Kraay, Aart (2005). Aid, growth, and poverty. In Peter Isard, Leslie Lipschitz, Alexandros Mourmouras, and Peter Heller (eds). *Macroeconomic Management of Foreign Aid: Opportunities and Pitfalls*. Forthcoming. International Monetary Fund, Washington, DC.

Kraay, Aart, and Claudio Raddatz (2005). Poverty traps, aid and growth. World Bank Policy Research Working Paper No. 3631, June, World Bank, Washington, DC.

Lofgren, Hans (2004). MAMS: An economy wide model for analysis of MDG country strategies. Processed, World Bank, Development Prospects Group, Washington, DC.

Lofgren, Hans, and Carolina Diaz-Bonilla (2005). An Ethiopian strategy for achieving the millennium development goals: Simulations with the MAMS model. Processed, February, World Bank, Washington, DC.

Rajan, Raghuram, and Arvind Subramanian (2005a). What undermines aid's impact on growth? IMF Working Paper WP/05/126, June, International Monetary Fund, Washington, DC.

Rajan, Raghuram, and Arvind Subramanian (2005b). Aid and growth: What does the cross-country evidence really show? IMF Working Paper WP/05/127, June, International Monetary Fund, Washington, DC.

Ravallion, Martin, and Shaohua Chen (2005). Hidden impact? Household saving in response to a poor-areas development project. *Journal of Public Economics*, Forthcoming.

Reinikka, Ritva, and Jakob Svensson (2003). *The Power of Information: Evidence from an Information Campaign to Reduce Capture*. World Bank, Washington, DC.

Sundberg, Mark, and Hans Lofgren (2006). Absorptive capacity and achieving the MDGs: The case of Ethiopia. In Peter Isard, Leslie Lipschitz, Alexandros Mourmouras, and Peter Heller (eds). *Macroeconomic Management of Foreign Aid: Opportunities and Pitfalls*. International Monetary Fund, Washington, DC.

World Bank (1998). *Assessing Aid: What Works, What Doesn't, and Why*. World Bank Research Policy Report. Oxford University Press, New York, for World Bank, Washington, DC.

World Bank (2004a). *Aid Effectiveness and Financing Modalities*. Report presented to the Development Committee in September 2004, DC2004–0012, World Bank, Washington, DC.

World Bank (2004b). *Global Monitoring 2004: Policies and Actions for Achieving the MDGs and Related Outcomes*. Report presented to the Development Committee, Spring Meetings of World Bank and the IMF, April 2004, DC2004–0006/Add.1, World Bank, Washington, DC.

World Bank (2005a). *World Development Report 2006: Equity and Development*. World Bank, Washington, DC.

World Bank (2005b). *Ethiopia: A Strategy to Balance and Stimulate Growth—A Country Economic Memorandum.* World Bank, Washington, DC.

World Bank (2005c). *Economic Growth in the 1990s: Learning from a Decade of Reform.* World Bank, Washington, DC.

World Bank (2005d). *Aid Financing and Aid Effectiveness.* Report presented to the Development Committee on aid effectiveness, September, DC2005–0020, World Bank, Washington, DC.

World Bank (2005e). *Economic Growth in the 1990s: Learning from a Decade of Reform.* Processed, April, World Bank, Washington, DC.

10
What is the Most Effective Monetary Policy for Aid-Receiving Countries?

ALESSANDRO PRATI and THIERRY TRESSEL[1]

At the 2005 G-8 meeting in Scotland, world leaders announced a $50 billion increase in official development assistance (ODA) to poor countries. The objective was to help poor countries achieve the Millennium Development Goals (MDGs) that emerged from the Millennium Declaration in 2000 and, thereby, reduce poverty. With foreign aid already representing a large share of recipients' GDP and the precise timetable of the surge in new aid yet to be decided, it is critical that aid-receiving countries be ready to manage the macroeconomic consequences of large and potentially volatile aid flows.

This chapter focuses on how monetary policy can enhance the effectiveness of volatile aid flows. There is growing evidence that such flows tend to be associated with real exchange-rate overvaluation, which hurts manufacturing exports and, ultimately, growth (Rajan and Subramanian, 2005a). Aid-receiving countries are well aware of this problem and tend to adjust their monetary policy stance to limit real exchange-rate appreciation and trade balance fluctuations. Such monetary response to aid inflows raises three questions: (i) does monetary policy have the intended effect of containing aid-induced trade balance volatility and real exchange-rate appreciation? (ii) if so, why?—that is, what allows monetary policy to affect *real* variables in aid-receiving countries? and (iii) under what circumstances does monetary policy improve welfare?

This chapter addresses each of these questions in a separate section. The first section presents evidence of aid volatility and of the effectiveness of monetary policy in containing the associated trade balance fluctuations. The next section discusses the features of aid-receiving countries that allow monetary policy to reallocate resources over time and across sectors by affecting the trade balance. The last section argues that the extent to which this monetary policy activism is welfare-improving depends on whether aid flows affect only consumption or also productivity growth.

Excluding the case of aid given for humanitarian purposes or emergency assistance, which has no reason to be saved, the last section proposes the following taxonomy. *If foreign aid affects only consumption*, then monetary policy should slow down consumption growth and build up international reserves when aid is abundant and deplete them to finance imports and support consumption when aid is scarce. *If foreign aid also affects productivity growth* and, thereby, future consumption, then monetary policy should take this productivity effect into account in responding to aid flows. If the effect of aid on productivity—net of possible Dutch-disease effects—is *positive*, then the higher productivity will contribute to support future consumption as aid dwindles. This implies that, in the face of a surge in aid flows, there would be a smaller need to accumulate reserves and the trade deficit could increase somewhat. Conversely, if the Dutch disease makes the productivity effect of aid *negative*, monetary policy should be more aggressive in containing the trade deficit and save resources in the form of international reserves for more productive future uses.

Aid Volatility and Monetary Policy Practice

Aid Is Very Volatile

Figure 10.1 shows that, in several countries, the average annual ratio of net official development assistance (ODA) to GDP is in the 10 to 30 per cent range, with some massive differences between minimum and maximum annual inflows.[2] Average annual absolute changes can easily exceed 10 per cent of GDP and, in some instances, they have plummeted by as much as 30–40 per

Figure 10.1

ODA flows in per cent of GDP during the 1990s (average, minimum, maximum)

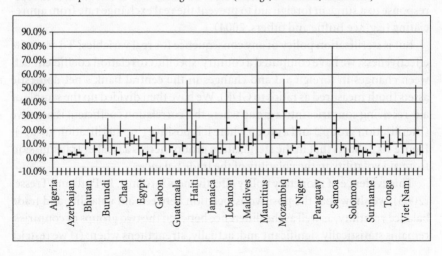

cent of GDP in a single year. These sudden reversals surpass those of net capital inflows in emerging markets, which reached, for example, 13 per cent of GDP in Mexico (1993–1995) and 24 per cent of GDP in Thailand (1996–1998).

In light of the critical role of foreign aid in supporting domestic consumption, there is little doubt that aid volatility has negative welfare implications for aid-receiving countries. Pallage and Robe (2003) estimate the median welfare cost of business cycles in developing countries to be between 10 and 30 times that of the United States. Arellano and others (2005) present numerical simulations showing that aid variability of the magnitude found in previous literature may have substantial detrimental welfare effects, albeit not large enough to wipe out the welfare benefits of the aid itself. This suggests that reducing the volatility of aid and, thereby, of consumption would yield considerable gains. There is also a substantial body of evidence showing that volatility has negative effects on long-term growth (e.g. see Ramey and Ramey, 1995).

MONETARY POLICY'S RESPONSE TO AID VOLATILITY

A widespread practice among aid-receiving countries is that of reducing the net domestic assets of the central bank in response to higher foreign aid inflows. This policy is dubbed *sterilization*. Over the period 1960–1998, we found 704 episodes—out of 1,935 episodes of foreign aid inflows greater than 2 per cent of GDP—during which net domestic assets fell. More recently, several African countries—including Ghana, Ethiopia, Mozambique, Uganda and the United Republic of Tanzania—have drastically reduced their net domestic assets in response to a surge in foreign aid to prevent the real exchange rate from appreciating (e.g. see Buffie and others, 2004).

But is sterilization policy of any consequence for real variables? To assess its effectiveness, we have computed a country-specific correlation coefficient between changes in foreign aid and changes in the central bank's net domestic assets (both measured as ratios to GDP). We have then divided up the sample of aid-receiving countries into a group where this correlation coefficient is negative ('sterilization group') and a group where it is positive ('no sterilization group'). Figure 10.2 shows that in the sterilization group there is a weaker transmission from aid volatility to the volatility of the trade balance.

This evidence of monetary policy effectiveness is robust. In Prati and Tressel (2005), we show that the positive association between aid volatility and trade balance volatility, as well as the difference between the two groups of countries, remains statistically significant and, actually, strengthens when: (i) we restrict

FIGURE 10.2
Aid and trade balance volatility (Countries with average ODA/GDP > 2 per cent)

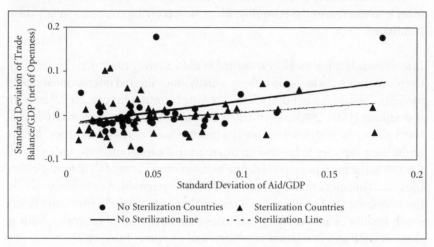

the sample to include countries with average aid-to-GDP ratios larger than 3, 4 or 5 per cent of GDP; (ii) we control for other variables that may affect trade balance volatility, such as trade openness (whose effect is already netted out in Figure 10.2), the volatility of commodity export prices, the size of a country (measured by population), the fraction of years in the sample during which the country was at war and whether a country exports oil; (iii) we use instrumental variables to correct for a possible reverse causation from trade balance volatility to aid volatility; and (iv) we take into account the *intensity* of sterilization policy by interacting the correlation coefficient between changes in aid and changes in net domestic assets with the aid volatility variable.

WHAT MAKES MONETARY POLICY EFFECTIVE?

In this section, we discuss why sterilization policy can modify real variables and, specifically, the trade balance in a typical aid-receiving country.

Characteristics of Aid-Receiving Countries

Prati and Tressel (2005) develop a stylized general equilibrium model where monetary policy affects real variables as long as the capital account is closed to both inflows and outflows and the prices of a country's traded goods are set in international markets. This model also shows that monetary policy could have real effects not only in the short run but also in the long run if aid inflows tend to shrink the tradable sector and, thereby, reduce positive productivity spillovers from it to the rest of the economy. Most aid-receiving countries satisfy these conditions.

International capital mobility is limited in aid-receiving countries
Countries receiving large aid inflows usually enjoy limited international capital mobility. First, only a handful of aid-receiving countries have no capital account restrictions (IMF, 2005). Even when the capital account is relatively free of restrictions, the high levels of official indebtedness of these countries *de facto* limits their capacity to borrow on international capital markets. Indeed, over the 1990s, the median external debt was about 80 per cent of GDP for the countries receiving more than 2 per cent of GDP in foreign aid. As a consequence, in the 1990s, the total of inward and outward private portfolio investments was much smaller in aid-receiving countries than in industrial countries, both as share of GDP and in relation to exports and imports (Table 10.1).

In this context, monetary policy controls the nominal interest rates because there are no capital flows that can offset the tightening or loosening of the monetary policy stance. For example, if the central bank raises domestic interest rates above international rates, foreign capital will not flow into the country to push rates back down. Moreover, domestic investors have usually no access to foreign financial assets. This restriction limits their saving instruments to domestic bonds and cash. As a consequence, any increase or decrease in the supply of public sector bonds must be met by an increase or a decrease of private non-cash financial savings.

Finally, governments of countries receiving large amounts of foreign aid are not allowed to save aid directly, nor can they borrow against future aid disbursements. Indeed, donors usually require recipients to spend development

TABLE 10.1
Private portfolio investments in aid-receiving countries

	portfolio investment assets + liabilities % GDP		exports + imports % GDP	
	Average 1990s			
	aid receiving countries	*industrial countries*	*aid receiving countries*	*industrial countries*
median	0.7	8.0	53.2	51.2
minimum	0	2.6	18.3	15.9
maximum	10.3	49.4	199.5	130.2

TABLE 10.2
Size of tradable sectors in aid-receiving countries (percentage of total exports and imports of aid-receiving countries)

	Exports % total exports	Imports % total imports
	Average 1990s, Countries Receiving Aid > 2 % GDP	
median	0.037	0.060
minimum	0.000	0.002
maximum	4.737	3.580

assistance when it is disbursed and aid flows are too uncertain to be pledged as collateral.

Aid-receiving countries are small open economies with internationally determined prices of tradable goods

Aid-receiving countries are open economies where international trade usually represents a large share of GDP (Table 10.1). Hence a large share of their domestic price index is accounted for by the price of tradable goods. At the same time, given that exports and imports of each of these countries represent small shares of total exports and imports of the products in which they trade (Table 10.2), the prices of their traded goods are likely to be set internationally. This implies that their domestic demand conditions are unlikely to affect their import and export prices.

Foreign aid can hurt tradable industries (Dutch disease)

Dutch disease usually refers to the adverse effects on the (manufacturing) traded sector of natural resource discoveries, or of foreign aid. Its origin is the over-valuation of the Dutch real exchange rate that followed the discovery of natural gas deposits in the North Sea, within the borders of the Netherlands, in the 1950s and 1960s.[3]

When part of foreign aid is spent on domestic non-tradable goods, the price of non-tradable goods rises relative to tradable goods. This real appreciation draws resources out of the tradable goods sector into the non-tradable goods sector. While this reallocation is not inefficient per se, the shrinking of the tradable goods sector will reduce growth *if the source of productivity expansion—* e.g., learning-by-doing (LBD) externalities—*is in the tradable goods sector.* In a recent cross-section study, Rajan and Subramanian (2005a) have found strong evidence that aid negatively affects the growth of tradable sectors. Specifically, they show that foreign aid reduces output growth of the more labour-intensive

FIGURE 10.3

Tradable industries grow less when aid is high, 1980s[a]

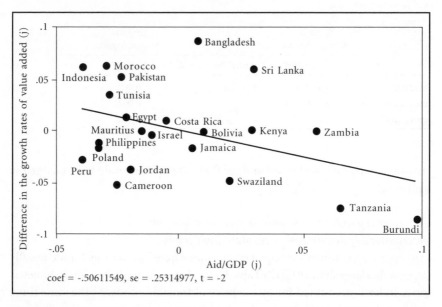

industries, which tend to constitute the export sectors of developing countries (Figure 10.3).

There are also several country-specific studies presenting evidence of productivity benefits from exporting. Blalock and Gertler (2004) show that Indonesian manufacturing firms became more productive by 'learning through exporting'. Van Biesebroeck (2003) finds that productivity of manufacturing plants in African countries increases after entering export markets. Fernandes and Isgut (2005) present evidence of 'learning-by-exporting' by young Colombian manufacturing plants between 1981 and 1991.[4]

Finally, Dutch disease concerns cannot be simply dismissed by observing that small manufacturing sectors and commodity-dominated export sectors limit the scope for productivity gains in aid-receiving countries. Manufacturing sectors actually account for non-negligible shares of exports, making up, for example, 15 per cent of exports in Tanzania and Kenya, 25 per cent in Ghana, and 90 per cent in Bangladesh (World Bank, 2002). Moreover, manufacturing export shares in several countries that successfully developed over the past 40 years were initially small and comparable to those of today's aid-receiving countries. In the early sixties, manufacturing exports represented, respectively, 2, 5 and 20 per cent of total exports in Thailand, Malaysia and the Republic of Korea (South Korea). At the end of the nineties, the same shares were 75 per

cent in Thailand and 90 per cent in Malaysia and South Korea. Finally, productivity gains (and/or quality improvements) could also take place in the
commodity-exporting sectors because commodities are often processed
domestically to meet international standards, creating some scope for positive
LBD spillovers.

How Does Monetary Policy Affect Real Outcomes?

But how do the characteristics of aid-receiving countries listed above allow
monetary policy to have real effects? This section describes the channels and
the mechanisms through which monetary policy can help manage volatile aid
inflows.

Does monetary policy matter for nominal magnitudes only?

In standard macroeconomic models, monetary policy only affects nominal
magnitudes in the long run (see Obstfeld and Rogoff, 1999: chapters 8 and 9).
The main exception is the case of high-inflation countries where inflation beyond a certain threshold has been shown to have negative effects on welfare. For
example, high inflation exacerbates frictions in the financial system (Boyd,
Levine and Smith, 2001) and affects the poor disproportionately (Easterly and
Fischer, 2001). The level of inflation is also generally included in indices of
'good policies' that may enhance aid effectiveness (Burnside and Dollar, 2000,
2004a, 2004b) together with fiscal and trade policies.[5] However, these are *not*
the channels through which monetary policy can reduce the impact of aid volatility and contribute to making aid effective. This effectiveness depends, instead,
critically on the monetary policy's ability to reallocate resources over time and
across sectors.

Monetary policy can redistribute resources over time and sectors
by modifying real interest rates.

Monetary policy can affect national savings when capital markets are not complete. This is the case when agents cannot borrow or lend internationally and
have access to a limited set of domestic financial saving instruments. In this
context, a monetary tightening (or equivalently an increase in the nominal
interest rate controlled by the central bank) compresses aggregate demand by
raising the demand for domestic bonds and reducing money balances. With a
closed capital account, capital inflows cannot undo this rise in nominal interest
rates. Moreover, aggregate savings increase as the central bank withdraws liquidity because domestic agents cannot substitute domestic bonds for foreign
bonds.

At the same time, the creation of base money through the improved current account and accumulation of foreign exchange reserves feeds back into the money supply and *partially* offsets the impact of the initial sale of government bonds. This offset is only partial because the demand for non-tradables also falls and the improvement in the current account is smaller than the reduction in aggregate demand.

Finally, to the extent that prices of tradable goods are set internationally, the fall in the aggregate price index that follows the reduction in domestic demand is less than proportional to the reduction in the stock of money. Therefore, *real* money balances fall (equivalently, *real* interest rates rise) following a monetary tightening, and national savings increase. Symmetrically, a monetary expansion would lead to a fall in real interest rates and a reduction in national savings. This implies that monetary policy can influence agents' decisions about allocating consumption over time.

A corollary of monetary policy's effectiveness in reallocating resources over time is its ability to reallocate resources across sectors and, thereby, offset Dutch disease effects. Given that the price of tradable goods is set internationally, aggregate demand changes induced by monetary policy affect the relative price of tradable and non-tradable goods (the real exchange rate) and, therefore, the relative size of tradable and non-tradable sectors.[6] For example, a monetary tightening compresses aggregate demand and puts downward pressure on prices of non-tradable goods while leaving the price of tradable goods unchanged. This real depreciation tends to increase the size of tradable sectors and prevent aid inflows from diminishing the associated positive productivity spillovers.

When Should Monetary Policy Take Action?

Monetary Policy and the Distribution of Aid over Time

Aid inflows tend to be associated with money supply expansions irrespective of the exchange-rate regime. Spending foreign aid requires donors or recipient governments to exchange foreign-currency-denominated aid into the domestic currency of the recipient. In fixed exchange-rate regimes, international reserves and base money would then increase at impact. This can be seen as a benchmark case as the large majority of aid-receiving countries have adopted either a fixed exchange-rate regime or a managed float.[7, 8]

Figure 10.4 illustrates how money supply and money demand determine the equilibrium trade balance for a given distribution of aid over time. We will use it to discuss the appropriate monetary policy response to a shift in donors'

FIGURE 10.4
Trade balance and monetary policy

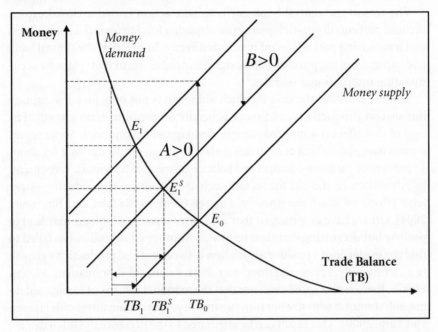

policies that leads to front-loading aid disbursements while keeping their total net present value unchanged. Recent donors' initiatives aimed at helping countries achieve the MDGs by 2015, such as the International Financing Facility (IFF) proposed by the United Kingdom of Great Britain and Northern Ireland, would have similar effects.[9]

First, consider the case in which foreign aid impacts only on consumption and has no effect on productivity. Suppose that the trade balance prior to the frontloading of aid is TB_0 and that, from the welfare perspective of smoothing consumption over time, the economy would need to raise current consumption and lower the trade balance to TB_1^S. This new allocation could be achieved by bringing the *right* amount of aid forward. Figure 10.4 shows, however, a case in which lack of donors' coordination leads to an excessive front-loading of aid (A) with an unwarranted expansion of money supply, current consumption and the trade deficit.[10]

To bring the trade balance back from TB_1 to TB_1^S, the central bank can undo some of the money supply expansion associated with the front-loading of aid. The appropriate sterilization policy would require the central bank to sell an amount B of bonds to the private sector. This sale would bring the economy to the new equilibrium E_1^S where higher real interest rates make agents augment their savings and a more depreciated real exchange rate reduces the trade deficit.

The reason the central bank needs to take action is that a closed capital account prevents domestic agents from acquiring foreign financial instruments and from saving part of the aid proceeds directly. In practice, the central bank ends up making the purchase of foreign financial assets in their place by accumulating international reserves.[11]

Second, consider the case in which aid impacts not only on consumption but also on productivity, and more generally on medium-term growth. The sign of this effect is a mooted issue in development economics. Some recent studies have shown that certain categories of foreign aid accounting for about 45 per cent of aid flows—budget and balance-of-payments support, investments in infrastructure and aid for sectors such as agriculture and industry—have large effects on *short-run* growth (e.g., see Clemens, Radelet and Bhavnani, 2004). Others have emphasized that *absorptive capacity* problems may lead to positive but decreasing marginal returns.[12] Another set of studies has failed to find any evidence of a positive association between aid and productivity growth (e.g., see Easterly, Levine and Roodman, 2004; Rajan and Subramanian, 2005b). Finally, there is also some evidence that the marginal returns of foreign aid do not only diminish with size but turn *negative* beyond a certain threshold (Hansen and Tarp, 2000). This result can be attributed to the presence of Dutch disease or to the potential corrupting effects of large amounts of aid on institutions.[13]

Given that productivity growth affects future income and consumption, there is little doubt that monetary policy should take the productivity impact of aid flows into account. If aid flows have *positive* productivity effects, the appropriate front-loading of aid is larger than in the case where aid impacts only on consumption. This happens because future growth would augment future consumption, thereby reducing the need for future aid. In this case, the consumption smoothing trade balance would be somewhat smaller than TB_1^S, implying that the central bank's bond sales would need to be smaller than the amount B shown in Figure 10.4. In other words, the central bank should engage in fewer sterilization operations and tolerate a larger trade deficit than in the case where aid flows impact only on consumption.

Conversely, if the marginal returns of aid on productivity decline or become *negative* beyond a certain threshold, then front-loading aid disbursements would curtail future consumption, and monetary policy should conduct bond sales in excess of B with the objective of saving more resources for future use and raising the trade balance above TB_1^S.

Figure 10.4 allows us also to discuss a possible scenario in which there is no frontloading of aid ($A=0$) although some would be appropriate ($TB_1^S < TB_0$).

This is a case in which the immediate consumption benefits of aid are large but disbursements are too back-loaded. Can monetary policy substitute for the donors and bring resources forward to boost current consumption? The answer to this question is positive, provided that the central bank has enough reserves to decumulate and to finance the larger trade deficit TB_1^S . Monetary policy would need to be expansionary with the central bank purchasing bonds rather than selling them. Domestic agents would use the additional liquidity to consume more tradable and non-tradable goods, causing real appreciation and a higher trade deficit. With unchanged aid and capital inflows, international reserves would then be needed to finance the latter.

What Are the Limits to Monetary Policy Effectiveness?

Individual characteristics of aid-receiving countries may vary considerably and with them the scope for monetary policy to take effective action in response to volatile aid disbursements.

As already discussed in the previous section, the key prerequisites for monetary policy effectiveness are a relatively closed capital account and an economy small enough to take the prices of tradable goods as given. In the few aid-receiving countries that have open capital accounts, monetary policy may either be ineffective or have effects opposite to what is desired. A standard Keynesian model with capital mobility would predict, in fact, that monetary tightening would not lead to real exchange-rate depreciation but rather to both *nominal* appreciation, as higher interest rates fuel private capital inflows, and temporary *real* appreciation, as prices remain sticky in the short run.[14] The evidence presented in the previous section on the ability of sterilization policy to contain trade balance fluctuations is, however, consistent with monetary tightening leading to real depreciation as a model with no capital mobility would predict.

Another issue is whether monetary policy effectiveness depends critically on the central bank's ability to buy and sell bonds. This is an important issue because many aid-receiving countries do not have well-developed domestic bond markets (Christensen, 2004), although the size of such markets has grown recently in several of those countries. In practice, this does not significantly limit monetary policy effectiveness because other forms of sterilization are available, including: (i) the central bank's issuance of its own debt certificates; (ii) higher reserve requirements, which, for a given level of base money, reduce the money multiplier and overall money supply; and (iii) fiscal surpluses or a shift of government deposits from the banking sector to the central bank, depending on whether the government banks with the central bank or not.

The possibility of using fiscal balances to sterilize the monetary impact of a surge in aid inflows raises the question of whether fiscal policy could not take responsibility for modifying aggregate demand and redistributing the effects of aid over time, leaving other goals to monetary policy. *In principle*, fiscal policy could be just as effective as monetary policy in managing aid inflows, especially if taxes and transfers are lump-sum. *In practice*, the volatility of aid flows makes fiscal policy unsuitable. Fiscal policy would need to change taxes frequently and in opposite directions to offset the large year-to-year swings in aid flows (Figure 10.1). This would be a daunting task even in countries with efficient tax and expenditure systems because there are much longer decision-making lags associated with fiscal policy than with monetary policy and because of likely political resistance to raising taxes and cutting expenditures. In aid-receiving countries, notoriously weak tax administration and public expenditure management systems would give even less latitude to the fiscal authority in timing tax and expenditure changes as required by the vagaries of aid flows.

An important limit to pursuing sterilization policy is the sterilization costs associated with bond issuance, which cannot be overlooked in practice. If the taxes needed to finance the differential between the interest rates on sterilization bonds and international reserves are distortionary or costly to be levied, sterilization would have welfare costs that should be weighed against the benefits of consumption smoothing. These costs would be even larger if high interest rates depressed interest-sensitive *private* investment that might enhance productivity. When sterilization is implemented through fiscal surpluses, it may involve other costs. The government may, in fact, decide to achieve the required fiscal surpluses by postponing the very public investment that the aid increase was supposed to finance (as opposed to reducing current expenditure). In this case, the loss of productivity gains due to public investment might offset the benefits in terms of smaller productivity losses due to Dutch disease. This implies that monetary policy cannot be seen in isolation from, and should be coordinated with, fiscal policy.

Finally, when aid flows are too back-loaded and monetary policy needs to be expansionary, insufficient international reserves could become a binding constraint. This constraint is all the more tight when aid-receiving countries keep international reserves for other purposes as well, including the need to cope with volatile terms-of-trade shocks and the risks of not being able to roll over short-term external debt. Table 10.3 shows that, indeed, the average aid-receiving country has only a limited amount of reserves that can be used to finance higher imports and consumption.

TABLE 10.3
International reserves in aid-receiving countries

	International Reserves In Months of Imports
	Average 1990s, Countries Receiving Aid > 2% GDP
median	3.46
minimum	0.01
75th percentile	5.30
maximum	36.00

CONCLUSIONS

This chapter points to both opportunities and risks for the conduct of monetary policy in aid-receiving countries. The challenge is twofold: while undoing some of the monetary expansion associated with aid inflows might help smooth consumption over time and contain Dutch disease, excessive sterilization may stunt current consumption and reduce other sources of productivity growth or factor accumulation. Choosing the appropriate monetary policy stance requires factoring in a multitude of elements, ranging from the benefits of higher current consumption to determinants of aid effectiveness and productivity growth such as the quality of institutions, corruption and capacity constraints. A reliable forecast of future aid inflows is, of course, another critical input to monetary policy formulation.

What is clear is that, in a typical aid-receiving country where aid flows are often disbursed in a typically haphazard manner and access to capital markets is limited, monetary policy decisions can have a vital bearing not only on nominal magnitudes but also on real ones such as consumption and productivity growth. When aid flows are excessively front-loaded, monetary policy can improve welfare by increasing gross national savings in the form of higher international reserves. Conversely, when aid flows are excessively back-loaded, an expansionary monetary policy can improve welfare, provided that the stock of international reserves is large enough.

While the theoretical arguments for welfare-improving monetary policy intervention are compelling, some perspective is in order. There are, in fact, limits to the extent monetary policy can correct the effects of an inappropriate distribution of aid over time. When aid flows are excessively front-loaded, sterilization costs may induce central banks to accumulate a less-than-optimal amount of reserves. By contrast, when aid flows are deemed excessively back-loaded, insufficient international reserves can prevent monetary policy from bringing resources forward.

Faced with these limits of monetary policy, donors could demonstrate a new found resolve and decide to coordinate their actions, minimize aid volatility and, thereby, reduce the need for monetary policy intervention. Increasing multilateral and bilateral donors' coordination in disbursing aid—a key object-ive of the Poverty Reduction Strategy Paper (PRSP) process introduced in the late 1990s—is then essential.

Allowing recipient countries to save aid directly for later use is an alternative to be considered if greater coordination of donor countries turns out to be an unrealistic objective. Donors could set up country-specific reserve funds in which aid is accumulated and then spent when aid flows or other resources dry up. The key challenge would, however, be the governance of such funds, which requires resolving the tension between predictable and timely assistance, on the one hand, and donors' desire to subject the use of the Fund's resources to conditionality, on the other. Indeed, for aid-receiving countries, international reserves are an appealing alternative, as they allow these countries to save resour-ces and use them at their discretion. Nonetheless, given that sterilization policy may be costly, there is still scope for future work aimed at designing a governance structure of aid reserve funds that might become acceptable to both recipients and donors.

Finally, the idea that there are circumstances in which some aid is better saved owes nothing to the notion that foreign aid might be too generous. Our results do not provide any indication that an increase in the *overall* net present value of aid can reduce welfare. They pertain, instead, to the welfare implications of the *distribution* of a given net present value of aid over time. From this pers-pective, the declared objective reiterated at the International Conference on Financing for Development, held in Monterrey, Mexico, in March 2002—to raise ODA to 0.7 per cent of industrial countries' GDP from a level that is cur-rently only about one third of that target—can only be welcome.[15]

NOTES

[1] This chapter was prepared for the UN/DESA Development Forum on 'Integrating Economic and Social Policies to Achieve the United Nations Development Agenda', held at United Nations Headquarters, New York, on March 14 and 15 2005. We are particularly thankful to Ratna Sahay, with whom we had many useful discussions that helped us think through the issues associated with monetary policy in aid-receiving countries. Manzoor Gill provided excellent research assistance. The views expressed in the chapter are those of the authors and do not necessarily represent those of the IMF or IMF policy.

[2] Bulir and Hamann (2002) and Celasun and Walliser (2005) discuss the fiscal implications of the volatility and (un)predictability of foreign aid.

[3] Theoretical models of the Dutch disease have been developed by van Wijnbergen (1984), Krugman (1987), Sachs and Warner (1995) and Gylfason, Herbertson and Zoega (1997), among others.

[4] By contrast, Adam and Bevan (2003) find that the impact of aid on the real exchange rate can be complex, and may not be large, in a model calibrated on Ugandan data.

[5] Easterly, Levine and Roodman (2004), among others, have raised doubts on the robustness of Burnside and Dollar's results.

[6] Of course, factors of production (in particular labour) must be relatively mobile across sectors for changes in relative prices to translate into changes in the size of tradable and non-tradable sectors.

[7] According to the classification of exchange-rate regimes in Reinhart and Rogoff (2004), during all instances of aid inflows greater than 2 per cent of GDP in the 1990s, the median exchange-rate regime was a de facto crawling peg with freely floating regimes accounting for less than 1 per cent of the observations.

[8] Foreign aid is often associated with an increase in base money also *in floating exchange-rate regimes*. When aid is aimed at budgetary support, the government usually deposits foreign aid at the central bank. Initially, this operation increases both international reserves and government deposits, leaving total base money unchanged. But, as soon as the government draws down the balance on its deposit account at the central bank, net domestic assets and base money increase.

[9] The IFF amounts to *front-loading* aid disbursements. Under the IFF proposal, donors would make off-budget pledges of future increases in their aid commitments that would be used as backing to issue AAA-rated bonds. Bond proceeds would be channelled through existing aid programmes. Over time, the IFF would draw down the donor pledges to pay off its bonds. Conversely, debt relief amounts to *back-loading* aid disbursements in a predictable, albeit potentially erratic, manner because the transfer of resources to recipient countries will materialize when future debt-service payments are due.

[10] Of course, this example does not apply to the case of humanitarian, emergency or post-conflict aid, where an aid-induced increase in consumption would merely return consumption to its pre-crisis level.

[11] International reserves increase because the deterioration in the trade balance from the initial level TB_0 is smaller than the additional aid inflow.

[12] Aid volatility worsens absorptive capacity problems. Consider the case of projects requiring repeated inputs over the years with donors disbursing aid in a single instalment or irregularly. For example, donors could disburse aid to build a school or a hospital, but leave recipient countries without a regular source of funds to keep the buildings in good condition or to pay teachers and doctors in the following years.

[13] Tornell and Lane (1998, 1999) and Sala-i-Martin and Subramanian (2003) stress that powerful groups tend to appropriate windfall earnings, leading to a 'voracity' effect. Similarly, Svensson (2000) and Torvik (2002) emphasize how aid may increase rent-seeking.

[14] Krugman (1987) develops a variant of this class of models where learning-by-doing externalities create the potential for Dutch disease. As in the analytical framework we used, these externalities allow temporary monetary policies to have *permanent* effects on competitiveness. In Krugman's model, however, the current account has to be balanced in every period. As a consequence, tight money leads to real *appreciation* because exports need to fall in line with the lower imports caused by the monetary contraction.

[15] Tripling ODA is viewed as a necessary step to achieve the Millennium Development Goals by 2015 (Heller and Gupta, 2002). The Millennium Development Goals (MDGs), which emerged from the September 2000 United Nations Millennium Declaration, are a set of measurable targets for halving world poverty between 1990 and 2015.

REFERENCES

Adam, C., and D. Bevan (2003). Aid, Public Expenditure and Dutch Disease. WPS/2003-2, Centre for the Study of African Economies, Oxford University, Oxford.

Arellano, C., A. Bulíř, T. Lane and L. Lipschitz (2005). The Dynamic Implications of Foreign Aid and Its Variability. IMF Working Paper No. 05/119, International Monetary Fund, Washington, DC.

Blalock, Garrick, and Paul Gertler (2004). Learning from Exporting Revisited in a Less Developed Setting. *Journal of Development Economics* 75 (2): 397–416.

Boyd, John H., Ross Levine and Bruce D. Smith (2001). The Impact of Inflation on Financial Sector Performance. *Journal of Monetary Economics* 47 (2): 221–48.

Buffie, E., C. Adam, S. O'Connell and C. Pattillo (2004). Exchange Rate Policy and the Management of Official and Private Capital Flows in Africa. *IMF Staff Papers* 51: 126–60.

Bulíř, Aleš, and A. Javier Hamann (2003). Aid Volatility: An Empirical Assessment. *IMF Staff Papers* 50 (1): 64–89.

Bulir, Ales, and Timothy D. Lane (2002). Aid and Fiscal Management. IMF Working Papers 02/112, International Monetary Fund, Washington, DC.

Burnside, Craig, and David Dollar (2000). Aid, Policies, and Growth. *American Economic Review* 90 (4): 847–68.

Burnside, Craig, and David Dollar (2004a). Aid, Policies, and Growth: Revisiting the Evidence. Policy Research Working Paper No. 3251, World Bank, Washington, DC.

Burnside, Craig, and David Dollar (2004b). Aid, Policies, and Growth: Reply. *American Economic Review* 94 (3): 781–4.

Celasun, Oya, and Jan Walliser (2005). Predictability of Budget Aid: Experiences in Eight African Countries. Presented at the World Bank Practitioners' Forum on Budget Support, May 5–6, Cape Town.

Christensen, Jakob E. (2004). Domestic Debt Markets in Sub-Saharan Africa. IMF Working Paper 04/46, International Monetary Fund, Washington, DC.

Clemens, M., Steve Radelet and R. Bhavnani (2004). Counting Chickens When They Hatch: The Short-Term Effect of Aid on Growth. Processed, Center for Global Development, Washington, DC.

Easterly, William (2000). *The Elusive Quest for Growth: Economists' Adventures and Misadventures in the Tropics*. MIT Press, Cambridge, MA.

Easterly, William, and Stanley Fischer (2001). Inflation and the Poor. *Journal of Money, Credit, and Banking* Part 1, May: 159–78.

Easterly, William, R. Levine and D. Roodman (2004). New Data, New Doubts: A Comment on Burnside and Dollar's? Aid, Policies, and Growth'. *American Economic Review* 94 (3): 774–780.

Fernandes, Ana, and Alberto Isgut (2005). Learning-by-Doing, Learning-by-Exporting, and Productivity: Evidence from Colombia. Policy Research Working Paper No. 3544, World Bank, Washington, DC.

Gylfason, T., T.T. Herbertson and G. Zoega (1997). A Mixed Blessing: Natural Resources and Economic Growth. *Macroeconomic Dynamics* 3: 204–25.

Hansen, H., and Finn Tarp (2000). Aid Effectiveness Disputed. *Journal of International Development* 12: 375–98.

IMF (2005). *Annual Report on Exchange Arrangements and Exchange Restrictions*. International Monetary Fund, Washington, DC.

Krugman, Paul (1987). The Narrow Moving Band, the Dutch Disease, and the Competitive Consequences of Mrs. Thatcher: Notes on Trade in the Presence of Dynamic Scale Economies. *Journal of Development Economics* 27: 41–55.

Obstfeld, Maurice, and Kenneth Rogoff (1999). *Foundations of International Macroeconomics.* MIT Press, Cambridge, MA.

Pallage, Stephane, and Michel A. Robe (2003). On the Welfare Costs of Economic Fluctuations in Developing Countries. *International Economic Review* 44 (2), May: 677–698.

Prati, Alessandro, and Thierry Tressel (2005). Can Monetary Policy Make Volatile Aid Flows More Effective?. IMF Working Paper forthcoming, International Monetary Fund, Washington, DC.

Rajan, Raghuram G., and Arvind Subramanian (2005a). What Undermines Aid's Impact on Growth. IMF Working Paper No.05/126, International Monetary Fund, Washington, DC.

Rajan, Raghuram G., and Arvind Subramanian (2005b). Aid and Growth: What Does the Cross-Country Evidence Really Show? IMF Working Paper No. 05/127, International Monetary Fund, Washington, DC.

Ramey, Garey, and Valerie A. Ramey (1995). Cross-Country Evidence on the Link between Volatility and Growth. *American Economic Review* 85 (5): 1138–51.

Reinhart, Carmen M., and Kenneth S. Rogoff (2004). The Modern History of Exchange Rate Arrangements: A Reinterpretation. *The Quarterly Journal of Economics* 119 (1): 1–48.

Sachs, Jeffrey, and Andrew Warner (1995). Natural Resource Abundance and Economic Growth. NBER Working Paper No. 5398, National Bureau of Economic Research, Cambridge, MA.

Sala-i-Martin, Xavier, and Arvind Subramanian (2003). Addressing the Natural Resource Curse: An Illustration from Nigeria. IMF Working Paper 03/139, International Monetary Fund, Washington, DC.

Svensson, J. (2000). Foreign Aid and Rent Seeking. *Journal of International Economics* 51: 437–461.

Tornell, A., and P. Lane (1998). Are Windfalls a Curse? A Non-Representative Agent Model of the Current Account. *Journal of International Economics* 44: 83–112.

Tornell, A., and P. Lane (1999). The Voracity Effect. *American Economic Review* 89 (1): 22–46.

Torvik, R. (2001). Learning by Doing and the Dutch Disease. *European Economic Review* 45: 285–306.

Torvik, R. (2002). Natural Resources, Rent Seeking and Welfare. *Journal of Development Economics* 67: 455–470.

Van Biesebroeck, J. (2003). Exporting Raises Productivity in Sub-Saharan African Manufacturing Plants. NBER Working Paper No. 10020, October, National Bureau of Economic Research, Cambridge, MA.

Van Wijnbergen, S. (1984). The 'Dutch Disease': A Disease after All?. *Economic Journal* 94: 41–55.

World Bank (2002). *World Development Indicators 2002.* World Bank, Washington DC.

11
Real Exchange Rate, Monetary Policy and Employment

ROBERTO FRENKEL and LANCE TAYLOR

The exchange rate affects any economy through many channels. It scales the national price system to the world's, influences key macroprice ratios, such as those between tradable and non-tradable goods, capital goods and labour, and even exports and imports (via the costs of intermediate inputs and capital goods, for example). The exchange rate is an asset price, it partially determines inflation rates through the cost side and as a monetary transmission vector, and it can have significant influences (in both the short and long run) on effective demand.

Correspondingly, the exchange rate can be targeted towards many policy objectives. In developing and transition economies, five of these objectives have been of primary importance in recent decades:

- *Resource allocation*: Through its effects on the price ratios just mentioned, the exchange rate can significantly influence resource allocation, especially if it stays stable in real terms for an extended period of time. Through effects on both resource allocation and aggregate demand, a relatively weak rate can help boost employment, which has been an area of concern in light of stagnant job creation in many developing economies over the past 10–15 years;
- *Economic development*: The exchange rate can be deployed, often in conjunction with commercial and industrial policies, to enhance overall competitiveness and thereby boost productivity and growth;
- *Finance*: The rate shapes and can be used to control expectations and behaviour in financial markets. Exchange-rate policy 'mistakes' can easily lead to highly destabilizing consequences;
- *External balance*: The trade and other components of the current account usually respond to the exchange rate, directly via 'substitution' responses, and (at times, more importantly) to shifts it can cause in effective demand;
- *Inflation*: The exchange rate can serve as a nominal anchor, holding down price increases via real appreciation and/or maintenance by the authorities

of a consistently strong rate. As will be seen below, it can also serve as an important transmission mechanism for the effects of monetary policy.

All of these objectives have played a role in recent policy experience. Use of the exchange rate to try to improve external balance has been central to countless stabilization packages over the decades, especially in small, poor economies. The inflation objective became crucial in middle-income countries in the last quarter of the twentieth century (and has become notably less urgent as of 2005). Along with capital market liberalization, fixed rates were significant contributors to the wave of financial crises in the 1990s.

In many ways, however, the resource allocation and developmental objectives can be the most important in the long run—and this is the central point of this chapter. We trace the reasons for this in the following section on channels of influence. We then take up the policy implications, contrasting the use of the exchange rate as a development tool in conjunction with its other uses (often in coordination with monetary policy) in maintaining external balance, containing inflation and stabilizing asset markets,

RESOURCE ALLOCATION, LABOUR INTENSITY, MACROECONOMICS AND DEVELOPMENT

Following Frenkel (2004), in this section, we trace three ways in which the exchange rate can have medium- to long-term impacts on development. We begin with overall resource allocation and then move on to the labour market and macroeconomics.

Resource Allocation

The traditional 2 x 2 trade theory model is a useful starting point. While this model *does* focus on the key role of relative prices, it *does not* take into consideration important non-price components of industrial and commercial polices. Both themes are woven into the following discussion.

The Lerner Symmetry Theorem (1936) is a key early result. Its basic insight is that if only the import/export price ratio is relevant to resource allocation, it follows that it can be manipulated by *either* an import *or* an export tax-cum-subsidy. There is 'symmetry' between the two instruments, so that 'under appropriate conditions' (at hand in the textbooks) only one need be employed.

A now obvious extension is to bring three goods into the discussion: exportable, importable and non-tradable, in a 'Ricardo-Viner' model. Two price ratios—say, importable/non-tradable and exportable/non-tradable—in principle guide allocation. The real exchange rate (RER or ρ naturally comes into play as the relative price between the non-tradable and a price-weighted aggregate of the two tradable goods[1]. These observations lead to two important policy puzzles.

The first has to do with 'level playing fields'. As applied in East Asia and elsewhere, industrial policy often involved both protection of domestic industry against imports by the use of tariffs and quotas, and promotion of exports through subsidies or cheap credits. In the case of a tariff on imports, the domestic price P_m becomes

$$P_m = e(1+t)P_m^* \qquad (1)$$

where e is the nominal exchange rate (defined as units of local per unit of foreign currency), t the tariff and P_m^* the world price. Similarly, if the internal price P_e for exports is set from abroad, we have

$$P_e = eP_e^* /(1-s) \qquad (2a)$$

where P_e^* is the world price and s is the subsidy rate.

The level playing field rests on the trade theorists' ancient obsession with setting the internal and external relative prices of tradable goods equal: $P_m / P_e = P_m^* / P_e^*$. This situation can be arranged if $t = s = 0$, or more generally, $(1+t) = 1/(1-s)$ The mainstream argument asserts that if all that industrial policy does is give more or less equal protection to both imports and exports, then its costs, administrative complications and risks of rent-seeking and corruption are unjustifiable. One might as well set $t = s = 0$ and go to a free trade equilibrium.

In a Ricardo-Viner set-up, where P_n is a price index for non-tradables, the price ratios P_e / P_n and P_m / P_n become of interest. Positive values of t and s move domestic relative prices in favour of tradable goods. From a mainstream perspective (Woo, 2005) this outcome can be interpreted as a justification for industrial policy.

The world, however, is a bit more complicated than that. If the home country is exporting a differentiated product, for example, a more appropriate version of (2a) is

$$P_e^* = P_e(1-s)/e \qquad (2b)$$

so that the foreign price of home exports is set by the subsidy and exchange rate. Presumably, a lower value of P_e^* stimulates sales abroad. Moreover, if the economic bureaucracy has the requisite motivation and organization, it can tie export subsidies to the attainment of export, productivity and other targets, and so pursue a proactive industrial policy. In such a context, import protection and export promotion serve different purposes: the former allows domestic production to get started along traditional infant industry lines, while the latter enables national firms to break into international markets.[2]

Now let us focus on the exchange rate. An increase in the nominal rate e would also switch incentives toward production of tradables, without the need for extravagant values of s and t. This simple observation is in fact a strong argument in support of the use of a depreciated RER as a developmental tool. If we define ρ as

$$\rho = [\mu P_m + (1-\mu)P_e]/P_n \qquad (3)$$

where μ is the weight in a tradable goods price index, then a high value of e means that the real rate ρ will also be weak or depreciated.

Of course, a weak RER may not be a sufficient condition for long-term development. For example, it may usefully be supplemented by an export subsidy or tariff protection to infant industries with their additional potential benefits mentioned above. Even without an effective bureaucracy, generalizing Lerner symmetry to a Ricardo-Viner world suggests that more than one policy instrument may be helpful because there are two relative price ratios that can be manipulated. The rub is that a strong exchange rate implies that commercial/industry policy interventions also have to be strong, with correspondingly high intervention costs. A weak RER may be only a necessary condition for beneficial resource reallocation to occur, but a highly appreciated RER is likely to be a sufficient condition for 'excessive intervention' in a situation in which development cannot take place. It is hard to find examples of economies with strong exchange rates that kept up growth for extended periods of time.

Labour Intensity

Continuing with the allocation theme, it is clear that the exchange rate will affect relative prices of imported intermediates and capital goods, on the one hand, and labour, on the other. Moreover, the RER largely determines the economy's unit labour costs in terms of foreign currency.

To explore the implications, we can consider the effects of sustained real appreciation on different sectors. Producers of importables will face tougher foreign competition. To stay in business, they will have to cut costs, often by shedding labour. If they fail and close down, more jobs will be destroyed. If the home country's export prices P_e^* are determined by a relationship like (2b), similar logic will apply to that sector. In non-tradables, which will have to absorb labour displaced from the tradable sectors, jobs are less likely to open up insofar as cheaper foreign imports in the form of intermediates and capital goods substitute for domestic labour. On the whole, real appreciation is not likely to induce sustained job creation and could well provoke a big decrease in tradable sector employment. Reasoning in the other direction, RER depreciation may prove employment-friendly.

In both cases, it is important to recognize that a new set of relative prices must be expected to stay in place for a relatively long period if these effects are to work through. Changes in employment/output ratios will not take place swiftly because they must come about via changes in the pattern of output among firms and sectors, by shifts in the production basket of each firm and sector, and adjustments in the technology and organization of production. Gradual adjustment processes are necessarily involved.

Finally, in the long run, if per capita income is to increase, there will have to be sustained labour productivity growth with employment creation supported by even more rapid growth in effective demand. Macroeconomics thus comes into play.

Macroeconomics

The question is how a weak exchange rate (possibly in combination with other policies aimed at influencing resource allocation among traded goods) fits into the macroeconomic system. Much depends on labour market behaviour in the non-traded sector. Following Rada (2005), we work through one scenario here to illustrate possible outcomes.

Assume that output in the tradable sector is driven by effective demand, responding to investment, exports and import substitution, as well as fiscal and monetary policy. The level of imports depends on economic activity and the exchange rate (along with commercial/industrial policies). A worker not utilized in tradable sectors must find employment in non-tradables, become under- or unemployed or leave the labour force. For concreteness, we assume that almost all labour not employed in tradables finds something to do in non-tradable production as a means of survival. Typical activities would be providing labour services in urban areas or engaging in labour-intensive agriculture.

If workers in neither of the two sectors have significant savings, their behaviour does not strongly influence overall macroeconomic balance, which is driven by investment, exports, saving from profits and changes in the magnitude of the import/output ratio via import substitution.

Now let us consider the outcomes of a devaluation. It will have impacts all over the economy, including a loss in national purchasing power if imports initially exceed exports, redistribution of purchasing power away from low-saving workers whose real wages decrease, a decline in the real value of the money stock and capital losses on the part of net debtors in international currency terms. Presumably, exports will respond positively to an RER depreciation, but that may take time if 'J-curve' and similar effects matter. Another positive impact on the demand for tradables will come from import substitution.

One implication is that for a given level of output, the trade deficit should fall with devaluation. If devaluation forces output to contract, as often appears to be the case in developing economies, import demand will decrease and reduce the trade deficit further still. In this case, real devaluation should presumably be implemented together with expansionary fiscal and monetary policies. As discussed in detail below, exchange-rate strategies must be coordinated with other policy moves.

If export demand and production of import substitutes are stimulated immediately or over time by a sustained weak RER, aggregate demand should rise and drive up economic activity and employment in the medium to long run.

So far, the analysis has taken labour productivity as a constant. Longer-term considerations have to take into account the evolution of productivity. Following Rada and Taylor (2006), and ultimately Kaldor in his 1966 Inaugural Lecture (published in Kaldor, 1978), one can show that the growth rate of employment must equal the growth rate of output *minus* the growth rate of labour productivity,

$$\hat{L}_t = \hat{X}_t - \xi_{Lt} \qquad (4)$$

where $\hat{L}_t$ is employment growth in the tradable sector, $\hat{X}_t$ is output growth and ξ_{Lt} is productivity growth.

Suppose that ξ_{Lt} responds to $\hat{X}_t$ along a 'Kaldor-Verdoorn' schedule of the form proposed by Verdoorn (1949) and Okun (1962),

$$\xi_{Lt} = \bar{\xi}_{Lt} + \gamma \hat{X}_t \qquad (5)$$

in which the productivity trend term $\bar{\xi}_{Lt}$ could be affected by human capital growth, industrial policy, international openness, population growth and other factors.

Finally, more rapid productivity growth may make output expand faster, for example by reducing the unit cost of exports. Combined with (4) and (5), this response means that we solve for the three variables in question. In this context, what will be the effects of real devaluation? If a depreciated RER stimulates net export growth, then ξ_{Lt}, $\ddot{X}_t$ and $\hat{L}_t$ will all tend to increase.

Outcomes may be less favourable if a new set of relative prices induces an exogenous upward shift in the trend productivity growth rate $\bar{\xi}_{Lt}$. If the direct effect of productivity growth on tradable output growth is weak, then it can be seen from (4) that that sector's employment growth could decrease in an example of productivity-induced labour-shedding.

What would happen to wages and productivity in the non-tradable sector? Let $\lambda = L_t / L$ be the share of tradable sector employment in the total. Then $\lambda \hat{L}_t + (1-\lambda)\hat{L}_n = \hat{L}$ where $\hat{L}$ is overall employment growth. Non-tradable employment expansion becomes

$$\hat{L}_n = \frac{1}{1-\lambda}[\hat{L} - \lambda(\hat{X}_t - \xi_{Lt})]$$

Let the elasticity of demand for non-tradables with respect to X_t be υ One can show that, even when taking into account the favourable effects on employment of a weak exchange rate that were mentioned above, a low demand elasticity υ and fast labour force growth $\hat{L}$ could mean that a strong export performance translates into weak or even negative wage and productivity growth in the non-traded sector. A case like this calls for fiscal and social policies intended to foster demand for non-tradables and compensate for the negative effects on income distribution and employment.

MACROECONOMIC POLICY REGIMES FOR A STABLE, COMPETITIVE RER

For the reasons just indicated, a competitive and stable RER can make a substantial contribution to economic growth and employment creation. Programming the RER, however, is no easy task. It is most directly impacted by the nominal exchange rate, which is itself influenced by many factors, but also depends on the overall inflation rate and shifting relative prices. Moreover, the RER cannot be the only macropolicy objective. In any economy, there are bound to be multiple and partially conflicting objectives. And all policies— exchange-rate, fiscal, monetary and commercial/industrial—are interconnected and have to be coherently designed and implemented.

The following discussion focuses on these exchange-rate coordination issues in the context of middle-income economies with at least sporadic access to private international capital markets. Although they are not addressed in detail here, somewhat similar questions can easily arise in low-income countries that receive official capital inflows, especially if they jump to levels of 10–20 per cent of GDP, as suggested in the discussion of the Millennium Development Goals (MDGs).

How, therefore, can policy-makers target the RER while at the same time controlling inflation, reducing financial fragility and risk and aiming towards full employment of available resources? Our focus necessarily has to shift from the 'real economy' to encompass monetary and expectational considerations. The principal emphasis is on the degrees of freedom available to the monetary authorities, if only because they have been at centre stage in recent policy debates.

What Determines the Nominal Exchange Rate?

To set the stage, it is timely to offer a few observations about how the nominal exchange rate fits into the macroeconomic system.

Theories that can reliably predict the level of the rate and its changes over time when it is not strictly pegged do not exist. (The fact that pegs not infrequently break down means they do not have 100 per cent predictive power either.) In the present circumstances of middle-income economies, it is not unreasonable to assume that a more or less floating rate is determined in spot and future asset markets: in effect, the spot rate floats against its 'expected' future values. The use of quotation marks around 'expected' signifies that we view expectations along Keynesian lines as emerging from diverse opinions on the part of market participants about how the rate may move. 'Beauty contests' that magnify small shifts in average market opinion and other sources of seemingly capricious market behaviour can easily come into play (Eatwell and Taylor, 2000).

With regard to the *level* of the rate, it is useful to think about a simple bond market equilibrium condition such as

$$i = f(e, \dot{e}^{\exp}, M) \qquad (6)$$

where i is the local interest rate, e the spot exchange rate, $\dot{e}^{\exp}$ the expected (as an aggregate of market perceptions) change in the rate over time and M an index of monetary relaxation. A high or depreciated value of e means that national liabilities are cheap as seen from abroad. It should be associated with high local bond prices or low interest rates. If expected depreciation $\dot{e}^{\exp}$ rises, on the other hand, foreign wealth holders will want to shift away from local liabilities and i will increase. Open market bond purchases will increase M and be associated with a reduction in i.

Over the past couple of decades, under conditions of external liberalization, most developing economies have been afflicted by high local interest rates and appreciated currencies. This unfavourable constellation of 'macroprices' is consistent with (6).

The *dynamics* of the exchange rate will be influenced by interest rates, because it is an asset price. One crucial question is whether lower domestic rates will tend to make the nominal rate depreciate or appreciate. If it tends to rise (or depreciate) over time, then exchange-rate dynamics can be a powerful mechanism for transmitting the effects of expansionary monetary policy into inflation by driving up local production costs.

Standard arbitrage arguments as built into interest rate parity theorems imply that the expected change in the spot rate $\acute{e}^{\,exp}$ should be an increasing function of the difference between domestic and foreign rates. If myopic perfect foresight applies, the expected change will be equal to the observed change (up to a 'small' error term). Hence a lower local interest rate should cause *appreciation* over time. On Wall Street, such an analysis of exchange-rate movements is called an 'operational' view.

A 'speculative' view is that the exchange rate will *depreciate* when the local interest rate decreases.[3] This view makes intuitive sense insofar as low interest rates should make national liabilities less attractive. It was perhaps first advanced macroeconomically by Minsky (1983) and can be made consistent with the parity theorems if it is assumed that there is a relatively strong positive feedback of expected exchange-rate increases into the domestic interest rate via the bond market equilibrium condition (6).

Recent macroeconomic history (Frenkel, 2004) suggests that the speculative view is the more accurate description of exchange-rate behaviour in middle-income economies.

Avoiding Catastrophes

The most fundamental justification for avoiding a persistently strong exchange rate is that it is an invitation to disaster. Exchange appreciation is always welcome politically because it may be expansionary (at least in the short run), is anti-inflationary and reduces import costs (including foreign junkets for those who can afford them). However, for the reasons discussed above, it can have devastating effects on resource allocation and prospects for development. Moreover, fixed or quasi-fixed strong real rates can easily provoke destabilizing capital flow cycles, as perhaps first described analytically by Frenkel (1983) and re-enacted many times since.

The existence and severity of these cycles is in practice a powerful argument for a stable exchange-rate regime built around some sort of managed float (detailed below). A floating rate does appear to moderate destabilizing capital movements in the short run and is therefore a useful tool to deploy. At the same time, the central bank has to prevent the formation of expectations that there will be RER appreciation, which can easily become self-fulfilling along 'beauty contest' lines. A commitment to a stable rate, backed up by forceful intervention if necessary, is one way the bank can orient expectations around a competitive RER.

Trilemmas

Possibilities for central bank intervention are often said to be constrained by a 'trilemma' among (1) full capital mobility, (2) a controlled exchange rate, and (3) independent monetary policy. Supposedly, only two of these policy lines can be consistently maintained. If the authorities try to pursue all three, they will sooner or later be punished by destabilizing capital flows, as was the case in the run-up to the Great Depression around 1930 and with the difficulties faced by Britain and Italy during the European Exchange Rate Mechanisms (ERM) crisis more than 60 years later.

The trilemma as just stated is a textbook theorem which is, in fact, invalid. Even with free capital mobility, a central bank can undertake transactions in both foreign and domestic bonds (not to mention other monetary control manoeuvres) to regulate the money supply, regardless of whatever forces determine the exchange rate (Taylor, 2004).

Nevertheless, something like a trilemma can exist in the eye of the beholder. There are practical limits to the volume of interventions that a central bank can practice, along with complicated feedbacks. Possibilities for sterilizing capital inflows or outflows are bounded by available asset holdings. Volumes of flows depend on exchange-rate expectations, which in turn can be influenced by central bank behaviour and signalling.

So how does the market decide when a perceived trilemma is ripe to be pricked? The fact that no single form of transaction or arbitrage operation determines the exchange rate means that monetary authorities have some leeway in setting both the scaling factor between their country's price system and the rest of the world's, and the rules by which it changes. However, their room for manoeuvre is not unlimited. A fixed rate is always in danger of violating what average market opinion regards as a fundamental. Even a floating rate amply supported by forward markets can be an invitation to extreme volatility. Volatility can lead to disaster if asset preferences shift markedly away from the home country's liabilities in response to shifting perceptions about fundamentals or adverse 'news'. Unregulated international capital markets are at the root of any perceived trilemma. It is a practical problem that must be evaluated on a case-by-case basis, taking into account the context and circumstances of policy implementation.

Monetary and Exchange-Rate Policies and Capital Flows

The implication is that, if it wishes to target the RER, the central bank has to maintain tolerable control over the macroeconomic impacts of cross-border financial flows in a world with relatively open foreign capital markets. For the sake of clarity, it makes sense to analyze situations of excess supply of and excess demand for foreign capital separately.

Large capital inflows can easily imperil macrostability. Indeed, central bank attempts to sterilize them by selling domestic liabilities from its portfolio may even bid up local interest rates and draw more hot money. Preservation of monetary independence in this case may well require capital market regulation. Measures are available for this task.[4]

They do not work perfectly but can certainly moderate inflows during a boom. Booms never last forever; the point is that the authorities can use capital market interventions to slow one down to avoid an otherwise inevitable crash.[5]

If there are capital outflows which are too large to manage with normal exchange-rate and monetary policies, the authorities certainly do not want to engage in recession-triggering monetary contraction. If the exchange rate has been maintained at a relatively weak level, the external deficit is not setting off financial alarm bells and inflation is under control, there are no 'fundamental' reasons for market participants to expect a maxi-devaluation. Under such circumstances, the way for the authorities to maintain a policy regime consistent with a targeted RER is to impose exchange controls and restrictions of capital outflows.

Contrary to IMF-style opinion that all runs against a currency must be triggered by poor fundamentals (even if they momentarily escape the notice of the authorities and IMF officials), it is perfectly clear that they can arise for reasons extraneous to economic policy—consider a political crisis, the fallout from mismanagement of an important bank or the impacts of financial contagion from a regional neighbour. In all such cases, outflow controls can be used to maintain an existing policy package in place, and they may not have to be utilized for very long.[6]

Monetary Policy

In a developmental policy regime, monetary policy must be designed in view of its likely effects on the RER, inflation control and the level of economic activity. There is nothing very surprising here—in practice, central banks always have multiple objectives. In the United States, despite paying lip service to controlling price inflation, the Federal Reserve certainly responds to the level of economic activity and financial turmoil (witness the stock market bubble and the narrowly avoided crisis in Long-Term Capital Management (LTCM) of the 1990s). In many developing countries, central banks intervene more or less systematically in the exchange markets. The proposal here is that these interventions should help support a developmentally oriented RER for the reasons presented above. That is, the nominal rate should move to hold the RER in the vicinity of a stable competitive level for an extended period of time.

Inflation targeting, on the other hand, is the current orthodox buzzword. The nominal exchange-rate and other policies should be programmed to ensure a low, stable rate of inflation. A trilemma-like argument also comes into play here. If exchange market interventions target the RER as opposed to the nominal exchange rate, and the central bank cannot manage the money supply, there is no nominal anchor on inflationary expectations: the inflation rate cannot be controlled.

As we have seen, in practical terms, the trilemma can be circumvented, allowing the monetary authorities to bring developmental objectives into their remit. But they have to take at least five important considerations into account in monetary management:

- First, many developing countries now have low to moderate inflation rates, demoting inflation control in the hierarchy of policy objectives;
- Second, are low interest rates likely to set off inflationary nominal depreciation (under 'speculative' exchange-rate dynamics, as discussed above)? RER targeting can help the central bank steer away from this problem;
- Third, shifts in aggregate demand likely to result from changes in the exchange-rate and monetary policy must be taken into account and appropriate offsetting policies deployed;
- Fourth, also as mentioned above, some mix of temporary capital inflow or outflow controls may be needed to allow the central bank to regulate monetary aggregates and interest rates rather than be overwhelmed by attempts at sterilization;
- Finally, unstable money demand and other unpredictable factors mean that the monetary authorities have to be alert and flexible. Indeed, 'inflation targeting' is a codeword for orthodox recognition that quantitative monetary and even interest rate targets are impractical. It is a means for giving more discretion in attempting to attain a single target.

The point being made here is that discretion can and should serve other ends. A stable competitive RER, in coordination with sensible industrial and commercial policies can substantially improve prospects for economic development. Surely that should be the overriding goal of the monetary and all other economic authorities in any developing or transition economy.

NOTES

[1] Just to be clear, we will treat the RER as the ratio of tradable to non-tradable price indexes. Real devaluation or weakening of the RER means that ρ increases. Equation (3) below gives this formal expression.

[2] Again, these are old arguments. Ocampo and Taylor (1998) provide a recent summary.

[3] To be more precise, the change over time in the spot rate $\dot{e} = de/dt$ will turn negative when i decreases if the operational view applies, and positive if the speculative view applies.

[4] For an ample menu, see the papers by Deepak Nayyar, Eric Helleiner and Gabriel Palma in Eatwell and Taylor (2002). Salih Neftci and Randall Dodd assess the possibilities of using financial engineering to circumvent controls.

[5] This danger also exists in poor countries with a boom in MDG-driven capital inflows, which could be suddenly cut off—by no means a geopolitical impossibility. The familiar "Dutch disease" analysis of adverse effects of foreign aid enters the discussion here.

[6] Argentina, for example, successfully managed exchange controls and capital outflow restrictions in mid-2002. The measures were transitory and were gradually softened as buying pressure in the exchange market diminished.

REFERENCES

Eatwell, John and Lance Taylor (2000). *Global Finance at Risk: The Case for International Regulation.* The New Press, New York.

Eatwell, John, and Lance Taylor (eds) (2002). *International Capital Markets: Systems in Transition.* Oxford University Press, New York.

Frenkel, Roberto (1983). Mercado Financiero, Expectativas Cambiales, y Movimientos de Capital. *El Trimestre Economico* 50: 2041–2076.

Frenkel, Roberto (2004). Real Exchange Rate and Employment in Argentina, Brazil, Chile, and Mexico. Paper prepared for the Group of 24, Washington, D.C., September.

Kaldor, Nicholas (1978). Causes of the Slow Rate of Growth of the United Kingdom. In *Further Essays on Economic Theory.* Duckworth, London: 100–138.

Lerner, Abba P. (1936). The Symmetry between Import and Export Taxes. *Economica* 3: 306–313.

Minsky, Hyman P. (1983). Monetary Policies and the International Financial Environment. Processed, Department of Economics, Washington University, St. Louis.

Ocampo, Jose Antonio and Lance Taylor (1998). Trade Liberalization in Developing Economies: Modest Benefits but Problems with Productivity Growth, Macro Prices, and Income Distribution. *Economic Journal* 108: 1523–1546.

Okun, Arthur M. (1962). 'Potential GNP': Its Measurement and Significance. Reprinted in Joseph Pechman (ed.). *Economics for Policy-Making.* MIT Press, Cambridge, MA, 1983.

Rada, Codrina (2005). A Growth Model for a Two-Sector Open Economy with Endogenous Employment in the Subsistence Sector. Processed, Schwartz Center for Economic Policy Analysis, New School University, New York.

Rada, Codrina and Lance Taylor (2006). *Structural Change and Economic Dynamics.* Forthcoming

Taylor, Lance (2004). Exchange Rate Indeterminacy in Portfolio Balance, Mundell-Fleming, and Uncovered Interest Rate Parity Models. *Cambridge Journal of Economics* 28: 205–227.

Verdoorn, P.J. (1949). Fattori che Regolano lo Sviluppo della Produttivita del Lavoro. *L'Industria* 1: 3–10.

Woo, Wing Thye (2005). Some Fundamental Inadequacies in the Washington Consensus: Misunderstanding the Poor by the Brightest. In Jan Joost Teunissen (ed.). *Stability, Growth, and the Search for a New Development Agenda: Reconsidering the Washington Consensus.* FONDAD (Forum on Debt and Development), The Hague.

12
Evaluating Targeting Efficiency of Government Programmes: International Comparisons

NANAK KAKWANI and HYUN H. SON

For about the last two decades, the consensus has been that economic growth is necessary but is, in itself, not sufficient for the alleviation of poverty. Other than growth, poverty alleviation requires additional elements. First, poor households need to build up their asset base in order to participate in the growth process. Second, growth needs to be more broad-based to reach all segments of society, including the poor. Third, short-term public assistance measures are required to protect vulnerable groups of society, because it takes time for the needy to benefit from the impact of a policy or strategy.

Implementing this agenda to reduce poverty requires methods or tools that can effectively reach poor households or individuals. One way of accomplishing this is by public spending on items like universal education, which can reach all segments of society, including the poor. Alternatively, it can be achieved through a direct transfer of resources to the poor. However, in practice, problems commonly arise because of the scarcity of resources. With fixed budgets, governments are often forced to make a decision to direct resources to specific groups of households or individuals in society. Targeting specific groups will achieve the maximum impact from a given budget or minimize budgetary costs to achieve a given impact. The attraction is particularly strong for transfer programmes that constitute safety nets because such transfers provide a benefit that is largely a private good for recipient households.

While targeting has its own merits, there are a number of methods that can provide resources to a particular group. Whereas the existing literature largely focuses on descriptions of individual programmes, comparative analyses tend to cover a single region or method of intervention (Grosh, 1994; Braithwaite, Grootaert and Milanovic, 2000; Bigman and Fofack, 2000; Rawlings, Sherburne-Benz and Domelen, 2001). A partial approach of this kind is not helpful for making broader assessments about the effectiveness of different targeting methods. This chapter attempts to provide a general framework to evaluate the targeting efficiency of government welfare programmes and to draw lessons from developing country experiences that are relevant for policy making.

A government programme may be defined as pro-poor if it provides greater benefits to the poor compared to the non-poor. Suppose there are two programmes, A and B, incurring the same cost, then A will be more pro-poor than B if it leads to greater poverty reduction than B. Utilizing this definition, Kakwani and Son (2005) developed a new index called the "pro-poor policy (PPP)" index, which measures the pro-poorness of government programmes as well as of basic service delivery in education, health and infrastructure.

The PPP index is derived as the ratio of actual proportional poverty reduction from a government programme to the proportional poverty reduction that would have been achieved if every individual in society had received exactly the same benefits from the programme. Having been developed to improve targeting, the PPP index provides a means to assess the targeting efficiency of government programmes. Furthermore, Kakwani and Son (2005) developed two types of PPP indices for socio-economic groups, namely "within-group" and "total-group" PPP indices. While the within-group PPP index measures the pro-poorness of a programme within a group, the total-group PPP index captures the impact of operating a programme in a group on its pro-poorness at the national level. The argument is based on the premise that the targeting efficiency of a particular group should be judged on the basis of a total-group PPP index.[1] Using micro-unit-record data from household surveys, the proposed methodology is applied to Thailand, the Russian Federation, Viet Nam and 15 African countries.

The chapter is organized in the following manner. The first section presents a brief description of the methodology proposed by Kakwani and Son (2005) in a non-technical manner. It outlines the poverty measures used in the chapter; the definition of the PPP index; the values of the PPP index attainable under perfect targeting; and the PPP index by socio-economic group. Technical derivation is left out in this chapter as it is detailed in Kakwani and Son (2005). While the following section presents empirical results for Thailand, Russia and Viet Nam, the penultimate section provides empirical analysis for 15 African countries. The final section summarizes the major findings emerging from the study.

METHODOLOGY

Poverty Measures

We measure the pro-poorness of a government policy by measuring its impact on poverty. If there are two policies, A and B, then policy A is more (less) pro-poor than policy *B* if it achieves a greater (smaller) reduction in aggregate poverty with a given cost. Aggregate poverty can be measured in a variety of ways. In this chapter, we will focus on a class of additively separable poverty measures. Foster, Greer and Thorbecke (1984) have suggested poverty measures that fall into this class. These include: a *headcount ratio*, estimating the percentage of people living below a poverty threshold; a *poverty gap* ratio, capturing the depth of poverty; and the severity of poverty index.

To formulate a poverty reduction policy, we need to make a choice of poverty measure. For instance, addressing the headcount ratio will require policies different than those for addressing the poverty gap ratio or the severity of poverty index. The headcount ratio is a crude measure of poverty because it completely ignores the gaps in incomes from the poverty line and the distribution of income among the poor. The severity of poverty index has all the desirable properties.

Pro-Poor Policy (PPP) Index

Suppose there is a welfare transfer from the government which leads to an increase in the recipients' income or consumption expenditure. Accordingly, there will be a reduction in poverty due to the increase in income. We define a government programme to be pro-poor if the poor receive greater absolute benefits from it than the non-poor. This means that the pro-poor government programme should achieve greater poverty reduction compared to a counterfactual situation where everyone receives exactly the same benefit from the programme.

The PPP index is defined as the ratio of actual proportional poverty reduction from the programme to the proportional poverty reduction that would have been achieved if every individual in society had received exactly the same benefits (equal to the average benefit from the programme). A programme is called pro-poor (or anti-poor) when the PPP index is greater (or less) than unity. The larger the value of the PPP index, the greater the degree of pro-poorness of the programme.

To calculate the PPP index, the programme does not have to involve cash transfers. As a matter of fact, a large number of government programmes consist of providing various services in the areas of education, health and other social services. Although these services do not provide cash to individuals, they do contribute to their standard of living. Hence, it can be assumed that if a person utilizes a government service, then he/she receives some notional cash. If all individuals who utilize a government service are assumed to receive exactly the same benefits (in the form of notional cash), then we can easily calculate the PPP index.

Perfect Targeting

The PPP index has the lowest value of zero if the government programme does not reduce any poverty at all, which will happen when all benefits of the programme go to the non-poor. This is considered to be the extreme situation of imperfect targeting.

On the other hand, perfect targeting may be defined as a situation where only the poor get all the benefits proportional to the income shortfall from the poverty line. Kakwani and Son (2005) define two different values of the PPP index obtainable under perfect targeting, depending upon how one defines the poverty line. One scenario is where every household has a different poverty line depending on the household composition and the prices faced by that household. In our empirical study of Thailand, the official poverty line varies with households, whereas for Viet Nam the poverty line is fixed for all households. In each case, the value of the PPP index under perfect targeting is defined differently.

In practice, it is not possible to attain perfect targeting because it is difficult to determine people's incomes or consumption accurately. We generally resort to proxy targeting, such as by geographical region or by other socio-economic characteristics of households. In this study, the targeting efficiency of a programme is judged on the basis of the value of the PPP index. The value of the PPP index under perfect targeting may be used as a benchmark to assess the targeting performance of government programmes. This methodology can also be used for ex ante formulation of new government programmes.

PPP Index by Socio-Economic Group

Taking the line of reasoning a step further, a decomposition methodology was proposed to explain the PPP index in terms of two factors: the within-group PPP index and the total-group PPP index. Suppose there are k mutually exclusive socio-economic groups. The within-group PPP index measures the degree of pro-poorness of a programme within the kth group. It does not tell us whether targeting the kth group will necessarily lead to a pro-poor outcome at the national level. Since our objective is to achieve the maximum reduction of poverty at the national level, we need to see the impact of targeting the kth group on national poverty. To capture this effect, another PPP index for the kth group was proposed, called the total-group PPP index.

The total-group PPP index shows that the pro-poor policy index for the whole country is the weighted average of the pro-poor policy indices for individual groups, with weights proportional to the share of benefits received by each group. It was proved that to reduce poverty at the national level, operating the government programme in some groups will be more effective than in others. This efficiency can be captured by the value of the total-group PPP index: the larger the value of the total-group PPP index, the more efficient the *k*th group in reducing national poverty. On the whole, the methodology presented can help us to identify the efficient groups from the viewpoint of improving targeting efficiency.

Thailand, Russia and Viet Nam

In this section, we apply our methodology, as briefly outlined in the previous section, to Thailand, Russia and Viet Nam. While the PPP index is applied to Thailand and Russia to capture the extent to which the welfare schemes of those governments benefit the poor, the PPP index is applied to Viet Nam to estimate the degree of effectiveness of basic services—including education and health— utilized by its population.

For all three countries, this study utilizes unit-record household surveys, and the analysis is based on per capita consumption expenditure. The surveys are nationwide and cover the periods 2000, 2002 and 1997–1998 for Thailand, Russia and Viet Nam respectively. Poverty lines are country-specific. While a single average national poverty line is used for Viet Nam, Thai and Russian poverty lines differ across households because they take into account different needs of household members by gender and age, as well as the different spatial costs of living by region and area in both Thailand and Russia.[2]

Welfare Programmes in Thailand and Russia

Thailand

In recent years, the Thai government has implemented a few social welfare programmes, including social pensions for the elderly, low income medical cards, health insurance cards and free school lunch programmes. These are means-tested and designed specifically to target the low-income group.[3] In this section, we examine whether these welfare programmes have indeed benefited poor people in society by using the PPP index.

Table 12.1 presents the PPP index for Thailand's social welfare programmes. As can be seen from the table, all four welfare programmes have a PPP index value greater than 1. Hence, we may conclude that all four welfare programmes benefit the poor more than the non-poor. Overall, the poor have greater access to these government welfare programmes than the non-poor.

Interestingly, the welfare programmes for low income medical cards and free school lunches have higher PPP index values with respect to the severity of poverty measure. Since the severity of poverty measure gives greater weight to the ultra-poor, the absolute benefits of low income medical cards and free

TABLE 12.1
PPP index for welfare programmes in Thailand, 2000

Welfare schemes	Poverty gap ratio	Severity of poverty
Social pension for the elderly	1.68	1.54
Low-income medical cards	2.02	2.12
Health insurance cards	1.29	1.25
Free school lunches	2.02	2.06
Perfect targeting	*6.77*	*10.31*
Universal social pensions	*1.21*	*1.24*
(for elderly over 65 years of age)		

school lunch programmes flow to the ultra-poor more than to the moderately poor.

We also calculated the PPP index in the hypothetical case of a universal pension system. Suppose that every elderly person over 65 years of age gets a pension from the government. Is this scenario more pro-poor than the actual pension system? The PPP index indicates that although a universal pension scheme for the elderly is pro-poor and is even more beneficial to the ultra-poor, the present pension system is far more pro-poor than the universal one. This implies that the current means-tested pension system provides more benefits to the poor than the universal pension system for the elderly 65 years of age and over. In this analysis, we have not taken into account the administrative costs involved in providing mean-tested pensions.

Perfect targeting is the ideal policy for poverty reduction. In practice, it is not feasible to operate such a policy because (i) the administrative cost is very high, and (ii) it is difficult to obtain accurate details on individuals' incomes or consumption, particularly in countries with large informal sectors. If the government in Thailand had succeeded in implementing perfect targeting, the PPP index would have been 6.77 for the poverty gap and 10.31 for the severity of poverty measure. Thus, although pro-poor, the Thai welfare programmes have much lower PPP index values than the values that would have been obtained with perfect targeting. This suggests that there is scope for improving the targeting efficiency of the Thai welfare programmes.

In the previous section, we mentioned two types of PPP indices by groups: the within-group PPP index and the total-group PPP index. As stated, the former measures the pro-poorness of a programme within the kth group, whereas the latter captures the impact of operating a programme in the kth group on its pro-poorness at the national level. The results are presented in Table 12.2. The total-group PPP index shown in Table 12.2 reveals that the welfare programmes

TABLE 12.2
PPP index by urban and rural areas in Thailand, 2000

	Total-group PPP index		Within-group PPP index	
Welfare Schemes	Urban	Rural	Urban	Rural
	Poverty gap ratio			
Social pension for the elderly	1.13	1.76	4.41	1.31
Low-income medical cards	1.44	2.10	5.60	1.56
Health insurance cards	0.70	1.39	2.72	1.03
Free school lunches	0.81	2.21	3.15	1.64
	Severity of poverty			
Social pension for the elderly	1.18	1.60	5.42	1.17
Low-income medical cards	1.34	2.23	6.18	1.63
Health insurance cards	0.61	1.36	2.83	0.99
Free school lunches	0.73	2.27	3.37	1.66

are more pro-poor in the rural areas than in the urban areas. Welfare schemes, such as the health care cards and free school lunches, are not pro-poor in the urban areas. This suggests that the government expenditures made on these programmes in the urban areas did not benefit the poor more than the non-poor.

It is, however, interesting to note that the within-group PPP index shows that all programmes are more pro-poor in the urban areas than in the rural areas. Thus, the two types of indices (total-group and within-group) present opposite results. The main reason for this is that welfare programmes in Thailand are better targeted in the urban areas than in the rural areas. Since the concentration of poor is higher in the rural areas, the impact of targeting the rural areas turns out to be more pro-poor at the national level. Thus, the two indices provide us with two different types of information about targeting. If our objective is to reduce poverty at the national level, then the efficiency of targeting a particular group should be judged on the basis of the total-group PPP index.

Russia

Russia has a well-developed social benefits system, of which the pension is the largest component. Table 12.3 shows the population receiving some kind of benefit. There are some persons who receive more than one benefit at the same time; those people are so small in number that we have not taken them into account here.

From Table 12.3, it can be seen that out of the total population of 143.32 million, 53.62 million are receiving some kind of government benefit, which

TABLE 12.3
Russian welfare systems, 2002

Welfare benefits	Beneficiaries (millions)	Percentage share	Per month cost (billion rubles)	Percentage share
Old-age pension	26.32	49.08	38.74	82.79
Disability pension	3.19	5.96	3.61	7.71
Loss-of-breadwinner pension	1.64	3.05	1.27	2.72
Social pension	0.27	0.5	0.26	0.56
Care for children under 18 months	0.84	1.57	0.41	0.88
Child allowances (under 16 years)	17.42	32.49	1.45	3.09
Unemployment benefits	0.45	0.84	0.31	0.65
Other benefits	0.95	1.77	0.2	0.42
Scholarships	2.55	4.76	0.55	1.17
All benefits	53.63	100	46.79	100

means that 37.41 per cent of the total population receives government benefits. This shows that the Russian social benefits system is very large in terms of population coverage. The old-age pension is the largest welfare programme, benefiting about 26.32 million people. The second largest programme is the child allowance, benefiting 17.42 million children. The disability pension is given to 3.19 million people.

The Russian government spends 46.79 billion rubles per month on welfare programmes (excluding administrative costs), of which 38.74 billion rubles go to the payment of pensions. The expenditure on child allowances is only 1.45 billion rubles, meaning that the child allowance per beneficiary is only 83.1 rubles per month. As the incidence of poverty among children is very severe, the child allowance is too small to have a significant effect on poverty among children. The government pays average benefits equal to 326.5 rubles per person per month. Our average lower poverty line for Russia is 1055.9 rubles per person per month, which means that the government pays benefits equal to one third of the poverty line income.

To what extent do government benefits go to the poor compared to the non-poor in Russia? This question is answered through the proposed PPP index. Table 12.4 gives the empirical estimates of the pro-poorness of each of the government welfare programmes that are currently implemented in Russia. As can be seen from the table, the benefits as a whole have PPP index values far greater than 1. From this, we may conclude that the welfare system in Russia tends to benefit the poor more than the non-poor. More importantly, the absolute benefits of the welfare system do indeed flow more to the ultra-poor

TABLE 12.4
PPP indices for the Russian welfare system, 2002

Type of government benefit	Poverty gap ratio	Severity of poverty
Old-age pension	2.20	4.13
Disability pension	2.18	4.16
Loss-of-breadwinner pension	2.09	2.40
Social pension	2.22	2.80
Care for children under 18 months	1.78	1.87
Child allowances (under 16 years)	1.19	0.79
Unemployment benefits	2.22	3.80
Other benefits	1.74	2.75
Scholarships	0.90	0.62
All benefits	*2.14*	*3.90*
Perfect targeting	*3.02*	*5.71*

than to the poor, as suggested by the value of the PPP index for the severity of poverty measure, equal to 3.90. Note that the PPP index for all benefits is the weighted average of the PPP indices for all 9 welfare programmes, with the weight proportional to the share of benefits accruing to people from each programme presented in the third column of Table 12.3.

Table 12.4 also reveals that if the Russian Government had implemented perfect targeting, the PPP index would have been 3.02 and 5.71 for the poverty gap ratio and the severity of poverty index, respectively. This suggests that although Russian welfare programmes are not perfectly targeted to the poor, their deviation from perfect targeting is not large.

It is important to note that welfare programmes such as the child allowance, given to those aged below 16 years, and scholarships are not particularly pro-poor for the severity of poverty index. This is evident from the result that the PPP indices of these two programmes for the severity of poverty measure fall far below unity. This suggests that the absolute benefits of these programmes do not flow to the ultra-poor. It further suggests that these programmes may require better targeting than the current system in a way that favours the ultra-poor living far below the poverty threshold.

Health Services in Viet Nam

Over the past decade or so, Viet Nam has enjoyed a significant improvement in the standard of living with its impressive performance in growth and poverty reduction. More importantly, its growth process has been pro-poor in a way that the growth benefits the poor proportionally more than the non-poor

TABLE 12.5
PPP index for health services in Viet Nam, 1997–1998 (poverty gap ratio)

Health facilities	Country-wide	Total-group PPP index		Within-group PPP index	
		Urban	Rural	Urban	Rural
		Poverty gap ratio			
Government hospitals	0.62	0.07	0.91	0.34	0.74
Commune health centres	1.17	0.27	1.23	1.38	1.00
Regional polyclinics	0.84	0.42	0.98	2.14	0.79
Eastern medicine facilities	0.96	0.04	1.15	0.21	0.94
Pharmacies	0.96	0.26	1.16	1.29	0.94
Private doctors	0.79	0.12	0.98	0.59	0.80
Health insurance	0.50	0.08	0.79	0.40	0.64
Perfect targeting	2.86				

(Kakwani and Son 2004). In this context, it will be interesting to see whether, along with a rising standard of living and its pro-poor growth, poor people benefit from utilization of health services.

Table 12.5 presents the PPP index for utilization of various health facilities in Viet Nam. As the results in Table 12.5 reveal, only the commune health centres have index values greater than 1. This suggests that the poor overall have greater access to commune health centres than the non-poor. It seems that commune health centres play an important role in providing basic health services to the poor in Viet Nam. Unfortunately, commune health centres do not provide quality health services because they are generally poorly staffed and equipped. Thus, the poor are not receiving quality health services as these are not provided by the commune health centres.

Public hospitals in Viet Nam provide higher quality care and are mainly utilized by individuals with health insurance. Utilization of government hospitals has PPP index values far less than 1, implying that public hospitals provide greater benefits to the non-poor than to the poor. That being the case, the poor are less able to access the quality health services provided by public hospitals.

Nevertheless, it is not surprising that the utilization of health insurance is not pro-poor because those covered by health insurance have access to government hospitals. Moreover, insurance coverage under the health insurance programme is more extensive for relatively better-off individuals. Having health insurance is positively correlated with the individual's income: while the insurance coverage rate is 9.2 per cent in the bottom income quartile, 24.5 per cent have health insurance in the top income quartile.

The results presented in Table 12.5 indicate that pharmacy utilization is almost pro-poor (0.96 for the poverty gap ratio). It is reasonable to assume that more highly educated individuals, and hence presumably those more aware of the risks of self-medication, avoid pharmacy visits. Pharmacy utilization therefore appears to be an inferior good for the high-income group since rich individuals go to public hospitals for their health care. On the other hand, pharmacy visits are a normal good for poor households.

Table 12.5 also reveals that, as indicated by the total-group PPP index, the utilization of three types of health facilities—commune health centres, pharmacies and Eastern medicine facilities—is more pro-poor in rural areas than in urban areas. This suggests that the government subsidies on these health services in the rural areas do benefit poor people more than the non-poor. In addition, the within-group PPP index indicates that, within the urban sector, sick and injured individuals from poor households receive far less benefits from the utilization of health care services such as government hospitals and Eastern medicine facilities. By comparison, the rural poor benefit more from utilizing facilities such as commune health centres, Eastern medicine facilities and pharmacies.

Educational Services in Viet Nam

In this subsection, we apply our proposed PPP index methodology to assess educational services in Viet Nam. Our prime objective is to find out to what extent public education at primary and secondary levels is pro-poor. We also attempt to find out whether free universal education will benefit the poor more than the non-poor.

Table 12.6 reveals that public primary education benefits the poor more

TABLE 12.6
PPP index for education services in Viet Nam, 1997–1998

School Types	Primary	Lower secondary	Upper secondary
		Poverty gap ratio	
Public	1.29	0.79	0.37
Semi-public	0.55	0.15	0.23
Sponsored	0.63	0.51	0.00
		Severity of poverty	
Public	1.31	0.65	0.23
Semi-public	0.19	0.08	0.09
Sponsored	0.14	0.26	0.00

than the non-poor. Benefits provided by public primary education are even more pro-poor for the ultra-poor. This is supported by the fact that net enrolments in primary school increased from 87 to 91 per cent over the period 1993–1998 (Nguyen, 2002). Coupled with this substantial improvement in primary school enrolment rates, changes in the allocation of public spending on education in the 1990s could have further favoured the lower levels of education. The share of public spending on education going to the poor increased from 16.5 per cent in 1993 to 18.1 per cent in 1998 (Nguyen, 2002). Although public schools at the primary education level are found to be pro-poor, other types of schools at the same level are highly anti-poor. In other words, primary schools that are semi-public or sponsored by the private sector benefit better-off children more than poor ones. This suggests that educational subsidies given to these types of schools are likely to benefit the non-poor more than the poor.

Table 12.6 also shows that lower secondary education in Viet Nam is not pro-poor, as indicated by the PPP index. This finding emerges consistently, irrespective of school type. At the lower secondary level, net enrolment rates more than doubled between 1993 and 1998, from 30 per cent to 62 per cent. However, for the population as a whole, 38 per cent of children aged 11–14 years old were not enrolled in lower secondary school, while 66 per cent of the poorest children in this age range were not enrolled in primary school. The disparity in enrolment rates between the richest and poorest quintiles has been highly significant over the years.

As would be expected, the PPP index shows that upper secondary schools in Viet Nam have far more children from better-off households compared to those from poor households. This is true for all types of schools at this level. There are no children from poor households enrolled in the upper secondary level schools sponsored by the private sector. Over the period 1993–1998, children from the poorest quintile experienced an increase in enrolment in upper secondary schools from 1 to 5 per cent, as compared to an increase from 21 to 64 per cent for the richest quintile (Nguyen, 2002). On the whole, much still needs to be done to achieve universal primary and secondary education. The question is whether educational outcomes can be pro-poor. The PPP index for universal education is now compared to that under the current education system.

Table 12.7 shows that universal education at primary and lower secondary levels in Viet Nam would provide more benefits to poor children than to the non-poor. The degree of pro-poorness of universal access to primary education among 6 to 10-year-old children would be almost as high as actually achieved by the current education system. Similarly, if lower secondary education were

TABLE 12.7
PPP index if universal education were to be provided in Viet Nam

	Poverty gap ratio	Severity of poverty
Primary	1.28	1.33
Lower secondary	1.08	1.06
Upper secondary	0.91	0.85

made universal for children aged between 11 and 14 years, this would provide a pro-poor outcome. This is in contrast with the actual situation, as indicated by the PPP index: the index is 0.79 for lower secondary education, whereas it would be 1.08 if lower secondary education were universal. At higher levels, universal provision is not likely to deliver pro-poor outcomes. The PPP index for upper secondary schooling is less than unity. In short, universal education at higher levels would not be pro-poor, but would provide greater opportunities to poor individuals aged between 15 and 17 years for upper secondary schooling to have greater access to higher education compared to the current situation. A better alternative would be to provide incentives to children from poor households to enrol in upper secondary education.

Basic Infrastructure Services in Viet Nam

Basic infrastructure services make significant contributions to people's well-being. Basic services, such as piped water and sanitation (e.g., sewerage systems, flushing toilets, etc.), have direct impacts on people's health status and overall well-being. Having access to other services, such as electricity and telephones, helps households increase their productivity for income generation. A number of studies reveal that a household's access to basic services is highly and significantly correlated with a lower probability of being poor.

As shown in Table 12.8, the benefits generated from all types of basic services go to the non-poor more than to the poor in Viet Nam. Poor households in

TABLE 12.8
Viet Nam: PPP index for basic infrastructure services, 1997–1998

Access to basic infrastructure services	Poverty gap ratio	Severity of poverty
Electricity	0.80	0.71
Piped and tap water	0.86	0.81
Collected waste	0.10	0.07
Sanitary toilets	0.10	0.05

general have much greater access to piped water and electricity than sanitary systems: the PPP index for water and electricity are 0.86 and 0.80, respectively, when measured by the poverty gap ratio, whereas the indices are only 0.10 for the sanitary facilities. As suggested in Table 12.8, benefits generated from sanitary services (collected waste and flushing toilets in this case) are highly skewed in favour of the non-poor. The benefits of all types of basic services are lower for the severity of poverty measure. This suggests that the ultra-poor have even less access to basic infrastructure services than the poor.

15 AFRICAN COUNTRIES

This section of our study utilizes unit-record household data sets from 15 African countries obtained from the African Household Survey Data Bank of the World Bank. The countries and years of the surveys are: Burkina Faso in 1998, Burundi in 1998, Cameroon in 1996, Côte d'Ivoire in 1998, Ethiopia in 2000, Gambia in 1998, Ghana in 1998, Guinea in 1994, Kenya in 1997, Madagascar in 2001, Malawi in 1997, Mozambique in 1996, Nigeria in 1996, Uganda in 1999 and Zambia in 1998.

The study uses national poverty lines for the 15 countries obtained from various poverty assessment reports. These poverty lines were originally very crude and did not take into account different needs of household members by age and gender. Moreover, the poverty lines were not adjusted for the economies of scale which exist in large households. To overcome these shortcomings associated with the official poverty lines, Kakwani and Subbarao (2005) made some modifications to the national poverty lines, taking into account the different needs of household members and economies of scale.

Targeting Children: Targeting vs. Universalism

According to Coady, Grosh and Hoddinott (2002), more than a quarter of targeted programmes in all developing countries had regressive benefit incidences. For instance, they found that the poorest 40 per cent received less than 40 per cent of poverty alleviation budget expenditures. Such ineffective targeting of poor households suggests that the overall impact on poverty of such spending has been much smaller than if well targeted. Moreover, the administrative costs involved in implementing any targeted programmes are very high. Much of the budget is spent on simply getting the resources to poor families. Consequently, the cost per unit of income transferred can be substantial. Transfer programmes seem to be administratively complex as they require resources to undertake targeting of transfers and to monitor the recipients' actions. In this context, one might argue for a scenario of universal transfers.

In this section, we estimate the PPP indices under a universal transfer programme for children aged between 5 and 16 years old. Under such a programme, every child that belongs to this age group is assumed to receive a certain amount of transfers, irrespective of the child's poverty status. The results are presented in Figure 12.1 and Table 12.9. From Figures 12.1 and 12.2, we note that the PPP index values with perfect targeting for the 15 African countries are quite small compared to the PPP index values in Thailand, Russia and Viet Nam. In fact, the PPP indices with perfect targeting differ little from the indices associated with universal transfers. This suggests that targeting may not be needed in cases such as these 15 African countries, where poverty is extremely high.

Table 12.9 carries two important messages. First, the results indicate that universal transfers will provide more absolute benefits to children from poor families than those from non-poor families. Second, a universal transfer scheme is likely to bring about an even more pro-poor outcome if implemented in rural areas where most poor children live. One exception is in the case of Nigeria where, in contrast, poverty is widespread in both urban and rural areas.

One possible criticism is that we do not compare targeted transfers with

TABLE 12.9
PPP index for universal transfers to rural and urban areas

Country	Poverty gap ratio				Severity of poverty			
	Universal targeting			Perfect targeting	Universal targeting			Perfect targeting
	Rural	Urban	Total		Rural	Urban	Total	
Burkina Faso	1.18	0.43	1.07	1.81	1.21	0.38	1.08	2.53
Burundi	1.12	0.28	1.09	1.59	1.16	0.23	1.12	2.11
Cameroon	1.28	0.60	1.09	1.54	1.32	0.50	1.08	2.05
Cote d'Ivoire	1.51	0.60	1.10	2.51	1.63	0.45	1.09	3.63
Ethiopia	1.13	0.73	1.07	2.37	1.14	0.74	1.09	3.42
Gambia	1.37	0.65	1.08	1.56	1.56	0.39	1.08	2.00
Ghana	1.39	0.54	1.09	2.24	1.47	0.42	1.10	3.03
Guinea	1.42	0.37	1.08	2.56	1.47	0.31	1.10	3.40
Kenya	1.25	0.29	1.14	1.95	1.27	0.18	1.16	2.53
Madagascar	1.22	0.65	1.09	1.57	1.29	0.57	1.13	1.95
Malawi	1.17	0.18	1.07	1.52	1.21	0.09	1.09	1.93
Mozambique	1.19	0.62	1.07	1.42	1.24	0.59	1.11	1.77
Nigeria	1.14	1.13	1.14	1.54	1.12	1.21	1.16	1.91
Uganda	1.17	0.25	1.06	2.00	1.20	0.19	1.08	2.75
Zambia	1.23	0.76	1.05	1.45	1.34	0.57	1.06	1.80

Figure 12.1
Pro-Poor Policy indices under universal transfers and perfect targeting (poverty gap ratio)

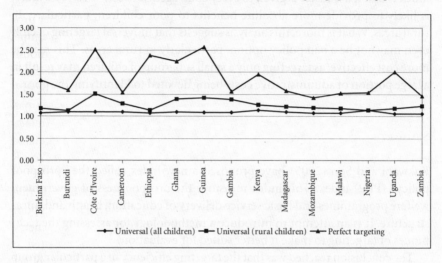

Figure 12.2
Pro-Poor Policy indices under perfect targeting for 18 countries (poverty gap ratio)

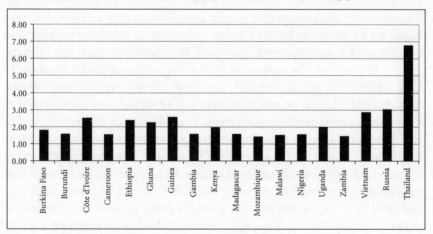

universal transfers. Nevertheless, the main implication emerging from the PPP index is that if a transfer is given to every child aged between 5–16 years old, it is likely to provide more absolute benefits to poor children, particularly in rural areas. What is more, this analysis suggests that universal targeting of children may not be a bad policy option, particularly in rural areas. This may be more cost effective, as targeting only a small subgroup of children may result in a large portion of administrative costs being devoted to identifying the poor.

SUMMARY

Kakwani and Son (2005) have proposed a new index called the "pro-poor policy" (PPP) index. This index measures the pro-poorness of government welfare programmes and basic service delivery of education, health and infrastructure. It is an attempt to introduce a methodology for assessing the techniques of targeting to make it better suited for evaluation.

The conclusion reached was that the targeting efficiency of a particular group should be judged on the basis of the total-group PPP index. If the objective is to reduce poverty, then social transfer programmes should be designed so that they lead to the maximum reduction of poverty under given resource constraints. To achieve this objective, perfect targeting would be an ideal solution. Two prerequisites are necessary in this context: only the poor get all the benefits, and benefits given to the poor are proportional to their income shortfalls from the poverty line income. To implement such a programme, it will be necessary to have detailed information of people's incomes or consumption expenditures. Such detailed information and the administrative ability to use it are, of course, not present in most developing countries. The policy makers, therefore, have to resort to a form of proxy targeting which makes transfers based on easily identifiable socio-economic characteristics of households; however, proxy targeting can never achieve complete targeting success. Hence, this study is an important methodological attempt to assess the targeting efficiency of government programmes by trying to find out how good the proxy targeting is compared to perfect targeting. Government programmes may be defined as pro-poor if they provide greater benefits to the poor than to the non-poor.

Using micro unit-record household surveys, the methodology was applied to 18 countries including Thailand, Russia, Viet Nam and 15 African countries. The major conclusions emerging from our empirical analysis can be synthesized as follows:

First, all four welfare programmes recently implemented by the Thai government were found to be pro-poor. In particular, welfare programmes designed to help the very poor—including low income medical cards and free school lunches—were shown to be highly pro-poor, benefiting the ultra-poor more than the poor. In addition, the study has shown that a universal pension for the elderly over 65 years of age is likely to be less pro-poor than the present old-age pension system. This suggests that the Thai government should continue with its present old-age pension scheme.

Second, the study found that the welfare system in Russia tends to benefit the poor more than the non-poor. Moreover, the absolute benefits of the welfare system do indeed flow more to the ultra-poor than to the poor, as suggested by the PPP index value for the severity of poverty index, which is higher than that for the poverty gap ratio. Additionally, the PPP index for all benefits is the weighted average of the PPP indices for all nine welfare programmes, with the weight proportional to the shares of each programme. The study found the Russian welfare programmes to be reasonably well-targeted. This is evident from the finding that the PPP indices of welfare programmes are quite close to (but still lower than) the index expected to be attained with perfect targeting. The study also found that welfare programmes—such as the child allowance, given to those aged below 16 years, and scholarships—are not pro-poor for the ultra-poor in particular. This suggests that these programmes may require better targeting than the current system in a way that would favour the ultra-poor living far below the poverty threshold.

Third, basic services—health and education—in Viet Nam were found to be mostly not pro-poor. Although government hospitals provide the highest quality of health care, the poor are much less likely to utilize them. This is, however, not true for commune health centres, which appear to provide more services to individuals from poor households. Unfortunately, the commune health centres do not provide quality health services because they are poorly staffed and equipped. On the whole, the poor have less access to quality health care.

In Viet Nam, public primary schools were found to be pro-poor. This was partly due to the increase in public spending on education for the poor in the 1990s. However, secondary education was not pro-poor. The study suggests that universal education at primary and lower secondary levels could provide more benefits to students from poor households, although this cannot be said for higher levels of education.

Fourth, ex ante simulations of universal transfers to school-age children in 15 African countries indicated that universal transfers would provide more absolute benefits to children from poor families than to those from non-poor families. In addition, the study found that a universal transfer scheme is likely to have even more pro-poor outcomes if implemented in the rural areas, where most poor children reside. This finding is true for all the countries except

Nigeria, where poverty is widespread in both urban and rural areas.

Finally, the study found that in the 15 African countries, the value of the PPP index with perfect targeting was quite small compared to the index values for Thailand, Russia and Viet Nam. The index value of perfect targeting for Thailand was far greater than for Russia and Viet Nam. In the case of the African countries, the PPP indices under perfect targeting differed little from the indices for universal provision. Therefore, we conclude that perfect targeting is not necessary for cases such as these 15 African countries, where poverty is extremely high.

NOTES

[1] It is possible that a programme may be well-targeted within group although it may not be considered as well-targeted at the national level.

[2] For a detailed discussion of Thai and Russian poverty lines, see Kakwani (2003, 2004).

[3] In practice, no programme can be perfectly means tested. It is important to know how much the deviation of a programme is from the perfectly means tested programme.

REFERENCES

Bigman, D., and H. Fofack (2000). Combining Census and Survey Data to Study Spatial Dimensions of Poverty: A Case Study of Ecuador. In *Geographical Targeting for Poverty Alleviation*. World Bank, Washington DC.

Braithwaite, J., C. Grootaert and B. Milanovic (2000). *Poverty and Social Assistance in Transition Countries*. St. Martin's Press, New York.

Coady, D., M. Grosh, and J. Hoddinott (2002). The Targeting of Transfers in Developing Countries: Review of Experiences and Lessons. Social Safety Net Primer Series, World Bank, Washington, DC.

Foster, J., J. Greer and Erik Thorbecke (1984). A Class of Decomposable Poverty Measures. *Econometrica* 52 (3): 761–66.

Grosh, M. (1994). *Administering Targeted Social Programmes in Latin America: From Platitudes to Practice*. Regional and Sectoral Studies, World Bank, Washington, DC.

Kakwani, Nanak (2003). Issues in Setting Absolute Poverty Lines. Poverty and Social Development Paper No. 3, June, Asian Development Bank, Manila.

Kakwani, Nanak (2004). New Poverty Thresholds for Russia. Processed, World Bank, Washington, DC.

Kakwani, Nanak, and Hyun H. Son (2004). Pro-Poor Growth: Asian Experience. Working Paper No. 1, International Poverty Centre, United Nations Development Program, Brasilia.

Kakwani, Nanak, and Hyun H. Son (2005). On Assessing Pro-Poorness of Government Programmes: International Comparisons. Working Paper No. 8, International Poverty Centre, United Nations Development Program, Brasilia.

Kakwani, Nanak, and K. Subbarao (2005). Ageing and Poverty in Africa and the Role of Social Pensions. International Poverty Centre, United Nations Development Program, Brasilia.

Nguyen, N. N. (2002). Trends in the Education Sector from 1993–1998. Policy Research Working Paper No. 2891, World Bank, Washington, DC.

Rawlings, L., L. Sherburne-Benz and J. Domelen (2001). *Evaluating Social Funds: A Cross-Country Analysis of Community Investments*. World Bank, Washington DC.

13
Targeting and Universalism in Poverty Reduction

THANDIKA MKANDAWIRE[1]

For much of its history, social policy has involved choices about whether the core principle behind social provisioning will be "universalism" or selectivity through "targeting". Under universalism, the entire population is the beneficiary of social benefits as a basic right, while under targeting, eligibility to social benefits involves some kind of means testing to determine the "truly deserving". Policy regimes are hardly ever purely universal or purely based on targeting, however; they tend to lie somewhere between the two extremes on a continuum and are often hybrid, but where they lie on this continuum can be decisive in spelling out individuals' life chances and in characterizing the social order. Indeed, how far a policy regime leans toward either of these options was a core feature of Esping-Anderson's seminal typology of welfare regimes.

This chapter is divided into two parts. The first part discusses the forces behind the shift from universalism towards selectivity in social policies to combat poverty in the developing countries. The second part—a review of the lessons from such policies—considers the administrative difficulties of targeting in the poor countries, the political economy bases of policy choices and the consequences of policy choices for individual incentives. Special attention is paid to cost-effectiveness, since advocates of selectivity in the fight against poverty raise this as the main argument in its favour.

SHIFT TO TARGETING

While the leaning was towards universalistic policies in the 1960s and 1970s, since the 1980s, the balance has radically tilted in favour of targeting in both developed[2] and developing countries. In the developed countries, this led to the shift from welfare to workfare states. In the words of Gilbert (2001), "Over the decade many social welfare policies have been redesigned to narrow the scope of recipients through means tests, income tests, claw-back taxes, diagnostic criteria, behavioural requirements, and status characteristics." Even in the more resilient cases of the Nordic welfare states, observers spoke of the "flight from universalism" (Sunesson and others, 1998). In the developing countries, the choice has been conditioned by the context of macroeconomic and aid policies, the centrality given to poverty in official discourse, and the unravelling of "social pacts" behind various forms of universalism and the consequent ideological shifts in both developed and developing countries.

Ideological Shifts

Ideologies play an important role in the choice of instruments used to address problems of poverty, inequality and insecurity. Each of the core concerns of social policy—*need, deserts* and *citizenship*—are social constructs that derive full meaning from the cultural and ideological definition of "deserving poor", "entitlement" and "citizens' rights". Although, in current parlance, the choice between "targeting" and "universalism" is couched in the language of efficient allocation of resources subject to budget constraints and the exigencies of globalization, what is actually at stake is the fundamental question about a polity's values and its responsibilities to all its members. The technical nature of the argument cannot conceal the fact that, ultimately, value judgements matter, not only with respect to determining the needy and how they are perceived, but also in attaching weights to the types of costs and benefits of approaches chosen. Such a weighting is often reflective of one's ideological predisposition. In addition, societies chose either targeting or universalism in conjunction with other policies that are ideologically compatible with the choice and that are deemed constitutive of the desired social and economic policy regime.

In the 1980s and 1990s, the rise of the Right, which privileged individual responsibility and a limited role for the state, had a profound influence in some of the key industrial countries. Mrs. Thatcher's insistence that "there is no such thing as community" touched on one of the most important ideological underpinnings of social policy—solidarity and citizenship. It is this neoliberal ideological position that has set the limits on social policy and underpins the preferences for "user fees", means testing, market delivery of social services or "partnerships" in their delivery. This ideology has also eliminated the equity concerns that have been central to all the successful experiences of poverty eradication. With ideologies of equality on the retreat, policies pushing for universalism, together with their accompanying redistributive measures, were bound to experience setbacks.

These ideological shifts in the North led to similar shifts in the South, where the attacks on the welfare state were extended to include the developmentalist ideologies with which it had strong conceptual and ideological affinities. In the name of developmentalism, socialist ideologies and nation-building, many Third World governments had tended to lean towards universal provision of a number of services, including free health, free education and subsidized food. For the aid-dependent or client state, ideological shifts reflected changes in the donor countries and international financial institutions (IFIs). Yet, the ideological assault on universalism was not only externally driven but had internal drivers as well. Like the developed countries, many developing countries were themselves also undergoing their own ideological convulsions that tilted the balance towards targeting. The case of Chile under Augusto Pinochet is the most emblematic of this internal shift. In many other countries, the nationalist and populist pacts that had underpinned universalistic policies were in disarray. Nationalist and populist ideologies had been undermined by both the mismanagement of national affairs by nationalists, some of whom had morphed into petty dictators and kleptocrats. Notions of solidarity and nation-building rang hollow in the face of increasing inequality and blatant self-aggrandizement. Technocracies that had arisen around these movements had been captured by both internal and external forces more inclined to liberal ideologies and their aversion to state provision. Current programmes on poverty reduction, such as the Poverty Reduction Strategies and the associated Poverty Reduction Strategy Papers (PRSPs), are tethered to the neoliberal ideology which is premised on self-interest and a fundamental faith in the market.

The Fiscal Constraint and the Quest for Efficiency

One other driving force behind selectivity was the fiscal constraint of the late 1970s that led to the perception that there was a need for budgetary restraint and, perhaps more importantly, to the overriding of all other considerations in the choice among possible social policies. "Fiscal crisis" also provided an excellent opportunity for the ideologically driven shift towards targeting because it sanctioned the view that targeting was the most efficient and commonsensical thing to do under the circumstances. Politically, it is much more convenient to deploy the language of cost containment and efficiency that comes along with budgetary constraints than to embark on a frontal attack on the legitimacy of universalism and its morally appealing language of rights and solidarity. In addition, it was argued that global competition called for changes in tax policies and the need to reduce "social wages" represented by social transfers. Not surprisingly, many of the debates on targeting in the 1980s revolved around restricting public spending so as to allow tax cuts, especially on traded goods, and remove other taxes presumed to be "distortionary" and, therefore, the cause of poor export performance.

The formulation for the case for targeting unfolds along the following lines: In the face of limited fiscal resources, it is better to target the resources to the "deserving poor". Governments are presented as if confronted with an exogen-ously given fiscal constraint and are enjoined to do their best under the circum-stances. However, we should bear in mind the close relationship between the macroeconomic regime and the choices made in the social policy arena. The fiscal constraint is not always exogenously given. In many cases, it is an outcome of deliberate attempts to limit the state, on the assumption that one can attack poverty with less money. As Besley and Kanbur (1990) observe, "Indeed, targeting has become a panacea in the area of poverty alleviation, whence it is suggested that policy makers can have their cake and eat it too—improved targeting means that more poverty alleviation could be achieved with less expenditure!" First, there is narrowing of the state's mandate and capacity by way of what Paul Krugman (2005) terms "starving the beast". Often, the most widely applied taxes and the easiest to collect (e.g., taxes on trade) are removed as part of adjustment policies.[3] This is then invoked to argue that, partly as a result of the fiscal crisis and retrenchment, the state has less capacity for providing universal services and is better off targeting both its limited financial resources and its much reduced capacity. The privatization of a whole range of social services, including education and health, was supposed not only to relieve the state of a heavy fiscal burden, but also to compel those who could afford to pay user charges to do so. In such markets, individuals would be induced to make the "right" investment in human capital, reflecting changes in demand in well-functioning labour markets.

Shifts in Aid

A fundamental factor pushing social policy towards targeting in the aid-dependent economies is the changing perception of aid and the centrality of poverty in policy discourse. In many countries, aid plays an important role in shaping social policy. Aid policies are embedded in the overall policies of the donor countries. Not surprisingly, then, any shifts in the ideological under-pinnings of social and economic policies in the donor countries were bound to spill over to principles of aid. First, many donor countries accepted the major premises of adjustment. The more critically inclined sought to give a "human face" to the adjustment process by providing funds that would be aimed at "mitigating" the "social consequences of adjustment". Such programmes were to be palliatives that would minimize the more glaring inequalities that their policies had perpetuated. Funds were made available to ensure that a so-called safety net of social services would be provided for the "vulnerable"—but this time, not only by the state (which had, after all, been forced to "retrench" away from the social sector) but also by the ever-willing NGO sector. Second, one reason for the preference for targeting is that aid is nowadays understood not so much in terms of helping developing countries, but in terms of helping the poor. In the context of "aid fatigue", it has become politically necessary to demonstrate either that aid directly reaches the poor or, even if it does not, that it enhances growth—which is good for the poor (the aid-growth nexus is not always so clear though, so it is argued that at least aid restructures public expenditure in favour of the poor).

In this regard, the World Bank, the bellwether in donor thinking, has advanced two somewhat contradictory positions. On the one hand, it has argued the need for a "pro-poor" policy stance and for measures to shift resources in favour of the poor during the growth process and to mitigate the negative consequences of adjustment policies. This position is succinctly stated in the 1990 report on poverty: "A comprehensive approach to poverty reduction…calls for a program of well-targeted transfers and safety nets as an essential complement to the basic strategy" (World Bank, 1990: 3). On the other hand, the Bank has advanced "the rising tide raises all boats" argument through the much publicized work of David Dollar and Aart Kraay, which, simply argued, is that "growth is good for the poor". The corollary point to this latter position is that, since the policies that the IFIs pursue ensure the requisite growth, there is really no need to pursue policies that directly address the issues of poverty. Although the second proposition was given considerable publicity by the World Bank, it is the former argument that eventually won political support and that underlies the choice of approaches for addressing poverty. Initially, safety nets and targeting were viewed as temporary, on the presumption that their need would be diminished by the high employment elasticity of growth putatively associated with structural adjustment programmes. However, over the years, it became clear that these measures were insufficient for the problems thrown up by adjustment and that their short-term nature was based on unfounded expectations about the effectiveness of macroeconomic policies whose negative effects they were supposed to temporarily mitigate. With the persistence of the problems, new approaches have been adopted, but such approaches have had to be compatible with the exigencies of both the ideological predispositions and macroeconomic policies favoured by the IFIs and bilateral donors. In line with the "new consensus" on poverty, many donors now lean heavily towards targeting—directly through projects that are specifically aimed at the poor, or indirectly through support to sectors that are likely to benefit the poor more than the well off. The PRSP process, upon which many developing countries have embarked and to which most donors now contribute, is squarely premised on targeting the poor.

Finally, there has been the rediscovery of efficiency as a primary policy objective, leading to the so-called new managerialism, in which concepts derived from the private sector replace the traditional ideas of public administration. This "new managerialism" accounts for the increasing willingness to delegate important policy-making powers to technocratic bodies that enjoy political independence, producing what has been referred to as the "contract state". This has spilled over to the national aid agencies, leading to the emergence of new arrangements for providing aid as features of the "contract state" being reproduced in the aid business. Such administrative arrangements, which call for "partnerships" involving the private sector and NGOs, have tended to encourage the "parcelization" and "projectization" of social policy (Tendler, 2004). This approach insists on a clear relationship between inputs and outputs, which in turn calls for a clear delimitation of tasks and of costs and benefits. These institutional arrangements have not only been driven by the new "targeting" approach, but have themselves given prominence to this policy option. Significantly, this rediscovery of efficiency has gone hand in hand with the downplaying of redistributive and transformative (or developmental) concerns.

Crisis of Universalism

The shift towards targeting also reflected the crisis of "universalism" in many countries, owing to a number of factors. As noted earlier, the fiscal basis of existing welfare regimes has been placed under severe strain since the 1980s. In the advanced countries, demographic shifts and widespread unemployment led to the realization that there might be fiscal limits to universal provision. In addition, in many countries, political transformations had undermined the political coalitions and the social pacts behind universalistic policies. Perhaps one major political weakness of universalism was the gap between its universalistic proclamations and the actual reach of its policies. In practice, universalism was stratified and tended to apply to social groups directly linked to the nation-building project (state functionaries, military) and to the industrialization project. Such stratification was most sharply drawn out in countries pursuing import substitution industrialization and was especially evident with respect to social protection.[4] Even prior to the crisis and the adjustment that undermined these policies, such "stratified universalism" was strongly criticized for urban bias and for creating "labour aristocracies" (Areskoug, 1976; Arrighi, 1973) while marginalizing large sections of the population. What had been touted as policies that would eventually encompass the society as a whole appeared as exclusive privileges "captured" by a few in privileged sectors, who were bent on blocking the extension of these programmes to other sections of the population. This opened the doors to the right-wing populism that treated these privileges as part of the rent-seeking that had wrought havoc on the policies of *dirigiste* states.

There are a number of observations that need to be made here. First, the factors that are said to have bedevilled universalistic policies are likely to rear their head even with targeting. As Figueira and Figueira (2002: 127–128) note with respect to Latin America:

> The problems of social policy in Latin America were not exclusively the result of centralism, the pretension of universalism, or statist and sectoral approaches. Thus, decentralisation, privatisation, and targeting are not their automatic solution. The problem in the region has been centralised authoritarianism, general inequality, rent-seeking political elites, and the bureaucratic weakness of states in coordinating and distributing services. These problems have not disappeared and their structural bases seem more present than ever.

Second, it should be recalled that the foundation of many of today's most successful universalistic welfare states was such "stratified universalism". In most "late industrializers"—such as Germany and Japan—welfare entitlements were directed at those parts of the workforce that were most crucial for economic growth, best organized, and thus politically most powerful: that is, skilled industrial workers (Manow, 2001: 95). Thus, for Germany and Japan, rather than extending universal social rights to a minimum level of subsistence to all members of the community, the states came into existence by granting privileges to groups whose cooperation in economic modernization and nation-building was deemed indispensable by political and economic elites. "Universalization" took place through the gradual extension of the "performance/achievement" model—hence, the importance of full employment as a labour market objective. The approaches were generally additive, i.e. over the years, new beneficiaries were added by specification of new eligibility criteria.

In general, late industrializers tended to climb the ladder towards universalism much faster than the "pioneers" of industrialization. The speed with which universalism spread was conditioned by the political regime in place. In democratic societies where labour was free, universalism was rapidly extended, partly by the necessity of forming coalitions between workers and peasants, as was the case in the Nordic countries. The important thing to recall here is that the underlying rationale of social policy in these "successful cases" was universalistic so that the tendency was to extend initially exclusive social rights for the employed to the rest of the labour force. This is in sharp contrast to current trends where the main preoccupation of social allocation is narrowing the scope of the coverage of social welfare. Structural adjustment programmes and PRSPs, driven by a "targeting" rationale, begin by dismantling the exclusive rights of formal labour on the grounds that this will lead to greater labour market flexibility and will attract donor funds for "pro-poor" policies.

Another criticism levelled against universalism is derived from the postmodernist emphasis on difference and diversity. The charge is that universalism has been used to create a false sense of unity which conceals the fact that it discriminated against certain social groups on grounds of gender and race, and that, through tutelage, it imposed, on new groups, standards set by the dominant group.[5] With respect to developing countries, these arguments have been raised more specifically in the context of gender and discussions on cultural diversity where purportedly universal policies have turned out to be parochial and reflective of fundamental biases (e.g. racial, gender bias). Implicit in most of these points of view is the need for selectivity that allows for "affirmative" action or measures designed for different groups. In its most extreme formulation, this perspective suggests solutions that would ultimately make any society incoherent because it sanctions something tantamount to unlimited relativism, and thereby eliminates any hope of discovering an agreed-upon theoretical and moral foundation on which to base allocation practices. Ellison (1999: 70) suggests that this "not only risks anarchy of competing claims from a variety of combinations of subject positions while offering no means of deciding among them, but also raises questions about how one can deal with those who seek to maintain, or alter, distribution outcomes at the expense of others". The postmodern approach runs into a cul-de-sac reminiscent of welfare economics which, by its insistence on the impossibility of interpersonal comparisons, was unable to say much that was useful in designing social policy. The most successful feminist movements have pursued a double-pronged approach by criticising the false universalism behind male-biased arrangements while insisting on universalistic social policies for eliminating forms of inequality in male breadwinner logic societies (Sainsbury, 1996). In addition, we find the most "women friendly" policies in societies that base their social policies on notions of social citizenship and in which universalism is also an integral part of social policies (Anttonen, 2002; UNRISD, 2005). This said, the criticism does point to dangers of totalizing categories and points to the need for a constant re-evaluation of the foundations on which universalism is built.

Exit Redistribution

The earlier focus on poverty was due to growing awareness of the economic cleavages within the developing countries and the rather discomfiting realization that only anaemic "trickle down" had occurred with economic growth.

This realization led to the calls for "growth equity" strategies. Although current debates on poverty pay little attention to equity, it is, at times, evoked in support of targeting. Indeed, in its more populist form, the current debate on the choice between targeting and universalism as modes of social allocation is couched in the language of redistribution. Targeting can be used as a means for flattening the distribution of income and as an administrative means to reach groups in society whose income falls below a defined level. One measure of universalism is precisely how flatly the income transfer is distributed across a population of different incomes. Indeed, one of the criticisms levelled at universalism is that it is not redistributive.[6] In contrast, targeting is portrayed as quintessentially redistributive, precisely because it is premised on the view that the social returns for a given level of transfers are higher for individuals or households at the lower end of the income distribution than at the upper end. However, in practice, the element stressed with respect to targeting is not its redistributive properties, but its cost-effectiveness. Indeed, the ideologies driving it are often distinctly opposed to equity and are guided by a philanthropic principle at best and, at worst, a mean-spirited paternalism. In any case, levels of equality are higher in societies pursuing universalistic policies than those that rely on means testing and other forms of selectivity. The point is not that there is some functional relationship between universalistic policies and redistributive policies in other areas but that there is an elective affinity between the preference for universalism and other measures, such as high progressive taxes. Thus, non-redistribution in transfers is more than compensated for by redistribution in taxation. As Korpi and Palme (1998) have argued, while targeted programmes may indeed be more redistributive *per unit of money*, other factors are likely to make universal programmes more redistributive. This is neatly illustrated by the example given by (Rothstein, 2001). As Table 13.1 shows, while everyone received the same

TABLE 13.1
The redistributive effects of a universal welfare state

Group	Average income	Tax (40%)	Transfers	Income after taxes + transfers
A (20%)	1000	400	240	840
B (20%)	800	320	240	720
C (20%)	600	240	240	600
D (20%)	400	160	240	480
E (20%)	200	80	240	360
Ratio A/E	5/1	(=1200)	(=1200)	2.33/1

Source: Rothstein (2001)

absolute amount in transfers, taxation is proportional to income. The consequence is a significant reduction in inequality ratio between A and E from 5/1 to 2.33/1.

Not surprisingly, in reality, societies that lean towards universalistic social policies have less inequality than those that prefer targeting. The argument advanced by Korpi and Palme is that institutions of welfare also act as intervening variables, shaping the political coalitions that eventually determine the size and redistributive nature of the national budget by defining interests and identities among citizens, the rational choices they make and the ways in which they are likely to combine for collective action. It is this that produces what they call the "paradox of redistribution": the more we target benefits at the poor only and the more concerned we are with creating equality via equal public transfers to all, the less likely we are to reduce poverty and inequality (Korpi and Palme, 1998: 681).

The main objection to universalism is, not surprisingly, often aimed at the redistributive policies that come along with it (tax structures, labour market policies, etc.). Stripped of these other redistributive measures, universalistic policies may actually be embraced by conservative governments, especially when they have, as is often the case, regressive taxation. This might explain why, even among the late industrializers, the push for universalism was not always made by radical movements but by conservative regimes concerned with social peace and nation-building a la Bismarck [7]

Targeting itself, almost by definition, leads to segmentation and differentiation. In service provision, targeting leads to the creation of a dual structure—one aimed at the poor and funded by the state and one aimed at the well-to-do and provided by the private sector. Or, as Amartya Sen (1995: 14) argues, "benefits meant exclusively for the poor often end up being poor benefits". One reason why such an eventuality is not taken seriously is that in many countries in which targeting has been effectively implemented, income inequality is already high, so that the segmentation in social provision does not raise eyebrows. Geographical targeting often leads to horizontal inequality so that the poor in one area might benefit more than the poor in non-targeted areas— assuming, of course, that the rich in the targeted area do not capture the resources. Such inequality can be explosive politically and is often the basis of ethnic conflicts. In many countries where ethnic, religious and cultural space is co-terminous with geographical space, such geographical targeting can lead to inequitable geographical selectivity.[8]

The Marginal Role of Social Policy

The shift from "development" to "poverty reduction" has impacted on how social policy is perceived in the context of developing countries and has contributed to the narrowing of the remit of social policies. The preference for targeting is thus often a reflection of the residual role assigned to social policy, which has come to be seen as merely an instrument for correcting some of the negative outcomes of macroeconomic policies. One implicit assumption is that social policy is only about poverty eradication, whereas in many cases, it has other objectives, such as national or social cohesion, or equity. Most of the arguments assume that social policies only lead to consumption, which reduces long-term growth. Universalistic policies are treated as part of the welfare state, as an end state attained only after crossing a certain threshold of economic development. Consequently, it is argued, poor countries should wait their turn before introducing such policies. Such a view is ahistorical. As Atkinson (1995) argues, expenditure that is considered to be targeting the poor, when judged solely by the objective of alleviating poverty, may well be directed at other objectives of the social security system. Historically, social policy has been conditioned by a wide range of considerations, including citizenship, nation-building, judgements on the sources of poverty and the conduct of the poor, faith in efficacy of the market, political ideologies, theories of human behaviour, bureaucratic capacities, overall economic strategies and international pressures and considerations. Indeed, in a number of countries, the relief of poverty was not even the most important motive for the introduction of transfers.[9] In developmental contexts, social policy has typically had a multiplicity of objectives that have included equity, social inclusion, nation-building, conflict management and human capital formation (Mkandawire, 2005b). It was part of a broad agenda of economic development and social transformation.

In a manner reminiscent of the Gerschenkron (1962) thesis on industrial policies, late industrializers adopted certain social policies and institutions at a much earlier phase of their development than their predecessors (Mkandawire, 2001). Indeed, the case of late industrializers—and low-income countries that have done relatively well in terms of social development—clearly suggests that universal provisioning of social services is one important ingredient (Vartiainen, 2004). Many European countries, for example, introduced flat-rate pensions at a comparatively early stage of welfare state development, when these countries had the same per capita incomes that Latin American countries had in the 1980s and 1990s (Stephens, 2002). In these cases, social policies have served not only as an instrument of development but also as a guarantee that the development process will ensure, contemporaneously, the wide range of "ends" of development and nation-building. A whole range of social policies can enhance long-term growth. The arguments range from the "human capital" effects, such as better education and health to policies such as land reform or targeted credit that may enhance the performance of markets that produce both equity and efficiency, which are good for growth. Finally, the social inclusion that social policies produce may contribute to political stability, which is a robust determinant of long-term economic growth. This aspect is particularly important in late industrializers undergoing radical social transformation (Vartiainen, 2004).

The narrowing of the goals makes current social policies singularly ineffective against poverty, their focus on poverty notwithstanding. In many ways, they suffer from the same weaknesses as the liberal regimes from which they draw their intellectual and ideological inspiration. Goodin (1999: 167) and others note that, compared to other "welfare regimes", "liberal regimes" are "strikingly bad" at combating poverty in every respect. This they consider "odd", given that it is liberals who are so "utterly fixated" upon the question of "what do they do for the poor". One consequence of the narrowing of the reach of social policy is the tendency to downplay the under-coverage of targeting. One well-known fact is that policies that have the greatest impact on poverty are not necessarily the most narrowly pro-poor, targeted ones. Indeed, in many cases, the focus on the pro-poor policies has diverted attention from the policies that have the most broad-based and sustainable effects against poverty. The success of the late industrializers of Northern Europe in conquering poverty lay not in explicitly addressing it but in addressing a whole range of issues that positively impacted on poverty or impeded the poor from bettering their situation—economic development in a broad sense, investment in human capital and equity were crucial to a rapid eradication of poverty. The issue was not targeting poverty but aiming at what Amartya Sen has termed "unaided opulence". Interestingly, Japanese economists close to the aid establishment have argued that the "pro-poor" focus detracts from the larger development projects, which alone can address the issue of poverty in a sustainable way. The Japanese argument partly stems from the view that the current PRSPs and their targeting of the poor diverges significantly from the experiences of the East Asian "success stories" in combating underdevelopment and poverty.[10] A similar point is made by Weiss (2004: 10):

> Some errors of targeting and some misappropriation are inevitable in any economic environment and more can be expected in low-income countries. Further, the very modest level of resources directed at the schemes would also limit their impact, even given far lower targeting errors. However the consistent picture,

which emerges from the available evidence, is that while some schemes may have had a modest positive effect on the poor, in our case-study countries trends in poverty reduction have been driven principally by macroeconomic developments—the rate and pattern of economic growth—rather than by targeted.

LESSONS LEARNED

The Problem of Administrative and Transaction Costs

The use of targeting involves some mechanism that discriminates between the poor and the non-poor. This being the case, there is always the danger of committing either type I errors, which occur when someone who deserves the benefits is denied them (underpayment, false positives), or type II errors, which occur when benefits are paid to someone who does not deserve them (overpayment, leakage). Thus, the ability to measure poverty and identify the poor is essential for designing any targeted transfer programme. There is no absence of theoretical models for achieving this, but as even the champions of this approach avow, targeting is usually faced with formidable administrative hurdles.

Most of the administrative constraints on targeting apply in both poor and rich countries, but they are invariably compounded in the poor countries where most people's source of livelihood is in the informal sector, people's "visibility" to the state is low and the state's overall capacity is low. Many studies clearly show that identifying the poor with the precision suggested in the theoretical models involves extremely high administrative costs and that the required administrative sophistication and capacity tend not to exist in developing countries (Srivastava, 2004). In a World Bank study (Coady, Grosh and Hoddinott, 2004a) of 122 targeted anti-poverty interventions in 48 countries, the authors conclude that while the median programme transfers 25 per cent more to individuals than would be the case with universal allocation, a "staggering" 25 per cent of programmes are regressive. Available figures show that the median targeting programme in sub-Saharan Africa transfers 8 per cent less to poor individuals than a universal programme (0.92) (Coady, Grosh and Hoddinott, 2004a).[11]

In recognition of the difficulties of implementing the kind of targeting implicit in the conceptual framework in its favour, there have been attempts to use other (less demanding) covariates of poverty through categorical targeting (geographic, demographic, gender, household, etc.). Other selection arrangements have also been resorted to, especially self-selection and community-based targeting mechanisms. Many of these arrangements are very blunt instruments to achieve the much touted efficiency of selectivity, and they simply shift the problem from one level to another.[12] They often lead to quite high type I and type II errors, in the sense that both under-coverage and leakage tend to be quite high. Often, attempts to reduce type II errors leads to increased commitment of type I errors. As Van Oorshot (2000) notes with respect to experiences in the developed countries, "Basically...it is the 'tragedy of selectivity' that trying to target welfare to the truly needy inherently means that a part of them will not be reached."

Analysis of geographic targeting schemes in Latin America and the Caribbean shows very high levels of under-coverage (see Tables 13.2 and 13.3). When the targeting is refined further for Mexico, the best that one gets is from the *localidad* level, where the leakage and under-coverage are both 37.3 per cent. The case of India, with its long history of interventions aimed at channelling resources to the poor, does not inspire much hope in targeting. According to Srivastava, the impacts have been "very disappointing", presumably because of serious under-

TABLE 13.2
Targeting in the Americas: the "success stories"

Country	Name of programme	Targeting accuracy for poorest quintile Q1	Under-coverage (% of poor not reached)
Brazil	Bolsa Escola	1.98	73
Chile	PASIS (old-age benefits)	2.67	84
Chile	SUF (cash transfers)	3.32	73
Colombia	SHIR (health social assistance)	1.68	26
Mexico	Oportunidades	2.9	40
USA	Temporary assistance for needy families (TANF) (cash transfers)	3.31	"About half of the eligible"
USA	Food stamps	4	Around 50%

Source: Peyre (2005)

TABLE 13.3
Leakage and under-coverage for state-level targeting in three countries (%)

	Mexico	Venezuela	Jamaica
Leakage rate	59.3	61.3	53.7
Under-coverage rate	61.0	59.8	48.7

Source: Baker and Grosh (1994)

coverage (so many of the poor are missed) and serious leakage (so many of the better-off benefit from the schemes). Poor implementation and weak governance are given as the key explanations for the failure of these schemes.

A sharper form of geographical targeting is community targeting, which presumably allows for better identification of the needy; however, community-based programmes also have their local political demands and prerequisites, their gender bias and their patronage and clientelism, and may run counter to the universalistic cultures of local communities.[13] They can, for instance, exacerbate local differentiation or be captured by local elites who may traditionally sanction discrimination (Conning and Kevane, 2000). In many cases, deliberate exercise of administrative discretion has led to the exclusion of women. It is in the nature of targeting that it vests a great deal of discretionary power in the hands of bureaucrats, who may use this capacity to manipulate the social and cultural entitlement aspects of targeted programmes.

Self-selection involves programmes, such as public works, in which the poor are more likely to participate than the non-poor. They are often accompanied by onerous and humiliating procedures often deliberately designed to discourage the "non-deserving". The measures used include rationing of food or health subsidies by queuing or inconvenient location of distribution centres, subsidizing inferior food staples or packaging in ways that are unappealing to the non-poor. The assumption is that the resultant costs to the poor are inconsequential to the poor themselves; however, there is considerable evidence that stigmatization comes along with such methods and, as a result, there are high levels of non-take-up, whereby people who are eligible for a benefit or service do not receive it (fully). In addition, the use of such stigmatizing instruments skirts the important issue of how equally the state relates to all its citizens.

Many studies on targeting perfunctorily acknowledge that it is expensive but then proceed totally oblivious to the fact that targeting is never without cost.[14] In order for this analysis to take on its full economic meaning, it will have to weigh targeting efficiency against economic efficiency that takes into account the total economic costs of a given amount of poverty relief. The few attempts at costing targeting confirm an Asian Development Bank Institute study of experiences in six Asian counties, which concludes: "With relatively high levels of leakage the expectation is that in practice most targeting measures have been high-cost means of transferring benefits to the poor" (Weiss, 2004). Both Grosh (1994) and Gwatkin (2000) show that the average cost of administering individual targeting schemes (with the best success rates) is 9 per cent, varying between 0.4 and 29 per cent of total programme cost. Other less efficient models (such as self-targeting or geographic targeting) are cheaper, e.g., the geographic model by 6 to 7 per cent, according to Gwatkin (2000), and by 7 per cent, according to Grosh (1994). The median costs of self-targeting schemes are 6 per cent of total programme costs. Rawlings, Sherburne-Benz and Van Domelen (2004) find that social fund expenses vary among countries by between 7 and 13 per cent. Coady, Grosh and Hoddinott (2004a) suggest that corruption and theft contribute more to total programme expenses than do legitimate administrative expenses. In light of the high levels of under-coverage, in measuring the costs of targeting, it is not enough to include only the budgetary costs due to leakage; the cost of under-coverage must also be factored in. Targeting implies a criterion for inclusion, which maximizes some welfare function, which involves a weighting of the two types of possible errors. Cornia and Stewart (1995) argue for a function that looks like:

Cost= α(overpayment) + β(underpayment).

They argue that, in conventional measures, it is implicitly assumed that $\alpha=1$ while $\beta=0$. They suggest instead that $\beta>\alpha$ would be the weighting that attaches importance to the failure to reach the poor.

It would indeed seem that targeting is a "luxury" which only countries with sophisticated administrative apparatus and substantive state reach can enjoy.[15] It does seem that, according to the logic of the argument for targeting, countries that need targeting (given their limited fiscal resources) cannot carry it out, while those that can (given their wealth) need not do so. In many successful late industrializers, it became self-evident that, where poverty was widespread, targeting would be unnecessary and administratively costly. Thus, the universalism in many countries was in fact dictated by underdevelopment—targeting was simply too demanding in terms of available skills and administrative capacity. In countries such as Norway, one reason for adopting universalism was pragmatism: according to Kildal and Kuhnle (2002), "The administrative costs of keeping the wealthy outside the system would eat up resources saved by income limits". A common feature of social policy in the successful cases of late industrialization is a leaning towards universalism in which benefits and services are treated as "merit goods" available to everyone as a right or obligation (e.g., compulsory education).

This, in a way, would be the conclusion that one would draw from the World Bank and neoliberal perspectives on development policy and state capacity in other areas. Indeed, the preference for targeting by the Bretton Woods institutions is rather paradoxical, especially in light of their aversion to targeting in many economic activities, such as selective industrial policies or credit rationing in the financial sector. Advocates of industrial policy have argued that, given limited savings or access to foreign exchange in developing countries, it is necessary to prioritize allocation of resources through "comprehensive planning", targeting, credit rationing and so forth. The dislike of the World Bank for such selectivity and targeting was partly based on the arguments that they would not be market conforming. Instead, it proposed "universalistic" policies— such as "level playing fields", lump-sum transfers and uniform tariffs — that applied to all. The more serious arguments deployed against targeting revolved around possibilities of *information distortion, incentive distortion, moral hazards, administrative costs, invasive loss and corruption.* It was asserted that governments did not have the knowledge to pick winners or to monitor the performance of selected institutions. In situations of asymmetric information, beneficiaries of such policies would conceal the information necessary for correct interventions. Selective policies and rationing of credit or foreign exchange produced perverse incentives, making it more rewarding to seek rents than to engage in directly productive activities. Furthermore, there was the ever-present danger of opportunism (moral hazard), and governments could not always guarantee reciprocal behaviour from those to whom they had extended favours. Developing countries were identified with weak administrative institutions, which could not be expected to manage the detailed requirements of selective policies. In addition to the purely technical problems, there was the question of the integrity of public institutions and the commitment of personnel. In such situations, the "targeting" of economic policy was an open invitation to rent seeking and corruption.

One would have expected, therefore, that, in the name of consistency, the World Bank would favour universalistic social policies because they are less bureaucratically cumbersome and more market conforming.[16] And yet, when it comes to social policy, such universalism is rejected on both equity and fiscal grounds. Instead, selectivity and rationing are recommended—apparently totally oblivious to the many arguments against selectivity raised with respect to economic policy. Suddenly, governments lambasted elsewhere for their ineptitude and clientelism are expected to put in place well-crafted institutions and to be able to monitor their performance. And yet, there is nothing to exclude the possibility that targeting in the social sector may be as complex and amenable to "capture" as targeting with respect to economic policy. It is certainly the case that the criteria for selection are at least as complicated, as controversial and as ambiguous as those for economic policy. Social indicators are extremely difficult to construct, and poverty has a multidimensionality that is far more complex than that of industrial structures. Amartya Sen (1995) has raised exactly the same arguments against targeting in the social sphere.

The Politics of Targeting

From much of the writing on targeting, there is often a perfunctory bow to the political nature of social policy, as the analysis proceeds with little consideration of the political economy of the choices involved. Targeting or means testing is thus treated as an administrative method whose function is to allocate welfare to claimants on the basis of available financial resources. However, the choice between targeting and universalism is quintessentially a political economy problem: it involves the choice of instruments for redistributing resources in society and for determining levels of social expenditure. These political economy problems are particularly poignant in the context of shrinking budgetary resources—that is to say, the context often used as an argument for targeting (however, much of the debate on targeting in many poor countries skirts this problem). Partly because the funds to be targeted often come from outside, as a fixed poverty reduction allocation, and are supposed to be disbursed by autonomous specialized agencies or NGOs, the tendency has been to conduct the discussion on poverty in a "non-political" or technocratic way. As a consequence, much of the time, it concentrates on the problem of disbursing external resources (aid), and not on that of generating the resources required for the task. Thus, such an approach does not deal with the relationship between targeting and the political economy of domestic resource mobilization, and rarely does it consider the variations in the budget that may actually be determined by the chosen method and pattern of distribution.

BUDGETARY IMPLICATIONS OF TARGETING

The usual assumption is that the amount spent on subsidies remains the same after introducing strict targeting, and that the targeted groups will therefore receive more. But in most cases, the total allocation to subsidies is reduced, and, in most cases, the switch to targeting leads to reduced effort. In situations where the focus has been on poverty alleviation, the level of efficiency in addressing certain aspects of poverty has outweighed efforts. Thus, "effort" and targeting are negatively related: countries with higher "efficiency" due to targeting have traded a good part of this by reducing "effort" (Korpi and Palme, 1998; Oxley and others, 2001). The "paradox of targeting" is that optimal targeting requires that an increase in the needs of some group be met by a reduction in the resources allocated to it (Keen, 1992). Targeting tends to lead to reduced budgets devoted to poverty and welfare, so that "more for the poor means less for the poor" (Gelbach and Pritchett, 1995). Thus, the more countries target benefits to low-income categories, the smaller the redistributive budgets they tend to have. Korpi and Palme (1998: 683) observe:

> Our paper suggests two empirically based conclusions. To paraphrase an old saying, if we attempt to fight the war on poverty through target efficient benefits concentrated at the poor we may win some battles but will probably lose the war. Universalism is not enough, however. To be effective universalism must be combined with a strategy of equality which comes closer to the preaching of Matthew than to the practices in Sherwood Forest.[17]

The experience in developed and middle-income countries is that universal access is one of the most effective ways in which to ensure political support by the middle class for taxes to finance welfare programmes. Indeed, one thing that emerges from the many studies of the "political economy of targeting" is that the optimal policy for the very poor is not necessarily a policy that targets benefits as narrowly and efficiently as possible (Gelbach and Pritchett, 1995; Moene and Wallerstein, 2001). Indeed, quite a wide range of political economy analyses, differing in assumptions about self-interest, altruism, distribution of risks, capacity of states, etc., reach the same conclusion, namely that "the optimal policy for the very poor is not necessarily a policy that targets benefits as narrowly as possible, once the impact of targeting on political support is taken into account" (Moene and Wallerstein, 2001).

For years, this "political economy" approach has been considered to have little relevance in many situations in developing countries where there is authoritarian rule. Quite a number of authoritarian regimes, especially the "developmentalist" ones, have succumbed to legitimation imperatives and pursued more or less universalistic policies.[18] Perhaps because of the view that, in authoritarian contexts, the pursuit of universalistic policies depends very much on the ideological and idiosyncratic proclivities of the ruler, such a political economy analysis has not received much attention in developing countries. However, with a growing number of countries increasingly relying on the democratic process to choose their leaders, politics assumes great importance. The importance of political economy even in the developing countries is illustrated by the case of Sri Lanka: after the Sri Lankan government introduced a targeted food stamp programme, the real value of the food stamps fell sharply during periods of high inflation, as the interest of the middle class shifted to other issues, and public support for the programme declined (Anand and Kanbur, 1991). In the late 1970s, the cost of a universal ration programme reached 5 per cent of gross domestic product (GDP), and the government was forced to cut costs by replacing it with a food stamp programme that cost only 1.3 per cent of GDP.

Finally, we should bear in mind that, often, initial choices map out the path that countries eventually take by setting societies' collective ideological predispositions and reducing institutional scope for manoeuvre. Choices made in the formative years can determine the future course of policies and practices (path dependence). Such choices entail institutions towards which interest will gravitate, severely restricting room for other options—including those that may have been universally accepted as desirable in the foreseeable future, though not feasible in the short run. The initial choice between targeting and universalism can lead to a political and institutional "lock-in" that can make departure from these initial choices difficult. As Evelyne Huber argues, one of the advantages of universalistic policies is that "they provide policy legacies that are more favourable to the maintenance of a redistributive and solidaristic thrust than particularistic and targeted schemes" (Huber, 2002).

The "Empowerment" versus Stigmatization Argument

Much has been said about the importance of "empowerment" in poverty eradication. However, effective empowerment demands the politicization of both poverty itself and the means to combat it. In the words of David Mosse (2004), "Making poverty a public, moral, and political issue is often the basis upon which the poor gain leverage by making power work to their advantage through enrolling elite interests, through pro-poor coalitions, and from competition between elite groups." The debate on poverty in the 1990s was closely associated with notions or "empowerment" and "participation". The World Bank, presumably influenced by the work of Amartya Sen, which highlighted the need to give "voice" to the poor, included three elements in its fight against poverty—"opportunity, empowerment and security". The OECD Development Assistance Committee (DAC) Guidelines on Poverty Reduction clearly highlights rights, influence, freedom, status and dignity as important components of well-being. The practice by most donors, however, has not paid much attention to the fundamental implications of such guidelines for social policies or the institutions for implementing such policies. Instead, they have insisted on forms of social assistance that were likely to be disempowering and even humiliating. As discussed above, such measures as community targeting and self-selection produce results that should be of concern to those advocating empowerment of the poor. The much bemoaned paternalistic and clientelistic practices of bureaucracies in the developing countries would be compounded in situations where local administrators wield power over matters of life and death, and where "minor potentates can enjoy great authority over the supplicant applicants" (Sen, 1995). Abuse and humiliation may become common features of citizens' interaction with the state, as in the unavoidable and insurmountable "procedural injustice" in certain administrative routines (Rothstein, 2001).

Political scientists remind us that, through processes of feedback, policies not only have a mobilizing effect on citizens, but may also affect the capacities of citizens for civic and political engagement (Pierson, 1993). Sen has argued that "any system of subsidy that requires people to be identified as poor and that is seen as a special benefaction for those who cannot fend for themselves would tend to have some effects on their self-respect as well on the respect accorded them by others" (Sen, 1995: 13). The process of means testing or identifying the "deserving poor" is often invasive and stigmatizing. Indeed, in some cases, relying on self-targeting in the design of programmes actually serves to increase their *disutility*. Given the growing attention now being paid to self-respect and empowerment, the danger of stigmatization inherent in targeting is an important policy issue.

While the literature on welfare policies in the developed countries pays considerable attention to issues of justice and dignity, this does not seem to be the case in that on developing countries. The possibilities of stigmatization are widely acknowledged but quickly passed over. In the context of extreme deprivation, it is tempting to subscribe to a "full belly thesis": that people do not eat dignity or democracy. However, there are serious issues of justice that must be taken into account in a poverty eradication programme that accepts John Rawls's argument that self-respect is "perhaps the most important primary good" on which a theory of justice as fairness has to concentrate (Rawls, 1971). Rothstein (2001) distinguishes between "substantive justice" (which seeks to answer the question: Are the goals of a particular social policy just?) and "procedural justice" (which seeks to answer the question: Can welfare policy be carried out in a fair manner?). He argues that selective programmes present serious problems of procedural justice because they allow administrators a wide field for discretionary action. This breeds bureaucratic abuse of power and opportunistic behaviour on the part of the clients.

Literature from political science also reminds us that "public policies can define the boundaries of political community, establishing who is included in membership, the degree of inclusion of various members and the content and meaning of citizenship" (Mettler and Soss, 2004: 61). We also learn from political science that "any policy that sets forth eligibility criteria for benefits or rights, or established guidelines for citizen participation, implies that certain individuals are fully included within the polity and others are not, at least not to the same degree" (Mettler and Soss, 2004: 61). In addition, not only do policies express mobilizing or pacifying messages, they enhance people's skills to play an active role in society. These features of socio-political arrangements are of great salience in new democracies, especially in ethnically diverse new states.

The "Perverse Incentive" Effects Argument

Ever since Thomas Malthus (1992), there has always been a concern over the effects of social provision on people's work habits and independence. A major criticism of the welfare state is that it breeds dependence of individuals on the state. In terms of both intellectual and ideological affinity, PRSPs draw on the liberal welfare regime whose primary goal is "alleviation of poverty", at least for the "deserving poor". The PRSP approach is preoccupied with "target efficiency" and the avoidance of creating "dependence" on welfare, which are seen to blunt incentives to work and therefore as inimical to overall economic welfare. However, targeting does not escape the problem of incentives. Indeed, one cost that is widely recognized in the literature is that of *perverse incentives* created by changes in people's behaviour in attempts to become beneficiaries of welfare policies, especially through perverse incentives on the labour supply of the poor. Individuals may avoid activities that may so improve their incomes that they are no longer eligible for public support. The high marginal effective tax rate can act as a disincentive to getting out of the "poverty trap": "through its disincentive effects, means testing tends to be dysfunctional with regard to social policy's broader aims of doing away with poverty" (Van Oorschot, 2000). Universal benefits, on the other hand, do not damage market incentives to take a job or save for one's own pension.

There is a second source of negative incentive of targeting that can be derived from broader notions of poverty, which include vulnerability as a key feature of being poor. One implication of taking vulnerability seriously is that, in measuring the efficacy of social provision programmes, it is important that the gains are weighted by the probability of their actually being received. Most of the measures on the efficiency of targeting are ex post, and if one of the objectives of poverty reduction strategies is to reduce the uncertainty that constitutes a major concern of the poor, it is important to consider the ex ante features of such programmes. This is particularly significant in light of the recognition of the importance of reducing the vulnerability of the poor. This welfare consideration builds on the concept of the "certainty equivalent of income" from the risk-aversion literature, which argues that households will prefer a steady stream of income to a variable one with the same mean. The poor, who are often risk averse, might prefer lower variability for a given value of expected future prospects. As Stefan Dercon (2001: 68) argues, what is essential "for any formal safety net and for any risk reduction policy, is that such a policy needs commitment and credibility. It should be permanent and transparent; moreover: it should be highly predictable." As we have seen, targeting typically involves uncertainty about whether rights to the ration will in practice be met or not, especially in situations of high probability of being excluded, even when one is among the 'deserving poor'. Targeted public provision implies serious risks faced by households to transform income and assets into outcomes, such as health and education. In addition, we should bear in mind that high consumption variability comes at a cost, not just in terms of current welfare but also in terms of long-term poverty alleviation: the choices made by households ex ante, and shocks ex post, may result in the poor being locked into low-welfare equilibria. Universal policies, on the other hand, try to reduce their vulnerability ex ante.

CONCLUSION

One remarkable feature of the debate on universalism and targeting is the disjuncture between an unrelenting argumentation for targeting and a stubborn slew of empirical evidence suggesting that targeting is not effective in addressing issues of poverty (as broadly understood). Many studies clearly show that identifying the poor with the precision suggested in the theoretical models involves extremely high administrative costs, and such an administrative sophistication and capacity may simply not exist in developing countries. The story of both the political and administrative difficulties of targeting is repeated so many times that one wonders why it is still insisted upon. Indeed, from the literature, it is clear that, where poverty is rampant and institutions are weak, what may be wrong is not the lack of appropriate data, but targeting per se. It is certainly the case that, in many countries, the shredding of the state apparatus has left it singularly incapable of effective targeting in the social sector. Most of the proposed refinements of targeting methods are likely to compound the problems that are often cited as constraints. An interesting phenomenon is that, while the international goals are stated in international conferences, in universalistic terms ("education for all", "primary health care for all", etc.), the means for reaching them are highly selective and targeted.

The need to create institutions appropriate for targeting has, in many cases, undermined the capacity to provide universal services. Indeed, in the most aid-dependent economies, the shift of funds from state institutions and ministries to "projects" run by a motley assortment of non-state actors immediately led to the unsustainability of activities that the state may have supported in the past or might wish to support now. We should also bear in mind that once institutions are set to implement a set of policies, "political capture", bureaucratic inertia and hysteresis can generate dynamics of their own that may eventually rule out alternative policies.

Social policies not only define the boundaries of social communities and the position of individuals in the social order of things, but also affect people's access to material well-being and social status. This follows from the very process of setting eligibility criteria for benefits and rights. The choice between universalism and targeting is therefore not merely a technical one dictated by the need for optimal allocation of limited resources. Furthermore, it is necessary to consider the kind of political coalitions that would be expected to make such policies politically sustainable. Many countries are undergoing democratic transformations. Consequently, the main political economy questions that may have been obviated by authoritarian rule were taken off centre stage. On the assumption that poverty alleviation is a straightforward and well-defined social objective, it should be easy to argue that, given budgetary constraints, resources should be concentrated on those in need. Both the objectives and the constraints are not as straightforward as suggested, however. They are both subject to political processes that determine what is to be allocated, to whom and for what reasons.

The current emphasis on targeting draws very little from historical experience, both in terms of what is political and administratively feasible, and of what have been the most efficacious ways of combating poverty. This is partly a reflection of the distance between development studies and the study of welfare policies in the developed countries. Consequently, there is a lot of reinvention of the wheel and wasteful and socially costly experimentation with ideas that have been clearly demonstrated to be the wrong ones for the countries in which they are being imposed. There is ample evidence of poor countries that have significantly reduced poverty through universalistic approaches to social provision, and from whose experiences much can be learnt (Ghai, 1999; Mehrotra and Jolly, 1997a; 1997b).

Although we have posed the issue in what Atkinson calls "gladiator terms", in reality, most governments tend to have a mixture of both universal and targeted social policies. In the more successful countries, however, overall social policy *itself* has been universalistic, and targeting has been used as simply one instrument for making universalism effective; this is what Theda Skocpol (1991) has referred to as "targeting within universalism", in which extra benefits are directed to low-income groups within the context of a universal policy design and which involves the fine-tuning of what are fundamentally universalistic policies.[19]

NOTES

[1] The author would like to thank K.S. Jomo, Shahra Razavi, Peter Utting and Sergei Zelenev for their comments on an earlier draft. I would also like to thank Alexander Peyre for his competent research assistance.

[2] On the shift away from universalism in the developed countries, see Gilbert (2001) and Van Oorschot (2000).

[3] An IMF study (Baunsgaard and Keen, 2004) covering 125 countries over the period 1975–2000 shows that, while high-income countries have recovered revenues with ease, middle-income countries have recovered only about 35–55 cents for each dollar of trade tax revenue they have lost, while low-income countries have recovered essentially none. Moreover, there is not much evidence that the presence of a VAT has, in itself, made it easier to cope with the revenue effects of trade liberalization.

[4] On Latin America, see, for instance, Figueira and Figueira (2002).

[5] For a useful discussion, see Ellison (1999).

[6] Thus, in Denmark, left-wing or Social Democratic parties often argue for more income- or means-tested benefits because they are more redistributive (Green-Pedersen, 2003).

[7] Green-Pedersen notes that in Denmark, right-wing or bourgeois parties often push for more universal benefits because they are more market conforming than income- or means-tested benefits. Writing about the USA, Pamela Herd observes that after decades of conservative attempts to scale back, conservative critics are now wrapping pro-market "privatization" policy proposals in the popular universal framework of Social Security and Medicare. While supporting key universal tenets, privatization proposals limit the redistributive elements of large social insurance programmes.

[8] A study (Jayne and others, 2001) on targeting in Ethiopia notes that the poor in the Tigray region of Ethiopia were treated more favourably than would be justified by its known levels of poverty. It then suggests that that such discriminatory practices could be eliminated using predicted per capita incomes. This suggests a rather poor understanding of Ethiopian politics and the current relationship of the regime to the Tigray region. In another study, Glewwe (1990) shows that if one used the standard approach to indicator targeting, maximizing poverty reduction, given a fixed budget for urban Côte d'Ivoire, would give all the budget to households born in one region of the country.

[9] As Jallade (1988: 248) notes with respect to France, "Social security was never primarily conceived as a tool to fight poverty. Security, in terms of protection against the risks and hazards of life, was its first, paramount objective."

[10] Indeed, many new democracies have tended to pursue rather orthodox economic policies as compared to much older democracies. This point is discussed, and some explanations suggested, in Mkandawire (2005a).

[11] Significantly, this study is cited as evidence that targeting works (Ravaillion, 2003)

[12] Ravaillion's (2003) observation in this respect is worth citing at length:
Policy makers seem often to have over-optimistic views on how well they can reach the poor by administrative targeting based on readily observable indicators. Here there are some sobering lessons from empirical research. Even using a comprehensive, high-quality, survey, one can rarely explain more than half the variance in consumption or income across households. And while household consumption is probably not a random walk, it is difficult to explain more than one tenth of the variance in future changes in consumption using current information in a panel survey. Add to this the fact that one must base targeting on observations for the whole population—not just a sample survey—and that there will be incentives to distort the data when it is known why it is being collected, one must expect potentially large errors in practice when using indicator targeting to fight chronic or (especially) transient poverty.

[13] Thus, in some localities covered by an Indonesian rice subsidy programme, rather than

limit the subsidized rations to poor households as the programme rules formally require, the community or its head chose to divide the ration equally among all households (Klugman, 1999).

[14] Thus, one study on Ethiopia concludes with the following observation: "Because information on targeting costs was unavailable, assessments of relative cost-effectiveness were beyond the scope of this article." (Jayne and others, 2001: 908).

[15] Even middle- and low-income countries with higher GDP do better at directing benefits towards poorer members of the population (Coady and others, 2004a).

[16] Indeed, the more consistent neoliberals have argued for universalism precisely on these grounds (Green-Pedersen, 2003).

[17] Korpi and Palme (1998) also show that countries with universal provision not only have higher budget expenditures, but also tend to have lower deficits than countries relying on means testing.

[18] On Korea, see Kwon (1999).

[19] A point well stated by ECLAC: "Since the lack of universal coverage mainly affects the poorest sectors, selectivity should be seen as a tool, or a set of tools, for guiding action, particularly in the allocation of subsidies aimed at ensuring access for the poor to social services and guarantees. That is why targeting, or selectivity, is not a social policy as such, but rather a method, which, if properly applied, enhances the effectiveness of universal social programmes. The fact that the principle of universality is translated into priority access to basic protection for the poor does not mean that selectivity, as a tool, represents "the" social policy. Targeting the allocation of subsidies to the poorest population, although essential for equity, does not work against the principle of universality, unless universal coverage is conceived as the uniform allocation of public subsidies across the board, independently of households' economic means (ECLAC, 2000: 78–79)

REFERENCES

Anand, Sudhir, and Ravi Kanbur (1991). Public policy and basic needs provision: Interventions and achievement in Sri Lanka. In Jean Drèze and Amartya Sen (eds). *The Political Economy of Hunger.* Vol. 3. Clarendon Press, Oxford: 59–92.

Anttonen, A. (2002). Universalism and social policy: A Nordic-feminist revaluation. *Nordic Journal of Women's Studies* 10 (2): 71–80.

Areskoug, K. (1976). Private foreign investment and capital formation in developing countries. *Economic Development and Cultural Change* 24 (3): 539–547.

Arrighi, Giovanni (1973). International corporations, labour aristocracies, and economic development in tropical Africa. In Giovanni Arrighi and John Saul (eds). *Essays on the Political Economy of Africa.* Monthly Review Press, New York: 105–151.

Atkinson, A.B. (1995). On targeting social security: Theory and western experience with family benefits. In D. van de Walle and K. Nead (eds). *Public Spending and the Poor: Theory and Evidence.* Johns Hopkins University Press, Baltimore, MD: 25–68.

Baker, J., and M. Grosh (1994). Poverty reduction through geographical targeting: How well does it work? *World Development* 22 (7): 983–995.

Baunsgaard, T., and M. Keen (2004). Tax revenue and (or?) trade liberalization. IMF Working Paper 05/112, International Monetary Fund, Washington, DC.
http://www.imf.org/external/pubs/ft/wp/2005/wp05112.pdf (27/09/05)

Besley, Tim, and Ravi Kanbur (1990). The principles of targeting. Policy Research and External Affairs (PRE) Working Paper WPS 385, World Bank, Washington, DC. http://www.wds.worldbank.org/servlet/WDSContentServer/WDSP/IB/1990/03/01/000009265_3960928225215/Rendered/PDF/multi0page.pdf (27/09/05)

Coady, D., M. Grosh and J. Hoddinott (2004a). Targeting outcomes redux. *The World Bank Research Observer* 19 (1): 61–85.

Coady, D., M. Grosh and J. Hoddinott (2004b). Targeting of transfers in developing countries: Review of lessons and experience. Processed, World Bank, Washington, DC.

Conning, J., and M. Kevane (2000). Community based targeting mechanisms for social safety nets. Processed, Williams College, Williamstown, MA.

Cornia, G.A., and Frances Stewart (1995). Two errors of targeting. In D. van de Walle and K. Nead (eds). *Public Spending and the Poor: Theory and Evidence.* Johns Hopkins University Press, Baltimore, MD: 350–386.

Dercon, Stefan (2001). Assessing vulnerability to poverty. Processed, Jesus College, Oxford, and Centre for the Study of African Economies, Department of Economics, Oxford University, Oxford.

Dollar, David, and Aart Kraay (2000). Growth is good for the poor. Processed, World Bank, Washington, DC.

ECLAC (2000). *Equity, Development and Citizenship.* United Nations Economic Commission for Latin America and the Caribbean, Santiago.

Ellison, N. (1999). Beyond universalism and particularism: Rethinking contemporary welfare theory. *Critical Social Policy* 19 (1): 57–85.

Esping-Andersen, Goran (1990). *The Three Worlds of Welfare Capitalism.* Princeton University Press, Princeton, NJ.

Figueira, C., and F. Figueira (2002). Models of welfare and models of capitalism: The limits of transferability. In E. Huber (ed.). *Models of Capitalism: Lessons for Latin America.* Pennsylvania State University Press, University Park, PA: 127–157.

Gelbach, J.B., and L.H. Pritchett (1995). Does more for the poor mean less for the poor?: The politics of tagging. Processed, World Bank, Washington, DC.

Gerschenkron, A. (1962). *Economic Backwardness in Historical Perspective.* Harvard University Press, Cambridge, MA.

Ghai, Dharam (ed.) (1999). *Social Development and Public Policy.* Macmillan, London, for United Nations Research Institute for Social Development (UNRISD), Geneva.

Gilbert, N. (2001). *Targeting Social Benefits: International Perspectives and Trends.* Transaction Publishers, New Brunswick, NJ.

Glewwe, P. (1990). Efficient allocation of transfers to the poor: The problem of unobserved household income. Living Standards Measurement Study Working Paper No. 70, World Bank, Washington, DC.

Goodin, R.E. (1999). *The Real Worlds of Welfare Capitalism.* Cambridge University Press, Cambridge.

Green-Pedersen, C. (2003). Still there but for how long?: The counter-intuitiveness of the universal welfare model and the development of the universal welfare state in Denmark. Centre for Comparative Welfare Studies (CCWS), Aalborg University, Denmark.

Grosh, M. (1994). *Administering Targeted Social Programs in Latin America: From Platitudes to Practice.* World Bank, Washington, DC.

Gwatkin, D.R. (2000). The current state of knowledge about targeting health programs to reach the poor. World Bank, Washington, DC. http://www.worldbank.org/poverty/health/library/targeting.pdf (27/09/05)

Huber, Evelyne (2002). Conclusion: Actors, institutions, and policies. In E. Huber (ed.). *Models of Capitalism: Lessons for Latin America.* Pennsylvania State University Press, University Park, PA: 439–480.

Jallade, J.-P. (1988). Redistribution in the welfare state: An assessment of the French performance. In J.-P. Jallade (ed.). *The Crisis of Redistribution in European Welfare States.* Trentham Books, Stoke-on-Trent: 223–253.

Jayne, T.S., J. Strauss, T. Yamano and D. Molla (2001). Giving to the poor? Targeting of food aid in rural Ethiopia. *World Development*, 29 (5): 887–910.

Keen, M. (1992). Needs and targeting. *The Economic Journal* 102 (410): 67–79.

Kildal, N., and S. Kuhnle (2002). The principle of universalism: Tracing a key idea in the Scandinavian welfare model. Presented at the First Conference of the European Social Policy Research Network on 'Social Values, Social Policies', Tilburg University, Netherlands, 29–31 August, and 9th BIEN (Basic Income European Network) Conference in Geneva, 9–14 September. http://www.etes.ucl.ac.be/bien/Files/Papers/2002KildalKuhnle.pdf (27/09/05)

Klugman, J. (1999). *Social safety nets and crises*. World Bank, Washington, DC.

Korpi, W., and J. Palme (1998). The paradox of redistribution and strategies of equality: Welfare state institutions, inequality, and poverty in the western countries. *American Sociological Review*, 63 (5): 661–687.

Krugman, Paul (2005). Deficits and deceit. *International Herald Tribune*, 5 March.

Kwon, H.-J. (1999). *The Welfare State in Korea: The Politics of Legitimation*. St. Martin's Press, New York, in association with St Antony's College, Oxford.

Malthus, T.R. (1992). *An Essay on the Principle of Population*. Cambridge University Press, Cambridge.

Manow, P. (2001). Welfare state building and coordinated capitalism in Japan and Germany. In K. Yamamura and W. Streeck (eds). *The Origins of Non-liberal Capitalism: Germany and Japan in Comparison*. Cornell University Press, Ithaca, NY: 94–120.

Mehrotra, Santosh, and Richard Jolly (eds) (1997a). *Development with a Human Face: Experiences in Social Achievement and Economic Growth*. Clarendon Press, Oxford.

Mehrotra, Santosh, and Richard Jolly (eds) (1997b). *Social Development in High Achieving Countries: Common Elements and Diversities*. Clarendon Press, Oxford.

Mettler, S., and J. Soss (2004). The consequences of public policy for democratic citizenship: Bridging policy studies and mass politics. *Perspectives on Politics* 2 (1): 55–73.

Mkandawire, Thandika (2001). Social policy in a development context. Processed, UNRISD, Geneva.

Mkandawire, Thandika (2005a). Maladjusted African economies and globalisation. *Africa Development* 30 (1&2): 1–33.

Mkandawire, Thandika (2005b). Social policy in development context: Introduction. In Thandika Mkandawire (ed.). *Social Policy in a Development Context*. Palgrave, London, for UNRISD, Geneva: 1–33.

Moene, K.O., and M. Wallerstein (2001). Targeting and political support for welfare spending. *Economics of Governance* 2: 3–24.

Mosse, D. (2004). Power relations and poverty reduction. In R. Alsop (ed.). *Power, Rights, and Poverty—Concepts and Connections*. Department for International Development (DFID), London, and World Bank, Washington, DC: 51–67. http://siteresources.worldbank.org/INTEMPOWERMENT/Resources/PPFinalText.pdf (29/12/05)

Oxley, H., Th. -Th. Dang, M. Föster and M. Pellizari (2001). Income inequalities and poverty among children and households with children in selected OECD countries. In K. Vleminckx and T. Smeeding (eds). *Child Well-being, Child Poverty and Child Policy in Modern Nations: What Do We Know?*. Polity Press, Bristol: 371–405.

Peyre, A. (2005). Successful targeting? The World Bank evidence supporting targeting. Processed, UNRISD, Geneva.

Pierson, P. (1993). When effects become cause: Policy feedback and political change. *World Politics*, 45 (4): 595–628.

Pierson, P. (ed.) (2001). *The New Politics of the Welfare State*. Oxford University Press, Oxford.

Ravallion, Martin (2003). Targeted transfers in poor countries: Revisiting the trade-offs and policy options. Processed, World Bank, Washington, DC.

Rawlings, L.B., L. Sherburne-Benz and J. Van Domelen (2004). *Evaluating Social Funds: A Cross-country Analysis of Community Investments.* World Bank, Washington, DC.

Rawls, John (1971). *A Theory of Justice.* Belknap Press of Harvard University Press, Cambridge, MA.

Rothstein, B. (2001). The universal welfare state as a social dilemma. *Rationality and Society,* 13 (2): 213–233.

Sainsbury, D. (1996). *Gender Equality and Welfare States.* Oxford University Press, Oxford.

Sen, A.K. (1995). The political economy of targeting. In D. van de Walle and K. Nead (eds). *Public Spending and the Poor: Theory and Evidence.* Johns Hopkins University Press, Baltimore, MD: 350–386.

Skocpol, Theda (1991). Targeting within universalism: Politically viable policies to combat poverty in the United States. In Christopher Jencks and P. E. Peterson (eds). *The Urban Underclass.* Brookings Institution, Washington, DC.

Srivastava, P. (2004). Poverty targeting in Asia: Country experience of India. Processed, Asian Development Bank Institute, Tokyo.

Stephens, J.D. (2002). European welfare state regimes: Configuration, outcomes, transformations. In E. Huber (ed.). *Models of Capitalism: Lessons for Latin America.* Pennsylvania State University Press, University Park, PA: 303–338.

Sunesson, S., S. Blomberg, P. G. Edelebalk, L. Harryson, J. Magnusson, A. Meeuwissen, J. Peterson and T. Salone (1998). The flight from universalism. *European Journal of Social Work* 1 (1): 19–29.

Tendler, Judith (2004). Why social policy is condemned to a residual category of safety nets and what to do about it. In Thandika Mkandawire (ed.). *Social Policy in Development Context.* Palgrave, London: 119–142.

UNRISD (2005). *Gender Equality: Striving for Justice in an Unequal World.* United Nations Research Institute for Social Development (UNRISD), Geneva.

Van Oorschot, W. (2000). Targeting welfare: On the functions and dysfunctions of means testing in social policy. In Peter Townsend (ed.). *World Poverty: New Policies to Defeat an Old Enemy.* Polity Press, London: 171–194.

Vartiainen, Juhana (2004). European 'late industrialisers': The Finnish experience. In Thandika Mkandawire (ed.). *Social Policy in Development Context.* Palgrave, London: 205–214.

Weiss, John (2004). Poverty targeting in Asia: Experiences from India, Indonesia, the Philippines, Peoples' Republic of China and Thailand. Processed, Asian Development Bank Institute, Tokyo.

World Bank (1990). *World Development Report 1990: Poverty.* World Bank, Washington, DC.

Contributors

Francois Bourguignon is Chief Economist and Senior Vice President, The World Bank.

Giovanni Andrea Cornia has been Professor of Economics at the University of Florence since 2000. Between 1995 and 1999, he was the Director of the United Nations University's World Institute of Development Economics Research (UNU-WIDER) in Helsinki. Before that, he held research positions in various UN agencies and the private sector.

Roberto Frenkel is Principal Research Associate at the Centro de Estudios de Estado y Sociedad (CEDES) in Buenos Aires and Professor at the Universidad de Buenos Aires. He specializes in macroeconomics, finance and development, and has published numerous articles and books. He has worked as a consultant for international organizations as well as for the Governments of Argentina and other Latin American countries.

Jayati Ghosh is Professor and Chairperson of the Centre for Economic Studies and Planning, Jawaharlal Nehru University, as well as Executive Secretary of International Development Economics Associates (IDEAs). She has published widely on issues pertaining to development, international economics, employment, gender and macroeconomic policies. She can be contacted at jayatig@vsnl.com.

Jomo K.S. has been Assistant Secretary General for Economic Development, Department of Economic and Social Affairs, United Nations, New York, from 2005. He was Professor at the University of Malaya, Kuala Lumpur and Founder Chair of International Development Economics Associates (IDEAs) until 2004.

Bernard Hoekman is Research Manager, Development Research Group, World Bank. He is also Research Fellow with the Centre for Economic Policy Research, London.

NANAK KAKWANI is currently the Director/Chief Economist of the UNDP International Poverty Centre, Brasilia. Before that, he was Professor at the University of New South Wales in Sydney for 30 years. He has published two books and more than 100 articles in international journals. His research areas include poverty, inequality, pro-poor growth, taxation, public policies, human development and MDGs. He was elected a fellow of the Australian Research Committee of Social Science, awarded the Mahalanobis gold medal for outstanding contributions in quantitative economics and is on the advisory board of the *Journal of Economic Inequality*. He has been visiting professor at many universities and consultant to the World Bank, UNDP and the Asian Development Bank.

GRACIELA L. KAMINSKY is currently a professor of Economics and International Affairs at George Washington University. She received her Ph.D. from MIT and was assistant professor of economics at the University of California, San Diego, and staff economist at the Board of Governors of the Federal Reserve System before joining George Washington University. She has been a consultant and Visiting Scholar at the IMF, the World Bank, and the Inter-American Development Bank. She has also been a consultant to the Banco de España and the Korean Center for International Finance and visiting scholar to the Banco de Mexico, Bank of Japan, Hong Kong Monetary Authority, and the Institute of International Economics, University of Stockholm. She was a visiting professor at the Department of Economics, Johns Hopkins University, Universidad de Los Andes (Bogotá, Colombia), Universidad di Tella and Universidad San Andrés, both in Buenos Aires, Argentina. She has published extensively on issues in open economy macroeconomics. In the last few years, her areas of research have been on financial crises, contagion, herding behaviour, the effects of financial liberalization, and mutual-fund investment-strategies.

SARBULAND KHAN was Director of the Office for Economic and Social Council Support and Coordination in the United Nations secretariat until mid-2006.

EDDY LEE is currently Economic Adviser at the International Institute of Labour Studies, International Labour Office (ILO), Geneva. He has a doctorate in economics from Oxford University and has published widely on topics relating to employment, labour and social policies in developing countries.

THANDIKA MKANDAWIRE is the Director of the United Nations Research Institute for Social Development. He is also former Executive Secretary of CODESRIA (Council for the Development of Economic and Social Research in Africa).

JOSÉ ANTONIO OCAMPO has been United Nations Under-Secretary-General of the Department of Economic and Social Affairs since September 2003. Prior to that, he served as Executive Secretary of the United Nations Economic Commission for Latin America and the Caribbean, Minister of Finance, Minister of Agriculture and in other portfolios in the Colombian Government. He holds a Ph.D. from Yale University, has taught in several universities and published extensively on economic and social issues.

ALESSANDRO PRATI is an Advisor in the Research Department of the International Monetary Fund (email: aprati@imf.org).

GUSTAV RANIS is the Frank Altschul Professor Emeritus of International Economics at Yale University.

ERIK REINERT holds a BA from the University of St Gallen, Switzerland, an MBA from Harvard University and a Ph.D. in economics from Cornell University. He is presently Professor of Technology Governance and Development Strategies at Tallinn University of Technology, Estonia, where he and his colleagues are starting a Masters Programme in historical/evolutionary economics in 2006. Reinert also heads The Other Canon Foundation based in Norway (www.othercanon.org). His main research area is the theory of uneven growth, i.e., the factors that cause world economic development to be so uneven, contrary to the predictions of standard economic theory.

HYUN H. SON has a Ph.D in Economics and is a poverty specialist at the UNDP International Poverty Centre. Dr. Son worked for the World Bank in Washington, DC, and held an academic position at Macquarie University in Sydney, Australia. Her research areas include, among other things, poverty, inequality, pro-poor growth and public policies. (E-mail address for correspondence: hyun.son@undp-povertycentre.org)

FRANCES STEWART is professor of development economics at Oxford University and Director of the Centre for Research on Inequality, Human Security and Ethnicity (CRISE) at Queen Elizabeth House, Oxford.

MARK SUNDBERG is Lead Economist, Development Economics Department, The World Bank.

LANCE TAYLOR is Arnhold Professor and Director of the Center for Economic Policy Analysis, New School for Social Research. He has written widely in macroeconomics and development economics, and has been a visiting scholar and policy advisor in numerous countries. His latest book is *Reconstructing Macroeconomics*, Harvard University Press, 2004.

THIERRY TRESSEL is an Economist in the Research Department of the International Monetary Fund. He holds a PhD from the Ecole des Hautes Etudes en Science Sociales (Paris, France). Before joining the IMF in 2002, he worked as a consultant for the OECD and for the World Bank.

L ALAN WINTERS is Director, Development Research Group, World Bank, on leave from Sussex University, Brighton. He is also Research Fellow with the Centre for Economic Policy Research, London.

Index